Also by Brad Kong

*Introduction to UnBrokable** (Chapter 1 to 5)
Intro to UnBrokable Large Print* (Chapter 1 to 5)

UnBrokable I* (Chapter 1 to 10)
UnBrokable II* (Chapter 11 to 20)
UnBrokable III* (Chapter 21 to 30)
UnBrokable IV* (Chapter 31 to 40)
UnBrokable V* (Chapter 41 to 50)
UnBrokable VI* (Chapter 51 to 60)
UnBrokable VII* (Chapter 61 to 70)
UnBrokable VIII* (Chapter 71 to 80)

Brad Short Story Collection I:

Robbery at Cyb Knight
How to Get Rid of Ladies
11 Girls I had Loved
Say No To TSLA
3 Ways to Avoid Divorce
15 Ways to Keep Your Teeth Healthy
5 Moments When I Felt Sorry For My Cat
Corn Dog Grandpas
Condo Chronicle
How to Lose 40 Pounds

15 Things You Didn't Know About Korea
3 Reasons Why We Need to Buy a Home Early
Why Are CDs Super Important?

Praise for *UnBrokable*

"This is the best book I have ever read. I am saying this only because Brad is my husband."

-Tsina D,
A housewife and teacher

"I cannot believe my dad wrote this much thick book. He must be a genius."

-Yuna K,
An elementary school student

"I am proud of my son who wrote a book in English."

-Mrs. Jin,
A wealthy woman

"Publishing this book is a celebration itself. Write your name on the next page if you bought this for a gift."

-Brad K,
A philosopher, writer, publisher and investor

Un*Brok*able*

Ultimate 80 Reasons

Why *People Go* ***Broke***
and Never Get Out of Poverty
Despite Working Hard

Brad Kong

Disclaimer

These are the full title and subtitle of this book:

UnBrokable*:
Ultimate 80 Reasons Why *People Go* ***Broke*** *and Never Get Out of Poverty* ***Despite Working Hard***

I wrote only "***Ultimate 80 Reasons Why Broke Despite Working Hard***" on the front cover *intentionally* for rhyme, simplicity and focus.

Un*Brok*able*

Dear ________________

This book is my gift for you.
It has been helpful for me, so I hope it will be helpful for you as well.
Thank you always.
Sincerely,

From ________________

For All the Honest Workers
Struggling Everyday

Foreword

So many books out there from Self-Help and Financial Gurus talk about personal finances in abstract terms. These are folks who make millions selling books telling us what to do. Here is something new and refreshing, however. The author relates his real-life experiences in personal finance. Not only is there a lot of good advice in here, it is an interesting look into someone else's life.

It seems we are at a time in history where everyone is struggling to get ahead. But then again, if we look back in history, it has always been this way. The inflation of today pales to that of the 1970's. The unemployment of a few years ago was nothing like that era, either. What is frustrating for so many is that even "making good money" people are living "paycheck to paycheck" and wondering where the money all went. I know I fell into this trap!

The author illustrates how people go broke even while making a hefty salary, and provides a guide to being "UnBrokable" - a term he has coined. And apparently it works - he retired at 40, not from selling self-help books (like so many Gurus do) but by being careful with money.

There is a lot here to learn from. And it's only just getting started!

Robert P. Bell
Georgia

USA

Mr. Robert P. Bell is a retired Patent Attorney, self-made millionaire and founder of the popular blog named Living stingy (http://livingstingy.blogspot.com). He has written in the last 15 years since 2008 and helped tons of people get out of debts and money problems. He is well known for his humorous witty but sharp writing style and has influenced myriads of writers including Brad Kong.

Contents

UnBrokable V*

UnBrokable VI*

UnBrokable* VII

UnBrokable* VIII

Prologue

Dying poor is a shame, especially in wealthy countries.
It is not all about money; it shows how we have lived.
-Brad Kong

This is me sitting on the Ferrari Modena in Miami, FL in 2003. Then, I didn't expect I would go abysmally broke and suffer for a long time. I had to work as a weekend dishwasher for 7 years from 2015.

Han Liu was a Chinese billionaire, the former chairman of Hanlong Group; the company is known for power generation and mining businesses in China. His assets were officially claimed at $6 billion USD by the time he passed away at the age of 49 in 2015. He was convicted of murdering 8 people and running a mafia-style gang for his businesses; he was executed by the law enforcement in China. The last words he left had been viral online: "Life is short; we don't have to live too diligently for more money. I will just have a small store next life and live happily with my family."

I agree with his lesson: I do not want to work to death, make a lot, spend more, leave a fortune to others and die; I do not want to *grind* myself to donate more. In the book *Psychology of money* by Housel, there is a story of a man named Read; he was a janitor for 42 years, made a fortune out of the stock market, left $8 million to a hospital and passed away. I know a similar case of Groner; she had worked as a secretary for 43 years, made profit out of the Abbott shares, left $7 million to a local college and died. They were undoubtedly honorable: But, seriously, what's the point? What would be the thing they regretted the most? What will they do if they can repeat their lives? As long as I have enough, **I conclude that the best reward I can give to myself is *working less.*** I may not need a luxury car or vacation, but I like to save myself from being offended by bosses and customers constantly for decades.

Coincidentally, I was in Chinatown Chicago the other day; it had some Korean shops, which were crowded. It took forever for South Korea to be wealthy. Ironically, once we[1] become rich, I found that we can make money out of it: *Being rich itself can be a new source of income.* I believe that a guaranteed way to stay prosperous is staying away from the reasons causing poverty.

---

[1] Not Koreans, but all of us who read this book

I bought my home in November, 2013. I didn't know it was the lowest price ever in the 21st century (source from Zillow).

My net worth has increased 8 times in the past decade. I had $80,000 CDs and some cash in the bank in 2013: How do I remember this? I bought my condo at full price of $60,000[2] that year; my real estate agent asked me to submit proof of funds in advance; I didn't know what to do, so I got a receipt from the ATM and gave it to her. Now I have over a $650,000 portfolio and savings, not including my residence, as of 2023. This growth has probably resulted from inheritance, investment success, salaries and frugality. But I would say that "not having rent or mortgages" after home purchase played the most crucial role.

I enjoyed my life; until I couldn't. And some of us may not since a recession may approach later in 2023. Maybe this book is not for the super-rich; probably not even for the

[2] It is more than $150,000 in 2023.

middle-class or mildly poor. I had been in a desperate situation myself, especially around 2009. My business wasn't doing well; the subprime mortgage crisis broke out; my car was a decade old; those horrible mechanics kept overcharging me amid despair; then my only daughter was born in 2010. I couldn't waste even a single cent for years, but I was able to manage to buy a small condo thanks to my parents; the only advantage was that all the house prices dropped significantly due to the heavy economic depression. I think this book is for those: **Unlucky people who have no idea how to get out of poverty.**

The Ferrari photo above was taken almost 20 years ago in 2003; back then, I had no idea how much financial troubles I was about to go through; I was in my late 20s, but stupid. Now I know that being wealthy is a combination of a ton of small skills and knowledge; we need some *luck*, too. On the contrary, I guess that being broke can happen easily anytime; it won't hurt to check real examples that cause financial hardships.

* * *

Charles Bukowski (1920 – 1994) was an American poet called "the laureate of American low-life" in the 1970s; he bought his first house 23 years *later* than me. His net worth was over $4 million by the time he passed away: How did this happen?

Mr. Bukowski was often considered a drunk loser, but I found out that he and I share more than a few things in common. First of all, we both started writing careers after our 40s; both had or have one daughter. We both had worked for low income physical jobs for a while; we both inherited some money from parents after becoming middle aged men. Also we both were born in foreign countries, originally.

But it shows that he bought his first house with a mortgage at the age of 58 in 1979; I bought my condo with cash at the age of 40 in 2013. Then, it took an extra 5 years for him to pay off his mortgage (which was fast). As a result, he ended up buying his house 23 years slower than me: What made him delay this long?

It is natural if someone goes broke when he or she does not have a job. But some live poor forever even though they work full-time. **More ironically, some live wealthy for good without having a job**: *How?* For instance, my mother was initially from a poor family (which is typical among old Koreans) and never had a job in the past four decades. But she has been in the top wealth class in the country for most of her adult life: What exactly happened? Having COVID for over the course of three years has been too long (I got my 5th booster shot the other day). I predict that a stock market crash may happen in Dec, 2023 or so.

* * *

Again, let me start this final *UnBrokable** by congratulating you: Picking up this book means that we are, at least, one step closer to wealth. This series will be a practical, unorthodox or alternative guide to stay out of *brokeness* and move forward to prosperity; we will talk about unique reasons, examples and facts; it is my memoir, too. **"*Brokeness*" (not brokenness[3]) is a noun meaning "the characteristic of being broke or not having enough money."**

Have you ever been broke before even though you have a job? Have you ever been short of money despite working

---

[3] *Broke**nn**ess* means "a condition in which something is badly damaged."

full-time? People may not get broke automatically, especially in wealthy countries; if some are poor despite the fact that they work to death, I think there must be reasons. What do you believe makes a person poor? **Why do some still rent an apartment after working 12 hours a day for 30 years?** I had witnessed a couple of those people closely for 7 years.

"UnBrokable*" may not be a word we can find in a dictionary yet as I coined it: **A person who cannot be financially broke is "UnBrokable."** The opposite of *Les Miserable.* I think that there is one big misconception in our lives: If we work hard, we will be rich. Nothing can be further from the truth; *in fact, I suspect that working longer can make us poorer.* I observed that some live painfully by exploiting themselves; "working longer" is one way.

This book is a collection of my own survival stories in a sense; I am a middle-aged man with a wife and a daughter from the Midwest. I think my American life can be divided into four periods since 1999.

1. Colleges: Cornell and SUNY at Buffalo (1999-2005)
2. Business: Cyb Knight Video Games (2006-2014)
3. Employment: A nursing home (2015-2022)
4. Writer (2022 - current)

Or I can divide my 24 years in America by jobs:

- College banquet (2001 - 2002)
- eBay and Amazon seller (2003 - 2015)
- Cyb Knight Games Owner (2006-2014)
- Nursing home dishwasher (2015-2022)
- Investor (2011-current)
- Writer and publisher (2022- current)

There are other jobs with licenses I prefer not to talk about now (pharmacy technician and medical coder). Also I have worked for myriads of small jobs since high school when I was in Korea: convenience store clerk, bar kitchen helper, military soldier, etc.

* * *

Out of all those jobs, the recent *weekend dishwasher* gave me the strongest inspiration to write *UnBrokable** series. The nursing home I worked at is within walking distance from my home. I had a chance to volunteer to work there one day in 2015; unexpectedly, that brought me a permanent weekend position. Then, I had not done anything for a year after closing out my video game store permanently in 2014. At the end of the work, they suddenly wondered (literally begged, if not forced) if I could do the job at least every weekend. Now I see the reason why as I asked similar questions to other volunteers or temp workers myself.

For some reason, those nursing homes always need employees while no one is excited to work there; I think they are at the top of the labor shortage pyramid in America. Since they suggested a reasonably good wage and plenty of free food from the kitchens, I accepted that offer. I had the job only on weekends for six years and on Sunday for a year; the total period was close to seven years.

I never liked that job much since it was physically hard, but have to admit that it has been helpful for my life in some ways. The first reason is that I had chances to meet a lot of people I would have not without it; there are types of people doing dishwashing for life. No offense, but **I think I was able to see some mandatory reasons they all had in common: the reasons why they keep getting broke and never get out of poverty.** I think I had good chances to take a look at their lives and listen to their stories. Some were *truly great* guys, regardless. Secondly, the job had brought me physical strength; I have lost a lot of weight, especially in the beginning and gained muscles continuously throughout the years. Thirdly, these weekend extra salaries, bonus and free food still helped me build up my savings faster.

There could be millions of reasons why people go broke: gambling, drug addictions, car accidents, being robbed, etc; we cannot help those who get into obvious troubles. **Nonetheless, there are millions of people apparently not doing anything wrong, but always being broke while working**; many have nothing left in their bank accounts after some payments are withdrawn at the end of month.

* * *

Do you know when I had the hardest time with money? While I worked at the video game store, my daughter was born in 2010. When a baby is born, parents need more money while physically exhausted to take care of the baby. Incidentally, the mortgage bubble burst in 2008 and I remember that severe depression came from 2009: The subprime mortgage crisis. I guess that businesses must have a hard time these days as COVID pandemic has been from 2020; the impact may not be over quickly. While I had wasted a massive amount of my parents' money to keep my store door open, the only good thing I did was buy a condo in full. Since the economy collapsed in 2008, there had been plenty of foreclosures, short sales and discounted houses on the market. Getting rid of my rent for good was the only upside during that era.

After having difficulty with money myself and watching people struggling, I started wondering what really makes honest laborers in trouble: **Is there any practical trap to make full-timers broke even in wealthy countries?** While working in the nursing home, I saw dishwashers still renting apartments even after *30* years of employment. They occasionally worked *double*, which means working up to 15 hours a day: **Where did all their money go?** I had been a renter myself for about fourteen years. I believe that I chose important but disregarded reasons.

Are you ready to jump into 80 chapters with myriads of episodes? **All the stories are either from my personal experience or true events that happened throughout history.** I hope this will be the longest book you've ever finished since you cannot put it down. By the time we reach the epilogue, I hope that we can be more mature, knowledgeable and a bit closer to wealth.

1

Drinking and Smoking

There is drinking and smoking behind all the poverty problems.

- Brad Kong

Alexander the Great (356 – 323 BC) was an emperor of the Greek kingdom of Macedonia, who had created the largest empires in ancient history; his territory stretched from Egypt to northern India then. The record shows that he had never been defeated in a war and considered the greatest military commander. While he had lived an extremely successful life in general, his sudden downfall seemed to come with his heavy drinking habit. The ruler impulsively killed "Cleitus the Black," who saved Alexander's life once at a battle, during a violent drunken altercation; it says the general Cleitus accused him of judgmental mistakes that night. The monarch deeply regretted it, but his severe alcoholism likely started from that point; it had gradually intensified along with the incidental death of Hephaestion, who was the king's childhood friend studying together under Aristotle. Alexander swam in a lake one day and developed a mild fever; he spent the next 12 days only on binge drinking and passed away possibly of malaria; he was only 33-years old.

Yoon is the 13th president of South Korea elected in 2022. He was a prosecutor general previously, but I found that he has an interesting record on Wikipedia; he had failed his bar exams 9 times straight; in other words, it took

10 years for him to pass the legal test after college. We all know that passing a bar exam to be a counselor is not easy. Still, I believe that most law students pass it after failing a couple of times in Korea (Kim Kardashian passed it after flunking three times while taking care of her four kids). Coincidentally, this president is *well* known for his *chronic alcoholism*; some believe that his numerous failures happened due to his heavy drinking habit, which started when he was in college.

James Cook was a British explorer and the captain of the Royal Navy in the 18th century. He has been best known for his three voyages to New Zealand and Australia across the Pacific Ocean; he found a lot of sea routes never known before and visited unknown islands as the first European; he visited Hawaii as well in 1778.

When the navy returned to Hawaii in 1779, it shows that the military had a surprisingly warm welcome reception from the natives. Coincidentally, it was a Hawaiian festival period to worship the Polynesian god Lono and they falsely thought that James was the deity who returned; the Navy decided to stay on the island for a month. Soon after, it turned out that the captain and crews had been drunk all the time, demanded too much alcohol, had fist fights with natives and harassed island women. As a result, the anger of the Hawaiians had grown.

One day, both parties had an exceptionally big quarrel over stuff stolen by Hawaiians from the English boats; the captain Cook tried to capture the King of Hawaii, "Kalaniʻōpuʻu" as a hostage to get their items back, but failed. Regretfully, the captain was stabbed to death during the incident in 1779; he was 50 years old; it shows that four more marines were killed during the brawl as well.

Did you know that it takes a lot of harvests to make a little amount of alcohol? That is why the Korean Joseon dynasty had occasional *prohibition eras*, especially when famines came. In a sense, making alcohol can be a global waste; drinking can promote our society to waste more food, including grains and fruits. I believe that money drain starts from drinking, smoking or frequently both; these two seem to be the most prevalent and common. **I think that it is important to stop draining money first before trying to figure out how to make more.**

* * *

Amy Winehouse was an English singer and songwriter. She was only 27 when she died of her noted alcoholism in London, England in 2011; it shows that her net worth was about $4 Million at the time of her death. Verne Troyer was an American actor and comedian; he was best known for his role of "Mini-Me" in the *Austin Powers* film series. He died at the age of 49 in Los Angeles, CA in 2018; his death was later ruled an alcohol poisoning. I feel sorry since he was just about to get noticed after a long obscurity in his career.

I have always thought that drinking and smoking are the biggest waste of our life. What I mean by waste includes *time,* too. I often reflect that, 'I have wasted decades of my life, but I have never done it on drinking, at least.' Sometimes, it costs our lives, too: *Is it too much if I imagine that Cook could have left Hawaii alive if he didn't drink alcohol?*

The *weekend* dishwashing job I had was like a Siberian death camp over the winter. I finished my army service by 1997, but still I don't see anything else I can compare the job with. Countless people quit within a week; I heard that a few even quit within 30 minutes. I truly wondered how some were able to keep it as full-timers for decades in that huge nursing home.

There were a couple of old Mexicans who were unpleasant yet diligent. Quite frankly, the amount of wages, tips and bonuses I had received was more than I expected before starting. Besides, they gave me plenty of free food from the five restaurants inside it, continuously; I recall that I didn't have to go to supermarkets for months, occasionally. Since most Americans spend a portion of salaries on food, the job was actually a deal. I assumed that it was how those Latinos were able to support their five children only by dishwashing; they get full benefits as full-time workers, too. **Regardless, the two old men were still renting apartments at the age of 60: *Why?***

* * *

There is an excerpt from the *Talmud*: A Jewish student asked, "Why are our pupils dark in the eyes?" A rabbi answered that, "It means it is better for us to see the dark side of the world first; if we keep seeing only the bright side, we can be too optimistic or even arrogant. We need to be humble to expand the brighter side."

Sadly, three ladies committed suicide together in Seoul, Korea in 2014: one mother and two daughters; this was not a common tragedy considering that all the victims were grown-ups. Apparently, they burned coal in their small room, causing carbon monoxide poisoning. It showed that the mother was a 60-years old eatery worker and got laid off a month before this suicide pact. The two daughters were in their 30s; the elder one was unemployed due to diabetes; the younger one had a part time job at a graphic novel publisher, but had suffered from small wage, debt and bad credit.

This demise had been all over the news and shocked the nation for a month in 2014. No one understood why this family could not get any support from the government at all. Eventually, the police concluded that the reason for this misery was financial hardship. A lot of investigators and reporters checked the house thoroughly and found one grocery check book by the mother in the end. Not everyone writes all the spending thoroughly like her, so I could see that she had been honest and punctual.

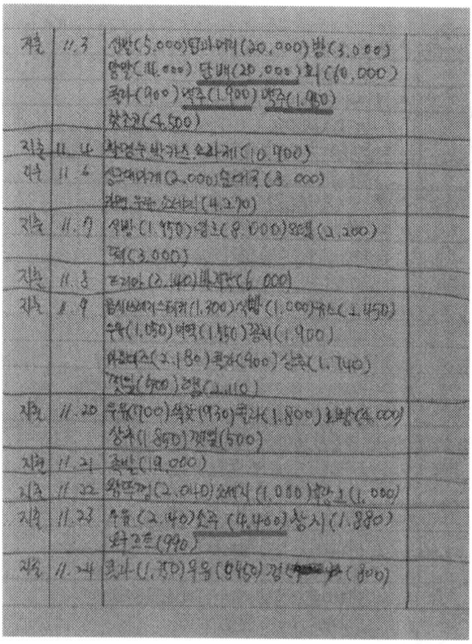

Still, I couldn't help that one item in their grocery lists grabbed my attention: Soju $4.40 (2014). Subsequently, I started wondering if their spending on cigarettes ($20) and beers ($1.90 and $1.95) was also necessary. I thought that they passed away due to extreme poverty. I had been desperate, but in my case, I couldn't waste a single cent for many years.

Soju is a cheap but popular alcoholic drink in Korea: a sort of diluted Vodka (a small bottle is $10 from Amazon in 2022). Different from wine or beer, it does not have any taste at all except alcohol; I saw that some Americans complained that it tastes just like ethanol from a chemistry lab, which it is. I believe it was invented when the country was a ruin after the Korean war in the 1950s; I also assume that the country did not have much harvest to make a drink properly. Unexplainably, it is still one of Koreans' favorite drinks nowadays.

Nonetheless, I suddenly felt different as soon as I saw these items in their purchases. "Why did they waste money on alcohol and cigarettes even when they were desperate?" I almost felt like they deserved the consequence. Then, this hitted me: **Were drinking and smoking the reason making them broke from the start?** After all, soju is not a food we need to survive; it does not have any nutritional value as it consists of only water and ethanol. I do not have every answer, but here is one thing for sure: If they did not drink or smoke, they would have saved the $28.25 in their pocket in 2014; little money helps when we are in despair. More importantly, alcohol is known to cause depression which can lead to suicides.

* * *

I have watched a documentary about Angel Falls in Venezuela. It showed that heavy rainfall drops on top of the fall mountain almost everyday; that is why the tops of mountains are flat by heavy rain beats. Then, it shows that water comes down through the falls, goes to streams, rivers and all the way to the oceans. **Then, I thought that**

drinking and smoking are similar to those rainfalls from headwaters. These two habits may create minor problems in the beginning (e.g. wasting ten bucks), but they can connect all the way to oceans of bigger problems (e.g. liver failure).

Paradise Fall in animation *Up* vs Angel Fall (source: Disney Pixar)

Another analogy I can take is the human population. If all the problems are all the eight billion population in 2022, drinking and smoking could be a couple of *Australopithecus* who lived 4 million years ago. Some may think they are wealthy despite keeping those habits; for sure, they could have been wealthier without those.

By the way, what I mean by "lose" includes *actual loss.* When I was in college in Korea, I lived in a home-stay in 1992. I still remember that the brother of the landlady complained that he lost $2,000 cash while he was drinking somewhere the other night. *I thought that losing that much is unbearable misery for me.* I personally do not drink or smoke at all; we will keep figuring out practical reasons we can improve without spending extra money in this series.

When I watched YouTube the other night; a popular Korean lady said all the expensive alcohols come out as *urine* after all. I also watched a documentary about a fallen celebrity in Korea; there is the man who used to be a top singer 20 years ago; he is poor now in 2023. It shows that he still wears a $10,000 coat and drinks $200 beers. One lady commented that, "The expensive clothes will stay at least; those expensive beers will only disappear with urine." Alcohol is beyond *useless* damaging organs, but the truth is virtually all types of drinks except water (e.g., soda, juice, coffee and tea) are bad for our teeth; water is the only liquid I put in my mouth personally.

* * *

The last dynasty in the Korean peninsula was the Joseon (1392–1897). It had had several *Prohibition eras* officially recorded and **the penalty for the violation was death**; cutting heads by a machete was performed on heavy drinkers in the 16th century; the record says that a high official named Yune was also decapitated. Then, this was the king's reason for the strict prohibitions: "People are starved to death as there is no grain left during famine. No one can eat a bag of rice, all at once. **Yet people can drink up a jar of alcohol overnight, which is made out of a bag of rice.**" In other words, it takes so much rice to make a small amount of alcohol and these can be consumed too quickly.

The issues of drinking and smoking often start with draining some cash. Then, the damage continues on with things like getting headache, getting fined for DUI, fighting, losing teeth, getting concussion, having kidney malfunctions, losing a liver, etc. There is a Chinese foot massage near my home; a middle aged Chinese couple own the place. I used to feel sorry for them since massaging feet must be a boring job; I do not believe they charge a lot, either. I saw them closing their business door one night; I noticed that they went straight to the liquor store across the street; strangely, I found my sympathy diminished: "Well, do they have enough money for that?" **While I owned my video game store, I did not have money to waste on anything: Not even a single cent.** Frankly, I had lost a little bit of money every month all the way through the eight years of the business ownership (except for several months).

I do not believe that the couple ever understand that drinking could be the reason they got stuck in that job. I have never tried the place since it always looked deteriorating; I am afraid that getting foot massages can make masseuse feel bad; window decals of the business were wearing off; I felt the business sinking with their habits. According to my experience, when owners do not drink or smoke, a store looks fresher even from outside; I know what my shop looked like.

* * *

I was in high school in Korea in 1989; it was 34 years ago as it is in 2023 now. At that time, the college entrance exam was exceedingly competitive nationwide and getting private tutoring from college students after school was popular. Korea was poorer back then and tutorings were not super expensive; a lot of college students did it for their part time jobs.

One day, my mother brought a college student for after-school tutoring. My mother was not wise; as a result, I ended up getting only lessons the whole day, instead of studying on my own; she is not the type of person who decides things on her own; she always does what others do, blindly, which I hate. Anyway, the guy was attending mechanical engineering in Seoul National; this college has been the most prestigious in Korea (like Harvard in America). Unfortunately, his lessons were awful and not helpful for my grades at all. Above all, he had a violent temper and unpleasant character; he was not a teacher material, to begin with.

But my parents were greedy; they thought that it was the best way for my brother and me. I felt like the parents thought my brother and I were the future income for them: My brother and I should get better grades and jobs, so we can support them with more money later on. Anyway, that guy was from Busan where is far from Seoul. Eventually, except me, all of our family *agreed* that the guy should stay in our house for his own college study and teach us in the evening.

When I think about it now, that guy was nothing but a garbage. Even though he was only 22, he smoked cigarettes crazily. One day, my smoker father visited his room and was shocked by how much cigarette odor was stuck in that room; that guy was a drinker, too. Since our home was far from his college even inside Seoul, I recall that he skipped his classes a lot; the guy complained that he got five F's during a semester since he made a lot of effort to teach us: *Not true.* Simply, he was a terrible student not doing his job: **He failed because of him.**

What shocked me later was that his parents turned out to be extremely wealthy. My mother's hometown is Busan, so I had a chance to visit his parents' house, while I visited my grandmother. I was surprised at the size of the house. I still remember he complained once in vanity that his parents got $8 Million USD fine from the IRS after a tax audit; it was believable considering the house. But, as a result of his poor grades, I learned that he could not study abroad in America despite the fortune of his parents. Korea is wealthier now, but it is still a small and monotonous country. A lot of people are eager to get out of there for many reasons. But I believe that his seriously bad grades were the reason to block him from getting better opportunities.

When I checked him last in 2016, he seemed to own an English kindergarten in Korea: **I personally think that this is a shame.** I guess the only job experience he had was tutoring, so he might have decided to go for it. I found out that his mother was a pharmacist[4] when I was at his house; seemingly, both of his parents studied well; I never liked that guy since he was physically violent to my brother and me. He was a loser who wasted youth on heavy smoking, after all.

The reason why drinking and smoking are horrible is for their long term effects; these will bring health issues later on; as a result, we can end up spending way more during our lifetime. Even for the super rich, our bodies are the most important assets. An asset is something that brings money to us; does it make sense that a bar owner damages his own place and complains about lack of customers? I believe that wealth

---

[4] Not Pharmacy Technician

building starts with protecting our foremost assets: Bodies. As Emerson once said, "the first *wealth* is *health*."

* * *

Summary

1. If you are serious about getting out of poverty, quit drinking and smoking first.
2. These two can bring millions of other problems.
3. These two consume a lot of time, too.

2

Having too Many Children

Human population does not have to be bigger than it is now.

-Brad Kong

Charles Dickens (1812-1870) was an English author who wrote *Oliver Twist* and *A Christmas Carol*. He and his wife Catherine married in 1836, when Charles was 24 and she was 21. From then until the time of their divorce 22 years later, *Catherine got pregnant and gave birth to 10 children*. It shows that Dickens' own childhood had been painful enough already. At the age of 12, with his father imprisoned for debt, he had to work in a shoe factory, pasting labels on jars of shoe polish for a few shillings each week; then, his parents had eight children and Charles was the second.

Although I don't personally expect my daughter would be a good money maker, which is perfectly fine, it seems Dickens had thought differently. Unhappily, none of his children turned out to be a successful writer like him and it says he officially lamented that, "having brought up the largest family ever known with the smallest disposition to do anything for themselves." In other words, he had to virtually pay everything for his children until he passed away. It shows that Dickens grew miserable about his marriage eventually: **The history reported that he resented the fact that he had so many children to support**; somehow, he saw it as his wife's fault. He did not approve of Catherine's lack of energy and began to indicate that she had never been his intellectual equal. In June 1858, Charles and Catherine filed for divorce, which was rare back then, and he started seeing a new woman named Turnan.

I have one child partly because I had a hard time, financially: Isn't it logical? No money, so I decided not to have more than I could afford. Unfortunately, a lot of people, especially poor ones, don't seem to think this way; some give many births no matter what. And I feel some fortify their poverty that way: **It almost looks like that they make sure to be broke for the rest of their lives.**

* * *

Regrettably, Jennifer and Sarah Hart couple murdered their *six* adopted children by driving the family's SUV off a cliff in Mendocino County, CA in 2018; all eight people were in the vehicle during the accident. Police found the bodies of seven people in or near the crashed vehicle; the county judge ruled that the body of one missing child was in the vehicle at the time of the crash, so a death certificate was signed on the missing child as well.

Toxicology results showed that Jennifer's blood alcohol content was over the legal limit; Sarah and two children had Benadryl in their bodies. Sarah had made Google searches to inquire about "the lethality of Benadryl" and "the nature of death by drowning;" her searches also included "No-kill shelters for dogs" as the family had two pets; apparently, this suicide had been planned in advance. It showed that Sarah told her co-worker that she wished someone told her that "It is okay not to have a big family."

Wikipedia shows that the couple had been struggling with and physically abusing the children for years.

I think it was very *noble* for this lesbian couple to adopt orphans; it's one way to take care of kids who need help without increasing the human population. Still, I think we should admit that taking care of children is extremely hard: *No reason to go too ambitious about it.* I know this adoption case is different from producing too many babies. Regardless, there are a lot of people having so many children no matter what (particularly low income or Latin American families). After the success of *Jon and Kate plus 8* shows, there are more couples giving birth to sextuplets and putting them on TV.

Personally, I do *not* consider producing a lot of babies an *accomplishment*; especially, there is nothing much for a man to do to make that happen; at least, women have to go through pregnancy and labor, but what does a man do exactly? Eating a lot of food is not an achievement; sleeping for long is not a success. From a point of view, all of these are just results caused by irresponsibilities of not controlling basic instincts.

* * *

I watched a documentary about poor senior citizens in Korea the other day; it shows that suicide rate in the country is the highest among OECD[5]s in the past two decades; this has happened, especially because of severe poverty among the elderly after retirements. They interviewed an old man who had been a construction painter for life. He lived in a small room in a decaying

[5] Organization for Economic Co-operation and Development: In other words, 38 wealthiest countries in the world.

residence; he said he watches TV all day and eats a small rice porridge twice a day from a convenience store; he and his wife had raised three children in that space though they all moved out as adults.

Suddenly, this idea hitted me: "*If he had only one child instead of three, could things have been better?*" I am experiencing that it costs a lot to raise one. Subsequently, I have wondered about this: "Korea is super crowded now; it's getting even more every year. Was it necessary for him to have even one?" The human population is increasing fast everywhere on Earth as of 2023: **More than ever**. This may be something we have to consider before moving on to the next stage of evolution.

* * *

Having too many children *blindly* can be a sin in a sense; at least, it can be a very selfish act as **our survival heavily depends on the death of other animals.** As much as our lives are important, their lives matter, too. I personally do not eat chicken, but it shows that over 50 billion chickens are slaughtered worldwide every year; others are butchered as well, including cows, pigs, sheep, goats, ducks, fishes, etc; certainly, livestock are not the only animals killed by humans.

Human population is expected to be over 9.2 billion by 2040, according to the Director of National Intelligence: **It means over 1 billion more humans will be created and added on top of the current population in the next 17 years;** this is an extremely fast increase in any animal population. People often suffer when they give birth and raise children physically or financially; I don't see a visible need for us to go through more pains while struggling.

I saw an Indonesian lady's video on YouTube the other day. She was the wife of a Korean man and it seemed the couple made tons of foods on a regular basis and donated them to poor children in Bali, Indonesia; it was supposed to be a humanitarian thing. One day, the couple bought a big pig (150 lb.) to kill and cook. I do not know why, but the lady was so elated with a big smile and tried to carry the pig with laughter with other villagers while the pig was screaming to death; I have never heard of such a horrific scream. I felt disgusted by her mindset: "Only humans matter and nothing else does." I think we ought to change our attitudes: **Humans will not last long by being offensive to others forever;** changing our views can be the only way we can make our survival a little longer.

* * *

There is a movie titled Brokeback *Mountain* starring Gyllenhaal and Ledger; one was the rich and the other was the poor. There was a restaurant scene; poor Ledger said that, "You forgot what it's like being *broke* all the time. Have you ever heard of child support?" Then, he burst into tears. The rich had only one child and the poor had three children (2 girls and 1 stepchild). There is a legendary old tale called *Heung-bu story* in Korea; there were two brothers; one was rich and the other was poor. The rich did not have a child, but the poor had nine children. Here is a question, though: *Do we have to have a lot of children from now on?*

It shows that the human population was about 300 million in the year of 1 (AD 1), when Jesus Christ was born, according to the book *8 Billion and Counting* by Scuibba. Now it is about 8 billion in the year of 2023; it represents 7% of the total population of humans ever born on Earth; she said that about 108 billion people have been born and died throughout the history of Earth.

The U.N. projected that the human population will be over 9 billion by 2040: *More than an exponential growth;* this explosion has never happened on Earth before. Delivering and raising a child is hard work for everyone, which requires a lot of sacrifices, too. When we sacrifice ourselves, I think someone else should get benefit out of it, at least: Do you agree? Otherwise, all of our sacrifices will go in vain. **Yet have you ever thought that no one gets benefit out of our rapid population growth?** What if we sacrifice for nothing? Is it possible that the Earth gets hurt or resources are depleted faster not "in spite of", but "because of" our hard work?

* * *

Have you ever thought that having too many kids can be a reason for a divorce? No one claims this, but it's highly likable, according to my experience and observations; it is important since people file bankruptcies because of divorces. I used to wonder why some parents get divorced long after having three kids; it takes several years for a couple to have multiple kids; I thought that they would have known each other well enough, before having many children. Now, as a parent, I can reasonably suspect that *having too many kids itself may be the reason to get divorced*: **For example, it is statistically true that mothers with twins have higher rates of divorces than one in America**; the rate gets even higher when parents have bigger multiplets. I believe that every marriage can be greatly different, depending on the number of children a family has.

In a sense, I feel that getting married is kind of similar to getting a job, especially for full-time housewives. If we suppose a housewife is a job, it can be heaven to hell, depending on the number of kids; to me, taking care of only one child itself is an enormous amount of work. Certainly, marriage life can be hell to heaven based on a lot of things; *the difference is that we can still decide and control how many kids we will have, at least.* We can inherit hardships from our parents, which often we cannot control. Still, in my case, I was able to decide how many kids I will have: **We don't have to create hardships for ourselves if we have a choice.**

Do you know how to avoid a divorce? From my point of view as a husband, it is crucial that the home should be a *livable place* for a wife. In other words, I believe a pleasant marriage means the amount of work in a household should be doable for a wife; at least, it shouldn't be a hellish amount. Otherwise, it is more probable that she may feel like giving it up. At least, those feelings happened to me in my previous jobs.

Certainly, a wife can still stay and do large amounts of work without complaining, even when her husband brings meager wages to home: *But why is this situation necessary?* What if we have a choice to make situations better? Isn't it better for wives to get little amounts of work to do? Isn't it *even better* if they do those while husbands are rich? Less women will file divorces in better conditions. **The job of a housewife is not strikingly different from jobs outside.** I think it is husbands' judgment to create livable environments for wives and avoid divorces.

* * *

Imagine our house is a restaurant; from a point of view, home is a place to make and serve foods. Then, which restaurant would you like to work at? A or B?

A

B

If the two households have the same income, I would choose to work at "A." Some restaurants have a crazy amount of customers with a lot of work to do; still, when owners pay employees well with benefits, many laborers stay despite hellish amounts of work; these are usually upscale restaurants.

In another type, pay is barely minimum, but they have a small amount of work to do. I have seen employees stay for decades in this type of restaurant; these places are often in big hospitals or nursing homes; a huge medical facility can have several restaurants inside. I used to work in one of those only for breakfast time for months; that was the *easiest job* I ever had; not many eat breakfasts compared with lunch or dinner, to begin with. Unless caring for more salary, working only four hours in the morning was ideal; they didn't care much about the number of guests eating; the facility made money out of care givings, surgeries or insurances, instead. I think that my home is similar to this situation: I cannot bring a huge income, yet my wife has less work with one child.

On the other hand, most restaurants on the streets do not pay employees a lot while having too much work to do. So many servers quit on a weekly basis; employee turnover is high and labor shortages are constant in those. I believe most families (60%), having wives with jobs and two children (or more), are in this condition; the high employee quitting rates are similar to the high divorce rates in America.

Conclusively, the most ideal option for a wife is that she gets paid a lot while having a tiny amount of work. Still, husbands can try to make the condition that their wives have little things to do, even when they cannot bring a lot of money home: *Planning wisely from the start could be cheaper than going through divorces.* Then, how can I decrease the amount of work for my wife? One way is having fewer babies. Here is the right question, though: **What blocks you from having *less* babies?** Personally, I do not see a disadvantage when my wife has less chores; frankly, I feel less guilty when I know that she's not having a hard time with child care.

* * *

I honestly do not know how others can take care of more than *one* child. I used to take my daughter everywhere by the time she got into elementary school: libraries, zoos, museums, aquariums, restaurants, malls, etc. I spent plenty of time with her outside during the summers and felt good about myself to be a great dad. I thought that, "I am such a great husband to give my wife enough time to take some rest." Unfortunately, it did *not last* long; I think I got exhausted after doing that for a few years.

Now it has been several years that only my wife has taken care of my daughter exclusively; I have gotten too tired; I just do not have energy any more to play with my daughter, not to mention bring her out; it actually requires a lot of energy when we think about it. Fortunately, we have a very nice lady next door and my daughter spends time with her frequently; more luckily, her mother visited this summer and she brought my daughter out to the farmer's market the other day, too. So I would say that four adults take care of one child now; it seems it really takes a village to raise a child. I am not sure if I am particularly bad with a child; all I know is I am very tired.

I think raising a child is hard in two aspects: Physical and financial. I just mentioned the physical part, but it costs a lot, too. I am from a wealthy family and got multiple financial support from my parents, but it has not been as cheap as I expected in the beginning of 2010. One question, regardless, tough: *Is it necessary to go through more of this hardship?* **Does anyone get benefits out of repetition?** No and *No one* really does: It is just our instinct to leave an offspring; no one seems to get particular benefits out of overpopulation.

First of all, I detest crowded places. I was not peculiarly like this when I was young. But after I became 40, I started hating crowdedness and loud noises more every year. During the COVID quarantine in 2021, I was happy to be in our library since I was virtually the only one in the building; others did not get out of their houses as much. I literally experienced from hell to heaven in the same spot. That is why I believe a country like Bangladesh is anguished: **Less because of poverty, more because of overcrowdedness.**

* * *

Currently, I am reading *12 Rules for Life* by Peterson. It's a top seller, but only *theoretically* well written in my opinion: No *practical* solutions. It shows that the author has been a professor at Harvard for almost 30 years; not many people are in that position and I felt his suggestions are not realistic to the bottom 50% in our society.

The book starts with a story about lobsters; they have been on Earth for over 400 million years. He explained that even they have a sense of social hierarchy deep in their brains; every animal has the sense instinctively, including humans. So he suggested that it is important for us to "stand up straight with our shoulders back." Apparently, this straight posture shows others the sign of a winner and will prevent possible conflicts with them. This may be a great scientific point, but wrong solution.

As he explained, Earth has too many animals, but too few ideal shelters and resources. That is why fighting happens everywhere all the time; in classrooms, Ukraine borders or wherever. According to the book, after fighting, the winners stand up straight and the losers shrink their postures; it says that this has happened throughout history on Earth. So is being bossy a good solution? I still believe that everyone gets hurt one way or another that way.

I think the better solution is that we should learn how to give up for more after having enough. I think that is what intelligent *Homo sapiens* should do; otherwise, there is no difference between us and lobsters. I believe having a showy posture may be effective to defend ourselves, at most; keeping the dominating posture, being competitive or working longer is not the answer; we will only get injured more if we keep exposing ourselves in brawls. I think we should lessen greedy attempts if there is no point in getting more; we are not the robin birds as in the book. It is time to think differently as modern humans who have evolved from the original *Sapiens* 300,000 years ago; no point to kill each other as *Australopithecus* had 4 million years ago.

People often put themselves in danger not because they need something, but because they want more: **Greed is the enemy.** While a few are excellent at keeping in good posture, others may lose more: these triumphs and defeats have caused misery for all of us; everyone loses this way in the end. **We should learn how to stop when enough is enough;** we should control ourselves to make things better for everyone; it includes every animal, plant or other life on Earth. I felt unpleasant that most books have been written only for humans.

I remember Peterson was once on a talk show and the host asked him, "How many children is ideal for a family?" He directly answered, "I don't think one is a good number." He said children can learn from each other when parents have *two* kids. This was nonsense as families do not live separately in a prison cell. I think he answered "two" since he has two kids. Or two is fine since Canada, where he lives, is totally empty. I don't think we can expect practical advice from a Havard professor for average fathers who worry about daycare fees. I strongly believe that one child *at most* a family is the way to go. Earth will be super crowded in the end; *this can only trigger extinction faster.* **Not reaching the stage of overpopulation is for both humans and other lives on Earth.**

* * *

The summary: "Having a lot of babies is the number one reason for poverty and social problems. Earth is already crowded and depleting enough that no one needs to have more than one baby any more. Regardless, 1.2 billion of the new population will be degenerated by 2040, so poor people don't have to try hard." We all know that humans have caused miseries on Earth; people talk about Jewish holocaust or African slavery. But did you notice that tons of animals are born to live only a couple of months and *butchered*? We can be vegetarians to help them. Or, more ultimately, we can have fewer babies.

The human population will be over 9 billion by 2040, regardless if I have one more baby or not; one more baby can contribute to killing an extra 100 chickens; meal issue for us, but it is a life or death matter for them. Simultaneously, I am glad I have only one child since I have been less stressed out financially. Conclusively, **I believe that having fewer babies is a win-win situation**: Good for relieving my stress, good for chickens and good for the Earth's environment, including limited resources.

* * *

In a sense, no one *needs* to have a baby any more: **No animal on Earth has such an obligation, to begin with.** My daughter was born when I still owned the video game store in 2010; it was a small store (900 sf). I barely made a monthly rent of $1,200 back then, so I could not hire any employee throughout the eight years. My wife taught at a music school two days a week; a huge music store had the school inside. She was popular that her schedules were all booked completely from morning till evening (no lunch break); I heard that, rarely, some artists didn't have a single student.

I had to do double duties on those two days: taking care of my store and daughter together. We set up a baby room with the "pack and play" crib from Greco in the back. I had a hard time whenever a good amount of customers flooded in, all at once. That had happened all along for the last four years of my store life. We never knew what would happen 10 minutes later in that place; it had been empty or crowded; I was busy with eBay sales[6], too.

The store had a big screen TV for video games; I used to watch reality shows like "Jon and Kate plus 8" or "Nineteen plus counting." I was curious how others can take care of 6 identical babies or 19 kids in a family. Taking care of only one had been more than a struggle for me (still *one* is hard even though my wife takes care of her most).

Eventually, humans have conquered the Earth and become the most dominant species. On a large scale, it is devastating that the top of the food chain is getting bigger. Most conflicts happen fundamentally because too many people share too little resources. On a personal scale, once we have a baby, we generally face two problems; first of all, we cannot work ourselves since we have to take care of the baby. Secondly, our spending becomes doubled for the baby while we cannot work.

* * *

Like many of you, I had pressure to have more babies in my 30s. It came from everywhere: parents, wife, friends, TV, social media, etc. Physically, I was able to do so. But I am glad I have stuck to my opinion and managed not to have more. In fact, having only one child turned out to be the best decision I have made, after all. I closed out my video game store when the lease was over in 2014. I took a

---

[6] I had been a top rated seller since 2003.

break for 1 year and found a job in the nursing home nearby in 2015. After working at the nursing home for 7 years, I decided to resign in 2022. The place had been worse every year and eventually filed Chapter 11 bankruptcy in 2023; it had so much waste all the time. I started the weekend dishwasher job as they requested; it was fine only in the first 2 years. Then, a horrible Mexican sous chef came and things got unnecessarily stressful.

I tried to transfer to other departments after getting a medical coder license in 2018; it did not work out for gender discrimination I suspect. The director of health information was a snobbish, unpleasant woman; I found out that all the workers and receptionists in that department were women: *every single one of them*. I did not make a big deal since it was not a high paying job or pleasant place to work, anyway; I learned that the woman director was fairly obnoxious during the job interview. I could see why so many women quit that seemingly easy job. Moreover, I believe that I was overqualified with a certificate which was not required. It was nonsense for me to try hard to share an awkward time with that boss.

COVID arrived two years later and the dishwashers got even shorter in that nursing home after 2020. I tried to transfer to a wait staff only to avoid the horrid sous chef, but it did not work out again for any reason I could understand. I had worked two positions for the last 8 months of my employment: the weekend dishwasher and weekday morning waiter; I was not able to transfer to the wait staff department completely for any reason. I felt it seems the entire managers in that nursing home tried to force me to be a dishwasher since it was severely short.

Finally, a new company came and took over only the entire dining department in 2022; I did not know there was a transfer deadline to the new company. I was scheduled to take a pharmacy technician exam around that time, which I passed at the first try. I told them I can still work as a dishwasher only on Sunday if they still need me. They said the transfer deadline had passed and suggested a slightly lower hourly rate; I am glad that I wrote a resignation letter and quit. It was a bad job in many senses: toxic chemicals to my skin, low quality managers, etc. Truthfully, I have been wealthy enough not to get any job at all by then; my investments have been successful all along; I have not been in a situation to need a job or to earn certificates.

Still, do you know what I was glad the most when I decided to get out of the nursing home completely? Having enough savings? Getting dividends and interest to cover my expenses? Having earned two certificates? My wife has been working all along? **Above all, I was glad the most that I have only one child to support.** During the 7 years, I had witnessed that good guys stuck in that dreadful job. Joe and Riccardo had four kids each; these two were nice guys, but had worked for two different jobs. I feel truly sorry for them since the working environment there was hostile, harmful and unfair: *Hell created by humans*.

We may start seeing more career changes from now on as people live longer. When people lived only until 60, I assume that people never really changed their professions and passed away after retirement. Soon, the average Joe like you and me will live up to 100; having a career change can be more common. Number of kids we need to feed will matter whenever we change our jobs for any reason: job loss, economic depression, better positions, ambitions, etc.

* * *

I think hardships have two types: ***given and created***. If we are born in a poor family or have a sick mother to take care of, these are given hardships. But if we create four children and struggle to support them, those are hardships created by us. We can have a hardship**: We do not have to create one.** There was a woman cook named Roza in the kitchen of the nursing home; she was a Cuban Mexican single mother with a lot of tattoos and piercings; I never liked her since she was *disrespectful* to dishwashers. She had a mother with liver cancer and five children to support (three different fathers). **Her sick mother might be a given hardship; her five kids were a hardship created by her**; I had heard her complaining about money, occasionally.

Still her action to create more kids could be beneficial for our society, right? Not necessarily. I recall that she eventually got fired in 2018; I believe the reason was drug related. I guess she probably has taken welfare checks since her Facebook shows that she has been at home with toddlers; it's not necessarily advantageous for our tax. And her children can be troublemakers later on as the mother was not sane: Building more prisons can be another tax loss. In conclusion, I do not believe that her actions to create five kids is inevitably favorable.

Nonetheless, are her children happy, at least? I doubt that since they had been without fathers or enough money. Conclusively, producing five kids might not be optimal for her own wellbeing, society or even children themselves; I don't think any baby wants to be born in that condition; no one gets benefit while Earth gets exponentially crowded.

Life is harsh already: true for all the animals here. I used to think that whatever happens in our lives is mostly luck; it's probable only until we become 20 years old. Now, at the age of 49, I can say this: **We are the ones who decide our own destinies.** *Having a hard time doesn't mean others get benefit out of it;* we can make our life grueling or we don't have to. At least, we have some choices.

* * *

Summary

1. We do not have to push ourselves to have a lot of children any more.
2. Regardless of whether I have one or two, the human population will be 9 billion soon. I know I would have had a way harder time if I had two.
3. We do not have to sacrifice ourselves more only to deplete resources faster.

3

Getting into Debt Too Easily

If money is a religion, debt is a cult.
-Brad Kong

Believe it or not, not paying a debt used to be a felony; it was common to go to prison for that. People still go to court when they file a bankruptcy: Why? It is a crime as I said. I use my credit card everyday though I have never owed any money; virtually, we cannot live without debt nowadays. Still, it's worth thinking one more time before signing up for a big one; basically, we pay more for the same thing in the end.

There is a book titled *Debt: The First 5000 Years* by Graeber. It explains that debt was invented during the Sumer civilization in Mesopotamia[7] about 3,500 B.C. I would say that this concept of debt is a pretty recent thing since it was systematically formed only 5,500 years ago. Humans started farming only about 10,000 years ago; however, we have been on Earth for as long as six million years. It has been pretty much normal for humans not to have any debt at all throughout history.

I think that the smartest thing I did *with money* was buying my condo with full cash in 2013. I know it is hard, especially when we live in the east or west coast regions in America; typically, the house prices there are three times higher than in the Midwest where I live. In 2008, the

---

[7] It is the south central region of Iraq in 2023.

subprime mortgage crisis broke out and I recall that it had lasted about five years. A huge amount of foreclosures and short sales came out on the market; these dropped housing prices significantly. By then, I had lived in rental apartments for about fourteen years. I had about $80,000 emergency fund my parents gave me after my daughter was born; I saved all in CDs at the bank initially. The price of a one-bedroom condo tanked to $60,000, so I bought it quickly.

One *advantage* when we buy a house in full is a *discount.* The nice Polish couple owners[8] said that they had two houses and were in need of cash. I got a $5,000 discount[9] immediately when I suggested a cash payment. I used to pay $900 a month for rent by 2013; a one bedroom rent is about $1,300 a month in my town as of 2023. Now I pay about $367 HOA fee (association fee) a month, so I believe I am saving about $900 a month; which makes the annual saving $9,000 a year after deducting about $1,700 property tax I pay as a condo owner. I have lived here close to 10 years now, so probably $90,000 has been saved only for not having a rent. I will save even more if I stay here longer.

It shows that the average lifespan of males is 78 years in America by 2020. I felt it's a little too much to spend 30 years on paying mortgages in that sense; it's like spending most of adult lives on paying for a house. I could have gone for a two-story house with a mortgage in 2012; I am glad that I didn't. In general, housing costs much more with debts. More importantly, I could have not been a writer if I

[8] I am glad they removed the stove in this unit, which was a fire hazard and makes this 850 sf condo even smaller. Without them, I would have not known that we even have an option to remove it.

[9] The original listing price was $65,000 in 2013.

had chosen that option; I could have worked for a medical coder job, which I do not care about, only to pay a home loan. *I just couldn't let myself waste three decades that way.*

* * *

Debts are everywhere nowadays: a mortgage, car loan or credit card balance; those are the major three types. Personally, I do not have any of those, though. I am using two credit cards all the time, but the balances are always close to $0 at the end of month. It is not like I am rich: I just don't spend more. Slavery from Africa might have been over 200 years ago; now people have created a new system. **In this brilliant structure, slaves do not even know that they are the ones.** It doesn't even matter if we are a black, white or yellow; if we are poor, financially illiterate or both, we just get sucked in. Some are willing to wait in line for hours to get into these traps; some show off they are in. Rarely, I wonder if some internet trolls don't know how to use a calculator; I felt *they must have not graduated elementary;* **We pay more for the same things with debt;** some are even proud to pay more since they believe that everyone in the world does the same thing; statistics show that only 65% of Americans have mortgages.

I argue that there is nothing really worth trying with debt. I know that we end up using debt somehow during lifetimes. But this idea should be the basic: ***No debt* or as little as possible.** Debt has a lot of names nowadays: balance, credit, margin, card remainder, etc; these are merely other names of leftover debt, business debt, investment debt and card debt; let's not get confused by fancy names. Having debt used to be considered a very bad thing decades ago; it has become a natural part of our lives now. I have never paid any interest on my two cards for a decade; in fact, I get cash backs from both every month; my spending limits are about $17,000 from both combined. I had a car loan 9 years ago, but the 3-year loan was paid off within 3 months in 2014.

* * *

It is proven that people cannot focus on their jobs when they have worries: How do we get constant worries? One way is having a debt; it can distract us regularly, so we may make less money in the end. How can we know if our lives are going in a positive direction? In my opinion, there are a couple of barometers to check that straight: our weights and debt situation. Are you lean? Then, more likely your life is in a good position; no one gets skinny automatically these days; foods are cheap and everywhere. Weight loss requires medical knowledge, controls and disciplines. Less likely we will spend a lot on medical bills in the future; this is a sign that our lives are headed in a better direction.

The other indicator can be our debt situation in my opinion; frankly, having any type of debt is not very good news to anyone, to begin with. Do you own a house outright without having a mortgage or rent? Then, definitely your life has been productive so far; you might not be rich yet, but on the way. Paying for a house in full requires financial knowledge, savings, luck and having strong wills as a majority get mortgages blindly. **While smart people try to hide their wealths, stupids pretend to have them with debts**; for example, some buy luxury cars with auto loans; this is purely idiotic from a perspective. I know a couple of Korean mothers whose children got kidnapped after pretending to be affluent[10]. Regardless, these can offend others for no reason while they lose money on loan interests themselves.

* * *

Unfortunately, I never really have had an ideal relationship with my father. But I admit that he has been right about one thing: **No debt.** He frequently said to me and my brother that, "Your dad does not have a debt." He has not been inevitably a pleasant person to deal with, but his voice changed tenderly whenever he mentioned this.

What he meant by "debt" was "business debt," by the way. Not using a debt to buy a house or car was out of the question to him (he always used full cash for those). If you know about old Korean men, you will understand what I mean. Regardless, what can I say? He is the one who made $20 M from scratch. Those old Koreans did not have anything since the Korean war ended less than 70 years ago; South Korea was a ruin 60 years ago just like Ukraine now. While most Koreans are not as rich as my father, it seems that the "no debt" policy has worked out for him.

I found this Buddhist maxim online: "Pain is not holding you; you are the one holding the pain. If you cannot save yourself, no one can. We are the result of the thought in the past; we will become the person in our thinking." The Dalai Lama once said, "Humans are created to be loved and stuff are created to be used. Stuff are being loved and humans are being used nowadays." I think this applies to materialism in general, but especially true to cars and houses.

---

[10] The movie *Secret Sunshine* is based on true stories.

* * *

There was a Korean internet community I used to go to; trolls there were stupid, spending-wise. It seemed they all made traditional and boring financial mistakes: Very typical lives, including full time jobs, mortgages, car loans, two cars, *two* children, wives with *no* job, etc. I had never expected a maverick, but I was amazed at how those people live monotonously without any twist at all. Funny thing was that some tried to argue with me despite the fact that they all pay double on their house with mortgages.[11] There is nothing wrong with it technically: Using a mortgage is reasonable when even the cheapest houses are too expensive (i.e., in San Francisco or NYC); trolls there shouldn't have argued that getting debt is better than the full cash payment.

In the community, I saw that some bought big houses with the hope that their house prices will jump up someday. Nowadays the single[12] population is increasing faster and less likely they will buy big houses for only one person in a family. I honestly do not think that house tags will go up more than inflation, but probably condo prices will increase more as single people prefer small units.

People are getting debts unconsciously. I think most tend to become frugal after being burned by a debt somehow. Honestly, I used to be a big spender myself, especially during the time I owned a business; during the *Cyb Knight* period, I remember that I owed up to $9,000 credit card debt once by 2009; it was a business debt, not

[11] It is mathematically true that people often make their house costs close to double with 30-year mortgages.
[12] People who is not married

really from personal consumption, though. My mother saved me once then and I have never had the same problem again so far. I live frugally even without a car these days.

I believe that the second biggest reason why people cannot quit a bad job is keeping a persistent debt; probably, mortgage is the common reason. In my opinion, buying a bigger house to show off could be a worse reason than having many kids, which is the number one reason, I believe, for putting up with a hellish job. **Debt will never bring us a profit.** I read some Korean trolls declaring that living in a bigger house means a higher quality of life; these are stupid. **Bigger houses only guarantee that we have more chores for the buildings;** we may or may not be happier as houses can be a nightmare, too; some building problems are impossible to solve. In reality, debt can seriously lower our quality of life. Please trust me that nothing is more important than peace of mind.

* * *

Summary

1. No debt or as little as possible.
2. Not having a debt at all is a perfectly *normal* thing.
3. See if you can buy a small house with full cash; a complete homeownership has been a life changing benefit for me.

4

Not Using Systems Already Paid For

We should use what's already paid first.
-Brad Kong

There is a group of movies titled the *007 series* (*James Bond* films); the first one *Dr. No* was released in 1962. Since then, 24 other *James Bond* films have been directed by 2021; the last one was *No Time to Die* starring Daniel Craig. There are thousands of action movies released worldwide every year; unfortunately, most fail commercially. Still, if a movie is titled with 007, it helps to beat the competition and bring millions of audiences to screens. The similar examples are *Mission: Impossible* or *Harry Potter* series. I think that one of the most obvious examples to use systems they already built is franchising.

The same thing goes for books. One of my favorite writers, Bryson has written 19 books as of 2023. Oddly, it doesn't seem any of his books have similarity to each other; one is about his childhood and another is about the universe or human body. In my opinion, he could have made more money if he had arranged his books in a type of franchise; for example, universe and body could be in *Bryson's science* series I and II. When readers see II in a book title, they automatically assume that there is I; this is automatic advertisement without spending an extra money. Besides, some bookworms have obsessions to collect everything in a series and complete them. Only a portion of authors do this even though many have published myriads of books. In the worst cases, some authors do not even use the same pen name. At least, Bryson used the same name, so people can find all of his works by it. I think we can apply this concept of "using what we already made or paid" to our personal finances, too; some are broke since they do not utilize it.

* * *

I think I am a library *maniac* by nature; I have visited more than 25 libraries in Chicagoland by 2023. While the one in Schaumburg is probably the best in Chicagoland, I found every library has its own ups and downs. One of my sanctuaries is the one in Wheelings; it's hidden, so no outsider goes there; it's in the newest building full of modern features. I like the one in Mount Prospect; it has the latest bestsellers from Korea; sometimes I wonder who manages the section since all are carefully chosen top sellers; I am sure the person actually read those. The one in Arlington Heights has decent interior designs; it is near multiple restaurants in the downtown of the village. The one in Oak park has a huge comic book section; the building has five stories and the entire second floor is for graphic novels. If you are Korean, you must visit the one in Glenview and Harold Washington in downtown Chicago; these two have massive amounts of Korean books; I think that only libraries in Korea have more than these two.

(Image source: Starfield Library)

The point is that **only *some* of us go to libraries while *all* of us have paid for them already with property taxes.** I used to work at a nursing home, which is only a quarter mile away from the big library I visit on a weekly basis; the place hired about 1,000 employees. Strangely, I have never run into any of my coworkers there in the last decade (i.e., cooks or servers). Actually, in this case, maybe I should say that I was lucky; meeting them could have been awkward since not everyone from the job was pleasant. Still, you know what, though? *Maybe those employees still work there since they never go to the library*; the facility clearly helped me get two new certificates[13].

[13] Medical coder and pharmacy technician.

By the way, do you know how I am certain that we all paid for the library *already*? Some may think that they are renting apartments, so have never paid property tax, part of which always goes to the libraries. **Rents[14] already include property taxes;** a portion of apartment rent is always property tax without exception; as a result, everyone has paid equally for libraries.

There are people spending money "first" no matter what; many do that unconsciously. *I think it is more logical to use "everything free" first and spend money if that is not enough.* For example, some people check the library first if there is a new movie coming out; they check if their friends have it. But others check Redbox *first* to rent it or go to Target, Walmart or Amazon to buy it; I think it is reasonable to do those if the movie is not available anywhere for free.

* * *

We have paid millions of things already while we don't notice: **Some never use those and spend extra money, being unaware of them.** Whenever I see my property tax bills, I can find that a good portion always goes to the community college nearby. There are a lot of students, including myself, going to a four-year university straight from high school, instead of finishing general courses in their community colleges; which were already paid for by their parents who are homeowners or apt renters. This is fine, but I just try to make a point that we have paid for something equally and some do not use it.

Also, on the bills, I saw that nearly $3 billion goes to the water supply system in our country every year; they spend an

[14] Apartment rent = property tax + rental company profit

extreme amount on ensuring the quality of water delivered to homes. Some still order water from Hinckley or buy it at Jewel with additional charges: *Spending double all the time could be the reason for brokeness.* I used to buy millions of water bottles from Sam's club, especially while I had the business. I still buy them from gas stations or convenience stores, instead of using a drinking fountain at libraries, malls or hotels, whose aquatic duct system we already paid for.

Another example is public transportation. Residents in Chicago get property tax bills showing city expenses twice a year and they will find a chunk go to public transits: subways, trains, buses, etc. Yet there are plenty of Chicagonians only driving cars as their sole rides. On top of the transportation charges they already paid for, they spend extra money on cars: car loans, insurances, registrations, parking fees, tickets, gas, repairs, washings, maintenance, accident costs, etc. It's double spendings; one is on public transportations by their property taxes and the other is on cars. I know some cannot live without a car for their jobs: delivery guys, construction workers, etc; most of us grab the car key mindlessly.

Whenever I check my condo property tax bill, I see that only about $1,000,000 goes to our library every six months; I have always thought that it's too small. The library has played a crucial role for this community as a real town square for residents; they have done fabulous jobs, especially compared with the ones in other villages. I insist that they deserve at least $5 million a year; this could be still tiny since over $12 billion are collected in this county every year. It is nonsense that the park district gets over $100 millions while the library only gets $1 M.

* * *

Another example could be the trolleys in this village. We have a big shopping area near my home; there are *free* trolleys connecting major spots: Woodfield mall, Street of Woodfield, Ikea, big strip malls, hotel convention center, etc. Many do not know about those, and only drive their own cars; I am the only passenger in the clean transit nine out of ten times. Without using them, everyone has to go through more traffic and parking jams as the area is often crowded. We had the COVID pandemic for three years by 2022. The federal government sent us stimulus checks during the period; some never got those since they didn't file taxes properly; some missed the $3,500 checks which they could have gotten legally.

The last example would be the swimming pool in this condo complex; we have a reasonably large one right in front of my unit. I have paid for the pool through the HOA association fee every month in the past 10 years. Honestly, I have never used it myself, which has been a total waste. But, after my family moved back in 2017, my daughter has stayed there up to 10 hours a day every summer. I think it is smarter to use it, instead of going to a village pool with paying an extra $10 fee. In fact, locals can come here for free, but some go to Atlantis hotel pool in the Bahamas with paying airline tickets. **Unfortunately, what they get mostly could be just waiting in lines**: lines for the hotel concierge, airline counters, rent car places, tour buses, etc.

How can we be wealthy if we keep spending money double all the time? Chicagoland has myriad CTA subway and Metra stations, and bus stops; not only free trolleys, there are also free vans for seniors. It is a walkable land, so I have lived without a car since 2017. If we are short of money even though we work hard, we may have to check if there is a spot we spend *double* on. There is a reason when our income disappears magically.

* * *

Summary

1. Do not spend money *first* for everything.
2. Check if there is something you have already paid for.
3. See if you can plan in advance to save.

5

Double Spending Lifestyle

If we are short of money while working day and night, something must be wrong from the basis.
-Brad Kong

Anders Hansen is a psychiatry specialist from the Karolinska Institute in Stockholm, Sweden. He accepted 100 volunteers before 2016 and conducted an experiment; he let 50 people do one-hour walking exercise three times a week for 12 months; he let the other 50 people do only stretching exercise without walking. When he checked all their brains, the result was striking: Hippocampus in the brains of walking people increased +2% on average while those of stretching-only people shrank -1%. **He suggested that walking helps our brains grow regardless of age and limits the dementias.**

What do you believe makes us walk less? Probably driving. Most Americans spend fortunes on cars: buying, fueling, repairing, cleaning, etc. Then, many spend wealths *again* on dementia treatments in the hospital later in their lives. **This is a *double spending* in a sense**: Car and hospital costs. *Is it possible if we live without a car and walk for brain health,* to begin with? Then, it's *double saving*: Saving from not owning a car and not going to a memory hospital when we get old. Some buy doughnuts, eat them and go to dentists. Or others do not buy a doughnut from the start and do not go to dentists as much. **I noticed that some people spend double or triple the money all the time for the same results.**

* * *

Those *who spend double* live rather on emotion than logic. Let's assume that everyone goes to the library everyday; I live about 1 mile from ours in town. I always go there by walking and it takes about 25 minutes; which is a good exercise itself. However, I notice that some go to the library by car, then go to the gym by car, spend money on gym membership and do walking exercises there. **It is *quadruple* spending for the same result: gas consumption; gym memberships and clothings; electricity on treadmills, etc.** Similarly, a lot of people go to work by car and go jogging after work: Why don't they just ride bicycles to work from the start, so they can save on gas and don't have to run after work?

On the contrary, I have witnessed some smart people do their hobbies at work. When I was in downtown Chicago the other day, I saw a construction site near the Willis tower; they were building a sort of ground expansion of the skyscraper. For about an hour, I had observed how the tips of new building frames were connected manually[15] by constructors. What struck me the most was a muscular guy trying to connect two huge beams by hand; he seemed to be the type of person going to the gym everyday; apparently, his job also provided him plenty of things to lift the whole day; he seemed to pursue his passion during work outside the gym as well. Another example is the Bloomingdale trail in Chicago. When I was on that walking bridge, I saw myriads of people go to work by bicycles or kick scooters.

* * *

I wonder how carnivore animals were created originally; it must be painful for them to survive; they havc to kill others whenever they need to eat; this is an offensive way of living on

[15] There is no other way.

Earth. On the contrary, the lives of herbivores or omnivores seem to be less hard as plants they feed on do not move. In this sense, the creatures living in the least offensive way could be scavengers; they just eat whenever anything edible is available. I read that lobsters live on the ocean floor and eat debris dropped from the surface or everywhere; it's an example of living in the least offensive way. I believe this is how they have survived for more than 400 million years: **Not bothering others, and being helpful to clean environments.**

Humans are wasteful; we have the most offensive way of lifestyle on Earth. It is not like poor people are frugal while rich people are lavish; we all are *wasteful* to some extent from an earth point of view. We do not see animals like humans in the wild: *Why?* **Wasteful animals must have been extinct already.** Nature does not allow being too offensive or wasteful; humans will be no exception.

Our agriculture started 10,000 years ago at the earliest. If humans become extinct within the next 100,000 years, that is not a long survival span for an average species; dinosaurs had gotten through for over 165 million years on Earth; they are still alive as birds. I agreed with a joke from a Korean biology book: If aliens visit Earth a million years later, their description of humans will be – *The shortest, but most impactfully lived species.*

People can live up to 100 years nowadays. When we check Wikipedia, we can see that a lot of people used to die before 40 even in the 19th century. Some know that the painter, Van Gogh, died at 37; did you know that his art dealer brother, who supported him financially, died at 33 as well? If we start living longer, I do *not* think we should live extravagantly any more: We should live frugally as much as we can from now; otherwise, we may not be able to keep our money all the way until we die at the age of 100. Simply, we have more years left to spend money than our grandparents. When we hear that an old person died, we automatically assume that he or she passed away naturally. **But it is possible that a portion of impoverished seniors' deaths can be actual suicides; which are conveniently reported as natural deaths.** Statistically, houseless or van dwellers die earlier since I suspect it is the only way to *graduate* from their pains; it can be true even for the entire human race on a large scale.

* * *

The weekend dishwasher job at the nursing home was physically hard, especially in the beginning. The place was only 1.2 miles from my home and it took about 30 minutes for me to get there by walking. After getting the medical coder license in 2018, I was wondering if I should keep the job or not even for weekends; it was mentally fine without much stress in the first few years. This is what I thought: 'I can consider it as weekend gym exercises for eight hours; *the only difference is I get paid and get free meals.*' It is true that I have lost a lot of weight and become more muscular since the job; I was more obese[16] and diabetic before. I had commuted strictly by walking[17] throughout 7 years to intensify my exercise. **Some spend money to lose weight while others get paid for the same result.**

It was hard for me to wake up early in the morning, especially during winters. I thought that it would be hard as well if I had to exercise in the gym for 8 hours a day during weekends. **We can skip the gym easily, but we cannot be late for work, so the job had been a better exercise**

---

[16] I used to be up to 165 pounds, but now I am 125 pounds as of 2022.

[17] I still had a brand new car for two years after starting that job

coach in a sense. During the 7 years, there had been extremely cold or snowy days, too: The horrible winters in Chicago. "Well, some go to Mount Everest after spending a fortune on equipment and sherpa; let me consider that I am doing outdoor climbing in Colorado now." The thirty minute adventures to work didn't look bad relatively; the commutes were over quickly. Additionally, that job has taught me why I should not waste money and go back to awful situations. I still feel sorry for people doing that for a living.

Particularly, I felt sorry for a Mexican boy named Omar; he was in his late 20s; he had done that at least for a decade only because he was born in a poor family. **It is sad that being born in poverty is a crime to get that kind of punishment**; the job was painful enough for me to consider it as a penalty, especially over the winters. I used to say to my wife that "*The only crime he committed was being born as the first son of the family*[18]*;*" he was such a great boy who accepted his hardship without a complaint and helped coworkers feel pleasant. I just hope Latinos would not breed blindly, so less children would get punished for no apparent reason at all.

When I was in college, there was a Ukrainian girl who had worked at Disney World for a summer. I assume she wanted to have a vacation there, but could not afford it completely; it seems it was smart for her to work there, get paid and enjoy vacation for about three months. I believe similar things can happen in cruise lines as well; if we do not want to spend money on cruise travel, we can work there, too.

To write this book, I could have hired low incomers and paid them to listen to their stories. I read a graphic novel "Jungle", originally written by Sinclair; it was about immigrants working

---

[18] His parents have five children.

in butcheries during the Great Recession in the early 20th century; I read that their hardship had been intensified after their child was born. It showed in the end that Sinclair actually hired the protagonist in the novel to listen to his story. Alternatively, **I think that the author could have worked in a factory himself and collected information for the book while getting paid;** some do the same thing with making money and others don't. If we keep being short despite working, I think we should check if we spend double on somewhere, somehow.

* * *

Summary

1. Try to walk instead of driving; walking can be a gas saving tool, but also a great exercise itself.
2. Try not to spend double for the same results.
3. It would be great if we can choose a workplace where we can use our passion.

6

Living in an Expensive Area

We can live in a cheaper place and
visit expensive places for travel.
-Brad Kong

Statistically, the east and west regions in America are about 3 times more expensive than the Midwest in terms of housing costs; I personally don't see a clear advantage to living there except that we can go see oceans easily; it is nonsense to pay more to get wildfires (west) or hurricanes (southeast). It seems to be more logical to move from the coasts to mid-America, which is actually happening now. It shows that Texas, Idaho and South Dakota have gotten the biggest moving-in populations since 2020.

I live in Illinois, which is also losing population every year; I believe it's due to high State income or property tax. However, only Chicagoland is still growing and I guess I will keep staying here for reasons. First of all, I think the living cost here is still *fairly low* even after considering higher income taxes. Strangely, property taxes are not that high for condos and townhouses in Illinois; I own a condo and it has been less than $1,800 a year after homeowner's exemption.

Secondly, I bought out my place when it was remarkably low during the subprime mortgage meltdown in 2013; I do not think I can find a residence with this quality in a decent neighborhood for this price any more. It's hard to let it go now since I obviously know I cannot get it back for the same price. Thirdly, the city of Chicago and vicinity have a huge population and have provided me plenty of places to walk around (walking has been my greatest joy). Besides, the city has well established public transportation systems, which help me live without a car now. I used to have symptoms of diabetes and walking has helped me fairly.

* * *

Can you live here?

I concluded that an expensive area may not be a good place to live *by nature*. Let's take Times Square in Manhattan for instance; it is probably the most expensive block in America and basically no one lives there. But let's imagine we can live there for *free*: Is it a nice place to live? I may suffer from noise, crowds, pollution or bright lights all the time. We have to spend more money on rent to live there, yet it doesn't provide us with more optimal conditions we can find in less popular places.

Although there is a difference between the displeasure intensities, I suspect expensive places are somewhat closer to Times Square; there is a reason why they attract more people. And living in a crowded place *must* come with discomfort along with financial burden. Sometimes, I go to downtown Chicago to walk around. I have always thought that I would not visit my village if I lived in Chicago. But you know what? That is the reason why I am happier to live in the suburbs. *Since no one visits my village for travel, I see more peace and less trouble.* I do not recommend anyone to live in a well-known place while paying more.

* * *

Mental comfort is more important than physical one; often people do not realize this. It was too hot yesterday as I live in Chicagoland and it was August, 2022. I thought I would go to a cool place to take a break, and had two choices: Rolling Meadows library or Barnes and Noble bookstore in Schaumburg. Do you know which place I chose? I ended up being in the Rolling Meadows library. It was all about mental comfort; I could stay in that virtually empty library for hours without caring about others' eyes. Barnes and Noble probably will not say a thing to me. Still I know I will get some mysterious pressure to buy a book or drink there (I am sure they don't intend this). Regardless, I just do not feel comfortable in a luxurious place selling something.

Everyone has his or her own sanctuary. When I think about it, this is not about physical comfort: This is always about mental comfort. I particularly like Rolling Meadows library only because no one really goes there; it is clean, but very isolated; most people do not know there is such a library in that area. Even if they do, outsiders still don't go there since it is small or does not have anything special; it is one of a few libraries in Chicagoland not having a single Korean book, for example. I like the library in our town as well, but the problem is it is too successful, popular or crowded; people come from everywhere and many of the staff know who I am. I feel physically comfortable, but mentally less comfortable: **I feel more comfortable when I am anonymous.**

* * *

Most people do not consider this mental comfort aspect *seriously* when they buy a house. I happened to be in our neighbor's condo unit in this building once and found out that they do not have any trees covering their windows (we both live on the top floor in this big building). In my unit, three windows are all covered by four trees. I felt like I was standing on a high platform in front of others while I was in my neighbor's unit. On the contrary, I always feel laid back, hidden or chilling in my unit.

In my opinion, it is not a coincidence that owners change every few years in that neighbor unit. However, the previous owner in my unit had lived here over 20 years until she passed away. Since the longer we stay in a house the more money we make, it is important to check if you can feel comfortable to stay for long before buying a house. Most people focus on checking how the house would look to others: Does it look fancy enough? Some people are not afraid of getting a bad debt (mortgage) to disguise themselves to be wealthy. They end up putting themselves in more uncomfortable situations including getting thieves or financial pressure after all.

* * *

Frankly, I have always thought New York City is the worst place to live in America. At least, I am in a position to judge that. I graduated from SUNY (State University of New York) at Buffalo myself and had chances to visit NYC about 30 times before graduation by 2006. The city has a big Korean community, too. This has been my conclusion about that city so far: Expensive, but dirty. I had chances to visit dozens of other cities in the U.S. as well. According to my experience, most of them were cleaner, cheaper or kinder than NYC.

A few places are more expensive than NYC, but at least it was nicer like San Francisco, CA. I could have settled in NYC if the cost of living was cheaper at least. But I thought it is absurd to pay more to live in a crowded and dirty environment. In NYC, you get smaller spaces for higher rents. Whenever I visited there, I always felt people were under more stress and unkind if not violent. And I noticed that overcharging came from everywhere from restaurants to bridge tolls. I remember I had more cloudy or gloomy weather than sunny there during many visits.

* * *

Have you heard of the "California exodus"? It shows that over 80,000 companies have moved out from CA in the last ten years from 2012: These include Tesla, Hewlett Packard and Oracle. They said that the reasons are high cost of living and State income taxes in CA: A lot of those companies are moving or have moved to Texas State in the Midwest of America.

There used to be a funny and nice Mexican dishwasher named Vincente during the time I worked at the nursing home. He was about 60 years old and had 5 children; he said three of his children live in California. Although I suggested not to, he wound up moving to California in 2019. I heard he worked in construction there now. Wildfires and droughts broke out one by one after he moved to CA, so I am curious if his decision was beneficial.

* * *

I originally planned to include two topics in this chapter: "Expensive regions in America" and "the local areas costing us more money." I think that I have lived in roughly four cities in the U.S. in the last 23 years since 1999: Rochester, Ithaca and Buffalo, NY and Chicago suburb, IL. As I mentioned above, I have never lived in NYC itself, but visited there continually while I lived in NY State for about 6 years. Eventually, I found out that NYC is far more expensive than even the rest of the cities in NY States: The farther from NYC, the cheaper.

There is one Korean community website I used to go to everyday. I used to get surprised whenever I heard their complaints about the cost of living in their cities in CA. An exceptionally large number of people on that site came from Silicon Valley near San Francisco, CA. I believe that it is the most expensive place in America as of 2022. The salaries and house prices they mentioned were unbelievable. I concluded that they probably get paid more, but ended up having nothing in hand as they spent more on mortgages or others after all.

* * *

In conclusion, I would say that the East and West coasts are three times more expensive than the Midwest in America. That applies to rents and house prices as well. But, why is this happening? **In my opinion, that is all about population.** Large amount of the American population lives along the East and West coastal lines and the middle part is pretty much empty in this country. High density of population drives housing prices higher along with other costs in those coastal areas.

Here is one important question, though. Do you get paid three times more when you work in East and West regions? **Absolutely not.** I think the minimum wages are the same if not lower in those areas. Since the minimum wage of Illinois is actually one of the highest in the nation, some jobs in coastal States actually pay less than Midwest. This is why people move to Texas crazily nowadays. Let me tell you what exactly happened to me.

* * *

I was about to graduate from State University of New York in Buffalo, NY in 2006. Most Koreans moved to NYC or surrounding areas after graduation, then. It is the biggest city in America after all, but more importantly, many big Korean communities are in those areas as well. But, at the same time, my girlfriend, who is my wife now, had studied for her doctorate program in Champaign, IL. Simply, I had to choose going to either Chicago or NYC after graduation in that year.

By 2006, I had made money out of my eBay business for about three years. eBay was a bigger business than Amazon once then and I noticed used video games were sold particularly well. EB games and GameStop were growing popular at that time, too. I thought that I can open a similar business to GameStop if I can get a small store space. Only difference is that I could sell games on eBay as well because I have been a power seller on eBay since 2003.

After checking some rents in Manhattan, NYC one night, I arrived at this conclusion: "There is no way I can go there." Store rents were like $10,000 a month for 500 sf space in 2006. I truly wondered what kind of business I needed to open there to make that much money every month (jewelry?). I ended up having a store space for $1,200 a month in Chicago suburb. And, the space was 900 sf, which is bigger than the 500 sf one in NYC I saw online. In a sense, my wife saved my life since she was the only reason why I even considered moving to Chicagoland, anyway. If I chose that area, my life would have been much different than now (probably more miserable).

I still remember that I saw one GameStop store in Manhattan when I was in NYC for the last time in 2006. Could they charge higher prices for games in Manhattan? **I don't think so.** Every brand new Xbox 360 or PS3 game was $60 everywhere in America even until I closed my store in 2014. If anyone charges more, players can always go to Amazon to buy them at $60 at most. But, does the GameStop in Manhattan pay more rent? Of course: **They definitely pay at least a few times more rent than those in other areas.** I really have no idea how they could survive.

* * *

Even though I made an example with businesses, we can apply this to personal finances, too. With the development in the modern technologies, people can do a lot of the same jobs everywhere in America now: Remote work. For example, people can trade stocks online everywhere without living on Wall street in NYC. Since traders make or lose the same amount of money regardless of locations, those who live in cheaper locations will make more profit after all.

One of the similar examples is the writer of the book titled *Pachinko*. I read that she is a Korean American writer living in Manhattan, NY. She will make exactly the same amount of money out of book royalty whether she lives in a countryside or city. **For sure, she will spend more to live in Manhattan, NYC.**

* * *

In the middle of this chapter, I mentioned that the second topic would be "the local areas costing more money". Regardless of the States, I think people tend to spend more when they live near shopping areas. I see some condo or apartment complexes built right on top of or behind malls (e.g., ALOFT at Glen Town Center or Roosevelt Collection Lofts). They look heavenly, but it is possible people can find some attractive, but not needed items easily when they walk around those malls.

Also, I think when people live in the middle of nowhere with nothing nearby, they tend to spend more on gas for cars. I think that it is cheaper to live near supermarkets or public transportations. Even if we work to death, if we do not see a single cent in our pocket, I think it's time to check if living in an expensive area (without a point) could be the reason.

* * *

Summary

1. Expensive places are often the worst places to live.
2. Buy a house for your comfort, not to show it to others.
3. See if you can live in a cheaper State for the same job.

7

Social Media Addiction

We may show too much to enemies.
-Brad Kong

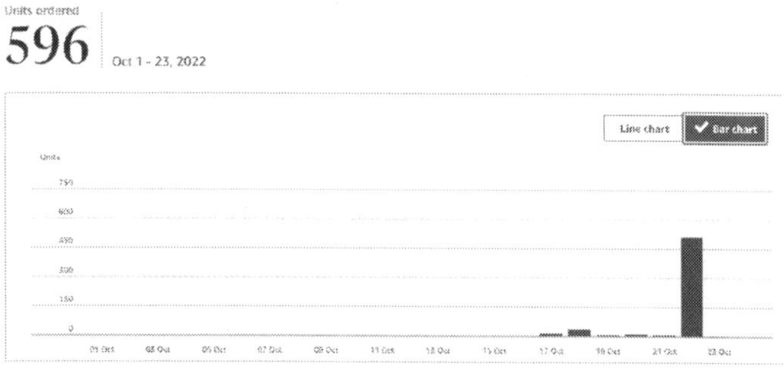

My very first book titled *Introduction* was released about three weeks ago (10/4/2022): The book was merely a short prequel, so it's not part of this series. And I sold 596 copies by at the end of October (you do not have to buy that book necessarily since this book *UnBrokable** I covered it). I had finished the 5-day free book promotion on Amazon that month; this means people were able to download that book for free for Kindles. Still, this is very *strange* since 520 copies out of the total were sold only on one day as you can see in the graph. I had five free book days in a row, but why did most customers come only one day out of five? Let me explain what happened.

First of all, I have to say that this book business is very comparative: Statistically, about 4 million new book titles are published in the U.S. alone every year; that is 11,000 new books every day. If you publish your own book today, chances are no one will notice anything for long. Amazon allows a 5 days free eBook promotion period out of every 90 days. So I made my Kindle eBook free to download during that period, but about 50 people or so downloaded it in the first four days.

I was frustrated since virtually no one wanted my book even for free. So I opened a new Instagram account lately and started advertising there every day. Certainly, I went there again to advertise yesterday, but I believe I used slightly different hashtag keywords (#freeKindleBooks) at that time. I don't know if it was the right hashtag (#) finally, but suddenly I saw that 520 readers had downloaded my free book within a day. I must admit that social media can be a very powerful marketing tool depending on situations: The best part was that it did not cost me anything.

* * *

Some people can ask this question: "What is the point of selling a lot of eBooks for free? You don't get any royalty out of it ($0.00 profit)." I think some do not recognize real *profit* here: Personally, I believe I made about $10,000 profit yesterday. Let me explain it to you why.

Product details

ASIN : B0BHF2LS8B

Publisher : Brad Kong; 1st edition (October 4, 2022)

Publication date : October 4, 2022

Language : English

File size : 738 KB

Text-to-Speech : Enabled

Screen Reader : Supported

Enhanced typesetting : Enabled

X-Ray : Not Enabled

Word Wise : Enabled

Print length : 81 pages

Best Sellers Rank: #257 Free in Kindle Store (See Top 100 in Kindle Store)
#1 in Two-Hour Business & Money Short Reads
#1 in Personal Money Management (Kindle Store)
#1 in Personal Budgeting

As I sold a lot of eBooks yesterday, my sales ranking on Amazon has been up to 257th out of millions of books as you can see in the figure above. Basically, this is how the Amazon system was built: As the sales ranking goes up, more and more people notice my book exponentially. I remember when my book was just released three weeks ago, the sales ranking of my eBook was like 2,000,000th. Let me ask you one question: How much money do I have to spend on advertisements to raise the sales ranking from 2,000,000th to 257th? I guess spending $10,000 on ads may make that possible. How nice would it be if I can make that happen without spending any money at all? What do I lose by giving out free eBooks, anyway? And I thought that it's better to advertise as early as possible since I just started this *UnBrokable** series.

Here is one issue we may have to address in this chapter, though: Most people do not use social media this way.

Honestly, many of us use them to waste more time, lose our jobs or even kill ourselves.

* * *

If it's alright, let me just give you a couple of extreme examples of people who died because of social media before moving on. It's important to check reality sometimes. We normally use social media without being conscious of any danger. I checked and found a couple of news very easily.

The Sun magazine shows that there was an English rapper named Mota Jr. Unfortunately, he was found dead at the age of 28 after getting diverse tortures in Sesimbra, Portugal in 2020. It shows that police found that he had frequently showed off his lavish "billionaire lifestyle" on his Facebook. They arrested three suspects, subsequently. I guess what the rapper had could be the "Like" addiction: Some people get extreme joy out of getting some attention or high *Like* numbers on Facebook. I found another piece of news.

Philadelphia Local News shows that there was a 50-year-old electrician named Tony Harris. He showed off $60,000 cash bundles on Facebook one day; three robbers visited him a week later and shot him to death in his home in Philadelphia, PA in October, 2015. In the case of the rapper, I guess he tried to promote his music or gain popularity at least. In Tony's case, I just don't see any point at all; it shows that he was a middle aged man, but I do not see much maturity here. I guess he would have been alive by now if social media was not invented.

Sometimes, I wonder if I am writing about too severe cases only. I know people usually do not get motivated by mild cases. Still, this is not a crime novel, so let me talk about a few more common problems for a while.

* * *

Believe it or not, *not losing* money is also a way of making money in my opinion. Those numbers on a ledger never lie: Not failing could be more than enough to be wealthy in real life. The same thing goes for time. We don't have to be stressed out to be productive, timewise. Often, not losing time is more than enough to be successful in real life. Have you ever felt exhausted for no apparent reason? Personally, I have: I think the internet, particularly social media nowadays, is a big black hole to devour our attention, energy and time in a harmful way.

I have had only one Facebook account I have not visited for a long time. Very recently, I opened a new Instagram account only for book advertisement[19]. A lot of writers, including myself, are frustrated since their books never really sell, especially in the beginning. If we can use social media wisely, I think it can be a free, but effective advertising tool.

* * *

Do you know what makes a woman attractive? In general, I think she tends to be more attractive when she does not show everything about herself: It seems a lot of girls do not realize this and act exactly the opposite way. Maybe some men like shy girls. But, regardless of specific

[19] Brad Book Cafe: https://www.instagram.com/BradBookCafe

cases, I think a girl tends to be more mysterious when people have no idea about her. Social media makes that unlikely or impossible: People can show bad things about themselves while they do not notice. Let's say that there is a garbage bag in front of our doors. We will not recognize it if it has been there for a year. We all have such a thing in our lives. You may not, but people will clearly see it in our photos.

* * *

I think internet addiction can be a more serious problem than most people think. One of the foremost reasons is that we have to inevitably meet those internet trolls (or cyber bullies). I think that we tend to meet or experience low quality people online more than in real life for one simple reason: Normal hard workers do not kill time there as often as losers. In my opinion, those trolls are the true bottom garbage class in our modern society: It is definitely a loss to meet those people frequently or on a regular basis and possibly get assimilated with them.

I have written on diverse web sites in the past 23 years; not many people (especially Koreans) appreciated me for my creative logical opinions. It has been a big waste for me although these articles have brought me a little bit of fame only in the internet world. Still I think I had met too many trolls or human trash and had suffered. Besides, writing online never brought me any financial benefit even though I believe it might help me improve my writing skills, somehow. I am more than glad that I bought 10 ISBN numbers ($295) finally in October, 2022: I decided to write and publish books from now on.

* * *

Believe it or not, our photos on our Facebook account will not make us look better in most cases: These will only get rid of any fantasy people may have about us. In my opinion, any photo can show more flaws than attractions. Unfortunately, these flaws can include those of our family, too. We can be extremely careful about choosing our own photos, but our family may not. They will still be in our friend lists or something like that and people can see their photos: Their embarrassments can suddenly be our problem. I strongly believe that social media will display something we do not want to show one way or another (eventually). If it does not show a dirty flaw, it can still show vanity or lavishness: These are flaws, too, in a sense. They can repel people who have a good feeling towards us.

* * *

Luckily, my wife and daughter do not have any social media accounts at all. Do you see my face in my book or web sites? Probably not. Frankly, I suggest you not post anything on social media unless for a business. This can make you look cool, actually: Not doing what most others do. A girl's attraction goes to the maximum when boys do not have any idea about her. Boys are stupid in relationships in that sense by nature: They will make their own assumptions and fantasies about a girl on their own.

One reason for this hypothesis is the *Mask Fraud* phenomenon in Korea. A lot of people wear masks due to the Corona Pandemics over the last three years and men automatically find that some girls look prettier when they cover their faces with masks. They joke that the girls are kind of frauds since most of them look far less attractive after removing their masks: "I was deceived by the girl! She is a fraud."

As social media gets popular, I believe a girl can only show more disappointing realities to boys online; for example, she can show their drunken father to boys on her Facebook. She could have shown him later if social media didn't exist. But she reveals him too quickly way before any relationship can possibly form with any boy. Boys will stop approaching a girl as soon as they see something undesirable. A girl may complain why she is still single at the age of 45 since she believes no man has ever approached her for life. The fact is that she might have blocked any approach by showing something distasteful about her online. Being single is fine, but I am just mentioning this just in case a girl wants a relationship.

* * *

Here is one more thing every (particularly) single woman should know: A lot of men believe that the *future face* of the girl whom they are interested in is her *mother*. In other words, the girl's mother is her future appearance. That is why men try to check the mother-in-law at least once before getting married.

Strategically, it may not be a good idea for girls to show her mother or grandma on Facebook too early unless they are ex-beauty queens. **No man is dying to get something, eventually turning out to be very ugly.** Without seeing her mom, men tend to imagine a looking fine old lady for the girl's future appearance on their own (again, men are stupid). They tend to self-hypnotize that "This girl will be a decent looking old lady later in life.": Without this illogical process, there wouldn't have been a marriage and humans would have gone extinct a long time ago. By seeing her mother directly via social media photos, he knows who he will get later in life for sure: He can hesitate or stop approaching. It is no coincidence that the single (unmarried) population increases super-fast now along with the emergence of social media.

I suggest you close all the social media accounts unless you need it for a business. We can make others jealous or angry while we do not intend to as well. We can offend poor people out of the blue even though we may not be that rich (a lot of photos are fake). Social media is the poor people's playground after all: Statistically, rich or educated people never go there for personal reasons very much.

* * *

I just mentioned that my wife and daughter never use social media. As far as I know, they have never even made an account before (My daughter does not even have a cell phone). I am the only one who used to post things on them a lot. Now I have only one Facebook and Instagram account left for my book publishing. The situation is that no one else in my family will put my personal information online; this is why you cannot find my face photo anywhere.

I believe control over the internet, including smartphones and social media, is crucial for success in modern days: We always make more money when we are in control; at least, we may lose less. Some people rush into the internet industry, found a company and make a fortune. Most of us probably cannot do this. Still, at least, we can control the amount of usage. Some people (especially the poor) check social media the whole day after getting an unlimited smartphone subscription plan: This is stupid as I have a minimum plan for $16.30 a month from Tracfone (500 texts and other things have been more than enough for me). Additionally, I think we should be concerned about which sites we can use to take advantage of the internet.

* * *

Some sites will help us make money: Fidelity.com, eBay, Amazon publishing, Google doc, etc. Fidelity and eBay have worked out greatly for me. I hope Google doc, Amazon publishing and Edit.org (self-book cover design) will work out for my publishing business from now on.

On the contrary, I think some sites will only help us waste more time: Snapchat, Facebook, Twitter, etc. These can just expose our private lives more without bringing much benefit or meaningful gain. Even worse is that some people have lost their jobs because of these. I think it's urgent to be aware of the danger by accessing social media.

* * *

I am not sure of other sites, but I used to know of a couple of smart people who used to go to *myspace.com* (an old social media site) a lot and remember they were very poor. One of these was one girl in my biology class at the university and I think she started using it even before 2005. At that time, most people didn't even know what social media was. I remember she was a white from Elmira, NY and she was unpleasantly and unnecessarily poor; all of her hometown friends and her fat sister who joined the site were poor, too. According to her postings, it seemed that she was the only one who made out to be in college among them.

When I checked her Facebook some years ago, I found that she was still poor even with two kids now: These types of people never get out of poverty by nature. I also noticed that people just cannot hide their poverty in their photos, especially when they have been broke for a long time. I could see that her husband had been out of work for quite a while (long and dirty hair). Maybe poverty and brokeness[20] have become her destiny since she had been with them for decades. Financially speaking, I think only Mark Zuckerberg makes money out of those social media: Still, did you know that he hardly posts anything on his FB account himself? The rest of us mostly waste time, energy or attention.

* * *

There are diverse ways to make money online nowadays. As far as I can see, writing articles on Google Doc and publishing them into a book with KDP at Amazon could be the smartest way to use the internet. Did you know that writers used to go door to door of publisher companies millions of times only to publish their articles? As a writer, I cannot imagine the level of hardships they had been through: I know there are a lot of obstacles we still have to overcome after publication (my book is not selling very well).

On the contrary, some people just check Instagram without a point indefinitely. How come they still do not know those photos online are all staged or fake? Just think

[20] Noun of being broke. Please do not get confused with brokenness.

of one person around you doing that whole day. Is the person smart? Probably not. Is she[21] rich? Never really.

I do not know why some people try to check their smartphones a second more. Technically, it's like they are the full time employees (slaves) for the internet advertisement companies: Their specific job is reading ads. **Checking social media consistently is like having another full time job without getting paid**: Some act as if they work for those internet companies except when they sleep.

Personally, I never carry my phone outside my home. I have lost a lot of things before, but I have never lost my phone only because of the rule (no smartphone outside). And, I think it's stupid and dangerous to carry it all the time to check: **We do not have to work for those internet companies voluntarily any longer.**

* * *

Although I opened an Instagram account for book sales recently, one Facebook account has been all I have almost for a decade. I could not close that one since too many of my Korean high school friends are connected via it (I have known them for over 30 years).

For sure, I have to say that Facebook has been helpful to find old friends; there used to be agencies finding people for customers in Korea (a sort of detective agency) and they used to charge a lot of money before Facebook emerged. That was one of the good functions of social media.

---

[21] No offense, but, statistically, women use social media way more than men do.

* * *

I already told you an odd theory that a person posting on social media cannot date or make a new boyfriend or girlfriend any more. Let me elaborate that with a couple of my personal experiences.

The nursing home I worked at had two upscale restaurants inside. I worked at the smaller one when I started the weekend dishwashing job in 2015. There was one young waitress in her early 20s; I did not like her very much since she had a very annoying loud voice. Eventually, I ended up hating her for diverse reasons.

When I checked her name on Google one day, her Facebook page came out. After I clicked it, these are the things I found.

- Her mother and she are alcoholics (holding big beer cans together)
- Her mother is a divorced single woman with four kids
- She is the second out of the four children
- She never went to college after high school
- Her mother does not have a job
- Her mother met a new man and they had the youngest son (4th child) together
- The man is a short Mexican working at an auto body shop in Chicago.

Isn't it too much information to show in public, though? I saw an unnecessary amount of profanity all over on her Facebook pages. I guess everyone could see what I saw. I will be surprised if anyone still wants to date her after seeing all of these.

Anyway, she was a Salvadorian descendant and eventually met a Mexican waiter boy in that restaurant. Both did not go to college, but had a baby in 2016. It seems they both quitted their jobs from the nursing home together before she gave birth. They were quite young in their early 20s, but apparently both did not have another job after quitting. Guess what? I saw all of these on her Facebook again.

Personally, I do not like this type of people: People having no job, no school, no income, but only having a baby. Who does not know how to make a baby? There is no hope for these types of people.

* * *

Let me give you just one more ridiculous example. After quitting the job at the small restaurant because of this unpleasant Salvadorian girl, I began working at the bigger restaurant from 2017 (only for the weekend). There was a white smoker girl server intentionally making loud noises in the kitchen. One day, she did not do her job at all and spent 40 minutes in the kitchen intentionally making loud noises to annoy me; I had to file a complaint report separately to her managers.

When I checked her name on Google, her Instagram page came out. Some postings had a bit of disputes with her ex-boyfriend. These are what I learned through her Instagram, surprisingly.

- She had one abortion and two miscarriages with her ex-boyfriend
- Her sister and she are both smokers and pot smokers

- Her parents' house was foreclosed in 2010
- Her sister was flying to Colorado to buy legal marijuana then while the house was foreclosing
- Her sister had a smoker boyfriend as well and broke up
- She never went to college, etc.

Apparently, there were five people in this family including three adult children: this girl, her sister and her older brother (all were close to 30 years old). Couldn't they work altogether to save their family house from foreclosing? The house looked like an ordinary one with three bedrooms, so the mortgage could have been $2,000 a month or something like that. **There is no cure for these kinds of people.** I would feel frustrated if my daughter spends money on an airline ticket to buy marijuana while I am in trouble.

I think these are examples of giving out a scary amount of information to the public: It would be disastrous, especially if these go to the hands of enemies. What would we get after giving out this information? Nothing! She also quitted the server job eventually and met an alcoholic husband with a tattoo and had a son. I found out about this on her Instagram again.

* * *

In conclusion, social media can be very dangerous things when we have an enemy. **The issue is that we do not even know if we have one or not.** We can offend someone while we do not intend to. Or some people are born hating everybody and I could be their target.

In the book titled *The Art of War*, Sun Tzu wrote, "If you know the enemy and know yourself, you need not fear the result of a hundred battles." Writing on social media is doing exactly the opposite of the quote: Showing yourself without knowing about an enemy. If you have a hard time finding a job, keeping a position or getting paid, see if this could be the reason.

* * *

Summary

1. See if you can leave your smartphone at home when you go out.
2. Let's give ourselves some alone time and breaks.
3. We can use social media for businesses only.

8

Having a Bad Reputation

A bad reputation can be a silent killer eroding our wealth.
-Brad Kong

I think that people get jealous the most when there is no hope to improve their situations: Some people live in a dead end for a long time if not forever. They often compare what they have with what others have now since there is no room to get better. Losers waste time on being jealous. Winners always look for more room to improve instead.

* * *

One weird thing about money is that paying more means getting worse sometimes. For example, choosing water as a drink is free in a lot of restaurants: Coincidently, it's the best for our body biologically or medically. If we choose a wine, it costs us way more (often more than a meal itself). Nonetheless, is wine more beneficial for our body than water? Not really. Alcohol is virtually guaranteed to be bad for our teeth and body: Still some people are willing to pay more for that. Coco Chanel once said, "The best things in our lives are free." Although I do not agree completely with this, **I must say that the less or least expensive things are often the best**: Not just OK for the price, but actually more beneficial than expensive things.

* * *

When someone mentions assets, people automatically think of cash generating assets only: stocks giving out dividends, bank savings giving out monthly interests, etc. But, if we define an asset as "something putting money into our pocket," I think there are other assets as well: experiences, intelligence or reputations. These three could mean more than just profits, but they will definitely bring us more money as well if we handle them wisely. The good news is that it won't necessarily cost money to improve these three.

* * *

I was passing by our village hall the other day and was surprised that over 2,000 people gathered to watch a concert; it was very unusual since I live in a small village. They said the singer was Keith Semple, who is famous with a song titled *7th Heaven* (personally, I have never heard of it). He was singing "It's My Life", which is a Bon Jovi song and singing was not hugely impressive to me; I stayed at the place for a couple of minutes and left.

When I checked his name online after coming home, I found he was an *American Idol* contestant in 2010. The music video of *7th Heaven* song had only 70,000 clicks on YouTube, so I assume that he is not extremely popular in general. Yet I would say that this can be a clear example showing the power of reputation. Only because he got famous once 12 years ago and has kept his fame well without much taint, he still attracts crowds and makes a good amount of dough overnight, which happened the other day: Being known to others (famous) is an asset. And, I think the other way around is also possible. We can lose money all the time since we have a bad reputation.

* * *

Being kind does not necessarily cost money. I found this quote in a book the other day: "Kindness can be one of the most powerful tools we can use in our life when we give it without expectation." I agree and believe being kind is one way to raise our reputation without spending extra money: It's not only about money, actually. We don't have to be kind to make more money, but **I still would call it social insurance purchased by our action**: We need help from others to survive after all.

* * *

There is one famous Korean maxim everyone knows: "A horse without legs runs for a thousand miles." Some people are busy building up a bad reputation more and more every day and staying poor for their whole life as a result.

There were several dishwashers in the big kitchen when I used to work at the nursing home: Most of them were great guys. Still, I particularly did not like two old Mexican dishwashers there. These two were kind of enemies with each other, but strangely had few things in common. They had acted unfair, rude or bully and had been a headache for me throughout the seven years of my weekend part time job. As a result, (naturally) they had pretty bad reputations, too.

In short, these two had stayed poor throughout their lives although both were almost sixty years old. They had been dishwashers for life since no one helped them to move in a better position. Both had been living in rental apartments by 2022 and never had a chance to get a mortgage or buy a house (both had never even seen a thing called a mortgage contract for lives). Actually, they are the ones who gave me the strongest inspiration to write this book.

For your information, these two were Mexicans from Mexico despite the fact that most Mexican men I met have been wonderful guys. I still did not like some Mexican girls and women, but that's fine. Let's talk about what exactly happened to me in real life.

* * *

What does make a person *disreputable*? What do you think? In my opinion, when people act too selfishly, they are sure to get bad reputations. **The extreme form of selfishness is betrayal.** Since I will discuss a couple of men in Chapter 33, let me give you examples of three women who gave me an idea of betrayal in the past decade. I believe these women have been exploiting many people, particularly men, and even betraying them in obvious and unpleasant ways.

* * *

There was a woman singer in Korea. I think she started her career when she was a teenager and had performed for more than 20 years by 2022. I remember I liked her new 7th album released in 2007 and found her blog website built for fans in 2011. Even though she used to be a teenage star, she was not any more as she was over 30 years old by then. I recall that she was pretty humble and replied to all the comments on that site in 2011. She replied to mine as well, which was impressive.

But, one day she got a minor role in a TV soap opera in Korea in 2012 or so. Suddenly, she deleted the site completely and acted as if nothing happened. She acted as if she had been a super-star all along: Personally, I found it very unpleasant. I felt she used the site only to check if she is still sellable in entertainments: Just popularity check site. Gladly, she never had been able to get her fame back and completely retired after 2020.

Still, when I dug more in 2020, I felt like this has been the woman singer's way of living a life. She had been a singer without any popularity at all for about 5 years since 2010. There were a couple of CEOs from entertainment companies helping her out to get some jobs in the industry. She was following those CEOs on her Instagram only while she had worked with them. When I checked the social media last time in 2020, she disconnected all these people and she was following no one: 0 following. Since she still has a good amount of followers as an old fallen star, she could have benefitted these CEOs if she just followed them. But, she was following no one even though it won't cost any money for her to help out these CEOs, somehow.

* * *

She also got married in a selfish way: As a result of her selfishness, I think she has been losing opportunities to make a fortune now. Strangely, she married a divorced rich man who has two kids already on his own in 2020. There has been rumor that she had extramarital affairs with this senior bald guy before his divorce.

In summary, she has not been on national TV any more in the last several years: I guess that she is out of the entertainment world for good now. It seems she has one child with him now (the man has three children total), but she cannot be on a family reality TV program, which is oddly popular in Korea nowadays. **I know it's not all about money.** But, if she got married to an honest single guy (who didn't have an ex-wife or kid), she could have made at least $200,000 a year now: Korean entertainments are big as you can see from the stardom of BTS or Psy. Now she has no income from TV, YouTube or whatsoever because of her dishonesty, selfishness and bad reputation.

In my opinion, she will probably get divorced one way or another. The husband may realize that money is the sole reason she chose him one day. I don't think there are other reasons why a single woman would necessarily marry a hairless man having two kids already from a previous marriage. Even if there could be other reasons, here is one thing for sure: She did not marry to support him and his two kids with her own money. Also he could think it is not fair that he is the only one making money all the time for her big spending: She is able to work, but does not. Unfair relationship does not last very long according to my experience.

* * *

When I was in college in Korea in 1998, I studied computer science as a minor. Since it was a minor instead of a major, I did not have many friends in those classes. There was one girl who approached me and asked many questions. I found out that she was accepted with the highest score in the CS department when she was a freshman later.

I remember there was one odd thing about her: She always backed off immediately whenever anyone asked her for help. My friend also said that this was the reason why he kept having distance from her: She does not help others back. I haven't seen her since 1999, but do remember her as an unusually unpleasant person.

* * *

Let me tell you what happened in the nursing home as well. Although I had worked as a weekend dishwasher for almost 7 years, I worked as a morning waiter as well for 8 months in 2021. The restaurant was slow in the morning and I worked for only four hours from 6:00 AM till 10:00 AM during weekdays. Simply, I had two part jobs for 8 months.

There was a young girl server who was apparently friendly in the beginning. I had good feelings about her initially, but ended up staying away from her. Oddly, she approached an old Mexican man in the kitchen too much (she was a Latina herself). He was one of the two dishwashers with a bad reputation I mentioned above. I didn't want to get close to anyone on his side (apparently, she was his side). As a greedy Mexican, the man had approached too many other women all the time, so I do not know what this girl was thinking.

When I resigned from the job in April, 2022, I gave my contacts to several coworkers. She helped me a few times and I knew she was attending a college with full scholarship, so I gave her my phone number and email address as well: I told her to use these as a reference when she applies for another job later on. I thought this is one way to help her without spending any extra money. While I didn't like her 100%, I thought she could be useful or helpful someday (because of her high academic performance).

And, surprisingly, she actually texted me a week after I quit that she was applying for another job in a hospital. And, she asked me to fill out 40 questions in a reference form for her. I did it gladly. And I said, "It does not cost me anything, so don't worry." But, strangely, her text got quiet as soon as I filled up the reference and sent it to the hospital. I did it quickly for her and even sent a confirmation photo to her. I ask for her email address just in case, so I can fill her in my reference likewise if I apply for another job. I asked twice, but she disregarded it after saying "Thank you."

What is this? Letting me know her email address would not cost her anything. I gave her email address, but she cannot? Why she cannot do the same favor as I did? I think it is a sort of a betrayal. I notice that her email address is on public record, after all. I just did not like her intention to take advantage of me, but does not want to do the same in such an obviously unpleasant manner. I always thought that her butt had been extraordinarily big and didn't feel good about her for no apparent reason: **My intuition was right.** I think being unpleasant can block any good opportunity from coming in. On the contrary, being kind can save us money and improve our money situations. It can connect us with good opportunities as well. I strongly believe we should do pleasant things, especially when it does not cost us any money.

* * *

I hate to say this, but my father has always been unpleasant to me for a long time. He has been pretty much angry at everyone all the time throughout his life. I personally thought it is a curse if someone is born with that much anger. While having been unpleasant, he has always wanted me to take over his fur business in Korea. I am glad I didn't since no one really wears fur coats any more. Regardless, he could have saved tons of money if he had a pleasant relationship with me. As I will write in Chapter 12, I believe I might have spent a lot of his money on possibly impractical education: Partly, I went to a few colleges only to stay away from him.

And I will talk more about one old Mexican dishwasher in Chapter 24: Everyone hated him at my work. He kind of reminded me of my father and actually gave me inspiration to write this book as I told earlier. I have to admit that he is a super hard worker (frequently, working 15 hours a day), but could not even buy a house at the age of 60.[22] He told me that he was paying $1,200 a month for his two bedroom townhouse to rent in 2021: The fact is that he has been only renting for 35 years and never even stepped in a bank to fill out a mortgage contract for life. I believe he has lost countless opportunities for being an unpleasant person.

* * *

I already said that we can still give our kindness to people even when we cannot give out money. **Helping others does not necessarily cost money.** I saw that my wife even gave a bunch of plastic bags to a kid who needs them on a regular basis. I think she is a giver by nature.

We do not have to save things unless we need them. Just help people as much as you can, especially when it does not cost you anything. I believe most people in the world are not a betrayer and our favors can come back to us inevitably.

* * *

Summary

1. Let's help others, especially when it does not cost any money.
2. Having a good reputation is not all about money. Still, we can be wealthier because of our actions ultimately.

[22] I bought out my condo with full cash at the age of 40.

3. Being disreputable blocks all the possible good opportunities.

9

Making Yourself Undesirable

A little thing can blow out the master plan.
-Brad Kong

It may be true that it takes a lot of money to be rich. But, believe it or not, I do not think it takes a lot of money only to get out of poverty. At least, I would say that it has not cost me a lot to stay away from painful situations so far (in the last 49 years). Maybe I am lucky, but just being frugal and not being wasteful have been enough for me to live beyond desperation.

* * *

Today I went to an Indian supermarket called Patel Brothers. I saw some Mexican guys collecting shopping carts in the parking lot. I felt truly sorry since this is one of the most killing jobs in America: A hidden painful job. But, still according to my experience, I would say that it didn't cost much money to get me out of that painful weekend dishwasher job. Maybe that job didn't bring me much dough to begin with. Or it's less expensive to live in the Midwest part of America. Or I solved my housing issue a long time ago, so I do not have high fixed monthly spending (e.g., rent or mortgage).

Yet this is my point: Do not aim to be rich. We can lose hope and give up early. Instead, focus on getting out of poverty: This will be a much more practical strategy. Things can be more achievable, life can be easier and we can be more content as well. Personally, I am living without a car right now: It has been true that staying away from lavishness and not being wasteful have been more than enough for me to stay beyond destitution.

* * *

Whenever I saw those Korean (loser) internet trolls, I could smell and detect two distinct characters from them.

1. Wasting time pointlessly (they don't try to learn new things or get information, but just waste time on being jealous)

2. Basically all of them have a rent or mortgage, which could be the biggest waste in our lives after all (not a single soul among them bought a house with full cash as I did a decade ago)

These 1 and 2 are not really separate things. These two virtually go together.

* * *

Do you know how to find out if we are living a good life or not now? Let's see if we can measure our weight. If we are skinny, more likely our life is in good positions now; probably, our finances are more than OK, too. If we are obese, less likely everything in our life is good.

Let's say that we meet an old friend for the first time in 20 years. Appearance will tell a lot of things about people (I am not talking about being born pretty or not). Sometimes, I see photos of old friends on Facebook and get shocked by how much weight they gained in the last several years: **This is really bad.**

Weight will tell more about a person since no one can change it quickly. If a person is skinny in his or her 40s, the person probably has lived a good life for a long time. If a fat friend has gotten skinnier, the person actually has improved (it's possible that the person has been wealthier, too). I can see that the same thing goes for celebrities as well. Why? No one really gets skinnier automatically nowadays. It requires control, exercise, mindfulness, medical knowledge or enough money: Combination of all these positive things will determine being obese or not.

Then why am I saying this now? I think losing weight is one way to make ourselves more desirable in the job market: **It won't cost a cent to lose weight.** Don't worry about the weight loss programs. Just fasting, skipping meals or eating less should be more than enough as I have lost 40 pounds myself in the last several years.

* * *

I personally have never really liked those artificial long nails some women have; these don't really make women look professional. Probably, everyone has to agree with me that skilled professionals like doctors or lawyers do not have those nails. Still, I do not think physical workers like restaurant servers or flight crews have those, either (these can be broken in physical workings). Then who does have those? I think some ladies not having real jobs have those: Instagram models, background dancers for pop singers, mystery shoppers or someone like that, for example. Mothers who have a baby would not have those (these can hurt their babies). So I would guess that these women with long nails didn't even produce a child along with no solid income. I think single men should stay away from those types of women. They can possibly hurt men financially or *even physically*; seriously, I feel that these nails can turn into weapons against partners if her mood swings in a bad direction.

* * *

There were two legendary baseball pitchers who debuted together in Korea in 1992: Chan ho Park and Lim. In general, the country is not really famous for strong baseball players. But these two had been exceptional superstars. Park had been the main pitcher in several American major league teams: New York Yankees, Los Angeles Dodgers, Texas Rangers, etc. Lim had totally reigned in the Korean pro leagues over a decade and some people argue that he had a better pitching skill than Park. But here is one difference between these two players.

It shows that the net worth of Park is about $40 M while that of Lim is less than $10 M. What has made an over $30 M difference in two net worth? Maybe the American leagues paid Park more than the Korean ones paid Lim. Another difference was Park had been in a lot of commercial advertisements while Lim had been in almost none: In other words, Park is much more handsome. Lim has gained *massive* weight as he got older.

I am not saying that we have to look pretty to make money. Still, I see that there are people ignoring or even abandoning their own hygiene, weight or appearance. Sadly, some turn themselves look *undesirable* for a job. But, surprisingly, they do that even with spending money sometimes: **Some spend money to look dangerous or ugly.**

* * *

Our attraction could be our biggest asset to survive. By rule, I would say that we make less money if we look, act, talk or smell unfavorably. Also, I think keeping a decency is important; humans are animals with basic instincts after all.

I know this can be unfair, but I think that our appearance will matter for any job we do in the future (even for a job which doesn't seem to require good looks). I know personality is more important and all that crap, but the truth is that our physical appearance will matter until the last day humans exist. While I believe plastic surgeries are overkill, I think it is important to make ourselves look as clean or neat as possible.

* * *

I notice that I perceive skinny girls attractive at first look: This is not something I can control. This is nothing but an animal instinct. I have thought about the reason why: Maybe I perceive they are healthier or less smelly; they may fart or burp less; maybe they look neater and cleaner than fat oily girls to my eyes. I am still not sure of the exact reasons, but, for sure, how I feel in a second is not something I can control. **Still, instead of making ourselves look good, I think it is more *crucial* not to look bad**; some people spend money to look bad; some spend money to get fat; there are people spending money to look less desirable and all these could be the reason for poverty.

* * *

Do you have any girl or boy you want to get close to or a job you want to get hired by? Frankly, losing weight would be one of the most realistic ways to make ourselves attractive: The best part is that it does not cost any money to do so.

My driver's license shows that I was 165 Lbs. I think I was that heavy in 2007; they just didn't change the record on the license. I have lost about 20 LBs due to kidney stones after 2008. Then, I have lost another 20 LBs due to one tooth infection in 2019; I could not eat very well because of one infected molar. I had spent over three years trying to cure it, but it was too late. Now the infected tooth is gone, but I am still 125 LBs now (5'7 feet).

Even nowadays I try to make myself look as skinny or handsome as possible. I don't really spend extra money on that: **I think this is just about respecting myself or not losing hope.** I was surprised that my money never went down in my bank checking account whenever I fast (not eating food for a while). It only made me realize that I had spent an incredible amount of money only on food my whole life; besides, it is true that a lot of foods we are eating are unhealthy and harmful these days.

* * *

There was a shooting incident in Highland Park, IL in July, 2022; it actually happened on July fourth. There was an Independence Day parade in the village and a person named Robert Crimo III (21) started shooting people from the roof of a building at 10:00 AM; six people were killed and thirty-six people were injured. The shooter was initially on the loose for several hours, but I could see that he would get caught quickly. I saw his photo on TV, and he has a few big and unique tattoos on his face and neck; these didn't look attractive at all. All I can say is that it is impossible to miss this guy if anyone sees him. He got caught five hours later that day.

* * *

Originally, the more specific subtitle for this chapter was "Making ourselves undesirable so that we cannot get a job." Actually, there are some people who do not need a job since they have more than enough money. Still, they will never know what will happen later since people start living close to 100 years nowadays; it is possible that they may need a job at some point in their life. Besides, some people even get a part time job only to kill boredom: I think this is more common in Korea than America (riches get jobs to kill time). **Regardless, I think not losing the capability of making money is important**; at least, being able to get a job without many restrictions would not hurt our life although working may not be necessary for some of us.

* * *

One of the reasons why some people may not be chosen for hiring could be a tattoo, according to my experience. I know a lot of people will not like what I am about to say, especially in America (no one really gets a tattoo in Korea). But, this is just one example and let me explain something based on what I have observed.

I notice that the big nursing home I worked at never really hired people with tattoos. If it does, these people must be placed in a position where residents cannot see them. Libraries or village halls will not hire tattoo people, either. We may be hired or may not. But, let me ask you a question: **Why do we have to limit ourselves?** Getting a tattoo is not free, anyway. It can come with pain or infection, too.

Tattoo parlors are generally located in low income areas. Whenever I saw these people with tattoos, I felt they have made themselves even poorer. **If we are broke, isn't it common sense to save all the money as much as we can?** There is no room to waste on anything. Why do they still spend money for tattoos or piercings and cannot even get hired as a result? I guess they may not have strong survival instincts.

* * *

When I worked as the weekend dishwasher, there was one annoying dining hall manager lady. I did not like her since she was unnecessarily demanding. She never missed a chance to ask a favor if anyone was around. But, what surprised me the most was that she had a big black tattoo on her chest. "How come such a person was necessarily chosen for the manager of all 30 servers? No one has a tattoo here." I assume she did not wear showy clothes during her job interview (it was visible only when she wore revealing clothes).

But you know what, though? She was gone for good after working only for one year in that nursing home: I was happy as if I got a promotion. Apparently, the company did not extend the one-year manager contract with her. I remember that she stopped by the kitchen one last time months after she couldn't get a job anywhere. It was an annoying visit, but she said she came there to re-applying for the job. I overheard her conversation with E, who was a nice black cook (the woman manager was also a black, by the way): I think that it was rude for her to show off that she will go to a mall on that day since everyone who heard that in the kitchen had plans to work the whole day for Thanksgiving (double pay).

And, it seems she did not understand the real reason why she virtually got fired: White wealthy orthodox seniors and a black girl with a breast tattoo do not match very well. The nursing home has alternative choices for employees. Still, I assume that it is a very little thing to blow out her entire career as she was a single mom with a son desperately in need of some cash.

* * *

When I owned the video game shop, people came to ask for a job until the last day it closed out. I had never put a "help wanted" sign, but people virtually had come every day for 8 years and two months. I think one of the reasons was that a lot of people knew that I was the only one working there. Or maybe they thought the job was a slow and easy one. I assume that over 5,000 people had come to ask for a job and some even filled out application forms which we never had: I just gave them empty A4 papers[23]. I was not able to hire anyone since business was not very busy, but if I did, the person could have been a winner who beat 5,000 to 1 competition.

I still remember one extremely fat guy who came and asked for a job (nothing wrong with what he did). He was actually a very nice customer in the beginning and brought a lot of his nephews to the store. I ended up not liking him as a customer since he tried to cut down game prices a little too aggressively.

At that time, he was like 400 pounds and I thought he may not fit into the space behind the cash counter even if I hired him. All of his teeth were completely rotten due to intensive soda pop drinking. I was relieved when I heard that he finally got a job for newspaper delivery. He said he was happy since the job has no aggravation. I remember his girlfriend and he worked for the Salvation Army during the Christmas season as well. They collected money in the red

[23] They just wrote their names and addresses on white papers.

bucket and came to the store to buy a couple of games. He had been a nice guy to talk with and these are all good memories now.

* * *

Now too many jobs are available everywhere since it is right after COVID pandemic period: I guess a lot of people have passed away or been hospitalized. We can self-publish books or YouTube channels, too (that's why job applicants are even shorter). Personally, I do not have any plans to be employed anywhere for the rest of my life: nonetheless, **I prefer to make myself somewhat employable just in case.** I believe those reasons above could be why some people are broke all the time even though they try hard.

* * *

Summary

1. We have to check "if we are employable or not" even when we are wealthy (just in case we need a job).
2. Some spend money to be undesirable to be hired in job markets.
3. That can cause poverty.

10

Marrying a Spouse Without an Income

Marriage does not guarantee happiness.
-Brad Kong

Quite frankly, I didn't plan to publish my first book *Introduction to UnBrokable** too early in October, 2022. My original plan was releasing an 800-page thick book titled *UnBrokable* (collection)* in January, 2023: The one book including all the 80 chapters. I have written more than 730 pages already by October, 2022. But one day I was curious how this book actually would look: Especially, I wondered about the margins on pages. If I do not keep enough margin in advance, I know readers can have a really hard time reading it. In the worst case, it would be like I don't publish any book at all since no one can read it. So, I decided to publish an introductory version including only five chapters only to see it in reality.

Then I realized it is quite easy to publish a book with Google Doc and Amazon KDP publishing as long as I have ISBNs. I decided to publish a series of books by ten chapters each instead of spending the next four months only on writing. I thought that I could eventually publish a thick book after combining all the nine small books: it will take similar time anyway. For sure, it costs a little more for extra ISBN numbers ($575 for 100 numbers, which means $5.75 per each number). But I thought that it's OK.

In conclusion, I have to say that I am hugely glad that I published the *introduction* book as a trial. I found that the right side margin on my pages is much narrower than I originally expected in the book design. I also discovered that I do not like this white paper option I chose (most novels are published on creamy paper). Yet I decided to keep those 12 pt. font, matte finish covers and a little bigger than 6x9 page size. We can have a spouse without an income (my wife doesn't have to work continuously). I would say that there are a lot of things we can do at home to make money nowadays.

* * *

According to my experience, whoever we get married to, we will face the worst moment, eventually. There is nothing wrong with the girl or your partner. This is just how it goes in a marriage or human relationship. Conflicts are inevitable when two people try to live together: In general, marriage struggles intensify more after a child is born.

I have two suggestions to stay in marriages in spite of conflicts. First of all, I think it's important for us to marry partners who provide more reasons we should not divorce. Maybe she makes or owns a lot of money; maybe she is an ex-beauty queen or still looks pretty; maybe she has a doctorate degree from a graduate school (just like my wife); maybe she is a good cook. The more reasons she can provide, the better it is. If we can avoid divorce somehow, we will be more wealthy. I see many men marrying fattish girls from low income families who have no job, degree or savings. She won't help husbands' lives very much. It is easier for men to get divorced from those girls and men will be poorer than ever if that happens. Secondly, go easy on having more kids. Both spouses will be more stressed out and have more conflicts as they have more children.

* * *

Love is the most important thing in the world, so we can throw our life for it, right? Or is it merely a hormonal interaction in our brain? Let's think about why it was created originally in the first place billions of years ago. **I think it's possible that it was initially created for animals to generate offspring.** Humans exaggerate too much to sell dramas, romance novels or movies nowadays. Wedding and jewelry industries are big, so sales people need to excite customers to do anything for their transient feelings (love). That is good, but there should be some limits. Otherwise, people can end up getting miseries without a point.

It is known that high levels of dopamine and norepinephrine are released in our brains during attraction; the same hormones are released while people take heroin. Bad drug called heroin strongly activates dopamine neurons; the same goes for nicotine and that is why it's extremely hard to quit smoking. So, in a perspective, being in love is like being addicted to drugs or cigarettes; just like we have to get out of these addictions to live better, we may have to give up some harmful women or relationships before it gets badly serious.

Realistically, I suggest men not to go too deep for women who are obviously below their league: If you sense it, just stop it even for a second. **There are women not showing any bright future;** you know you only go down together if you get more involved with her. Some women are smokers and drinkers; some women don't have a job or have a job incomparably worse than male partner. Let's take Nicolas Cage as an example; he has been married five times by 2022 and got divorced four times. None of the women he got married to was a famous actress or performer like him; most had trivial jobs like waitress, makeup artist or background (extra) actress; getting married to Cage was probably their biggest achievements in their lives. Instead of surrendering to the emotion, he should have been just friends with them since divorces must have cost him a lot of money and pain.

* * *

I am not a relationship expert, but I think that here is something all single males need to know: It's better for us to get married with a woman who has been genuinely into us (rather than someone you like more). The life after marriage will be more likely heaven in this case; if not, it may be far from hell at least.

Don't stick to a woman not interested in you or force her to get married to you: just stop it completely. Don't think that changing her mind is an accomplishment; it is possible she is not really a prize from the start; it is possible she is merely a nobody (compared with you) while you were just not her type. It is possible we can lose a chunk of money or do a lot of chores and drudgeries without much benefits after marriage in those cases.

Strange thing is that a girl is not a low quality one only because she is into you. Also, a girl is not that great only because she is not interested in you. **Rich girls can love you or poor girls can be not interested in you.** Forget our emotions for a second and let's see if we can make a rational decision. Otherwise, our whole life can go down the drain along with our money.

* * *

Still, I am not sure if it's a good idea to marry a too diligent woman; I am married to one, so it's a little too late for me to wonder about this now. She may want you to participate in house work together, but it's just hard for me to keep up with her frequency or intensity of cleaning sometimes (all the time, actually). If you take some break, she may say that it's not fair for her to work solely and preach that marriage cannot survive this way and all that crap. **Alternatively, you can try to reduce the total amount of work in the house** (which is what I am doing): having less babies, eating one meal a day, no car, living in a condo, so no yard work and so on.

Still, if your wife is industrious enough to make money while taking care of home and child, that is a truly great help for your life: Super women do exist in real life as I am seeing one every day. To justify myself, I have to say that I do not create extra work for her at least; **I have used my brain to reduce the total pie of work at home even before slicing it.** Statistically, husbands get wealthier much faster when their wives have a job. It is up to you, so see which type of a partner you would like to go with in the end.

* * *

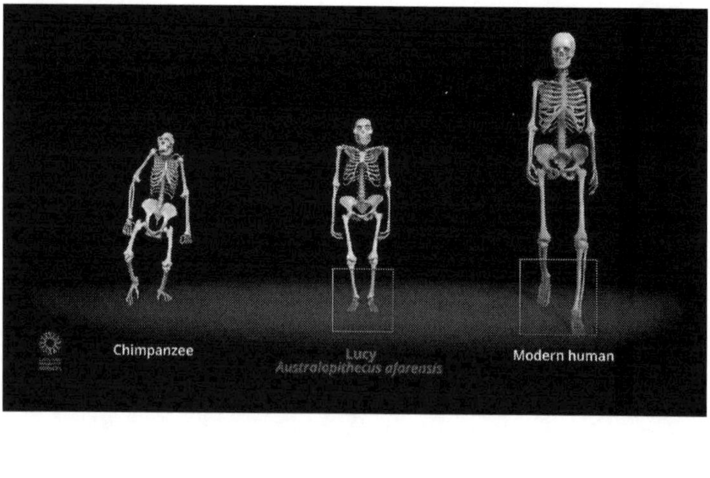

In the book titled *12 rules for life*, Peterson pointed out one interesting fact: **While human skulls have been changed**

drastically by evolution in the last six million years, chimpanzee skulls have remained about the same. Humans and chimpanzees share a common ancestor called Hominini, who existed about six million years ago. The skulls of Hominini and humans are so different. But, the skulls of Hominini and Chimpanzees are relatively similar.

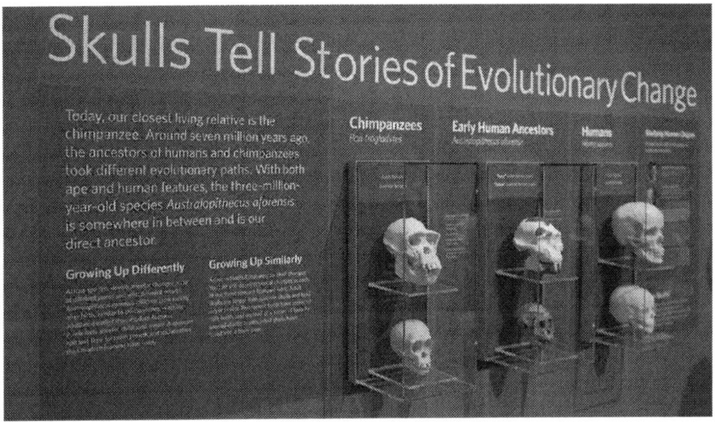

Anthropologists believe that this difference has happened because human females are more selective to find a partner than chimpanzees; **scientists believe only half of human males have been able to leave an offspring, somehow.** Human ladies always try to find a better man even nowadays: smarter, stronger, richer, more handsome, etc. Or they just do not get married. And the offspring in the next generation possibly would "look a little better" this way. That is why the skulls of those two species are very different as a result.

Yet here is one question: Are those ladies all good enough for men who they are trying to find? Unfortunately, according to my experience, I strongly do *not* believe so; **many women are more disqualified than men even though a lot of men are still willing to accept them.** Consequently, divorce rates are high in every country; meeting the wrong partner is expensive and costly, especially to men these days.

Let me explain what I have learned after dating human females for over three decades in the modern era.

* * *

Above all, I have learned that it is extremely hard to find a woman who men can really trust; I am not even talking about money issues. I just included this topic since it is true that we can save wealth faster if we find a good partner; it is also important that our wives do not waste a lot of money. I am lucky in that sense since my wife is a reasonable spender and money maker (not completely, but I cannot expect she would be exactly like me); above all, she is one of few people I could trust comfortably so far.

Some people might stay broke since they live alone. This can be especially true for women since many go for easy, but low paying jobs as Dr. Peterson suggested: Men dominantly go for hard, dangerous, but high paying jobs. Also, a lot of women take care of their child or elderly for free; they do this for years if not decades. It does not usually happen to many men: No pay, no work, strictly. Shamefully, I myself don't remember that I have worked for an hour without getting paid (except the Army service).

Traditionally, women or girls have a role to sacrifice themselves for their families (which I don't think it's fair). It has been like this for millions of years and still goes on, unfortunately. Some stupid old men keep having more babies and use their older daughters as free babysitters. It's like these girls have a full time job already regardless of school while the entire family gets poorer. It reminded me of one fat stupid Mexican dishwasher: These types of old men are usually idiotic, greedy for women and stingy for family all the time. Smart men figure this out already and prefer not to have many babies. **I think it is the man's fault if his family is poor and has a hard time this way.**

* * *

Some people get poor since they marry the wrong spouses: a spouse without any income, a spouse spending a lot of money, a spouse wanting too many kids, etc. If I have to choose only one of these, I would rather choose living alone. Finding a spouse who is making a lot of money, being frugal and wanting only one child has been almost impossible to me: **I think less than 10% of all women in the world are in this category.** Some women are nice, but they do not own or make that much money (which I don't blame necessarily). If they do, they are not frugal, trying to have many kids or something like that.

Strangely, in Korea, I heard that a lot of Korean women quit their jobs right after marriage; **I feel some young ladies get a job only to lure a man**; they just pretend to be productive top class bride, but do not do anything right after marriage (except getting fatter); I do not understand why housewives are so common (a few times more than other countries) in that country despite the fact that Koreans are diligent people in general.

* * *

Even more strange case is Mexican women in my opinion; One Latino old man (janitor in the nursing home) said some tend to have a lot of kids no matter what. I believe life can become hell easily with too many kids this way; it doesn't even matter if you are rich or not in these cases; we will be guaranteed to live a troublesome life since kids will bring us troubles continuously. The Mexican floor cleaner (nice guy) said that some Latina women actually leave a man if he refuses to have more kids: **This is crazy and brainless.** This seems to be nothing, but it can be a serious matter in case these women have our own child.

For White or Black women, let me not tell much about them here. In my opinion, they have too many unknown negative factors, from the perspective of a Korean man, possibly spoiling our marriages instantly. For example, some white or black women scream a lot which I have never seen among Korean women. I do not know the reasons, but all I know is I cannot live with someone like that since I cannot be startled every day.

* * *

In a general financial sense (regardless of race), there are so many luxury wedding or bridal shops in America: Which gender are the customers? Men or women? **The fact is that men can get into debt even before they start a marriage life with some women** (Trump is stupid)**.** Some women may be good people; nonetheless I think many have unfavorable factors well-hidden and men usually find those when it's too late: The divorce statistics support this theory. If you enjoy the minesweeping game, you can marry any woman. Here is my conclusion as a whole, though: **Living a single life may be better unless we are sure to meet good partners.**

* * *

I think this chapter should have included the topic, "making your partner incomeless" as well. I am not trying to be a male gold digger here. Still, there is no reason to get married to a woman without a job when 80% of women graduate college and 90% of women have jobs somehow nowadays. Let me tell you my story.

I think many people find this weird, but let me just say it: Strangely, many Korean men (especially old ones) not only allow their wives not to work, but they promote wives to stay at home without a job. It sounds absurd, isn't it? Why do they want their wives incomeless? I am a middle aged man myself, but have never understood these old generation farts. All I can assume is that they may try to dominate money power in the family completely. All I have observed is that those grandpa Korean men, who prefer jobless wives, are not necessarily wealthy. **In fact, many of them are poor.** And, for sure, they are stupid enough to get stuck in traditional ideas.

And they do the same thing to their children as well. When I was a teenager, my father always made sure that I did not get a part time job during summers. **Did he give me any money to compensate for that? Not really.** I had been broke without a job then. I still do not understand this as a 49 years old man myself.

If my daughter gets a part time job during summer, I will probably worry. I know it cannot always be pleasant to be at work. But, I think she should learn it her own way and I have to wait until she does not want to do those types of jobs any more. **Still, I think it is stupid to be poor altogether in families while their spouse or children are unemployed.**

* * *

There is one Korean community website I used to visit. There was one particular troll garbage who was wasting time for posting nasty comments on many articles. I had never seen him post any article with his own ideas for years. This is what I found out about him after reading comments: He works for an IT company (unverified); he has a "huge" mortgage debt; he has a few auto loan debts; his wife and he never went to college in America (no money for education, but a big debt for a house and cars?); they have two kids; he is an alcoholic; no side income; no investment profit; calling cleaning ladies once a week (extra spending); his wife has no job.

His wife does not have a job? **Of course not.** No smart woman gets married to such a troll to begin with. Yet he calls for cleaning ladies for his jobless wife, so now I can say that he is classified into the "Pong-pong men" category.

Pong-pong men is a new slang created lately in Korea. Originally, pong-pong was a popular brand of dish soap in the country. So it implies men who do dishwashing. More specifically, this is what they try to imply: There are gold digger women trying to find profitable husbands; they are often sexually promiscuous and have no particular job, assets or education; they are like food leftovers and those men are cleaning them in the final stage only because they were "fascinated" by their beauties. I can translate that slang to "Slave men (for gold diggers)" in English.

This "Slave men" has been a big issue lately with high inflation: Lives have gotten harder in the country since the Corona Pandemic came in 2020. Korean men started realizing that giving all their salary to wives and getting a small allowance from them is not right (shocking to Americans, but many Korean men have lived like that). For example, those husbands give $3,000 monthly salary to their wives and get only $500 allowance from them: The wives have total control over the salary. I do not know why they do that, but anything can be possible when you live brainlessly as I will discuss in Chapter 26.

* * *

While Koreas have their own problems, I believe Americans have a little different problem. As I stated in the middle, some men make their wives unworkable: One way is by having too many kids[24]. This happens particularly a lot in the Mexican population in this country.

Do you know how many babies can make a mom *immobile*? Surprisingly, I think the answer is *two*. Two kids can require double the amount of work from a mother. But, more importantly, day care costs of two often exceed mom's salary, so it does not make sense for her to go to work.

When I worked at the video game shop, I had seen couples talking over the phone to each other to get permission to buy a video game. I remember mostly they had two kids in the family. I thought that they had financially suffocating lives. I did not want to live like that with counting nickels and dimes every day.

My wife had a very nice coworker lady and she gave my daughter a couple of dolls from the American Girl brand years ago. Wife and daughter went to downtown Chicago the other day and bought a clothes set for the dolls. I asked the price and they did not answer. When I checked online, it seems it is $38. That is fine since it had clothes, nice quality shoes, a cupcake and other accessories as well. It is once in a while, anyway. But, if I have two daughters, these will be $76. I do not think I want to spend that much for a couple of doll clothes.

I personally think I am happy with one child. I might have felt empty if I did not have my own family. But, I know having two kids is just too much for me. Maybe I do not have a lot of

---

[24] Birth rate in Korea is very low. I have one child myself and this is very common in Korea.

money. **However, I do not want to push myself to make a lot after creating reasons, either.** Please know that no one will give us a medal of honor only because we have two children instead of one: No one will care. As I mentioned in Chapter 2, Earth has over 8 billion people already and the human population is growing very fast now. Nevertheless, more money cannot be a cure for every problem. I like to talk more about how to avoid divorce or stay in marriage in Chapter 46 later on.

* * *

Summary

1. Never push yourself to get married.
2. Always stay awake. Don't do things only because others do them.
3. There are more jobs to work at home with flexible schedules nowadays.

11

Auto Addiction

70% of Americans do not need to own a car.
-Brad Kong

While I used to own the video game shop, the owner of Maria's massage visited me one day. She gave me a couple of coupons and explained that these are extremely good deals; I felt so much desperation in her eyes. I believe she needed to pay store rent, but no one visited her parlor. I almost thought that I would help her out once, but suddenly didn't feel like it: Why? I saw that she was getting in her car parked in front of my store and it was a mint Infiniti QX80! That was the biggest SUV the luxury brand makes and it was over $60,000 then in 2011.

Virtually, everyone owns one car in America. Even though automobile and gas prices are not necessarily cheaper compared with other countries, everyone just owns one. This means living in America costs more even because of automobile ownership. I personally have lived without a car since 2017 (I had had two cars for 18 years before that). Getting rid of my cars was one of the best decisions I have made my whole life and I would say I am much happier now than when I had one.

Owning a car will expand our chances to spend more money (often unnecessarily). There are online purchases with *free shipping* everywhere nowadays (e.g., Amazon);

major supermarkets just have started *free* grocery deliveries as well (e.g., Whole Foods, Walmart and Kroger). **I don't think we need a car necessarily to shop any more.** Since we can go somewhere like a mall by car easily, we just end up spending more money every weekend. Moreover, owning a car itself costs unnecessarily a lot even when we do not use it for months.

* * *

I think walking is important since it shows that it can develop our brains; scientists say that it can prevent dementia or other mental related diseases as well. I don't think people believe this, but I still can see that I am getting smarter every day even at the age of 49; I believe brain development continues for a really long period of time. I remember I didn't even know how to take the subway right when I was in high school; I could not understand how the subway map works. And, I see that a lot of people are still at that level of mental capabilities.

Sometimes, I see people who cannot figure out passcodes in the libraries: the two digits of our birth month and the last two digits of our birth year (totally four digits). Sometimes, it takes 20 minutes for some people to figure that out.

There was a group of four Mexican families who took the 600 express bus to downtown Chicago with me the other day (about 15 people in total). It took 15 minutes for them to figure out how much they have to pay for bus fares; it took another 30 minutes for them to figure out how to buy and pay CTA subway fares after the bus trip, additionally. I guess I used to be like them 30 years ago. I could see that they were all drivers not familiar with public transportation. And, I am pretty sure there are people who cannot understand how self-publishing a book works on the web, either. This is my conclusion: **We can be poor, but must not be stupid.** Being stupid is more likely a permanent condition and we cannot expect to be wealthy that way.

Missing chances to develop your brain (by walking less) is a big loss. The Japanese Brain Institute also strongly recommends walking to develop our brains and this is its slogan: "Get off one station earlier on the subway and walk." As I said, I have lived without a car since 2017 and walked all the time. I am not sure if I have been smarter only because of walking; still I can realize that I finally understand things that were not clear before. I can see that I am the fastest person using ATMs or self checkout machines in a supermarket (I have not seen anyone faster than me for years). Besides, I often get good ideas to write while I walk. **I think that not having a car is a way to maximize our brain activity and exercise mandatorily while saving money.**

* * *

The famous Chinese actor Chow Yun-fat is known not to own a car; it shows that his net worth is $714 M in 2022. The well known Japanese billionaire Takashi Kotegawa (a.k.a. BNF) also said he does not own a car, but rides a bicycle in Tokyo. I checked their (both men's) interviews a little more thoroughly; Chow said he does own one car even though he *rarely* uses it; he lives in Hong Kong and mostly he rides subways. BNF said he has one car only in his hometown in the countryside, not in his mansion in Tokyo.

Anyway, I would say **Americans own too many cars as if these are free;** it costs the same or more to own a car in this country than Korea. In other words, people spend more money to live in North America than those living in Asian countries solely for auto related costs; Americans make pretty much the same amount of salaries if not less. My family of three (3 people) have lived without a car in a Chicago suburb for five years now in 2022; except for calling Uber sometimes, I guess we have lived just fine.

Owning a car causes all sorts of problems; it can cost something beyond financial expenses, too. One of the most ridiculous stories I ran into was the case about Sandra Bland: in my opinion, she virtually died only because she owned a car and was a smoker. Regardless, people generally do not have much chance to meet police officers unless they drive a car. I read a book titled *Talking to Strangers* written by Malcolm Gladwell the other day; this book starts with an episode regarding the death of one young lady.

* * *

Sandra Bland was a 28-year-old African American woman from Naperville, Illinois (I used to live in that city). She graduated from Texas A&M University in 2009 and had diverse jobs before she died. In July, 2015, she was driving to start her new job in Prairie View, Texas and got pulled over by a traffic cop named Encinia. I actually watched the whole footage on YouTube and it seems everything started as a routine traffic stop for a signal violation; the police asked for license and registration, etc. And then, suddenly things got pretty bad after she started smoking in front of the officer; I assume the officer was a nonsmoker. He asked to put off the cigarette and she refused; they started arguing more violently; the officer got offended, and she got arrested and transferred into a jail.

Surprisingly, she committed suicide by hanging in the jail three days after she was booked into the place.

Let me ask you one question: **Would she be alive by now if she was a non-smoker?** I have strongly suggested not to smoke if we need to save money in the first chapter. But, I just did not realize it can cause a death like this at that time. Or would she be alive now if she did not own a car at all? Is it too much to ask although officer related deaths increase nowadays, somehow?

I know some people really need a vehicle for their jobs. But, in my opinion, too many people just have too many cars for no compelling reasons; there are plenty of alternative choices nowadays, but people don't even consider those from the start; many do not have a plan to live without a car to begin with; they just own cars unconsciously (just like our parents did) and these bring a full spectrum of problems into their lives. In finance, a car costs a chunk of money, big enough comparable only to housing costs. We cannot live without a house, but I believe 70% of Americans can live without owning a car.

* * *

To be fair, I like to make sure that I am not blindly only on the police side. In 2003, my girlfriend, who is my wife now, and I went to Miami, FL from Champaign, IL by my new car then: the greatest road trip in my life. On the way back from Florida, we planned to stop by Charleston, SC since I heard it is a famous tourism city. Not long after I crossed the South Carolina border, I was stopped by a traffic cop, and he said I was driving too fast. It was amazing that the local highway had a 30 miles speed limit; he said I was driving 45 miles, which is still pretty slow for any highway in common sense; he also explained that I do not have to go to court, but have to send a $52 fine for the ticket by check, which is fishy and unusual. I felt like I just got robbed of $52 for nothing (probably $100 value in 2022).

When I think about it now, these crooked South Carolina highway patrols were there intentionally; probably, it was a tourist trap for many first time visitors. It is not natural that I got into a local road with a 30 miles speed limit suddenly as I had driven all along at 65 miles on the highway from Florida (it must be a sudden speed limit drop spot). I believe many people make the same mistake as I did on that spot; these fraud SC cops just chose newish cars with foreign license plates (non-South Carolina) only to make $50 easily. Since these low quality people ruined my day, my wife and I canceled the Charleston trip and decided to go home directly through Georgia. Later, I heard a lot of Americans complaining about the similar experiences. I am glad I did not spend a single cent more in that State and got out.

* * *

I believe this black lady, Sandra, might have a similar situation as I had. According to the report, the police car was driving very fast and pushing itself right behind her car, so she was yielding the lane for it. And then, she got pulled over by the cop for not turning on the signal light for yielding; simply, this guy stopped her for nothing (I am sure he did it for everyone). It was unfair and upsetting, but I believe she should have acted a little bit cooler; I did not tear up and throw out the ticket to the South Carolina police in 2003.

Regardless of this incident, apparently, she had written a lot of articles against the police regarding black rights movements before she passed away. I still believe it's better for us to remember that these officers are humans, too. Writing more tickets does not bring them more salary, so it is worth being polite and explaining things a little bit; I do have some experiences where traffic officers did not write me any ticket and moved away in several States. She did not have to act rude bluntly or start smoking right in front of an officer at that moment.

Or better yet, maybe not owning a car can solve *all* the problems I just mentioned so far. I know Sandra's story is not about car ownership. But let me tell you one thing for sure: **Personally, not owning a car for the last five years has gotten rid of 30% of my life problems.** Let me explain what happened to me in the last twenty-three years and what made me decide to get rid of my newish car in spite of having an auto ownership of 18 years.

* * *

The first car I had was a brand new Hyundai Elantra. I bought it in the year of 2000 and had kept it for 13 years. The second car was also the newest model of Elantra in 2013. Maybe I bought the brand new Hyundai twice since I am from Korea, originally. But honestly I liked the designs of both models. I kept the second one for about 4 years. So, in summary, my car ownership had been about 18 years total though I rented cars before and after.

Throughout the ownership, my biggest horror always had come from mechanics. Have you heard of "Trauma from mechanics?" Probably not since I made up that word. Getting ripped off and over-charged years after years (or even decades), I had strange symptoms that made me feel freaked out even with getting the smell of mechanics: You know the mild gas smell from the working area of mechanics. Cars went back from mechanics in worse condition many times even after spending a chunk of money for repairs. I had to squeeze my budget crazily since I had been short of money in the 2010s. Many mechanics replaced original good factory parts with cheap after markets even after getting $1,500 payment for repairs.

I particularly had a hard time after my first car became over 10 years old in 2010. In that year, my daughter was born and economic depression came. The store could not make a lot of money, but I had to keep pouring money into my old car while mechanics didn't do anything.

I should have replaced my first Hyundai by then. Monthly payment for a brand new car could have been cheaper. For some reasons, I thought it is wise to keep an old car with healthy repairs. Honest repairs improving the car condition never really happened throughout my ownership of 18 years.

* * *

I was in college when I bought my first car in 2000. I remember it had been great for about 7 years. The first frustration came after the timing belt change in 2005. The dealership said they will give me a loaner car and asked me to leave the car for a day for repair. They suggested a strangely lower price of $375 even though $500 was common for timing belt change then. You know what? They did not change it.

When the timing belt change session happened in 2005, I was about to finish up college in Buffalo, New York. I planned to move to Chicago to start a new business permanently. I thought I will visit NYC one last time since I got a new timing belt just now, anyway. After parking my car in Manhattan, it did not start again. I spent so much money on towing, getting a new timing belt and replacing the damaged cylinder. It took a few days to repair in Manhattan. I had to go back to Buffalo by bus and flew back to NYC via JetBlue plane to pick it up. I think the total damage was about $3,500.

Horror from mechanics did not stop there. In fact, it was merely a start. Whenever I went to any car related place (usually mechanics), I spent a chunk of money just like nothing. I felt like American consumption starts with car ownership. Once we have it, we must spend a good amount of money somehow, anyhow or somewhere. Even a low life's excuse to ask for money is "gas money".

* * *

I will explain more details in chapter 13, but I live in a walkable neighborhood now. Though one of our neighbors, Jim, had lived without a car for the last 30 years, I thought that it was crazy to live without it in the beginning. How can I, right? **I guess we are all addicted to cars to some extent.**

I used to have chronic back pain when I had cars. That is long gone years ago after starting walking, exclusively. And, I am much thinner and notice that I have way more free time as well. It takes time to wash, clean, maintain, fill gas into or repair a car. I do not have to visit the DMV, insurance office, police station or court, either.

* * *

How can an ordinary honest citizen be a criminal quickly? I think driving a car makes the chance for it ten times higher. I do not drink, but drinking at a bar and coming home is not really a crime. With a car handle in our hands, it is (serious one). Some good people can be hit and run criminals. These may be bad people by nature or not just good at driving.

I used to rent a car every month right after removing my car in 2017. Renting vehicles has become less and less and almost none now in 2022. My wife uses Uber whenever she needs it (about once a week).

When I used to own a store, there was a nice, but poor maintenance guy working for the plaza landlord. He is Polish and had three daughters and four cars. He had two jobs and his wife worked all the time. But they had been flat broke all the time. Later, I learned that he eventually lost his house in 2014 (foreclosure) though his family had paid a mortgage for it over 20 years.

If you work to death, but do not see any money left, see if your car ownership could be a reason. It is sad to see that someone lost a house over a few junk cars. Humans have lived with a car for over 7 million years. One car a person is wasteful, toxic and unhealthy: This does not happen in most countries in the world.

* * *

Summary

1. It's not necessary for everyone to own one car.
2. 30% of my life problems have been gone after I sold my car in 2017.
3. It has been and will be manageable to live without a car thanks to IT technologies.

12

Pointlessly Expensive Educations

There is a difference between education and spending money on tuition.
-Brad Kong

I am not really a rich person yet. I do not know how to put this exactly: I have wealthy parents, but have not had a close relationship with them for decades now. Thankfully, they gave me some money after my daughter was born in 2010. So I was able to buy my condo with full cash payment, which is the best thing I have done with money I believe. Although I have had a healthy amount of savings all along, I had chances to own a low income business (video game store) and work in low income jobs (dishwasher and medical coder). I would say that I have been in a position to observe and compare rich and poor people more closely in detail.

* * *

I believe writing is the only way we can truly live forever in a sense. When we think about famous people throughout history, we can see that one half of those people are writers or people who wrote something impressive. Except for some famous kings, conquerors or generals, probably six out of ten people we learn during history classes are writers: Shakespeare, Balzac, Cervantes, Dickens, Hugo, etc. Even among famous kings or queens in the past, some tend to get more famous than others when they had written something: Aurelius, Caesar and Napoleon are examples.

There have been some famous painters or composers throughout human history as well; still I believe that these art and music fields require highly specific skills or talents (e.g., Michelangelo). I believe writing is the most realistic way for ordinary people like me to leave something before I pass away. Most people do not realize this and focus on making a little more money during their lifetimes and die: **Making more money than we need can be a waste of life.** From a perspective, writing after school years can be one way we can truly start thinking without worrying about spending too much on tuition.

* * *

I have a weird theory that **a little bit of success can actually be harmful.** I am not saying that we should not try hard. But, I think it could be better for us to be successful completely or just fail, technically. One example of mediocre successes could be a job like a dentist (no offense, but just hear me out).

If we are totally good at studying, I think we can go to medical school, especially with a scholarship. Or if we are not good at studying at all, I think we may just start working early; some people build up wealth faster that way. A dentist could be in the middle of nowhere in a sense; they are not extremely good at studying or not academically bad enough to give up studying. Dental schools are notorious for high student loans: A lot of people graduate dental schools with huge amounts of student debt. Yet they don't make enough salaries like Medical doctors. There are so many dentists in America that virtually every strip mall has at least one practice already (our town square mall has five practices including oral surgery, kid's dentistry, orthodontics, etc). I have gotten overcharged before, so maybe I am writing about them negatively. Still, I think this could be an example that **a little bit of success can hurt us more than no success at all.** I think I myself have wasted a lot of my time and my parents' money since I had studied just a little bit well.

* * *

It may sound controversial, but let me say this: I think some people are poor since they are not smart enough. Here is one good news everyone should know in spite of that fact: Not many geniuses are born naturally. I strongly believe that people can get smarter as we make some effort toward it. In other words, smart people are made: **Being smart is achievable.** What kind of people make more effort for it? I believe people with stronger survival instincts do that.

There is a difference between being wealthy and being smart: Being wealthy can be temporary, but being smart can be permanent. I saw on the news that a Korean company sold a floating liquefied natural gas (FLNG) vessel (a big gas mining and purification ship) to Mozambique for $3 Billions. Are Koreans able to make this only because the country is wealthy? No, they are smart. There are rich countries not knowing how to make things: One example is Qatar; the GNP of this country is often number one in the world. Someone joked online that the king of Qatar gave out super cars to every citizen there once, but we all know that the country doesn't know how to make a vehicle.

* * *

There is no TV in my house; everyone in my family reads books mostly. For some reason, all the books my wife reads are fiction; John Grisham and James Petersons seem to be her favorites. All my daughter reads are a kind of children's diary series: Dork diaries, Diary of a Wimpy Kid, Garfield fat cat series, etc; strangely, she also reads a lot of catalogs from *Lands' End* clothing repeatedly. She is an elementary student and interested in modeling in the future, which is understandable. We have too many of those catalogs since my wife buys clothes from them occasionally.

I never read fiction unless it is a graphic novel; I am very much interested in what actually happened in real life and how we can solve any issue if there is one. I am particularly interested in poverty or hardship poor people have to go through nowadays: Charles Dickens and Victor Hugo were the same and they wrote *Oliver Twist* and *Les Miserables,* respectively. I read Korean books as well, but a lot of books I read are self-help books. It sounds ridiculous, but I am reading *12 Rules of Life* written by Jordan Peterson in the Korean version since the language is easier for me; I am writing reviews about the book in English, though. I strongly believe reading is the best education, regardless; reading habit would be the most valuable inheritance that my daughter would get from me and my wife.

It is not arguable that education is the key to success: Still, what I mean by education is actual processes of educating ourselves; keep thinking, reading books, writing articles, going to libraries, etc. Some people, especially Korean trolls, seem to make the mistake that education is spending money on tuition or getting degrees from well known schools (Ivy Leagues); these two are not the same things. In my opinion, true education virtually does not cost money; meditation, discussion, interpretation, translation and realizations are all free. We just need enough time to be alone.

* * *

I was stupid back before 2006; I had followed the major trend of education blindly for most of my life. Probably the biggest waste of my parents' money on me was those English programs for non-native speakers in American colleges.

There are plenty of ways we can learn English nowadays. But, for some reasons, attending ESLs[25] in the U.S. universities were popular in Korea in the 1990s. And, these were expensive.

While most students attend only one ESL for a year or so, if not none, I have attended three. And, total periods were about 2.5 years.

- RIT: 6 months (1997)
- Cornell: 1 year (1999)
- SUNY at Buffalo: 1 year (2000)

Probably, wasting money on education is definitely better than other wastes like drinking or smoking. Maybe I learned some good English, western culture or system. Maybe these helped me graduate college with a Bachelor degree. But, these were expensive including room and board and I still regret that I had wasted a chunk of my father's money.

* * *

Cornell was the most expensive out of those three and I remember I had wasted the biggest amount of tuition on attending that stupid Ivy League. The city of Ithaca was so small that I felt suffocated all the time for the whole year. I had visited NYC a lot during that era in 1999. I was overly stressed out and skipped the classes often, which is unusual for me.

[25] English as Second Language

Only good thing was I met my wife at Cornell. Surprisingly, she came to the ESL by scholarship, which is rare. After that, she eventually finished her master's degree at University of Ark Fayetteville and her doctorate degree by full scholarship at UIUC. She has helped me a lot in the last 23 years and that includes giving birth to my daughter.

It is unusual that a man with a college degree is getting married with a woman having a doctorate degree. Maybe the program was worth the tuition after all. Regardless of her degree or income, I realized that it is extremely hard to find a good woman I could really rely on.

* * *

Contrary to the above, I have examples of less expensive, but great education, too. While I was working at the nursing home for almost 7 years, I was able to get two certificates from two different institutes: Medical Coder from AAPC and Pharmacy Technician from PTCB. Honestly, this was possible partly because I was a full time dishwasher only for one year and the weekend part timer for the rest of six years. I had spent most of my time studying at the library by myself.

The Medical Coder license was called CPC[26] and it was given by AAPC (American Academy of Professional Coders). Luckily, AAPC did not require me to take their online courses, which could have cost me $3,500. They allow people to take and pass their exams without course registration. In 2016, all I did was buy their text book for $100. I bought one more

[26] Certified Professional Coder

book[27] and other required references (CPT, ICD-10-CM, HCPCS, etc) from Amazon and studied for about 2 years by myself. The exam fee was about $350 for 2 attempts and I passed it on the second try.

It was great since the total amount I spent was less than $1,000 to get that great certificate. You are welcome to take their $3,500 online course, which is still not hugely expensive. But, that was totally optional. It was good to have a library near home.

* * *

In the case of a Pharmacy Technician license, the PTCB required me to take one of the online courses from an organization they approved. There are hundreds of those online schools available. At first, I thought it was a sort of trick to make more money out of me: "I can study by myself. Why do I have to spend money on tuition again?"

But, it turned out that the online course was only $200 for 5 months in 2021 (RxTechExam.com). If you cannot finish within 5 months, there would be an extension fee of $100 a month. I was able to finish the online course within four months. The course was extremely helpful and I might have not passed without it as the exam was hard. The PTCB Exam was $129 in 2021 and I finished at the first try at Pearson center in Illinois.

Private education businesses have been booming especially in Korea nowadays. It is particularly more popular and expensive in Korea than America. **Getting a good education is one thing, but spending a lot on it is**

[27] "Step by step Medical Coding" by Carol J. Buck

another. But, if you have a lot of money like my father, maybe it is one place we can pour some money in. After all, these are all unique and valuable experiences to me.

* * *

Summary

1. Spending a lot on tuition doesn't necessarily mean getting a good education.
2. True education can cost nothing even though it may require a lot of hard work.
3. I know one Korean troll who never graduated from a college in America, but spent a lot on mortgage debt and car loans here: Stupid. **Still, it's better for us to waste money on tuition rather than anything else.**

13

Not Imitating a Billionaire

The fastest way to get out of poverty is to imitate a billionaire.
-Brad Kong

This can be the most hidden secret to being rich in my opinion: **Reducing the years to pay a rent or mortgage during our lifetimes.** A lot of people are not concerned with their spending first hand and focus only on incomes: This is a plain mistake. Let me give you a couple of actual examples.

First of all, this could be the case in my life unless I move to a new place. I bought out my small condo with full cash when I was forty years old in 2013. I have not gotten any rent or mortgage in the last nine years. Let's take a look at my life financially by age.

0-20 years: Living free at my parents' house ($0.00)
20-40 years: Mostly rents
40-100: Home ownership (HOA fee up to $348 a month in 2022)

It seems I can manage to spend only 20% of my life on paying rent, which had been much higher than my current condo association fees (HOA). On the contrary, this can be the typical financial lives of mortgage payers in America.

0-20 years: Living free at my parents' house ($0.00)

20-40 years: Rents
40-70: Mortgages
70-100: Rents again (downsizing)

I can explain more later, but a lot of Americans pour money only on their houses for decades and end up having only those as savings after retirement: Often, they do not have anything else significant than their big paid off houses. So occasionally they sell them and move back to rental apartments. **In this case, these people can spend 80% of their lives on paying rent or mortgages**: These are huge financial wastes.

Here is one more problem: As medical technology develops, it is possible that average people can live up to 120 years old after the year of 2050. Then, some can spend more than 80% of their lives on paying rents or mortgages. Ideally, buying out even a small condo with full cash *early* and living *without paying* rent or mortgage for the rest of our lives sound like a good strategy. Do you know who else took this strategy? **Warren Buffett.** This billionaire ($108 B net worth in 2022) bought out his house with full cash of $31,500 at the age of 28 in 1958 and has lived there for over 65 years now in 2022: **It seems he will end up spending less than 8% of his life on paying rent.**

* * *

Here is one important question for you: Why do we have to make a lot of money? In my opinion, the premier reason why we need to make enough money is to protect ourselves from being in pain: Poverty always will come back to us as a pain. It can be a mild or severe pain; that pain can come to us tomorrow or 30 years later. The pain could be something like not having enough money for medical treatment (physical pain) or working in a hellish job (conditional pain). There are jobs where nine out of ten people quit within a week (I have been one of these for almost seven years). Still some people keep working for good since there is no other choice for them; they curse millions of times every day, but still go to work.

I didn't write a fantasy novel right above. We have an obligation to keep ourselves from going through terrible things. Most people have more chances to get out of a hell in their early ages and less in their late age. But, eventually, for one way or another, **some people may end up having no way to exit a hell forever.**

* * *

A lot of people mistakenly think that getting rich is only done by working hard or saving money. Nothing can be further from the truth. It requires some luck, ability to figure out and take opportunities, financial knowledge or having some useful human connections. **Being wealthy is a combination of diverse constructive things.**

Let's take "buying a condo with full cash" as an example. I had some money prepared in the savings account: Cash preparation was hugely important, but that was not all. I was lucky to have a housing market crash in 2013 and smart enough to take that opportunity. I knew one real estate agent who is the mother of my friend and she helped me quickly to grab a nice deal (other agents didn't move for no apparent reasons). I knew how to tell a good condo from bad ones within an hour. I had some financial knowledge to figure out that not having a mortgage is a much better deal (not a little better, but much better). I knew how to use a relatively small condo space to the maximum for my family of three.

After all, buying out my condo with only a single payment was a total combination of the random luck, opportunities, cleverness, decision making, knowledge, skills, people connections and money (mostly luck). Not having a mortgage or rent has saved me from tons of money waste since 2013.

* * *

Being rich and being decent are two different things: I would say that **noble people are less likely to move by greed.** Some people may look wealthy, but they actually have more debts than others; this is just a result of greed and desires to own things; these people are in the lowest block in the personal finance pyramid. Having some control over desires makes people decent and respectable. I have one child though I could have ten if I really wanted. For whatever it is, I think people who don't do "a thing they can do" look cool and honorable.

* * *

"What is the difference between being broke and being poor? **Being *broke* is temporary while being *poor* is eternal.**" As Kiyosaki quotes in *Rich Dad and Poor Dad,* what we may need is an asset, not necessarily a job; the examples of cash earned by assets are interests, dividends, book royalties, etc (assets are things putting cash in our pocket). Personally, writing a book means trying to build one more asset while I am getting some interests and dividends every month.

I am sure that many people still do not understand this asset concept. When I think about it, the best thing my wife did to me financially was introducing this book *Rich Dad and Poor Dad* in 2006; she read this book to me in the Border bookstore (all these store chains closed out now) and I ended up buying it. I had a chance to get small fortunes several times since 2006 and ended up living only on interests after putting all the money in the bank. Without that book, I could have bought some sports cars or something.

The most controversial concept in the *Rich Dad* book is whether a house is an asset or not: Kiyosaki strongly suggests that a house is not an asset, but merely a liability (debt or spending). And I am totally on his side. If we are not sure what to do in real life financially, I think the easiest thing is to see what a rich man does and try to imitate him. For example, it shows the net worth of Kiyosaki is over $100 million. He may be correct, moneywise. I am not going to trust some internet trolls having huge mortgage debts. **I personally believe it is a loss to buy a too big house.**

On the contrary, there are people like Ric Edelman who suggest paying mortgages as long as possible (40 years). According to Suze Orman, these types of financial advisors are nothing but *frauds*; they just want your mortgage money now, so they can use it for their investments. I see that sales of this guy's book is hardly ranked within 100,000th on Amazon while *Rich Dad and Poor Dad* is still ranked within 100th in August, 2022 since the second edition was published in 2017.

* * *

I do not want to *waste* my life *pointlessly* now: **At least, not for now.** I want to enjoy it with a bit of control for now (hopefully forever, but I am not sure). I know some Koreans go to the Philippines or Thailand, and enjoy the lower costs of living there; there is no future for these types of people in my opinion. We cannot make money when we mingle with bar girls or compare ourselves with extremely poor people in poor countries.

There is a travel writer named Park; he cannot speak or read Thai much even though he had stayed in the country for more than 12 years; he and I are the same 49 years old as of 2022. I think we are still too young to start looking down, enjoying our little achievements and indulging ourselves mindlessly: I am not saying that we should live *diligently* (I do not have a job, anyway). I just feel that it is too early for people of my age to start wasting life by comparing ourselves with unblessed people after little successes.

It is a good thing to enjoy our lives; I will never work for a company for the rest of my life. I am just saying that there should be some bottom limits; I do not want to feel proud after placing myself next to people from Southeast Asia. I may be richer than people in Africa, but can be settled in the low income class in North America that way: We should stop comparing ourselves with people with deprivation. Stop visiting impoverished countries unless you have a specific business. **Being wealthier only because we were born in America instead of the Philippines is not an accomplishment.** I don't know why I have been interested in Thailand travel a bit lately, but I decided to visit Thai restaurants once in a while instead of walking around and drinking in Pattaya for real. It is better for me to have that moment of looking down, indulging and being wasteful *as late as possible*: It is better for us to *delay* realizing a fruitless harmful desire if we cannot remove it.

* * *

According to the book titled "Outliers" written by Malcolm Gladwell, the richest man who has ever existed in human history is John D. Rockefeller; experts estimate his net worth is over $500 billion USD in 2020. The record shows that this is what he used to say repeatedly when he was alive: "Do you know what the biggest joy is in my life? Getting the dividend check every month." I think I have gotten my stock dividends and bond interests for 11 years now as of 2022. These used to be less $100 a month in 2011, but over $2,000 a month now in 2022.

* * *

I believe the easiest way to get out of poverty is by imitating super-riches. Statistically, most super riches were not born rich: there is a reason why they became one. We do not necessarily have to be millionaires by imitation. **I believe getting out of poverty is more important than being rich.** Does it make sense that we can get out of poverty at least after keeping copying what billionaires did when they were poor?

The first day I bought a stock was in 2011; my daughter was one year old at that time. I remember I bought a $100 amount of Pitney Bowes stocks. I had owned the video game store at that time and made twice more money out of eBay sales than store sales. Whenever I sell a game, PayPal lets me print out a shipping label through its site. "Pitney Bowes" logo was always on the top part of the shipping label. I thought the company would be profitable since millions of items are sold only on eBay every day. Besides, the stock has given out good dividends, anyway.

After buying the stocks, my interest in stock investments had grown. I have been particularly interested in dividend stocks since then (check UnBrokable* X book about why, later). When we save money in a bank, we get interest every month. When we own a stock, we get a dividend (every month, quarter or year depending on the dividend stocks). **Interest and dividend are basically the same things.** Only difference is we have to buy dividend stocks since half of stocks in the market do not give out dividends (for example, TSLA or Tesla stock does not give out a dividend).

* * *

In the 2010s, I was obsessed with Warren Buffett for no apparent reason (he was a more popular figure in general, then). He was the second richest person in America and a long term dividend investor at that time (still 4th richest next to Musk, Bezos and Gates in 2022). But the Wikipedia article on him helped me big time in an unexpected way. I had rented an apartment at that time and thought I would buy a big house with a mortgage someday (like most American chumps). **But I learned that he bought his house with full cash of $31,500 in 1958 and still lives there for over 60 years.** I thought that was very unique and intriguing.

I had about $80,000 cash in Bank CDs, which my parents gave me for an emergency. I was interested in a three-bedroom house in a village called Roselle and it was about $200,000 in 2012 ($100,000 huge price drop thanks to the subprime mortgage crisis since 2009). But, unfortunately, this means I still need a $120,000 mortgage debt to buy that house ($200,000 house - $80,000 cash = $120,000 debt). No one would have given me that amount of mortgage since my business was not extremely doing well. But, even if I got it, I could have been in a situation to pay $2,000 a month for 30 years: Not an ideal life I have ever imagined.

Strangely, several months after that, I was able to find a one-bedroom condo in my current village for $60,000. It is a way better area than Roselle to begin with. It was 2013 and the economic depression had stayed for more than a few years since 2009. In Particular, condo prices dropped a lot.

Still, this was my concern: 'I have never seen anyone buying a house with full cash for one time around me. Do I really have to go for this condo?' I truly wondered. Actually, I was even nervous and afraid since no one around me did it. I had reached this conclusion eventually: 'This billionaire did it for a $31,500 house. Let me just imitate him. I can move out later if I am not happy with the place. Who knows if I can end up with $7 M since he made $70 B this way.' You know what? It turned out to be such a great decision when I think about it now in 2022: **The best thing I did with money so far.** Let me explain why.

* * *

First of all, this 850 sf one-bedroom condo has not been very small as I thought. I have a wife and a daughter, but we do not live together all the time for personal reasons (when you think about it, this is actually true for a lot of families for colleges, travels, jobs, military, etc). Certainly, it is enough for me, but even when we live together, we reasonably divide the space into three sections: Usually, living room for wife, bedroom for daughter and walk-in closet for me. The walk-in closet is about a room size in this condo: We already have bought enough space saving furniture from Ikea and renovated this house.

Secondly, since I use the full cash, I could get some discount on the house. It was originally listed for $65,000, but the previous owner discounted $5,000 immediately for a cash deal within a day. This condo is about $150,000 now after having lived here for 9 years since 2013. With mortgages, there is not really a discount for any house: people often pay more than cash buyers to begin with, not to mention mortgage interests.

Thirdly, I have saved tons of money by not paying rent or mortgage interest. Often, some people pay a house price close to double than original prices with a mortgage. For example, some people ended up paying $270,000 with a mortgage for a $150,000 house.

Fourthly, I was able to sell my car and live a car less life since 2017. Usually there are more facilities around a large condo complex (500 units in this case). We have 3 super markets nearby. And I found my nursing home job within walking distance as well later on. I sold my car for $7,000 and have never worried about gas for the last five years. FYI, there has been no supermarket near the house in Roselle I was interested in, originally.

Fifthly, HOA for condo increase has been much lower than APT rent or house upkeep cost increases. I think I have saved about $2,000 every month compared with renters (especially in CA) and it has been 9 years. Rent can increase $100 a year, but my HOA association fee has been increased only by $70 in the last nine years.

Lastly, the library happened to be very close to home, coincidently (this was just luck although I found out that it's quite important later on). I was able to pass two exams for certificates while working at the nursing home for weekends. Even publishing these books could not have been possible unless I lived close to our library. **Benefits have been great only because I copied Buffett once.** Maybe there is a reason why he is in that position.

By the way, I learned that Roselle is a worse area than I thought in the beginning as time goes on. Library was not close to the house, but it had been particularly outdated (one of the worst in Chicagoland). And blackouts have been frequent in that area since all the electricity lines are in the sky while those are underground in my village.

I am glad I did not choose that single family house in Roselle though it even appeared in my dream once. I still remember that I woke up in the middle of night from the dream of that house. When I see it, it is just a dull common house now, but I do not know why I wanted it so badly in 2012. This could be the lesson here: **Not everything I want badly is a good thing.** Having a debt with that house could have been a big regret by now. I will talk more about this in Chapter 45 “Being impulsive” later.

* * *

Summary

1. Check what financial decisions billionaires made when they were poorer.
2. Personally, the smallest house in the village turned out to be still big for my family. I am glad that I did not spend more or go into debt for a bigger home.
3. What we really want can be a bad thing: our intuitions are not always correct.

14

Being Too Religious

Honest religions never ask for money.
-Brad Kong

Some countries like Afghanistan are poor because of the dominance of Islamic religious zealots like the Taliban. Many of those people care more for Allāh instead of making ends meet for their family. I think that most Indians agree that caste social classification is the huge obstacle for their economic growth as a whole in the country: The caste originated from Hinduism 3,000 years ago. I think being religious beyond common sense can be a reason for poverty.

I believe religion was created to benefit people, originally. Let's take the old Egyptian religion for instance; I read that people in old Egypt used to worship the God of the Sun 5,000 years ago; they called the god "Ra", the ancient Egyptian deity of the Sun. **This makes sense since all the lives on the Earth grow thanks to the sunlight, basically.** When you think about it deeply, you will see that the photosynthesis of plants is the origin where all the wealth comes from. In fact, the concept of wealth was created only after accumulation of leftover crops happened; Yuval Harrari explained this well in his famous book titled *Sapiens*.

When I was in the Field Museum in Chicago, I saw quite a good amount of cat mummies in the Egyptian collection:

This means they also deify cats or treat them equally like humans at least; this makes sense to me, too. A cat is a very unique animal catching and eating only mice without touching plant crops; you know that sparrows and mice have been the biggest problem for farmers for thousands of years. Simply, there is no more ideal animal to protect our harvests than cats. **It seems what ancient Egyptians did makes more sense to me than what we are doing now.**

* * *

I am not a very religious person, but here are a few things I decided to do for our society. First of all, I decided to concern less-privileged people from now; I may not be able to donate any money since I do not have much now. Still, I can write easy books mostly about poverty for them; I hope they will read those and help themselves to get out of there. For sure, I will think about struggling people and study them to improve conditions.

Second, I can stop eating meat at least; these will truly benefit other animals on the Earth. Personally, I have never liked meat as food since I was young; my mother always tried to feed me meat since she had believed it's healthy, but it never worked out. I hope I can save all the animals in the farms, but that may not be realistically possible. Most people think about only other humans when it comes to charity: This is totally wrong. **I hope people will learn that other animals are as important as humans soon.**

* * *

Karl Marx once said that, "Religion is poison." Also, the German philosopher, Arthur Schopenhauer once said,

"Religion is the masterpiece of the art of animal training, for it trains people as to how they shall think." It is surprising if I agree with these quotes since I believe I am a kind of religious Buddhist. My mother and wife are really Buddhists; I am not that religious like them, but I am reading books written by many Buddhist monks.

Still, I candidly believe religion has been modified for a governor to control the majority of low class people for a long time: It does not matter which religion it has been. Everything has been utilized by humans for reasons. In fact, so many religions have been created and demolished for thousands of years. There have been so many weird practices as well in many places. It is up to us how we can react to them. Regardless, I think we should be very careful if a religion asks us for money, somehow.

* * *

I apologize for Indians if anyone reads this, but, honestly, the most cruel religious practice I have heard so far is "Sati" in Hinduism in India: it shows that a wife, who is alive, will be burned to death together with a husband if the husband passes away first before a wife does. It is not like the widow killed the husband; she just dies together, actually being burned together, with the dead husband *for nothing.* Every human can produce some productive outcomes, so killing a woman this way is just a waste of the working force in a society.

When a country is extremely poor while its people try very hard, there is a reason. I know Indians are extremely hard working in general. No offense, but it seems to me that India has a lot of severe corruption in the country including the old caste system. I hate to say this, but this could be why the country rarely wins a gold medal in the Olympics in spite of having more than 10 billion population. Being wealthy is not just about money. **In a sense, wealth tells if a society runs in a fair constructive way or not.**

* * *

Some people are broke all the time since they get too involved in a religion. We are living in the 21st century now. An average hard worker is not supposed to be broke, especially in America or Korea. **I heard some people donate all the money they have to some cult Christianity in Korea.** Let me tell you what happened to me about 30 years ago.

Personally, I have had negative experiences with Korean Churches all along throughout my life. Christianities in the country are much different from those in America. The only common thing is that they have the same Bibles in the Korean version in their churches.

Before starting, I have to mention that South Korea really has a surprisingly large number of churches (most people do not know this). These are mostly small chapels, but the numbers are unbearably many compared to other countries. I am sure half will disappear if governments charge property tax on them. Good portion of these are nothing but money grabbing greedy organizations.

Those Korean churches have been even in America for a long time, but they do not accept Americans to visit them: churches for Koreans only. Isn't it weird? These will never be a place we can stop by comfortably and pray. In Particular, we will never be able to see a black or Mexican there since churches assume the poor probably do not have money to donate.

Since money making is their priority, all they focus on are advertisements and propagations. They will ask Koreans to join in crazily (stalking). I hardly go to Korean supermarkets, but if I do, these church people are always there. They are a little more aggressive forms of Jehovah's Witnesses we can see on subway stations in America.

When I was in college in Korea 30 years ago, there was a church guy who followed me everywhere on the campus. **It was painful for me to be stalked by a man and learn why stalking is a serious crime.** He did not care whether I was studying in the library or taking exams in a classroom. He even checked my exam schedule and waited outside the classroom. Maybe he hoped that I would give them some money or bring some friends to join their church eventually.

* * *

There was one Korean guy's blog I used to visit. He was an IT computer technician working in an American high school and his wife owned a dollar mart. Both were Christians.

A Korean minister visited their dollar mart on the day it opened. And he wrote that the person suggested donating the entire first day sales to the Lord. The guy wrote that he donated it gladly and was ashamed that he could have not thought about it before the minister suggested.

I honestly was disgusted for two things. The minister did not care for how hard it is to run a small business. I think that he took a chance to make more money since asking for an extra donation usually works well on the opening day of a business. Apparently, this blogger had trouble with money for a long time even before opening the store.

Second, I was amazed how a human can be such a voluntary slave without having any common sense at all. What do you mean we could have done that before the person suggested? **What do we really owe?**

When I checked his blog last time, the dollar mart had been closed for good after being in business only for a few years. He wrote that he had been packing a lot of stuff at home since it is highly possible to move out from his house: Foreclosing his own home. FYI, there had been a lot of foreclosures back in 2011. I could not find any posting about moving out after that, but I could see that he had been worried about money a lot in numerous postings.

* * *

Religions definitely help our lives on some occasions. There is a Buddhist monk[28] YouTube channel I enjoy watching[29] and it helped me a lot when I needed some inner peace. I may talk about this later, but he is the one who made me decide to apply for a dishwashing job in the nursing home years ago.

When I think about it now, I am glad that I started the job 7 years ago even though last Sunday was my last day in April, 2022. The place is nearby, so I have lost a lot of weight by walking to work for years. I had worked as a full timer for 1 year and weekend part timer for 6 years. I have studied at the library next to the nursing home building and passed two exams for certificates: Medical Coder and Pharmacy

---

[28] Pomnyun

[29] I am not exactly a Buddhist, by the way.

Technician. And, I planned to get one more certificate later on: AWS Cloud Practitioner (instead, I am writing books now though).

Before getting the job in the nursing home, I thought there are types of people doing dirty jobs for us. Now I know they are not different from me: We are all the same weak people. Seven years of the experience fixed my arrogance well and I believe this mental growth is the biggest achievement I have gotten from the job.

I do not want to live uptight always. But, as I will explain in the next Chapter, there have been many people taking advantage of me whenever I lowered my guard a little bit. I think we may have to decide what situation we will be in and how we can handle these people.

* * *

Summary

1. Being religious and being obsessed with unhealthy beliefs are different.
2. Some "leaders" have modified religions to take advantage of honest people.
3. If a religious person asks for money somehow, watch him or her out: There is a difference between being generous and being stupid.

15

Being Gullible

Don't be a too nice guy.
-Brad Kong

I hate to say this, but I think we should be careful when we give a favor to anyone. Some people will truly appreciate our help. Others may take more advantage from that moment. One fat black boy stepped on a bus I was on in south Chicago the other day; he delayed the ride to ask for a free ride to the driver (I cannot believe someone is poor that much). The generous African American driver granted him, but that obese boy started eating his dinner on the bus which was very unusual. I was truly disgusted. He learned how to take advantage at such an early age (teen); usually, hopeless, but bold old people do what he did. I did not say a thing since I knew he would get off soon since it was getting out of black area. **Getting into a habit of taking advantage of others can make us poor, ultimately.**

* * *

One of the most horrible ways to be gullible is "cosigning the guarantee (Bo-jeoung)" in Korea. I know we can get a cosign from our family or friend when we buy a vehicle in America. But I believe it's a little different there: More strict and *predatory*. Victims usually cosign any type of debt for family, relatives, friends or even for acquaintances in that country; this is a horrible legal system to put anyone in hell when the duped cosigner gets betrayed. **I am not sure why victims do those since cosigners do not seem to get**

any benefit in any case: They only take responsibility when things go wrong. I saw one documentary regarding those victims one time and it was horrid; they put their own children in deep poverty and misery by doing something they didn't have to do. I saw that many YouTubers posted comments saying "*never* to cosign anything" in Korea.

* * *

In his bestseller titled *The 48 Laws of Power,* the author Greene suggests not to trust your friends *too much.* It sounded weird in the beginning, but when I thought about it, it made sense somehow: **What do we exactly know about our friends?** Technically, they are sort of strangers from other families we have been close to. He took the example of Michael III of the Byzantine Empire in the 9th century. He was murdered only when he was 27 by a close "friend" named Basilius (Basil I) in the stupidest way possible in my opinion; he should have not given too easy "chances to get murdered" to his *actual enemies, who was* disguised as a friend.

Michael III was originally the Byzantine Emperor in the mid-9th century (842 - 867); Byzantine was a huge empire back then and its territory included Italy, Greece, and Turkey combined currently in 2022. Since Michael III became the emperor when he was only 2 years old, his mother and uncle Bardas governed the country basically; the record shows that it had been just fine for 12 years and Bardas was the excellent governor. Then, the family feud started as Michael III got older. The mother of Michael III interrupted her son's private life too much, so Michael III killed one famous politician named Theoktistos on his mother's side himself and sent his mother to an isolated convent for good.

While Bardas had been a self-controlling politician, it shows that Michael III had been a mere alcoholic living a prodigal, vain and wasteful life since he was 15; naturally, these two didn't get along very well. The emperor (Michael III) met a person named Basilius on the street somehow and they became close buddies. It shows that Basilius was simply a refugee who was illiterate with no education; still, he had strong physical power and was good at handling horses. Eventually, Michael III used Basilius to kill his uncle Bardas, who was the head of the army at that time. As a result, Basilius became the prime minister of the country instead of Bardas. It shows that it took only 9 years for him to be in the highest position in the empire military from a humble and uneducated peasant.

It shows that Michael loved Basilius like a brother. Basilius kept asking for more salary and the emperor doubled, then tripled it: Basilius' power and wealth had only grown. But, surprisingly, when Michael III asked him to pay some money back to the emperor himself one day, Basilius refused. It was a wakeup call for him: **Michael III suddenly realized that this "peasant horse boy" had more money and power than the emperor himself.** The bad news was that Basilius also detected that the emperor started changing his mind.

After having heavy drinking one night, Michael III awoke and found himself surrounded by Basilius and his soldiers. The emperor's head was cut off on that night, placed at the end of a long pike and displayed to the public by Basilius in 867 A.D. Maybe this is a fair conclusion for a guy who killed his own family (uncle) and got an unqualified stranger in the highest position: Still, I feel 27 was too early an age to get murdered. I believe drinking played a major role here again as I suggested in Chapter 1; the similar assassination case is the one of Julius Caesar by Marcus Brutus: Nonetheless,

Caesar (55) died at least when he was twice older than Michael III (27) since there was no alcohol involved in the morning.

* * *

Some people buy *Tesla* stocks only because they seem to be popular; they do not analyze the company report or check if the stock price is "too high or not" at a certain moment; they just buy since everyone buys. Some people buy gold because the news says the gold price will go up; some people buy coins since there are people who claim to have made a fortune out of that investment. There are diverse types of coins nowadays: *Bitcoin, Ethereum, Doge coin, Luna* coin, etc; these mindless people don't even care which one they go for; they just buy since these look to be easy money making opportunities.

I personally have never bought a coin. I usually buy stock from a company only if I use any product from that company, and if I am happy with it. These give me more confidence in the company and help me hold its stock longer, which generally brings me better investment outcomes in the long run. No one uses these coins in real life every day: **No one uses them at all.** I personally believe coins will be recorded as one example of hoaxes in the 21st century (just like Tulip mania in the 17th century). And, unfortunately, something serious happened to a family in Korea related to one coin in 2022 before this mania has been completely over.

* * *

A family of three committed suicide in Wando Island, Korea in June, 2022: They were father (36), mother (34) and daughter (10). Technically, it was a partial murder since the police believed that the parents killed their daughter first with sleeping pills. Then, they drowned themselves together in a new Audi sedan into the sea. The ocean police finally found the car with three bodies inside on 6/29/2022. The news shows that the father had an incredible amount of debt because he lost a lot of money on crypto coin investment; the one was called Luna coin. Also, they found the family had lived lavishly driving a luxury sedan even though they did not have much income. Conclusively, I would say the debt was the reason for family suicide overall.

This incident was particularly shocking to me since I have a wife and a daughter myself. Coincidentally, the girl's name was the same as my daughter; my daughter's name is not supposed to be popular, but, surprisingly, I see it everywhere all the time these days. Only difference is that I do not own a car at all. And I have never invested in anything like coins. Also I do not rent a house like them; I have owned mine outright in the last nine years since 2013.

In general, I think that the father was merely stupid. First of all, parents do not have any right to decide the fate (dead or alive) of their child; it is better for us to learn early that our child is a totally different human being on his or her own. Luckily, I think I realized this when my daughter was one year old; it is too arrogant if parents think they have the right to interrupt the destiny of their child: **No one has such a right.**

In this case, it shows that the deceased girl had "two pairs" of grandparents (from both sides of parents) and plenty of relatives, so she could have lived just fine with their help. Besides, when the father commit suicide alone, all the debts are gone *legally* in Korea; people do not ask money from dead people in that country; debt is not automatically inherited to the child as long as she give up the entire inheritance from her parents legally: It is $0 to inherit in this case. Maybe the father could have sold the car and given the money to the rest of his family before he died: **Stupid people are as harmful as wicked people.**

Coin investments are booming nowadays. I saw that Matt Damon said, "Fortune favors the braves." in a commercial. We have to buy some coins since he is a reliable guy, right? Larry David also made a funny commercial about one crypto trading website. Maybe I should sign up since he is super rich himself, correct? Let me tell you one thing: **These frauds go extreme; they will do whatever it takes to make us hooked.** They would not just try; they would do extreme things. Personally, I believe cryptos and coins are useless craps; no one uses them after all. People get blinded by their own greed and will do stupid things as always.

* * *

I originally planned that this chapter includes the "being too generous" topic. Financial crimes are big nowadays. One of the guys I used to see in the Korean community site I used to frequent said his wife had lost $500,000 through voice phishing. He said the victims include even a Harvard professor and he does not know how this exactly happened.

Though nothing really happened while I had worked in the nursing home for seven years, I had been involved with diverse types of minor crimes while working in the video game store. I am glad I shut it down permanently in 2014: No worries any more. Here is what happened.

* * *

First of all, we[30] had a lot of shoplifters. I think I called the police over 30 times during that 8 years. Then, we had a couple of identity theft problems with credit cards; probably, I have lost $130 or so for two new games. And I had ATM deposit fraud once. Gladly, Chase covered $1,000 I lost. It was not their fault at all, but they gave me $1,000 cash out of their pocket. I guess I will stay with them forever. And, lastly, we had a robbery at a gunpoint in 2009.

I believe the gun was a fake during the robbery in November, 2009. At that time, my pregnant wife was next to me. The robber hit my eyes for no reason and got all the money in the cash register. I believe it was about $160 (about $200 value in 2022). This made me wonder if I have to keep the store open permanently. Soon, I decided not to renew the lease and the store was closed 5 years later in 2014. I had countless ugly customer problems as well, but let me not talk about it here now.

* * *

When I think about it now, I was a too nice guy when my store opened in 2006. I did not want to spend $2,000 for security cameras which turned out to be extremely necessary. I had been the only employee for a long time until my wife came to give me a hand from 2007. The store had been in pretty much vulnerable condition as a whole.

Before opening the store, I had 3 months of free rent. That was a trick from the cunning landlord. The landlord was a strangely unpleasant lawyer every tenant did not like. He took one month of security deposit in his pocket

---

[30] Actually, I was the only employee and owner.

when our 8 years' lease was finally over in 2014. So it was like I got two months of free rent, but I spent that for store set up and construction. The rent was $1,200 a month in 2006. I think I spent about $30,000 including game purchases for the opening in 2006.

Do you know who came first as soon as we opened the store? A customer with cash never came for a long time. I could not make any sales in the first 10 days until Javier Martinez (a good Mexican boy) came.

But, strangely, a lot of people still came and these were mostly sales people, advertisement ladies, job seekers, shoplifters and potential other criminals. They all came to take advantage of the "Cyb Knight" store somehow. While most people were great and tried to help us, there had been people always trying to take advantage continuously.

* * *

Shamefully, I had never really donated a lot of money for my whole life and probably would not a lot from now on as well. I learned that corruption in non-profit organizations was severe at that time. I got trillions of phone calls from those places in the store and heard that they actually put 90% of donations in their pocket and give only 10% to poor people.

I guess I will just pay more than enough taxes instead of giving money to some charities: Governments help poor people with their tax money, anyway; these help include free or discounted housing; food stamps, coupons or SNAP cards; Medicare, Medicaid, etc. In a sense, **paying only huge taxes (without donating at all) makes my charity spendings easier and simpler** than creating and handling diverse foundations in case I become a super-rich. Besides, **I do not have to worry about tax audits if I focus on paying more than enough taxes.**

There was a lady named Pippa Bacca in Italy. She tried to cross Europe via hitchhiking to show how the world is a peaceful place in 2008. Twelve days after she started the trip, she was found dead in Gebze, Turkey after getting raped: She was only 33 years old. Justly, it shows that the murderer, Murat Karataş, was caught and had life sentence in prison. We can be good people. But I don't think we need to be too nice or generous beyond reason. I suggest we should check if this could be one of the reasons why we got nothing in our pocket despite working hard.

* * *

Summary

1. We can be nice: We don't have to be too nice.
2. Frauds do extreme things to deceive people.
3. We have an obligation to protect ourselves first before anyone else.

16

Not Going Against Destiny

If we stay in poverty too long, it can stick to our lives and never get off.
-Brad Kong

There is a movie titled *The Hurt Locker* starring Jeremy Lee Renner (Hawkeye in Marvel series). This main actor is an American soldier in Iraq and his particular job is disassembling bombs: the leader of U.S. Army Explosive Ordnance Disposal (EOD) unit. He survived many dangerous missions and went back home safely in the end. However, he was bored with routine civilian life and started another hellish mission with the Army again.

Believe it or not, a lot of people live like this. They get back to bad relationships, horrible jobs or poverty again and again until their lives are over. How can we get out of this vicious downward spiral? How can we be different from a hamster running in a spinner in a cage? **My recommendation is to have a habit to try something new whenever possible**. This could be the mindset: Let me try everything at least once in my life. I think we can start with trying a new restaurant or menus. Maybe we can try to read a new book we would never imagine reading before.

* * *

Do you know why most lottery winners go bankrupt several years after winning? I think they failed to challenge their destinies: They didn't resist and went back to poor destinies. If we live in poverty for more than a decade, it can become our fate; some people feel comfortable being poor. Some winners probably would have felt uncomfortable having a lot of money suddenly; they spent it quickly or even gave it away to others until they felt comfortable like before.

I think the other way around is also possible in a sense. There are people comfortable being wealthy. Actually, they probably cannot put up with not being wealthy or having enough money. They can be broke temporarily, but always come back to be comfortable financially. Above all, they just do not like the feeling that they are inferior or poorer than others. Finally, they feel relieved or normal only after having some money saved.

* * *

There used to be a girl server named Vanessa when I worked at a small restaurant in the nursing home in 2015; I believe she was about 20 year-old Latin American; I saw that her parents were originally from El Salvador and divorced on Facebook; her mother has four children from a couple of relationships and she was the second child; she has one older brother and two younger brothers.

I do not remember that she was a very nice server; she made a lot of hustle and bustle unnecessarily in the kitchen. When she brought a large amount of dirty dishes to the dishwashers, she often slammed those on the counter, so a few broke occasionally. I did not like one of the female managers there and these two were close friends; they made my life very uncomfortable, then.

She ended up quitting the job in 2016 and I found out that she was pregnant already and has one son at the age of only 21 on Facebook later; it seems that was the reason for her quitting although the family was poor. The father of the baby was a Mexican boy waiter working in the same restaurant.

I thought this is too early to start and expand a family since all they had were just a couple of high school diplomas. I believe both were only 21 years old. **In my opinion, it was way too soon for a man to get into a "prison" called marriage.** I am not blindly against marriage, but I guess it is true that prison and marriage lives share some common points (good thing is that both provide stable lives, too). In 2016, both did not have any higher education, job or income, but only ended up having a baby. For your information, I don't necessarily consider having a baby early as an accomplishment (As I said in Chapter 2, there is not much for a man to do to make this happen). Let's be honest: Who does not know how to make a baby? It was not extremely hard for me, at least.

I saw her photos only with her son without the waiter boy on Facebook last year in 2021, so I assume they might have gotten separated already. **I knew it was too much to ask for a 21 years-old boy to stick to only one woman for the rest of his life from the start.** I know this is what a modern marriage requires nowadays, but does that honestly make sense to you (in a sense of animal nature)? Alternatively, I think a man can marry a little later in his life after he learns that there is nothing much special or fantastic about other women. I don't think shackling a young boy by social rules works out very well all the time.

As a result, it seems she just followed the destiny of her divorced mother exactly. Only difference is her single mother has four kids and she has one for now; both seem to be alcoholic, too (on Facebook). Statistically, Latin

Americans tend to have more babies at a young age here. I cannot blame all the Mexican descendants since some men never get married. Here is one important question, though: Could she go against her destiny? Could she go against the general trend of Latin Americans in America? Could she try to be a little different from her mother? I notice that every single one of her friends is Latinas on Facebook. Maybe she could not see beyond the Hispanic trend or customs. Is this what's happening to all of us by chance (not seeing anything beyond our surroundings)?

Instead of blaming this waitress, let me talk about myself for a while. I have a father who has made an incredible amount of money in Korea. That is good, but he also has unnecessarily showing off and feisty characters. **Am I going against my destiny?** I think I do not spend money to show off like him, at least (I do not own a car). Still, do I inherit his bad characteristics only instead of his money making skills? He got divorced, but am I a good husband or parent to my own family (my father has been a clear pain)?

I think I may be selectively aggressive from now on. I have never liked my father since he had been angry all the time. Still, I cannot be generous to everyone since there are obvious assholes existing. I think it's important for me to be awake as often as possible and act reasonably based on situations.

* * *

Some people reject happiness by habits. Some women reject a great guy because he looks too good to be true. They strongly believe this cannot be real since nothing *great* has happened to them for their whole life. Often, they do not try anything new; for example, many have never been really out of their home States. I am not saying that we need to be risk takers: **I am saying that we should not go back to our original bad destinies since we are so comfortable with them.**

Believe it or not, some people choose misfortune voluntarily: The common point is that they are familiar with misfortune somehow; the most common case is that a lot of them have had unfortunately bad childhoods. **Some choose bad lives they are familiar with rather than happy lives they are not familiar with.** Whenever a good thing happens, they think it cannot be true, subconsciously; they think they do not deserve it, and then avoid it. I think I used to be one of those people: I kept the weekend dishwashing job for almost seven years even after I got wealthy; it took quite a while to let go of drudgery. I was not comfortable living only on dividends and interest, even after I have done that in the last 11 years now.

It is important to notice this in case it is happening to us: it is possible that we live unhappily for nothing right now. **It is crucial for us to have a habit to try something new unless it is dangerous**: I think it is an efficient way to *break old destiny* and put ourselves in new possibilities. I will not try skydiving only because I have not done it before. But I can try African vegetarian food, a new Indian restaurant or writing as a new career. I have not published a book before until I become 49, but who knows if I can make more money out of that job?

Did you know that a criminal usually commits the same types of crimes repeatedly? I watched a police program on YouTube the other day; one guy was arrested for uploading photographs of minors; the officers unlocked his smartphone and said the guy had five photos again. Later, they found out that he had been arrested for the same crime three times before in the last twenty years; he was in prison for years for similar convictions like child assaults, etc. I guess he failed to go against his own character and destiny.

* * *

As I said, if we stay in poverty too long, it can attach to our life as if it is a superglue and will never get off; it is important to get out of poverty ASAP. I know some people always look poor no matter how much they try to take care of their appearances; they look poor even in Mercedes; they look poor in new clothes; they can look poor in a library, too. Especially, I notice that their fat never goes away. Before this happens, I think we all should get out of poverty.

Some people never go against their destinies and stay broke for lives: They surrender to poor destinies and live like slaves. Let me give you three unique examples.

* * *

There was one boy's pop singing group in Korea in 2003: It had three male performers. They were not extremely popular, but reasonably famous I believe. Probably, they had been on national TV about 10 times a year in the 2010s. And, I could see articles about them in entertainment sections on internet news.

What was the most unusual about them was the *lead* singer guy. ***Strangely*, he was well known for his exceptional poverty in 2003.** I am not sure of the exact reason, but I do not think they made a huge amount of money to begin with. The news I read was something like this: He could not afford his car, so he had to sell it. It showed that it was the hardest decision since he could not be on public transportation since he was a public figure. I read another article that his fans collected cash in a paper box and gave it to him at the end of one meeting. Fans said, "Do not misunderstand us. We just know your situation and want to help you only once." I guess it all happened by 2004 or so and I forgot about this for a long time.

I believe it was 2017 when I found him with a wife and six kids on TV again. I watched some family reality shows on YouTube. At that time, my daughter was seven years old. I wondered if I was the only one having a hard time raising a child. For that reason, I used to watch those child care programs occasionally. I did watch some American shows like "Jon and Kate plus 8", but I watched some Korean programs as well. Those usually showed the daily lives of large families (parents with a lot of children).

At first, I thought the guy in the reality show was not the guy (lead singer) in the boy's pop group. It was a long time ago, anyway. But, as I watched more than 20 minutes, I realized that it could be the same guy who I remember. When I checked Wikipedia briefly, it was him!

I was totally shocked: **What six kids?** People who never had a hard time as a head of family will not understand me. And, for the first time, this idea struck me: **Is there anything like a poverty destiny?** Are some people born to be poor throughout their lives? Why do they go back to poverty again even though they have a chance to get out? **He didn't necessarily have to have six children.**

I know some people never get married or have only one child since they had a hard life. For instance, Oprah once said 70% of black ladies in the U.S. are singles. I think she exaggerated the number, but I believe about 40% of black women are singles in America. And I think that is reasonable if they believe they have lived hard lives all along and do not want to pass the asperity to the new generations. Population is increasing crazily nowadays, anyway.

In a sense, this Korean singer blindly sentenced himself to be poor for the rest of his life. The interview showed that his parents were actually upset when he had the third child. They worried how he could raise them all. I can understand if he had been wealthy for life, but apparently he had suffered greatly with money all along. Has he been following his "original poverty destiny" mindlessly for decades?

* * *

Another example is Lupe, a Mexican girl who I used to know at work. I think she was about 22, studied at a community college and worked as a CNA at the nursing home in 2018. She was a little fat, had a tattoo on her lower back, which is not necessary in my opinion and had some taste of luxury goods (e.g., expensive wallet).

She said that she was originally born in Chicago, but her parents got divorced when she was a baby. So she had lived with her mom as a single child, but her mom passed away when she was in early teens. Her father remarried and had three sons separately in a new household (stupid and irresponsible in my opinion). So she had three step brothers, but lived by herself except getting little help from father and relatives. She had lived pretty much for entire life in South Chicago: a dark and dangerous area.

Social media shows that she met a fat Puerto Rican boyfriend in her late teens: A guy with spider web tattoo on his neck. They rented two rooms on the third floor of a very old house and the rent was less than $500 a month in 2018. That was less than half of the average one-bedroom apartment in Chicagoland then ($1,200). The boyfriend looked tough, but could not get any job or help her with money: A useless guy from a financial point of view. **I guess that all these had been a "*given* hardship" for her so far**; the first type of two hardships I explained in Chapter 2. I guess none of these had been her fault by 2018.

* * *

I really wish the story would go in the direction that they both get jobs, make money, buy a small condo and get out of South Chicago. But, unfortunately, it went in exactly the other direction.

To everyone's surprise, she gave birth to a son out of the blue in 2019. It was sudden since we didn't even notice she was pregnant. She was pretty chubby and maybe that was why (I am not sure). Even more surprising was that the baby was a black boy while her boyfriend (fiancé living together) was a *white* Hispanic from Puerto Rico. It seems he did not realize this until the baby became a couple of months old or so. It is hard to recognize everything on a very newborn. She used to post photos of the baby and her boyfriend napping together or having a good time on Facebook. But I saw that the guy unfriended her and completely disappeared one day: **I think he realized that the baby was not his.** Still, this is not all the story.

In 2020, she suddenly posted a photo of her new born daughter. **Apparently, she got pregnant again right after her first son was born**: That was really fast in my opinion. She wrote on social media that finally she got one prince and one princess or something like that.

Apparently, she found a new boyfriend who is the father of the daughter: A young Mexican guy without any hair, but with lots of mustache and beard. I could see that she will have a hard life. The new boyfriend's Facebook showed only photos of his daughter: Not the black son. The situation would be like he will stay with Lupe only to take care of his daughter, but will not consider the son as his child. **He can act selfishly or unfairly for that reason in the future**: "I am supporting someone else's child as well for you." She may have to put up with a lot of crap since he is the one who gives her a favor. I found out that they all moved out to California on Facebook in 2021. I cannot find her Facebook page any more as I have never made a Friend with her on the site. She showed all these publicly before 2021.

Just like the Korean lead singer, she probably was born in a poverty destiny as well. Statistically, Latin Americans produce more babies than other races in North America. But, does she need to follow the trend, tradition or custom because she is a Latina: Not necessarily. **She did not seem to recognize or resist her given destiny.** She had kept giving more births in her (already) hard situations and made sure to stay poor firmly. All I remember about her now is that she had a hard time paying rent and complained about it many times even before having the first child.

* * *

I guess that this concept of "going against destiny is necessary" worked out *great* in my case. Most people do not know this, but Koreans drink alcohol way more than Americans: Possibly, more than any other people in the world (I am serious). If you visit Korea, you will see way more alcohol drinking bars, restaurants and salons (aka Karaoke bars with ladies): All these are places dedicated to alcohol consumption.

Not only there are more, but the kinds of drinking places are diverse for poor to super-rich people in the nation. Also, the country has places called "room salons" providing assistant women with alcohol: These are common there, but there is no such a thing in America (it is translated to Karaoke Bar, occasionally). **Personally, I do not drink or smoke at all.** I have never been in a "room salon" for my whole life (I have seen it from outside). Do I have to follow the popular trend only because I was born in Korea? Absolutely not. I do not like alcohol by nature, but even if I do, I will never spend a lot of money on them (I heard these are super expensive). We will discuss more about this in Chapter 18 later on.

* * *

Let me give you the last example with the story of my friend, Joe. Even though I did not like Vanessa or Lupe very much, I have liked this guy and always felt deeply sorry for him. And I found that his case is outrageously unique: **He could have let go of his poverty destiny for good, but unnecessarily caught it at the very last moment in his life.**

Joe was about 55 years old when I first met him in 2015: A big fat white guy with an easy going character. He had a wife with four kids. He worked for two dishwasher jobs every single day to reduce his family's credit card debt (about $30,000) then. His first job was from 6:00 AM to 2:00 PM; his second job was from 5:00 PM to 9:00 PM. It was the second job where I met him.

I was working at a luxury restaurant in the nursing home every evening for only four hours in 2015. He was always very tired and leaned himself against the dishwashing machine all the time. The job was hard for me even as a part timer: I cannot imagine how hard a life he had lived. He was such a very nice guy that he always stopped his van whenever he saw me walking on the street. I did have a brand new car by 2017, but I always walked to work only because the work was close.

* * *

Joe said the first job he got was street sweeping in downtown Chicago. He was a teenager at that time. I do not think there is a street sweeper any more, but we know Joe is an old guy. Probably, he is 63 in 2022. And, then, the first serious real job he got after that was automobile assembly technician at Saturn factory. Apparently, his life had been fine during those 30 years of employment. He eventually met a nice lady and got married at the age of 42. **Even though he married a little late (42), he ended up having 4 children.** And, then, Saturn filed bankruptcy and has not made an automobile any more as you already know. His debt had piled up after being laid off from the high tech job. He still had to pay a mortgage for his two-bedroom condo and had 4 kids to feed on top of it. He got a dishwasher job after that, but had to work two jobs to reduce the credit card debts.

Do you know how hard the dishwashing job was? I have always thought it was a hell made by humans: Very intensive hard work combined with mental and physical stresses. Dishwashers are the lowest class in a kitchen in a sense: Everyone disrespects and bullies them all the time. I simply cannot imagine if someone has two of these jobs. Dishwashers seem to live on the Earth like everyone else, but actually they go through *hell* every day.

Here is one important question, though. He was not married until at the age of 42: Couldn't he just let go of the chance to get poorer? **Did he have to grab the chance at the last moment and produce four kids, so he had to work to death for two jobs?**

Joe finally got a heart attack in 2018. I learned that it can happen by mental stress as well. I think he took a 6-month break, got unemployment benefits and came back. I always felt he may be destined to work hard throughout his life, somehow: **Maybe creating 4 kids would have been one way to follow his destiny.**

* * *

I feel people who are destined to work hard even create works to do so. Some are not comfortable having easy lives. Some even intentionally make their situation poor, so they can work more. They do it subconsciously, so no one can really notice. This is why we need to get out of poverty quickly; before we feel comfortable with it; before it becomes our destinies.

Honestly, this has been what I felt about myself all along. Even when I got enough stock dividends every month, I worked for a dishwashing job handling garbage. I even created excuses like "This is good for my own exercise or society needs this" or something. **The truth is that I was not comfortable having an easy life.**

Eventually, I was afraid this "working hard for no reason" style would become my destiny.

* * *

I have spoken about three examples, but let me just add one more before finishing this up: Kim K (social media celebrity). She might not have been very poor, but I assume that she might have lived a hellish life so far. The bad news is that she may have to continue living like that from now on. In my opinion, she also failed to challenge her own destiny somehow.

We all know that she had repeated relationships, break ups, marriages and divorces until she got the third marriage. I do not think she had a happy life until her third marriage: Having too many relationships is like having too many wars in our personal emotional lives.

When she had wedding with the famous rapper for the third time, I thought she was finally done with all those relationship headaches and would live peacefully from then. But, to my surprise, she ended up having four kids in 2022. These four kids can bring her all sorts of problems from now on. I am not saying that they are bad kids: Probably they are good kids. But I know what usually happens in a family of a single mom with four kids: Problems, problems and more problems to handle alone. **In my opinion, she did not have to make her life that way.**

I felt like she lived a loud noisy life too long and that kind of became her destiny. Instead of cutting that boisterousnesses off, she created more. These will be permanent since there is no divorce with our own kids.

* * *

Even if we are born to live noisy destinies, I think we can challenge them if these are not good for us. The opposite example can be Paris Hilton from a view. It shows that she got married to a rich guy and she does not have a kid as of now in 2022. She may finally have a peaceful life now even though she used to be a sort of vain troublemaker: **She challenged her original destiny in a sense.**

Whenever I lifted heavy garbage cans in the nursing home, walked to work in the snowy winter instead of driving, or rode a bus to a poor village only to try to eat a famous hot dog in that area, this question used to hit me sometime: **'Why do I live like this?'**

I thought, 'Am I supposed to live poor in my current life? Is this the reason why I am having hard times and living stingy despite all my savings?' The fact was I have had more than enough money for over a decade. 'Maybe I had lived a poor life too long, so I cannot cut it out? It has become my permanent destiny now?'

* * *

One day, I decided to quit the nursing home job and become a writer. So far I am much happier since I have worked less than five hours a day for writing: Not like working 13 hours a day as when I worked for dishwashing. Still, it's weird that I worked for that job even when my savings had been increasing fast. If having this self-publishing works out fine, maybe I can make more money than before as well.

Conclusively, I am glad that I had the chance to help elderly people for almost 7 years. But it had been painful for me and I could not do it forever. **I do not think we should continue our lives blindly only because we have lived that way so far.** I do not think we should be afraid to be different from our own folks. We should not live by suggestions even though they are from ourselves: Our wrong destinies can suggest something wrong.

Remember this: I think we should know what we like, what we do not like and what makes us painful. We should think outside the box in the third perspective every now and then: In other words, we should look at ourselves as if we look at someone else. I think we will make a better choice that way.

* * *

Summary

1. Do not continue living your life as before mindlessly.
2. Keep a habit to try something new all the time; it can help us change our destinies. At least, it can make our lives more diverse and colorful.
3. Don't be diligent unless there is an obvious reason for it: Not doing anything can be an excellent strategy, sometimes.

17

Giving up a Little Too Early

A miracle happens sometimes.
We need to give it enough time, so it can find a way to us.
-Brad Kong

Giving up is a cool and wise thing depending on the situation. **I think that one efficient way to get out of an addiction is giving up or delaying.** There is a very popular Korean community website named dcinside.com. I used to write a lot of articles there and was a sort of celebrity on that site by 2009. After all, it was pointless for me to write on that site any more at one point; the internet trolls there started offending me in diverse ways (e.g., making prank calls to my video game store at that time, etc). Still, it was hard for me to stop writing all at once since I got millions of readers for my articles free without spending any of my money.

How did I quit writing there eventually though? I always thought I would check that site *later*: **Delaying was the key and it worked out fine for me.** The site was not necessary for living, anyway. I eventually ended up quitting visiting there and it has been almost 13 years since I haven't been on that site by 2022. No professional really writes there, so it was pretty much a waste of my life as a store owner back then.

* * *

Yet there are people getting incredible losses from anything since they *gave up too early*. For example, the record shows that the Jewish writer Anne Frank, who wrote *The Diary of a Young Girl*, passed away only when she was 15 in Bergen-Belsen Nazi concentration camp in Germany in 1945. **Surprisingly, history shows that she could have been saved by the English army if she managed to survive only a few weeks longer.** These types of things happen everywhere all the time. This could be the reason why some people stay poor as well.

* * *

There is a group of young, but fat women in Korea; they call themselves feminists; Koreans call them twisted feminists in general ("*Maegal*" in Korean). Coincidently, I notice that many women in this group are obese; their favorite celebrities are plump, too. Regardless, from my perspective, they seemed to *give up* on themselves too early; they gave up on being pretty, meeting a nice guy, starting a family or whatever (which is fine I guess). **Still, I felt like they gave up on them too early**; abandoning their bodies to be in whatever weight is merely one sign of their neglect: Negligence is basically from losing hope. I honestly do not believe that they can be happy even as singles on their own.

* * *

There is a company named CVR Partners; it makes nitrogen fertilizers for agriculture and its stock ticker (symbol) is UAN. I bought 120 shares of this company stock for $10.30 each in 2015; it was a great *dividend stock* back then and I spent about $1,235.00 to buy all those shares. The bad news was that, suddenly, the stock price dropped

90% out of the blue in 2017; an even worse thing was that the company did a 10-to-1 *reverse split*. **As a result, I had only 12 shares of that stock with a 90% loss from price drop for five years since 2017**: To break even, the stock price had to go over $103, which seemed to be impossibly high back then (after reverse split, 120 shares for $10.30 each became 12 shares for $ 103 each). **It was one of those failed investments for 7 years since 2015, after all.** I just did not sell those off since there was no point. And then, all of a sudden, a miracle happened.

The price of this UAN stock suddenly jumped up to $107.25 on 1/18/2022 (out of nowhere, miraculously). It was way over $103, so I sold all of these shares on that day; **I made +$52.82 profit, conclusively.** I heard that fertilizer could not be imported from China any more due to some trade disputes with that country. That is why this U.S. fertilizer company stock jumped up only for a few days. I am glad I did not give up too early and sold them all for 90% loss. Waiting for 7 years after the purchase of the stock had been too long, though.

This chapter is a little lengthy, so you can skip it to the next chapter after reading only bold sentences and summary. Lately, the novel titled *Pachinko* written by one Korean author has been a big hit and a series of dramas based on that book was released by Apple TV. I read that the book describes life stories of four generations of Korean immigrants. I thought my life story is as good as theirs and I can write an epic chronicle about my life once. I hope you will enjoy this, especially if you are a fan of memoirs. **I made a small fortune (about +$20,000) out of PBI stock in January, 2021 and I will tell you what exactly happened.**

I

Before starting this chapter, I would like to make sure that I am not writing this to blame a company or someone. I just would like to explain what happened to me, so I hope you will not make the same mistake. **We will see how I made a small fortune eventually out of a long loss.** Also it would be great if some companies can learn something from this as well. This is my honest experience as an investor. I do not know why some people do not change things in their company for a decade while others change things too frequently.

* * *

There is an American technology company called "Pitney Bowes" in Connecticut, USA. It is a publicly traded company and its stock ticker is PBI. This cooperation is best known for an online postage machine called "SendPro". If you sell an item online, you can print out postage with this machine and drop the package at the post office. Simply, that machine had made my online sales much easier.

I had invested a lot of money in this company from 2011 to 2020: Simply, I had owned a $65,000 amount of PBI stocks by 2020 (about 6,300 shares). I had bought this company's stocks little by little whenever I had chances or extra money for almost nine years.

I thought this company had a bright future in the beginning: Online sales had helped my retail video game store from the start all the way up until it was closed in 2014. I opened my shop in 2006 and we had made a lot of used items sales on Amazon, eBay, Half.com, etc. **Before Pitney Bowes made delivery tracking systems**

integrated in PayPal, which is connected with eBay, keeping USPS tracking numbers on receipt papers was an extreme hassle.

* * *

Before 2009, I had to go to the post office and wait in line whenever I sold an item, mostly on eBay. If I chose to use certified mail for my packages at the post office, they used to give me tracking numbers on green receipt papers at that time. **After selling dozens of items, I didn't even know which tracking number papers are for which items I sold, exactly.**

The biggest problem was fraud buyers. There were dishonest buyers online and they lied to eBay or Amazon that they did not receive an item they bought. These online companies ask sellers to provide tracking numbers showing proofs for the deliveries to those customers' addresses. If sellers could not find the exact tracking numbers on papers, they took money out of sellers' accounts. A lot of amateur sellers stopped selling online for this reason almost until 2009.

This happened to me a few times as well (about 3 times by 2009). **I just did not have the luxury *not to* sell online.** I invested so much money in the retail store already by 2006 and the retail store itself did not do very well all along. Store rent was relatively cheap ($1,200 a month by 2014), but the location did not bring us enough foot traffic. Well, you get what you paid for, right? Still, I had good feedback on eBay and Amazon, so I was able to make more than reasonable sales throughout 8 years: Often online sales were twice bigger than store sales in many months. But the problem with fraud buyers still remained by 2009.

After Pitney Bowes invented the computer delivery tracking system for online sellers, I did not have to worry about those fraud buyer problems any more. Its software lets me print out postage on eBay and PayPal sites automatically with my own computer and printer (not on Amazon, though). FYI, eBay and PayPal were basically the same company since PayPal was spin-off from eBay in 2015.

The tracking numbers were saved together with items sold on eBay after 2009. **I could easily provide tracking info to eBay by clicking a link next to an item, so disputes with those frauds were resolved in my favor.** Also good buyers have been able to check delivery status of their items by clicking tracking numbers as well. Tracking is merely a natural part of online purchase nowadays, but it was innovative technology for sellers at that time. In general, inquiry emails about delivery status have decreased dramatically after 2009. That was great for time saving since I had to work by myself in the store most of the time.

* * *

I remember that I sold a lot of my items particularly on Amazon in 2007 and 2008. No site had that kind of postage generation and tracking integrated system for small sellers like me before 2009. So I used the "Stamps.com" service separately with a $15 a month subscription fee then (Stamps.com merely copied Pitney Bowes Technology, after all). I did not like Stamps.com very much since they upgraded software once in a while for any reason and it made my computer freeze unnecessarily.

But I remember that the Pitney Bowes software integrated in eBay had been always working smoothly. And it was free with eBay sales (no subscription fee). **As online sales literally saved my store, I thought everyone might try to do online sales someday.** "As it saves my life, it can save others' lives as well," I thought the company had a strong bright future.

I invested originally $100 for this company in 2011. PBI was one of S&P 500 company stocks back then until 2014. And it came with the highest dividend among S&P 500s as well (I remember it was up to 12% a year at one point). I probably invested up to $30,000 by 2015 (I had got my dividends continuously every three months). **And I finally ended up investing $65,000 on PBI stock by 2020.** FYI, this stock had always come with dividends until I sold them all in January, 2021.

* * *

But I was at risk of losing -$40,000 in 2020 since the company suddenly did not do very well particularly after 2015. It sounds ridiculous, but that was the reason why I ended up owning so many PBI shares by 2021: **I had bought more and more shares simply because the stock price had kept dropping every year.** It is called "averaging down": Some buy more shares when a stock price gets cheaper. An average purchasing price of a particular stock can get *lower* this way, after all. Let me explain this concept briefly, so everyone can understand this book.

For example, let us say that we bought 100 shares of A company stocks for $500: The average purchasing price of the stock is $5 a share ($500/100 shares = $5/share). Then, let's suppose the company did not make a lot of profit, so the stock price dropped to $3. If we buy 100 more shares, our average purchase price becomes $4 now: We have 200 shares of A company stock with $4 average cost a share ($500 + $300 = $800 and $800/200 shares = $4 a share).

Sometimes, I think people do this when they have faith in a particular company. They may believe, "The stock price of this company will go up to $20 someday. I will make more profit by lowering the average purchase cost now." **In my case, more likely I did it because I believed I could get out of loss at least by lowering my average purchase price.** I thought I could sell it all with a little profit someday even though I had suffered from the loss from 2015 to 2020.

* * *

I remember the Pitney Bowes did just fine until 2014: The stock price was up to $28, then. I thought that I was a visionary investor (the next Warren Buffett). I was happy, optimistic and invested about $30,000 on PBI by 2015. But when the stock price dropped to $12 in 2016, all I hoped was getting out of the investment without loss. **I was desperate and bought more and more shares whenever the price dropped even more continually.**

These were risky actions since we can lose everything if the company files a bankruptcy. Some people commit suicide for this reason: Some lose all. A $65,000 is still a huge amount of money to me (or to anyone) as I have a portfolio having just little over $600,000 even now in 2022. It was even a bigger amount of money at risk then since I remember that my portfolio was about $420,000 by 2020.

* * *

The latest CEO came to the company in 2012 and the company stock price had been downhill since 2015.

Apparently, the tracking system was invented long before he came to the company. I can see that he is still the CEO of the company as of 2022. I personally do not understand how he has managed to keep the position in the last ten years: I heard that he always gets a 90% approval rate with votes at the annual stockholder meeting. It is about a $600 Million market capital sized company and hires 10,000 employees. I absolutely have no idea about how politics works in that company. **All I know is I had miserable five years since my stocks had dropped abysmally after 2015.**

I checked a lot of information while I had suffered from the $40,000 drop out of the $65,000 investment by 2021. One thing I noticed was the CEO still had gotten paid $10 million salary including benefits every year despite the long term loss: I thought it was a lot of wage considering the stock price drop. Probably his salary had been $1 million a year, but the huge benefit had been added on top of it. He was certainly not the type of a person willing to get paid $1 a year like Steve Jobs or Donald Trump. He had been paid a lot regardless if the company was suffering or not. **I ended up making $20,000 profit only thanks to "Wall Street Bet" from Reddit** (I finally wrote "Thank you post" to them in 2022), but it could have been a big time loss for me that I would never be able to get over for my entire life.

* * *

While the stock price had been in a downturn in general, it got particularly ridiculous after Covid pandemic hit in 2019: **The PBI stock price was as low as $1.80 in 2020.** I understand it was not completely the PBI's fault: I know most company stocks crashed in the beginning of 2020. But the PBI stock price was up to $28 in 2014. As a result, it had been like over 90% gradual drop for the 6 years until 2020.

But, miraculously, I ended up making about $20,000 profit out of selling all the PBI stocks in 2021. I sold out all the 6,300 shares on 1/26/2021 (Tuesday): I remember that it suddenly went up to $14 in only two days (1/26/2021 to 1/27/2021). You should be able to check the records. This is surprising since PBI stock price went back soon and it is only $3 even now in November, 2022.

This is the key point of my PBI investment: "-$40,000 *possible loss* (2020) Vs + $20,000 *actual gain* (January, 2021)"

You can see there was a $60,000 difference over the course of just a year: I was losing $40,000 out of the $65,000 PBI investment in 2020, but I ended up making +$20,000 profit in 2021. I am glad I did not give up one year early (that almost happened, though). And I believe this could have happened if I didn't choose a dividend stock (PBI always has come with about 3% dividends). It was extremely lucky to get out of that loss in general.

* * *

When I think about it, everything started with opening the video game business in 2006. At that time, I remember that I happened to watch the news about an old lady in Lake Forest, IL in 2010. Her name was Grace Groner and she left $7 Million as inheritance when she died in 2010: It shows that she only bought three shares of Abbott Laboratory stock in 1935. **It made me interested in investment in dividend stocks** (by the way, Grace had lived until 100, so she fits my topic in Chapter 25).

Along with the news and several financial books I had read back then, my business eventually put me into PBI stock purchase in 2011. Whenever I sold an item on eBay, the shipping postage label showed the Pitney Bowes logo on top. **Without eBay sales, personally I would have not known that there is such a company:** There would not have been +$20,000 capital gain in 2021 or an extra +$8,000 dividend income from 10 years' investment on the PBI stocks from 2011 to 2021.

I will tell you why buying a stock paying dividends played an important role for my gains later. Personally, I think that it is crazy to buy a stock without a dividend when there is one with it. Do not buy a stock as if we gamble. We need some safety nets: Dividend income. I suggest people address stock investment as if they invest in saving accounts. That is my advice especially for beginners. First of all, let me get back to 2006 and tell you what happened in detail in chronological order.

II

As I mentioned in previous chapters, I graduated from college in March, 2006. **I have already been a power seller on eBay since 2003.** I received a Bachelor of Science degree in biology. My GPA was only 2.6 out of 4.0, so I decided not to go to graduate school (more likely, I was not able to). I decided to go to Chicagoland to start a business instead of New York City since my girlfriend studied in a doctorate program in Champaign, IL. I told you where I met her already in Chapter 12: She eventually gave birth to my daughter later in 2010 (my wife now in 2022).

Before leaving Buffalo, I sold virtually everything from my rental apartment via Craigslist.com. It was easy since a lot of new college students were looking for used furniture or TV for the new semester. One Ukrainian girl contacted me and brought some cash with a lot of her friends. I remember one of her friends was a biology instructor at University of Buffalo.

After finding a new apartment in Rolling Meadows, IL, I moved everything from Buffalo by my Elantra. I thought the apartment was a little too expensive while the size is also bigger than I need ($900 a month in 2006). But I did not have much choice since I did not know anyone at all in Chicagoland. It was a cold winter in March and I had to find some place quickly.

I did not rent a U-Haul truck when I moved into that place, then. The distance is about 500 miles between Buffalo and Chicago. Above all, I was not sure if I could drive a big truck for such a long distance. Secondly, I did not have much extra cash to spend on renting a truck. **So I decided to use my car twice to bring everything left to Rolling Meadows from Buffalo.** I brought my cat on the second trip: I remember that he was very tired in his cage and slept a lot after that 10-hour trip. And I remember I had back pain for about two weeks because of too much lifting heavy stuff. I remember I bought a new huge table from Meijer supermarket and assembled it for my new place. I bought a new mattress as well and brought it myself by car to save some money on delivery charge, too.

I was all by myself and had to do everything on my own. **I have been through a lot of hardships even though I**

have wealthy parents (I don't think I can write everything in this series). I still remember that I saw one Mexican lady moving a broken down car on her own on a busy Arlington Heights road in 2009; she struggled, but her car hardly moved. **I cannot imagine what really poor people have to go through.** Maybe that motivated me to write this book.

* * *

The apartment was pretty looking initially, but turned out to be a bad one since the management had raised rent every year and I found mice a few times inside. And the rent did not include any utility at all. It is not that they raise rent because of inflation: **They raise it because tenants tend not to move out once they settle.** Not only is it bothersome for residents to move out, moving out costs money, too. Pretty much every landlord is a little deceptive in that sense. And this is why we have to buy out even a small condo with full cash no matter what instead of going for a bigger house with a mortgage. **Unless we own something completely, these types of deception (raising rent as if there is inflation all the time) will never stop.** We can keep leaking money until we get out of rent or mortgage.

And that apartment complex had window stickers for resident cars. It was my fault that I did not take it seriously and did not attach it. Just like in Buffalo, they had plenty of spaces to park, anyway. But the stupid Redmon towing towed my car out of the blue one night. **It was simply immoral since there was no assigned spot in the complex and more than plenty of parking spaces available**: This company was no good and they did it only for money (the miserable $65 in 2007); what they did was not helpful for anyone. When I visited the apartment office the next morning, they had no idea of who towed what overnight. I believe I spent $100 totally only to pay for a taxi and towing charge: Pointless spending.

I still remember the taxi driver had a very hard time finding the towing company, then. I felt sorry for him. He was a middle aged man, but definitely a beginner driver. Navigation was not available for most taxis in 2007. He said it is OK not to pay, but **I paid him since he tried hard.**

* * *

I remember that it took about two months for me to find the "ideal" location for my store. The web site, "Loopnet.com" was truly helpful. I drove around everywhere in the beginning of 2006, but soon I found it was pointless. An empty retail space is always available somewhere. I did not know which one was good. I read a book titled *The Complete Idiot's Guide to Starting and Running a Coffee bar* at that time. **It gave me the idea of compatible businesses**: "We should open a business close to related businesses (so these businesses can help each other). We cannot open it in the middle of nowhere." I ended up opening the video game store right next to an internet gaming cafe thanks to that book. I feel sorry for Borders bookstore as I had to return the book after reading since I was pretty much broke, then.

In May, 2006, I opened my video game shop at a local strip mall in a Chicago suburb. One lawyer owned the strip mall and the price of the entire plaza was about $5 Million. It was huge, but in a slow location. I did not like him much while I owned my business (no tenant did). But I cannot hate him necessarily now since the management suggested the lowest rent in Chicagoland ($1,200 a month by 2014).

Without it, my business would not have survived for eight years.

I am not sure I will go into more detail, but my rent dropped down to $1,100 a month in 2012 when the management bought the J exercise business right next door. The business made incredibly loud noise for aerobics (outdated fitness exercise in my opinion). **Those three woman owners were honestly the most stupid people I have ever seen.** They made only a lot of noise instead of making money. They charged very little subscription fees to members, but they never had enough customers for five years. Their situation was like me in Chapter 45: Making only enemies instead of money. Only difference is I was 29 then and these women were in their 50s in 2012.

* * *

My poor mother gave me $30,000 initially for my business start-up in 2006. She has been wealthy, but too generous for her two stupid sons (one is me, obviously). I got two months free rent out of three years of the first lease contract and spent most of the money to set up the store. **I had no idea about wholesalers, but found one within driving distance nearby**: It was a sort of miracle since America does not have that many video game wholesalers to begin with. My business saved a lot of money by not paying delivery charges since we were able to pick up new games on our own.

I thought that I would make a lot of money out of refurbishing used games if I could get used video games reliably: How to make that happen could be owning a small store. **A small store can be a marketplace for customers to trade used games before buying new**

games (just like GameStop). I know I made way more profit selling used games than new ones on eBay.

The size of my store was about 900 square feet and the initial rent was $1,200 a month in 2006. As I said, I opened it right next to an internet café where a lot of guys gathered to play PC games (e.g., *World of Warcraft*). Again, it was a good business plan to locate my business right next to a compatible one. The cafe was eventually closed out in 2012 and I suddenly saw a huge decrease in foot traffic. **I still feel grateful to Eddie who founded the gaming place originally in 2004.** Not only was he a great business man and neighbor, he was a great customer, too. He brought his uncle and nephew to our store and they bought several video games: Usually Nintendo DS Pokémon series. I visited the Sushi restaurant his parents owned to give his family some business. I truly appreciate that we had a more profitable 6 years out of 8 thanks to him.

* * *

Basically, this is how we made money in our store. We sold a lot of brand new games, accessories and consoles (systems) for little profits: I remember the profits were no more than 10% for brand new items. This was probably similar for all the game retail stores. But the more important thing was that we accepted used games, accessories and systems for store credits. **Customers traded in used stuff they did not want any more and got discounts on new items they bought.** After cleaning those used stuff, we sold them for much higher profits than brand new items we buy from wholesalers: We often sold used items *online*.

We made about $7 to 8 profits whenever we sold a brand new game by 2014: We used to get Xbox 360 or PS3 games for $51 from a wholesaler in Elk Grove, Illinois. And we sold them for $57.95 + tax (which is $63 after tax) even though most other places sold those for $59.99+tax: **We sold $2.04 cheaper than even Walmart or Target** (deep discounters), not to mention GameStop.

Some people suggested that it was ridiculous we were selling things even cheaper than big corporations (e.g., Bestbuy, etc). But I thought that it was fair since we obviously paid less rent and had no advertisement cost. We had customers' visits only via word of mouths. We had coupon magazine advertisements in 2006, but these turned out to be a complete waste of money: I hate the Indian Pizzeria owner who suggested that. I am not sure if he had any monetary gain out of the referral, but it definitely caused loss on me. **I decided to spend those few hundred dollars on game discounts instead of advertisements; we did it until our store was closed out in 2014.**

Personally, I just did not feel comfortable charging the full $59.99 to gamers. I knew it could be a lot of money to some people. The strip mall had a low income apartment complex right on the back. **I think I was nervous that we might lose regulars if we charged in full.** Still, we did not see a lot of customers even with $2.04 discounts on new games since the store location was a bit invisible and obsolete.

* * *

Before moving on, let me explain how the store credit system worked exactly in that business. Let us say that there is a new game selling at $60. If a customer wanted to trade in one used game, we could value it for $10 store credit if we could sell it for $15 on eBay ($5 profit).

Then, the customer pays the rest $50 for the $60 game because he traded in one used game: It is a $10 discount on a new game since the person traded in a $10 used game. It was just like GameStop. But, there were three differences from these competitors: GameStop, Play and Trade, etc.

First of all, we suggested way more credit than those corporations. With careful calculation, I concluded that we do not lose money even if we give out enough store credit on used games which customers traded in. Especially when they buy a used game after trading used games, we made the maximum profit. It was better for us to just keep the reputation of generous store credit by giving out a lot. **The reputation was an advertisement itself.**

Secondly, we did not have a cash option for trade in: "More credit, but no cash" for used game trade in. Simply, customers could not sell games for money while they could use them only as store credit for discounts on new items. That was the *best store policy* I had ever made since those street craps for asking for more cash disappeared magically. Before that policy in 2007, there had always been arguments about cash amounts. It was pointlessly tiring. More importantly, the store had kept losing a lot of money to give out cash and never made money before 2007. **After setting up a "store credit only policy (no cash for used games)", arguments disappeared and cash drains in the store stopped as well.** I noticed that we ended up having more quality gamers as our customers, too.

Thirdly, we sold refurbished games after cleaning the used games which customers traded in. We had two Azura disc cleaning machines: One in the store and the other at home. This company used to build CD DVD cleaning machines with price tags up to $10,000. We had two of $600 machines by 2014 and suggested $1 disc cleaning service as well: That was popular. **We always cleaned used game discs, changed dirty game cases and sealed those with new plastic shrink wraps**; these looked like new. We sold those as refurbished games, but the prices were the same as just used games in other stores.

* * *

I still remember one of the worst customers we had was one Nigerian guy. He was a middle aged short guy and had strange habits to buy games at aggressively discounted prices and returned all for full prices in a couple of weeks. He gave me a lot of headaches. In the return case, customers only can trade in those for credits only, but he did not understand and insisted his way. I re-wrote all the store policies only for him. I almost called the police on him and it could have been the first time I called the police even though no one stole anything. What a shame on him. **I even went to his apartment only to ask not to come to my store again.** This is a great shame since most stores try hard to get customers. “What kind of monster are you since the store owner seriously begged you not to come? Why do you cause this much trouble even in a small, trivial local store?” I lived in an apartment close to my store then and he lived in the same apartment complex where I lived.

I am still not sure of his exact job, but he obviously had a small income, but large expenses: Two kids, two cars, two-bedroom apartment rent (which was much bigger than my one-bed rent), smartphones, etc. I will never understand this type of person. What is the point of having an argument to see who is going to call the police first at a game store? I told him that I will call the police if he does not walk away. He said he will do it first for the buyer's right or something. Why didn’t he just walk away and save some money since he certainly earned a meager wage? What is the point of going through all that confrontation to begin with? To spend money? **He obviously cannot make money out of buying games.** Probably, he has been living in that low quality apartment with a huge rent in the last 9 years. If rent is a waste of money, his larger two bedroom rent was a bigger waste. There is no cure for these types of idiots.

III

I explained how our online sales worked with the Pitney Bowes system in the beginning of this chapter; that was the core part of this investment disaster in 2020. I was on the verge of losing about -$40,000 in my portfolio thanks to investment on Pitney Bowes stock in 2020. I had four painful years from 2016 to 2020.

This could have been my first major loss if a miracle did not happen in January, 2021. I have lost money before, but none of it has been a big amount. Currently, I have 100 company stocks and 42 company bonds in my portfolio as of November, 2022. I think about 10 companies had filed bankruptcies and the total loss had been less than $8,000 in the last ten years. I have gotten about $20,000 in dividends and interests a year in the past 11 years, so that loss was not really significant (acceptable). But a $40,000 loss solely on one company stock could have been really big.

For your information, I have bought most company stocks for 100 shares per company except PBI. Now I buy more than that nowadays, but it has been like this for quite a while, especially before 2015, so the loss has not been that big. In 2020, my situation was like I would be more than happier if I could get my $65,000 back without loss. **Instead, I got $85,000 back from the PBI investment on January 26th in 2021 (+$20,000 profit).** Do you know what happened on that day?

There is a community website called Reddit and it has a subgroup called "Wall Street Bet (r/wallstreetbets)". Three million members were there in 2021 even though I heard more than 11 million members are there now in 2022. **What I heard was that these investors had united all their powers together and focused on buying certain stocks for some reasons I do not understand completely**; sometimes, they call it "pumping" or "short squeezing".

One day, these three million members decided to focus on buying Pitney Bowes stock out of the blue. I am still not sure why they decided that (I asked around and no one knows why). $5 PBI stock then suddenly became $14 only for two days starting from 1/26/2021. This was like a miracle to me. I could not believe my eyes when I checked the Dow graphs on screen on that day: "What is going on?"

I was relieved for a moment, but I had to make a quick decision: "Do I have to sell all the PBI shares now? Or wait longer?" **Fortunately, I decided to sell all the PBI shares as soon as I saw the profit hit about $20,000.** It was 2:30 PM in Central time (Chicago), which was 30 minutes before the stock market closed. I would not have made that decision unless PBI stock had been a headache to me for over five years.

And, above all, I am glad I was not very greedy on that day. I realized that my decision was correct only a couple of days later. Suddenly I saw that the PBI stock went down back to $5 to 6 ranges and it has been like this in the last two years now ($3 to 4 in November, 2022).

I am glad I did not give up on PBI stock too early when all my friends and online trolls recommended selling them. They all said there is no hope for the company and I can get $0, which means $65,000 loss. **I am glad that I stuck to my own idea.** Also I am glad I did not hold on to the stocks too long to get more profit. I thought that $20,000 profit was plenty, especially considering these shares were a five years old headache: I knew that was "enough". Conclusively, I am glad that I sold all out when I had a little chance on one day in January, 2021.

I am not writing this to blame the company or the CEO. It is over and I do not plan to buy the stock again unless something happens like the management retirements. Maybe the company can learn something from my story to improve the situation. **I like to thank Wall Street Bet one more time and wish my best luck to all the members.**

IV

Here is one question: Did I really make money because I was patient? *No*: **Absolutely not.** I strongly believe the secret was that I bought "dividend" stocks from the start. If this is alright, let me give you some basic ideas.

Dividend to stock is like interest to the bank. If we have some money in a bank, the bank will give us interest every month. Interest and dividend are basically the same things: I would say that only the names are different, primarily. **When stocks give out interest like savings accounts in a bank do, they are called *dividend stocks*.** Only difference is that banks give out interest every month, but stocks give out dividends usually every quarter, which means every three months. So we get most dividends every three months although some give them out once a month or once a year depending on stocks.

Not every stock is a dividend stock. According to my experience, usually about half of stocks in the entire markets are dividend stocks. This rate changes all the time as new companies come out or old companies go away. These are the examples of dividend stocks in 2022: Apple, Pfizer, Wal-Mart, Intel, AT&T, Target, Microsoft, etc. And these are non-dividend stocks as of now: Tesla, Facebook, Google, Amazon, Netflix, etc.

* * *

Personally, I only buy dividend stocks. If a stock of the company I am interested in does not have a dividend, I buy bonds of the company, instead: The examples are Google (Alphabet), Amazon, Berkshire Hathaway, etc. Their stocks do not have a dividend, but their bonds have reasonable interests. **Bonds give out interests, which is the same as dividends.** As I said, basically, only the names are different.

In my case, if a company does not have a dividend stock or bond giving out interest, I just do not buy anything from the company. For example, Facebook stock does not have a dividend nor the company has a bond. I have never bought anything from the company. FB stock price dropped crazily this year, anyway.

Why are dividend stocks important? In my opinion, investment is like we are putting money that could have been in the bank into stocks. Let us say that we bought $1,000 of "A" company stock. **We could have put that $1,000 into a bank and gotten interest every month safely.** There is no real reason to risk losing that money even a little bit in the stock market.

Alternatively, if we buy dividend stocks, we get dividends as if you get interests in the bank. Often those dividends are bigger, if not much bigger, than bank interests. For example, Annaly Capital stock (NLY) gives 11% dividend a year while bank interest is 3% a year nationally in 2022: That dividend was like 3 times bigger than an average bank interest. Then I believe it is worth investing in the stocks and risking money. Annaly is the biggest mortgage REIT (Real Estate Investment Trust) in America now and considered a safe investment. If we can buy that NLY at some lowest points on some days, **we can make money out of *both* stock growth and dividends** (It was only $6.65 on 4/23/2022).

Some people say that non-dividend stocks are growth stocks and better than dividend stocks: In my view, these people are idiots or gamblers. A stock which is growing is a growth stock: **Not having a dividend does not guarantee a growth of any stock.** I notice that usually poor people bet on only stock prices without considering dividends. It is a well known fact that rich people are more likely to go for dividends. I learned that there is no cure for poor gambler internet trolls.

* * *

I could not have endured five years of depression with PBI stock price without getting their dividends (3-6% a year for 10 years). **I gave PBI stock enough time for price recovery since I am getting dividends, anyway.** The $65,000 I put into PBI stocks would have been in a bank to give me interests. Instead, I had gotten interests in the name of dividends from the company. There was nothing I had been losing only because of the PBI stock price drop. I did not have any plan to sell it any time soon as long as I get dividends.

While I had gotten dividends for a long time (10 years), the stock price jumped up for one day and I made +$20,000 profit, too. Sometimes, we have to give enough time to a miracle, so it can find a way to us. I strongly believe it is the right approach to put money into dividend stocks as if we do in savings accounts. At least, I think we should do it with most of our money unless we are crazy gamblers.

V

Originally, I did not decide to write a book because of money in April, 2022. An important idea hit me one day: "What would happen to the world 500 years later? People will not even notice that I existed then." **I guess that I did not want to be oblivious completely.** I thought I could write about my own stories at least while I am still alive. Besides, my desire to get out of the hellish kitchen in the nursing home got particularly stronger in the beginning of 2021.

I had problems with my job at a nursing home for a couple of years from 2020. There was one short Mexican sous chef giving hard times to everyone. He was just a poor cook himself after all, so I can ask him to bring my food if I have a chance to see him outside later on. Another problem was management interrupted me moving forward to a better job inside the nursing home.

I had the medical coder license, but they never had really an opening for that job for years. I had the pharmacy technician license as well, but the small pharmacy store in that nursing home was owned by a different company called Symbria and they did not have an opening, either. The dining service I worked at had kept preventing me from transferring to the wait staff department. They tried to use me only as a dishwasher. Not only is this not right, but not even legal. I felt like I was trapped in a swamp there. The dishwasher job was way harder than the waiter even though people get paid exactly the same in both ($16.24 an hour in 2022). I thought holding me in one place was ridiculous.

Luckily, I have been in a situation to get enough dividends and interests from my portfolio every month by 2022: At least, enough for living (about $2,500 a month or more). My wife has been working as well and I have only one child to support. **I thought I could try to be a writer since that gives me more meaning.** People may find my book at the library 500 years later and recognize that I had lived on earth once. I thought it is better for me to start a little early before turning 50; I still have 51 years left if I live until 100. Who knows if I can make more money with writing as well, anyway?

* * *

I did not plan to publish a hardcover book in the beginning. It was not in my interest to charge more money to readers. But I found three reasons why I may keep publishing a hardcover version also.

First of all, there are readers who prefer or even buy only hardcovers. I always buy paperbacks mainly because it is a little cheaper. But we do not know everyone's preference and I did not want to lose a reader for that reason. I assume it pays about the same whether I publish a book in hardcover or not. I can charge more, but it costs more to publish hardcovers, too. Regardless, I can simply suggest more choices for readers.

Secondly, I learned that hardcover books last longer. Believe it or not, I found that books have expiration dates and it shows that some hardcovers last about 50 years while some paperbacks last 20 years. I hope my book can last longer, so someone can also find it long later.

Thirdly, expensive hardcover prices make paperback prices look cheaper. I know it is not my primary concern to get financial gain out of publishing, but I kind of hope that more people will read my books. I think they can buy my paperbacks with less resistance to the price barrier.

Fourthly, I can use up my ISBN a little faster. I plan to buy 100 ISBNs all at once since that discounted price is way cheaper (1 ISBN is $125 while 100 are $575 in 2022). I am not sure if I can write 100 books any time soon. Maybe I can use one more for a hardcover version when I have 100 in hand. For your information, we need two ISBN for a hardcover and a paperback respectively in publishing.

* * *

Maybe some people wonder why I try to write a thick book. You will see my final collections will be obviously thicker than others. When I checked Amazon's top seller list, I noticed that a lot of them are thick books. For example, the horror novel titled *IT* written by Steven King is 1,150 pages. I am not a famous guy: Honestly, I don't think I can write way better than others. **But I thought I can write more than others at least.**

In a sense, I have done this for everything throughout my life. I had never shown any excellent talent in a field or achieved a superior goal for my whole life. But I think I have tried harder than others at least: I usually have done more. If this series is successful, one of the reasons why would be simply that I have written more than others. **I am good at finishing things completely over a long period of time.**

Talent can be important. But I believe luck comes to a person who prepares and tries harder. Readers may choose a thicker book not only because they can get more knowledge with less money, but also they know this writer has written more and tried harder: Again, I am not famous yet, so I have to write more at least. **Also, I think having a long term vision and giving enough time for luck to come to us are important.** Maybe that is why I was able to make a profit out of a fallen company stock or have enough savings to support my family without working at a relatively young age.

Now it is May, 2022. The news said that a lot of people started coming out of their houses for fun even though 300 people die a day because of COVID 19 (Coronaviruses). I still stay at home mostly nowadays and wait for my fourth

COVID vaccination. I don't think it is over until it is over. I suggest not to give up too early or move too fast: **I strongly believe that a little bit of patience can make a huge difference.**

* * *

Summary

1. I had PBI stock and sold all for +$20,000 profit in Jan, 2021.
2. If I sold all the shares one year earlier in 2020, I could have lost -$40,000.
3. Do not give up too early.

18

Preferring Other Stuff to Money

Buying more things is like getting more pain.
-Brad Kong

In my opinion, **the best way to quit a bad habit can be stopping spending money for a while.** When I think about it, all the bad habits cost money: drinking, smoking, drugs, playing video games, etc. On the contrary, a lot of the good habits do not really cost any money: meditation, eating small, losing weight, sleeping early, sleeping longer, walking, etc.

* * *

I think it's important to have a savings account to deposit our experiences: Let's call it an *experience account*; we do not deposit money in this account, but deposit new experiences. This account may not be visible, but will be a great asset for our life. What I mean by a new experience is not necessarily an expensive one. Visiting a foreign country may be a new experience. But, going to a different restaurant can be a new experience, too. Even if it's the same brand restaurant, we can try to go to the one in a different location. Or we can try a different menu, at least.

I have always tried to save money no matter what for my whole life. But I guess that I have a little more than half of my life left until I die as of 2022, so I decided to spend some of my money from now on: More specifically, I decided to let my money go a little easily as long as I try something new. In my opinion, there are a few reasons why we have to keep doing this and depositing new experiences in that account.

First of all, this habit of trying something new helps us not get stuck in a bad situation forever. I witnessed that some people had worked for dishwashers for 30 years: It's a harder, but lower paying job, but they had been too comfortable with it. I know they will never change their job since some are 60 years old already (almost retirement age). **If we keep trying something new or different by habit, I think we have more chances to get out of a bad job, too**: A cook at least in those people's cases. People may get out of a terrible relationship more easily as well if they have a habit of trying something new. I am not saying that we have to change things frequently; **It may be more important for us not to get stuck in a bad situation.** Sometimes, we have to go against bad destinies; a habit of trying something new can help.

Second, this collection of new experiences can make our lives happier. **One Korean psychology professor said it's essential to have diverse experiences to promote our happiness.** There are things we will never know unless we try it; there is clothing we will never know how it looks on us unless we actually try it on. Our life can get better little by little as new experiences accumulate. It can make our life more diverse and colorful.

* * *

I have a weird theory that we can experience more heavens when we do not spend money: When we stop spending money, lives get simpler, easier or quieter; spending money can make our lives more painful, complicated or disorganized; consumption can eat up our time, too.

Stopping spending money is like traffic clearance for personal finance in a sense; sometimes, we have to wait half an hour or so until there is no traffic jam on a highway. It was medically proven that not eating any food for one day a week is good for our health; people may do that not because they do not have money, but for health reasons (*intermittent fasting).* **I strongly suggest that we should not spend money "a day a week (1 day out of 7 days)" for the same reason**; we have to give ourselves intermittent breaks from spendings; it would be great if we can make this lifetime habit. Regardless of finances, this can make our lives more pleasant and optimal.

* * *

I think it is a waste of life to spend more time working to make more money than we need: ***It can be a life loss despite an extra monetary gain.*** Which one of these is the most important? Life, time or money? This is what one Buddhist monk said once: "We own everything only temporarily; there is nothing we can bring after we die. In a sense, we *borrow* everything only until we die."

Some people misunderstand that they can still own things if they can pass these to their children; this is merely a *mistake.* Let me tell you the biggest misunderstanding in human history: **Our children are not us** (my daughter is not me). They may appreciate our inheritances, but I guarantee we do not own our stuff through offspring.

In fact, our great grand kids may not even know our full name correctly; I am saying this since I don't; I do not think my father knows the name of his grandfather, either. People spend a lot of money to buy things more than they need; **some even get debt for those.** They waste their whole life to make money or pay debt just for some stuff.

I have always thought that "preferring money" to other things makes our life simpler or healthier. Certainly, it can make us wealthy, too. We do not have to go crazy to save money, but this may be generally true. We would not feel ripped off by saving money, at least. Let me give you some examples of why a little affection for money is beneficial or even can save our lives.

* * *

Let's suppose that there is one man trying to quit smoking only to save money. He is addicted to smoking, but he loves money too much, so he decided to quit. Isn't it one example that preferring money made one's life healthier?

There was an actor named Paul Walker (1973-2013). When I checked his profile in Wikipedia, I was surprised that he and I had more than a few things in common: He was born in the same year I was born (1973). He studied Marine Biology and I have a Bachelor of Science degree in biology. He had a daughter with his girlfriend and I have one daughter, too. But here is one difference: He died in a sports car accident in 2013. Actually, I was shocked that the Porsche totaled was the exact model I was interested in (Carrera GT). I even like the exact color (mouse gray), so **I wondered if there is such a thing like the same *astrological destinies*.**

But let me suppose that Paul really loved money more than anything else: Saving money and getting interest out of it was the biggest joy in his life. Is it possible he would have not owned a sports car from the start and did not get into the accident? **No spending money, no sports car and no accidents?** It was not Paul's fault since he was in the passenger seat when the accident happened in 2013. I am just taking an example, but I see similar types of cases everywhere all the time: Not spending money saves us from having a lot of pain.

* * *

When my wife used to study in Champaign, IL, I visited her by bus once when I still studied in Buffalo in 2003. I got bored, so we decided to go to St. Louis by rental car. I remember we had a big fight out of the blue near Saint Louis that night. She finally got out of the car and walked into a late night restaurant in the suburb. I followed her and had to order an expensive menu (which I did not want) only to stay there with her for a while.

I assume that a lot of stress, including spending extra money for that unnecessary St. Louis trip, accumulated and that caused a fight. I felt we would have not had that fight if we just stayed in Champaign. **What if we stayed in Champaign since we were stingy to save money?** You can trust me on one thing: I believe that a reasonable love for money can make our life actually better. Any type of consumption can bring us a sort of trouble to some extent.

Believe it or not, I do not think that not having enough money is a huge problem: In fact, spending money can cause problems more often than we assume. **Conclusively, if we can live as if we do not own money, I believe it can even save our lives.**

* * *

I read a self-help book titled *The subtle art of not giving a f*ck* written by Mark Manson the other day. It starts with stories of Charles Bukowski, who had been considered the *laureate* of lowlife writers in the dirty realism genre. I did not expect it in the beginning, but as I researched more about him, **I learned that this poet and I have more than a few things in common.** I know I just started my writing career in 2022 and have never been successful yet: Nonetheless, I almost felt like I am him only without drinking and smoking habits.

1. **Both he and I started writing careers in our late 40s.** I just finished my "first four books" at the age of 49 in 2022: *Introduction to UnBrokable*,* that of the large print version, *UnBrokable* I* and *UnBrokable* II.* Bukowski became a full time writer at 49 and published his first novel titled *Post Office* at the age of 51 in 1971.

2. **Both had worked for diverse physical drudgery jobs for a long time.** Bukowski worked in the post office for more than 10 years. I borrowed his first novel, *Post Office,* from the library out of curiosity months ago. And I learned that the post officer's job is extremely hard, overall. I did not know that they have a time limit to finish all the deliveries, which makes the job even harder.

I also felt that life had been generally tougher in the 1970s than the 2020s. I myself worked as a weekend dishwasher in the nursing home for almost 7 years. I often thought that it was the most intensive labor in the world since there was only one dishwashing place for five restaurants in that huge nursing home. Tons of dirty pots and dishes were gathered in the dishroom from everywhere. I just kept that job since pay was fine and it was pretty near my home. Before that, I had been through a good amount of other dull fatiguing jobs: Convenience store clerk, kitchen helper, military soldier, banquet server, online sales packers, etc.

3. **Both had or have *one* daughter.**

4. **Both inherited small fortunes after 40.**

5. **Frugal**

6. **Immigrants**

* * *

Nonetheless, I found out that he and I have three major differences also.

1. **Bukowski had been a heavy alcoholic and chain smoker**. I just don't see a single photo of him without holding a beer bottle or cigarette in hand. On the contrary, I have never been a drinker and smoker for life *mainly* to save money (I don't do these for teeth health nowadays, but I just had to save money *from anywhere or everywhere* for decades).

2. **I bought out my condo 23 years earlier than him.** It shows that Bukowski bought his first house with a mortgage at the age of 58 in 1979. I bought my condo with full cash at the age of 40 in 2013. **But that was not all.** It shows that Bukowski bought it with a mortgage although he paid that off within five years (which is super-fast). Still, that means I became a complete homeowner 23 years earlier than him: I remember that I got my deed right after my payment in November, 2013. Paying rent 23 years less is a great saving.

3. **Bukowski had to pay child support.** It shows that Bukowski had been married twice and had to send money for child support to his ex-wife every month. It seems he had hard times because of it, especially in the beginning of his writing career. I have been married once.

Why does "no drinking or smoking" matter? **Sadly, Bukowski passed away when he just started making a good amount of money.** He died at the age of 73 in 1994: As a late starter, he finally started making steady income only from the 1970s and suddenly died of cancer. Couldn't it be better for him to spend some of it while living a decade longer? It takes forever to be a successful writer and living until 90 is *possible* nowadays.

And why does "buying out my own space" *early* matter (even if the size is small)? **I can use the expensive "rent money" right now.** It shows that Bukowski had lived in the Carlton Way apartment for 5 years before he bought his first house in 1979. Google shows that the rent of Carlton Way starts from $1,900 a month in 2022: I am paying $350 HOA a month as a condo owner (it has been up from $280 to $350 in the last nine years). **Isn't it better to use this extra $1,550 a month right now?** Who knows how long it would take for me to be successful? What if it never happens? I don't want to be hungry now and get $10 M later a few years before I die. I want to enjoy my life a little bit now: At least, I do not want to suffer.

* * *

Actually, Bukowski's story in that book by Manson inspired me greatly a year ago in 2021. He started his writing career at 49 and published his first novel at 51. I just turned 49 this year. Can I start writing as a full time author like him? I had to resign from the dishwashing job since a new company called Morrison took over the dining department in April, 2022. They refused to transfer me over with the same rate, so I decided not to go with them.

I could have applied for other jobs, but honestly, I did not have any desire to repeat another company life after decades of work. There have been bad bosses or coworkers all the time. Wages will be little, work will be hard and worst of all, no one will really appreciate or even recognize how much I sacrificed myself for work after I die. **I thought I can finally have a chance to leave something**: At least, some writings or books. It can be meaningless for me to work in pain and totally vanish in 50 years as if I have never existed.

It must have been hard for Bukowski to find a publisher in the 1970s (actually, I feel sorry for every writer during that era). It must have been hard for everyone to write with a typewriter back then. Things are much easier nowadays with computers for writing and self-publishing. I do not even need an editor nowadays (thanks to Google

Doc and Grammarly). I thought that I could try to write a book at least once. Using computers is almost free, anyway.

* * *

I imagine that Bukowski's life could have been a little easier if he was a super-stingy person: "I want to save money. Let me quit drinking and smoking since I want more money." Then, he might have not gone through divorce or cancer therapies in his life. **Preferring money surprisingly can make our life simpler and more enjoyable than we have imagined.**

Records show that he claimed to have $90,000 in his hand by the time he made the first contract for his first novel in 1969 (He was 49 in 1969); $90,000 in 1969 would probably be about $500,000 in 2022. I read that people think that is a probable claim for him to own that much money since he got the money out of selling his father's house and had been frugal for life.

That was kind of a similar situation to me. I got some money from my father and bought my condo when I was 40 years old in 2013. I think he could have bought a small condo a little faster if he did not waste that money on drinking, smoking, etc. The public record shows that Bukowski bought his first house for $80,000 in San Pedro in 1979. If he didn't waste his parents' money ($90,000), he could have bought it at least with full cash. **Then, he could have been 18 years slower than me, at least**: He is 23 years slower since he had to get a new mortgage contract and paid it off in five years. I think poor people get poorer in this type of downward vicious cycle.

* * *

I recommend that we should put all our money in dividend stocks and savings accounts in a bank. Live as if we do not own any money. We have to see how long we can live without spending. When our refrigerator is completely empty, we will start losing weight. **Losing a little bit of weight is considered healthy, anyway.** Again, preferring money can make our life simpler and better.

After putting all the money in stocks and saving, I think we should try to get as much dividend and interest as possible: **Life paying interest can be hell, but life getting interest can be heaven.** I already have over $600,000 in a stock portfolio and bank CDs and get at least $20,000 interest and dividends every year as of 2022: **It is like I have a job paying me $20,000 a year without working.** I prefer to keep my finances this way instead of buying some stuff that possibly will bring me headaches.

* * *

Summary

1. All the good things often do not cost any money; all the bad things usually cost money.
2. Not spending money for a while makes our lives better and simpler: We can try this one day a week.
3. Buying out even a small condo early can be a good idea. We can use the extra money now instead of *later*.

19

Keeping a TV

Having TV is like spending our money to get their advertisements. -Brad Kong

Lately, I am reading a book titled *The Cafe on the Edge of the World* written by John Strelecky. It shows that more than 4 million copies of this book have been sold and I found that it has a short, but strong message: Commercials convey false messages that "buying stuff will make us happy." As a result, people buy more, need more money and work longer: **This is really a vicious cycle and inevitably ruins people's lives.** Let me ask you a question: How do people get most advertisements?

* * *

TV is the center of the universe in many households nowadays: I guarantee you that this is never a good idea for many reasons. But, especially in a financial sense, TV is a well-designed temptation machine: **Urge to buy things.** If we are short or broke for no apparent reason, I think we should get rid of the TV in the living room first. We can save some money out of electricity and have some quiet evenings as bonuses. It's possible that we will feel like ourselves and wound up having a sane mind finally. **Getting rid of TV merely means we cannot watch it on a big screen TV in the living room**: My wife and daughter have never had a problem watching TVs with their iPad, iPhone or Chromebook whenever they want.

They still have helped me have quiet time by using earphones and headsets.

* * *

There is one thing we need and learn when we read a book regardless of genre: Patience. We may learn that we cannot finish everything quickly. I am a very slow reader myself and not necessarily trying to be a fast reader; I believe we all have our own natural speeds to understand things (the speeds are all different depending on people). This is a great virtue in the age of rushing: **Not everything can be done easily, conveniently or instantly**; we may have to take some time to finish it.

The richest man in the world is Elon Musk according to Forbes in 2022 ($193 B); it shows that grew up reading two books a day, according to his brother. It also shows that Warren Buffett spends five to six hours a day reading five newspapers and 500 pages of corporate reports; Bill Gates reads about 50 books a year (one book a week).

If we are serious about getting out of poverty, I think we may just read books after getting rid of TVs; I do not know how to say this in a better way. I know it is extremely hard to make such an overwhelming change to remove something; most of us probably have watched TV for our whole lives. But what can you really lose? We can watch TV any time online, anyway; we only save electricity, cable subscription fees or TV costs themselves. Maybe we can save some eye doctor fees by visiting them less frequently, too. **Most importantly, I think we may feel more sane, be ourselves and realize where we are now.**

* * *

Nothing is more important than peace of mind in my opinion. The worst part of TV is it makes us buy a lot of things; it shows you direct and indirect advertisements all the time. The more we buy, the less we will have peace of mind. Our wallet will get thinner: **I believe we feel more comfortable when we sit on enough money.** Personally, I have never liked TV since I was a teenager. I used to, but I do not go to movie theaters any more: These are just not good for my eyes to begin with. I believe that quitting watching screens for mental health and stopping eating sugar for our bodies are the same things.

The second worst thing about keeping TV is it will never give us a break. Watching a screen is a work in a sense; it can provide continuous more work after we are done with our day job. We may realize how tired we are after turning off all the screens. **The last time I had a cable TV subscription was March, 2008.** That was about 14 years ago since it is 2022 now. I still have the old CRT TV in brand new mint condition which I bought in 2006, but it has never really turned on since 2008. We used to connect a Blu-ray DVD player to it, but the last time was 2014. So the last time I turned on our TV was about eight years ago. The Blu-ray movies kept giving me physical headaches, so I eventually had to sell it off on eBay.

I have had a peaceful life for quite a while and passed two difficult exams in the last five years: Medical Coder and Pharmacy Technician. My daughter's grades from school have improved noticeably after my wife and she moved back into my place in 2018. **Wife said that my daughter used to get poor grades while she lived with her grandpa who owned a TV.** Having no TV is important. Eventually, my writing career has launched after my mental exhaustion stopped and meditation started.

* * *

In 2007, I still worked at the video game store and my mother visited me in my rental apartment in Rolling Meadows, IL. She stayed for about a couple of weeks and I ordered cable TV service only for her just in case she would get bored. I remember she watched the home shopping channel a lot. **When I think about it now, the cable TV order was a total waste of money.** I saw that she played with my cat (who died in 2020) just fine even though she never had a pet for her whole life. She could have had a relaxing two weeks' vacation without a TV for the first time in her life.

My father watched a lot of TVs when I grew up. He has been a self-made millionaire all along since the 1980s. Just like many Korean fathers, he never had any hobby costing money. This generation really started everything from the rock bottom after the Korean war which ended in 1953. They know what real famine was like and it is impossible for them to spend any extra money only to enjoy lives. Naturally watching TV has become their sole hobby: **Only three national channels had been available in Korea until the early 1990s and these were free with air signal reception by antennas.** I was born in the 1970s and lived with him only until I graduated from high school in 1991. The house had two TVs: One in the living room and one in the master bedroom of our parents.

My brother watched a lot of TVs, too. But, for some reasons, I have never gotten into that bad habit. In fact, I really hated it when everyone else watched the TV in the living room altogether while I was studying in my room. They pumped up the volume, regardless. They should have gotten rid of TVs instead of getting extra tutors for my study at home. I explained this in Chapter 1 already, but they could have saved tons of money if they did it so. **They lost double the money on electricity bills and tutoring fees.** Since they kept threatening me to improve my school grades while they kept interrupting my studying environment with the TV noises, they ended up making me a complete enemy. When I think about it now, these people are complete idiots in that sense; they were rude, stupid and thoughtless. Maybe that is the reason why I live without a TV now. **I do not want to repeat what they did to me to my own daughter.**

* * *

We are living in an era having too much media now. By that time when my family had been crazy about TVs, there was nothing else: No Internet, for example. Radio, TV and movie theater were the only electronic media in the world in the 1990s. Maybe there were some analog newspapers, magazines, books, etc. I guess that life had been simpler and healthier back then.

But, suddenly, the Internet came out of the blue in the late 1990s and there have been too many electronic media hurting my brains now: Computers, laptops, smartphones, HDTVs, iMax theaters, Digital Dolby theaters, etc. **There are more and more things to watch every day.** Even TV was simpler back then (only 3 to 4 national channels by air via antenna). Now even hundreds of cable channels are not enough, so some people order Netflix or something like those with extra subscription fees. On top of that, I can borrow new movie DVDs at the library for free or at a RedBox rental machine for $2 (2022). There are too many devices, too much media and too many screens to watch. No wonder I feel insane and get headaches all the time.

Currently, I have a 16 years old CRT TV in brand new condition and I am glad I did not buy a HDTV after that (I just keep this for antique value). I have already wasted a large portion of my life on the Internet. The big problem is that our quiet time to think about daily issues is diminishing. Rather, people get more and more advertisements through all these media and end up spending more money even while getting broke.

* * *

As I said, technically, watching the media for a long time is like working for another job. Physically, mentally and biologically, I think watching is working. Watching TV or social media becomes like our second job while we do not get paid at all. I have been tired for no apparent reason in the last decade (due to the internet). We are all addicted to some extent and keep watching those non-stop 24/7.

While we do not have a TV in my house, my family has two desktop computers, two notebooks, one iPad and two smartphones. My wife has a strange habit of carrying her iPad everywhere. She agreed not to have a TV, but she's watching TV all the time on the internet (particularly CNN news).

We had a bit of an argument the other day since she did not understand my letter to one government agency. She said she thought it's for my previous job. I told her, "Why do I make an effort to write a letter to my previous job I quitted two weeks ago? I am done with them and don't care what they do now." She clearly showed severe symptoms of confusion: She lost her mind. **Ridiculous thing is that she did not get heavy exhaustion from working hard.** She just got it from watching too much internet.

* * *

It is a long story, but I do not borrow free DVDs from the library or go to the movie theater any more. I used to borrow new release movies all the time and go to the AMC theater with my daughter every Tuesday since the ticket is $5 only on that day. She and I used to watch a lot of animations together. But I just don't do that anymore after 2021. I think I have been burned out by watching too much media already. I hate those uniquely unpleasant headaches after watching a couple of movies in the theater. It used to happen to me after watching Blu-ray movies as well. **I thought it was nonsense to get sick after spending money.**

Also I just got a new Dell desktop computer in April, 2022, but I decided not to download the PC game *StarCraft II*. I used to play *StarCraft* a lot when I was in college in the 2000s and even *II* is *free* to download now. **But I decided not to download it to play.** So there will be no TV, video games, DVD, movie theater or social media other than businesses from now. Nowadays, I only borrow books from the library and listen to some audiobooks from YouTube. I can save some money that way, but more importantly, I can have some alone time to think.

* * *

As I mentioned earlier, having a TV is like having their advertisement machine at home. In that sense, those companies should have given us one TV for free, but most of us just bought it at a high price voluntarily. The machine will maximize our shopping desires: We may get poorer and poorer while we do not notice. A lot of IT companies provide us one email or social media account for free. YouTube provides free videos without subscription fee; we are watching their advertisements for them on YouTube. **But, in the case of TV, we do not get a free TV; we voluntarily exhaust our attention to watch their advertisements.**

I heard that Nazi used to provide free radios, so German citizens could listen to the addresses of Hitler every evening. **Modern slaves do not think that way.** We just buy expensive TVs willingly with our own money since it is fun. Some do not care if they get headaches, red cheeks, bad vision, high blood pressures, expensive bills, too much ads from TVs or media. They just buy since it looks like it is fun.

* * *

If we go broke for no obvious reason, I think it's time to get rid of those TVs, DVD players, Netflix, Disney plus subscriptions or whatever: **Just remove them completely out of your life.** Sell them for cash, so make some money for now and eliminate all the future risks and spendings.

See if you can make some time to think alone quietly: I think that keeping sane minds and figuring out solutions to any problem in our lives are priceless. In real life, I don't think anyone can truly help us unless the person is exactly in our shoes: **This won't happen since the person is not me.** I think we all need to figure out a specific solution for our unique situation ourselves, somehow. I think it's time to shut off everything and start using our brains.

* * *

Summary

1. We can get rid of the big screen TVs from our house. We can still watch plenty of TVs on the small screens.
2. The Media often keeps us from having sane minds.
3. Let's recognize that TVs are supposed to be free since we watch their advertisements for them.

20

Traveling in Too Expensive Ways

True travel is the one to our minds. We do not have to go for extravagant vacations.
-Brad Kong

There is a psychology term called *anchoring effect*: A cognitive bias whereby an individual's decisions are influenced by a particular reference point called anchor. **In other words, a ship does not move far away from an anchor.** Let's suppose that you used to drive a Mercedes a decade ago and now you drive a Hyundai; you may feel miserable since you are driving such a cheap car now. But let's say that you used to ride a bicycle, but now you drive a brand new Hyundai; you may feel proud since you are driving such a shiny expensive car. Depending on where we put our anchor, we may feel the new Hyundai is a cheap or expensive car.

There are a lot of people visiting Thailand, the Philippines or India nowadays (personally, I have not been to any of these). Many Westerners, Americans or Koreans visit those for prostitution or beach parties secretly. In my opinion, visiting those may not be such a good idea especially when we are young. **Starting comparing ourselves with poor people in impoverished countries from an early age will never help us financially.** We can end up being in a poor class in our own countries; in other words, we can be a poor white compared with other white people in America. On the contrary, if a Korean visits only European countries, I believe he or she has more chances to be in the wealthy class at least inside Korea. He (or she) will start comparing himself with richer Europeans, subconsciously. We don't always have to live uptight or try to grab as much money as possible. But we do not have to expose ourselves to extreme poverty in poor countries unless there is a specific reason (e.g., a business trip). Alternatively, I think we can start visiting poor places after we become old if we have to visit these.

* * *

I used to dream and planned to live in France, Thailand and Peru for one year each. I had stayed in Korea for 26 years of my life; now I have lived in America for 23 years since 1999. So if I stay in America for three more years after 2022, I will be in the situation to have stayed in both countries for the same length of time, which is 26 years each. I thought it would be great if I can find another different country to live in: A nice new country not related to Korea or America much. **I thought that it would make my life diverse and interesting.** For some reasons, I do not like very short trips by nature; if I have to go somewhere, I prefer to stay at least for one year in a country. Still, it seems the biggest problem looks to be language barriers.

Now I have changed my mind a little bit. I heard that these French are arrogant and discriminate against other races. Some Koreans complained that the waiters do not take orders even in upscale restaurants: **This is not acceptable as I had been a server myself for years.** I know they have lots of art museums, but so what? I am not going to take art exams or something similar again for the rest of my life; school days are over a long time ago. I have been to the Art Institute of Chicago a few times with my daughter, but that's mainly for her education. I don't particularly enjoy looking at those, frankly; it's probably similar to others, too. If you do not agree, it's possible that you are brainwashing yourself now.

And I heard that the weather in Thailand is too hot and air quality is very bad. I think the northern Chiang Mai area may be cooler, so I hope that staying for one year would be possible a long time later; a lot of Koreans actually do one month staying in the country nowadays; I heard that it's getting popular. I like to visit Peru for one year as well, but the high crime rate would be the big repellant from visiting there; it is hard to keep or store one year expenses safely in South America.

For now, I guess I will just go to Thai or Mexican restaurants occasionally; unfortunately, I don't remember I have seen a French restaurant in Chicagoland. Instead, I guess I will go to big or little museums more frequently, especially when these are free.

Strangely, I am eating a lot of Indian Thali or other instant foods from Swad or Haldiram nowadays; $7 Thali at Ghareeb Nawaz used to be my favorite. But I noticed that, if I spend a little more money ($3 more), I can find a good amount of quality Thali places on Devon Ave (e.g., Sukhadia or Annapurna). Regretfully, I do not have any plans to visit India as of now. I guess visiting those restaurants could be a way to travel to India in a cheaper and safer way.

* * *

Honestly, I have never thought that I will immigrate or settle in a country poorer than Korea permanently; I do not want to travel to countries restricted for dangerous reasons. Let's forget about the money for a second; visitors can be murdered there, in fact.

I remember reading on the news that there was one Korean law student visiting a slum in India after passing his bar exam, and being robbed and murdered. I could not find that result on Google any more since too many similar cases happened and millions of results were coming out altogether. I am mentioning this since stupid Koreans go everywhere now and their government keeps spending a lot of tax money to get them out of hostages.

* * *

I just watched diverse videos interviewing White expats (people who live outside their native country) settled in Thailand on YouTube; they mostly did not look good to me and some planned to move back to their home countries even after staying for decades. I noticed that most of these did not look normal; they were all super tanned, tired and hardly spoke out of exhaustion; they exactly acted like homeless in America.

Sometimes our appearances say many things: **Regardless, it doesn't seem to make sense to live in poorer countries than our own.** Some tried to build a business, but it must have been harder for them in a country having less funding with more language barriers. It only makes sense when Thai people try to move into wealthier places like Europe or North America to survive.

* * *

I know it can cause some controversies, but let me just say this: I strongly recommend not to travel to poor countries especially when we are *young*: particularly Thailand, the Philippines and India. These three are *poor* people's *favorite* destinations. We don't have to start our world travel looking downward on impoverished countries. I realized that tourism in poor countries often suggests only *consumptive* pleasures: Killing time, partying and enjoying superficial things at low prices. I think it's much better if we can *start* our world travel as a learning experience; visit museums, art galleries or historic sites in once prosperous wealthy countries. **Where we set our viewpoint at early ages can be influential throughout our lives.**

I saw so many people (especially Koreans) living in poverty for life after frequenting poor countries; **they tend to be in the low income class in their home countries.** For example, Americans who retired in Thailand are often plumbers or warehouse workers; no CEOs or Doctors really do that. If we have some businesses or relatives to visit, I guess that is fine; actually, that is more than a good enough reason. But I cannot recommend visiting poor countries without a purpose; do not go to Thailand for crazy beach parties, massage parlors or hotel stays. Alternatively, I think we can do that at least after we get rich enough or old.

* * *

Let me talk about Thailand just for a minute; the tourism in that country is all about pleasures as far as I can see: foods, women, night lives, drugs, etc. It is not a good idea to set our life in that direction especially early. **People may not see much difference in the beginning; they may see a huge difference later in their lives**; these visitor people can end up being much poorer than their own peers who do not visit there at all.

Thai people are known to have lavish lifestyles for no apparent reason (no Instagram result for frugal Thai): I believe it is because this country does not have winter. I found one Korean guy settled in Thailand with his Thai wife on YouTube; he's selling Korean churros in a Thai flea market, but the couple drove a brand new mid-size SUV. **I didn't get the feeling that he would ever be out of poverty.** For your information, rich Koreans would not even eat the food he was selling, not to mention making it for living: I think he had a too luxurious spending style considering what he did for a living.

And, let's just be honest. What is the main reason for men to visit these countries? Prostitution. I know that not every single man visits there for that reason. But, in the case of Thailand, it has had the reputation of a red-light district of the world for decades; it has a surprisingly higher HIV infection rate compared with its neighbors: Statistically, Thailand is the major root cause for HIV import to South Korea.

* * *

In the case of the Philippines, the Kopino problem is particularly serious among Koreans; Kopino is the term to describe a person having Korean and Filipino parents (usually, the fathers are uneducated Koreans). **A lot of Koreans went there for nothing (no specific business), made babies with local Filipina and ran away.** Recently, I watched one poor Korean boy selling peanuts on the street in the Philippines on TV; the reporter asked his nationality since he looked different from a typical Filipino; he answered that his father is Korean. It's unimaginable if my son lives like that. I didn't even know the Philippines is that close to Korea until I checked on the world map recently.

* * *

In the case of India, we have to admit that it is just environmentally filthy (no offense); still millions of people defecate on the street due to the lack of sewage systems. I suspect that the main reason is government corruption on tax. I have seen that a lot of people, especially Koreans in America, complain that they felt unpleasant more than a few times after mingling with Indian people. I had similar experiences before; some act as if they are in the high class in caste and I am in the low class; this is total nonsense since I am not even from the country and probably never will be. I used to have great respect for that country since it might be spiritually high at least.

But, after reading about their custom called "Sati", I kind of gave up my last hope: Apparently, sati is a custom of burning a widow alive in the funeral with her deceased husband. I read that it used to be more common until banned by the British in 1829; horribly, it is said that it is still rarely performed. I do not believe no other country has this kind of custom (certainly not in Korea) and it shouldn't be encouraged anyhow. I have never thought that the UK is necessarily a great country, but I believe she is absolutely right in this matter.

Still, Wikipedia shows that "bride burning custom has been recognized as an important problem in India, accounting for around 2,500 deaths per year as of 2004." Just in case you didn't know, bridal burning is another type of horrible violence (burning wives). In my opinion, this can be kind of a mild form of sati and probably has evolved from it; burning a person is the most extreme form of violence as you know. I don't think it's a good idea to visit poor countries only because we are bored or broke.

* * *

Certainly, money is not everything in our lives. But, when we keep visiting poor countries, a poverty spirit comes to us. If we visit repeatedly, the spirit will stick to our life and never come off. **Koreans visiting poor countries are the people in the low income class in Korea.** I have not seen or heard that super-rich Koreans visit the Philippines; if they do, most likely it is for business reasons since Samsung phones or Hyundai cars are sold everywhere.

I just used the term, "spirit", but we have to admit that humans are animals deeply affected by environments. Poor people have more reasons to be poor than wealthy. If we keep exposing ourselves to those and become familiar, we can become one of them after all: **We become poorer after spending all that travel money.** If we have to do that, I think we'd better do it at least after we become solidly wealthy. Nonetheless, I have witnessed many American men going bankrupt after spending up all their life savings in Thailand. Let me give you one actual example.

* * *

There is one travel writer named Park. He is the same age as I am, but I believe it was a kind of mistake that the first country he visited was Mexico. He visited many countries only in South America and wrote the first series of books about it (three volumes). Then, he visited poor regions in China and wrote his second series. What does he do now? He lives in a small village in Thailand without having money or family. He has never married, and I can see that he worries about money a lot according to his blog. He is in his 40s now, but where would this go from now?

Typically, these types of people never get a job in low income countries. They just make some dough in Korea and stay as long as they can in those poor countries. If he visited the USA for the first time in his life 30 years ago and visited Europe next, would his life be a little different now? Possibly since Koreans in America are generally wealthier than those in Korea. The same goes for Americans: Americans in Switzerland may be wealthier than those living in Cambodia. I explained that the first world trip can set up our viewpoints and influence our lives for good.

In a sense, I am truly blessed that I happened to start my international travels with wealthy countries: USA, Denmark, Finland, Netherland, Japan and Canada. I did not realize this at that time, but these destinations were for all my studies or businesses. **I am just glad of this, not because I want to be rich, but because I had avoided a chance to get the poverty influence.** The experience in our early life goes forever: People in the low income class may have visited poor countries. **Or vice versa; we become poor after visiting deficient countries multiple times.**

For my international travels, I visited the USA for study in 1997; Denmark and Finland for business in 1998; the Netherlands and Japan for layovers in 1998; Canada for tourism multiple times from 1999 to 2005 (mostly Toronto while I stayed in Buffalo, NY for 5 years). I have lived in South Korea for 26 years in the beginning of my life and the USA for 24 years after that by 2023. Living in another country for decades is also a kind of travel since life is a journey, right?

* * *

The first time I went to Europe was in 1998. That was pretty much the first memorable international trip I had. I went to RIT in Rochester, NY by airplane the year before in 1997. But that was purely for study. The six months in Rochester were great, but let me skip that part for now if that is alright with you.

I still lived in South Korea in 1998 and my father had owned a fur import business for more than 25 years at that time (he might still have it). **His company used to import gray mink furs from Denmark and white fox furs from Finland.** He was eager to find someone to inherit his business then, so asked me and one of his favorite employees to go on one international business trip together. It was the right timing before I graduated from a college in South Korea.

* * *

Quite frankly, my father had a pretty unpleasant hot temper and I had never gotten along with him for life. For some reason, he had always been ready to be angry for anything. Often, there was no particular reason for his anger and I believe he should have controlled his temper even if there was a reason. That is common sense, but I don't think he was really fitting into common sense ranges. He had done whatever he wanted to his family only because I was too young to live on my own, then. He was only good at making money, which was fine: I understand not everyone is good at everything. **I don't think we should expect any perfection from anyone.** But the only problem was he had kept approaching me to ask to take over his business years after years even until recently: Unpleasant and unreasonable pressures.

Fur business has been clearly dying in Korea. Did your mom wear a fur coat today? Yes, or no? Does she even have one at home? Probably not. In fact, the fur businesses have been dead everywhere in the world for decades now. In general, clothing productions move from wealthy countries to low income countries: For example, Vietnam makes T-shirts instead of Singapore. You know South Korea is getting wealthier every single year. And the fur business has had another critical disadvantage in my opinion: **Global warming.** Even the super-rich will not wear it unless the weather is *extremely* cold. Have you ever tried on a fur coat before yourself? It had been invented for extremely cold weather originally, not for mildly cold ones.

In a sense, I am glad that he had a fur business, not a smartphone business. If I wanted to work with him, I would have done that already, regardless of a business type. It was a good excuse not to work with him: Fur had been a dying business. Honestly, I am glad he did not have an IT business since I could not have a good excuse to stay away from him. I feel sorry for all those young people having bad fathers: **I was glad that I was not in a situation where my father actually has a visionary business to inherit**; I am happy that I did not have to wonder if I had to work with him or not.

Nonetheless, I feel blessed that he made so much money, gave some to his two sons already and gave me a chance to take a look around Northern Europe once in 1998: **Denmark, Netherland and Finland.** I was young then and thought that I would be visiting Europe every few years later in life. But that certainly has not happened so far by 2022. It was the only time I had been in Europe though I am 49 now in 2022 and I do not know when I can get out of this Illinois State again. Once we are settled with our own family and busy with jobs and investments, I learned that it's nearly impossible to move around as before: We have to try much harder even to get out of our houses with a child.

* * *

I believe we (father, the employee and me) used KLM airline to Denmark in 1998. I liked the employee, Young-hu, from my father's fur company. He was two years older than me, had a nice character and was kind to me probably because I was the son of his boss. I never had a problem with him for two weeks even though I had been with him all along from airplane seats to hotel rooms. But I had a hard time with my father if I had a chance to see him for a second. I do not know what's wrong with this old man since he had a business seat in the plane far from us and stayed in a separate hotel room as well. **I felt like he existed only to make others painful.** Maybe that is what all the fur business is about: Maybe that is what all human beings do on Earth.

I remember the Kimpo National airport in Korea was like a bit of a flea market in America in 1998. Korea built a totally new airport (Incheon International) in 2001 and it is in the world's best class now in the year of 2022. But it was still a little poor country back then before the year 2000. We were in a duty free shop and the retail glass counters were just like the ones we can see in flea markets here: Nothing fancy. I believe these duty free girls tried to sell something like Ginsengs and said something in Japanese and my father answered, "I am not Japanese."

Japan was an outstandingly richer country back in 1998 though it's about the same as Korea now.

* * *

I think it took about 15 hours to get to Copenhagen airport in Denmark. The customs officer said, "Good Evening" in perfectly educated English. My father's sales agent guy (American) came to pick us up: I heard father bought a lot of furs from him every year. That agent was a very nice, tall and fat Jewish guy. I met a lot of Jewish rich people in the fur trading center buildings and learned that we do not have to be unnecessarily aggressive all the time to get wealthy. As a middle aged man, **I suspect that having a hot temper actually makes us lose money.**

I believe it was pleasantly warm in Copenhagen although it was January, 1998. I would say it was like mild Busan (south) weather in Korea. I spent most of the day in the huge warehouse handling tons of fur stocks. The place was ample and they gave us hotel quality nice meals for free. Basically, hundreds of buyers came from all over the world and billions of dollars of purchases were made within a couple of weeks. There were a lot of auctions for fur packages from morning till evening. Young-hu and I helped my father to get all the stock samples to check and move them back to their original places.

I felt sorry for all those animals since probably about 200,000 minks are massacred every year and their skins were removed, dried, processed and packaged there. Also I thought it's more waste than most people assume since no one eats mink meat at all: Those animals were murdered purely for fur reasons. I think humans are very selfish. Although this was not the primary reason why I decided not to work with my father, I am glad that I had not been part of it to begin with. I personally hope people keep wearing regular coats other than furs (e.g., paddings). Still, I will never be able to blame my father since I have lived happily for 49 years thanks to his money. **He had done what he had to do to get out of extreme poverty in Korea back in the 1970s.** It is more than a luxury to talk about animal rights for his generations.

* * *

Luckily, I was totally free in the evening in Denmark and Finland (for a one-month trip). There were about twenty Korean fur buyers only until 1998 in the fur wholesalers club. The number of buyers had been getting smaller since then and virtually my father was only Korean when I saw him last in Toronto, Canada in 2005: Chinese have become the majority after 2005. My father hung out with these old Korean business people in the evening and Yong-hu usually stayed in the hotel room. **I had a chance to check around Denmark freely for a day myself.**

The first thing I noticed was people sleep extremely early in Denmark. Basically, **I remember that the entire city of Copenhagen was closed after 6:00 PM every day** (impossible in Korea or America). I could see that Scandinavians are the utmost morning people. Even most restaurants were closed, so I truly wondered where people eat their dinners. Only some Chinese restaurants and strip bars were still open. Soon, I learned that Denmark is an erotically open country.

When I walked around in the dark pointlessly, I found one place which looked like an adult movie theater on the street. I remember it did have a smaller movie screen and Danish people gathered watching adult movies. The general atmosphere was safe and friendly, though. It was definitely not like an American skid row.

What was unique was the drinking bar: There was a bar serving beer and other drinks in the theater. The bartender was a lady and she was totally naked. It was a bit old lady when I was there for the first time. But the bartenders were different young girls when I went there two more times. In Particular, the third girl raised her leg and put her foot on the bar whenever a customer ordered a drink. I felt she tried to expose her body a little bit more.

Also I remember I found a sort of Asian place for that type of atmosphere in Denmark; these were the only places open, anyway. When I entered, I saw a small Asian lady behind a bar and she completely exposed her breasts; I saw that she served drinks and spoke with a Danish man.

Then, another tall pretty girl came, so I had a chance to talk with her. She said she is originally from Malaysia and it is 800 Danish Krone to spend some time with her. In currency, 800 Krone is like $112 USD, but it was 1998; that was 24 years ago, so it must be at least 2,000 Krone by now ($250 USD in 2022). She lifted her skirt and showed her butt, but I could not do anything. Actually, I had to leave the country for good only after our business. I just had a friendly talk with her for a while. When I think about it now, it is surprising that Malaysian people go all the way up there to make money. I saw some erotic book stores on the streets, but these are pretty much all I remember about my trip to Denmark in 1998.

* * *

Summary

1. I do not think it's a good idea to visit poor countries for fun, especially early in our lives
2. We don't have to work hard all the time. Still, we do not have to look downward and feel better after comparing ourselves with impoverished people.
3. I don't think we should immigrate to poorer countries than our own hometowns: Nonsense can make us miserable one way or another in the end.

21

Spending Too Much on Pets

I hope we can help all the lives on Earth.
-Brad Kong

This chapter is dedicated to my old cat, Oscar Yang Kong (2003-2020): *Born on the street, buried in the wild.*

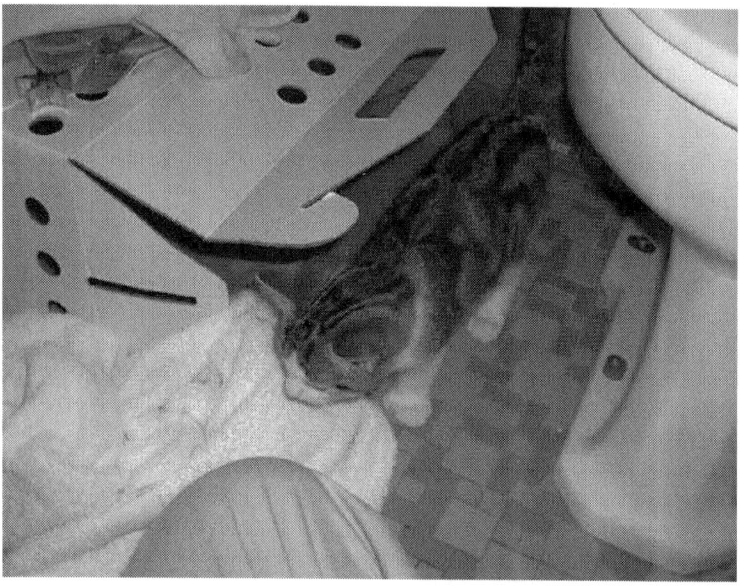

The day I adopted him in Buffalo, NY in November, 2003: He was 3 months old; the paper box was from Erie SPCA animal shelter.

The day we buried him in a Chicago suburb in September, 2020; he was covered by my sweater, which was his favorite; he died of blood cancer at the age of 17 (86 years old in human age).

There is a Canadian documentary titled *Cat Ladies* directed by Callan-Jones released in 2009. All of the cat owners in the film were single ladies in common; they had up to thirty cats respectively in their households. I think it's noble to adopt feral animals, but it may cost to take care of that many. It is said that losing a child is the biggest sorrow; I believe that all pet owners can guess the feeling as they take care of their pets like their children; unfortunately, most animals don't live very long. I have good memories with my cat; he had given me plenty of comforts while he had stayed for 17 years.

When we have a pet, I think we can have a chance to observe the entire life of an animal; I felt that life stages of a cat are similar to those of a human. When I got him in 2003, he was very active and vibrant. After he became an adult, I noticed that he had spent time sitting and looking around more every year. One day, we realized that he got unusually slower after getting blood cancer. Eventually, he could not move at all on the last day of his life. I am sure he had a hard time; I guess I had made a lot of mistakes all along as a first-time pet owner.

A human is a weak animal physically; no one can survive alone in the Amazon jungle. Eight billions of weak humans have gathered and built a safe society now; no one has to worry about getting attacked by a tiger on the way to the supermarket. I think we should be happy about it and celebrate. However, I don't think we should be overly excited: We should not increase our population fast, expand territories excessively and deplete resources: **We should not exploit the Earth.** When we control ourselves and help others, *Homo sapiens* may last a little longer.

* * *

I don't know why I wanted a cat so badly in 2003. I was 29 years old and was in my junior year at the University of Buffalo. I failed all the applications to graduate schools before coming to Buffalo; as a result, I was late for my second undergraduate degree in America. Weirdly, a lot of bad things happened around those years: The darkest era of life (2000-2003). Ironically, the Ferrari photo in the prologue was taken around that time, too. Buffalo was a cold and deteriorating city: a lot of snow, shockingly freezing temperatures and countless car accidents over the winter. Nothing fancy on the campuses, but tuition[31] was the lowest in America, which I am still glad about.

---

[31] It was up to $6,000 a semester without scholarship by fall, 2005.

I moved to an apartment in Cheektowaga, NY from the one in front of North Campus since rent was a little cheaper[32]; I thought I needed a change to get out of bad luck by 2003. Yet I have to say that the move was kind of a mistake; the new area was a bad slum which I didn't realize in the beginning; it was far from the north campus where I studied mostly, too. The north had a lot of new libraries and most of my classrooms, where I had spent most of my days there until I graduated.

Basically, I was alone in the silent but cold apartment in the middle of nowhere in 2003. Sometimes, I spoke with my girlfriend[33] over the phone, who studied in Champaign, IL then. I remember she clearly said once that, "I think you are very lonely." In the worst out of the worst situation, my cat came into my life; **I would say he literally saved me from getting into more troubles.**

* * *

I have never liked people looking for purebred animals; I hate people buying, selling or smuggling exotic animals; the fact is that a lot of those animals die on the way. I like people adopting pets from shelters, including SPCA: I am pleased that I was one of them. It's a bad idea to buy pets at the mall or from commercial breeders: **We do not help animals that way;** these people don't care much about welfare of animals. Often, they push some female animals to get pregnant to get certain breeds repeatedly. Besides, we will definitely overspend on getting pets that way. I know it costs a lot after adoptions[34] since I had my cat for 17 years.

[32] $420 by 2003

[33] She is my wife now.

[34] I got him for $65 at Erie SPCA in 2003.

By chance, have you heard of pet plastic surgery? It shows that cosmetic procedures may include wrinkle removal, tail docking, ear trimming, declawing in felines and debarking in canines; **I heartily oppose feline declawing since it is extremely painful for cats.** *Personally, giving my cat scratchers had been more than enough.* My girlfriend, who is my wife now, called him Yang; cats are called *"Go-yang-yi"* in Korean, so Yang was the short name from it. Later on, she made another name for him: Oscar. I guess she didn't want to go through the hassle of explaining his unique name whenever visiting hospitals.

Do you know what was the best thing my cat had done for me for almost two decades? **He had helped me stay at home longer.** Then, I had a strange habit of driving around for nothing: *Stupid joy rides* on slippery roads during Buffalo winters. I cannot describe all the minor accidents that had happened vainly; a lot of expensive but unpleasant damages happened *unnecessarily* while I was broke, including auto repairs and traffic tickets. It wasn't that I quitted driving around as soon as I had the cat: **Still, my joy rides had been less than half suddenly.** Who would know what could have happened if I had stayed outside twice longer pointlessly? I remember I slipped off on highways many times; it is probable that he saved my life.

Unfortunately, Oscar had blood cancer in the end. I especially cherish the memories of the first few months in 2003 and the last months in 2020. He looked OK pretty much throughout his life, but suddenly got worse a month before he passed away. I hated it, but we had to go to the vet to have him euthanized: he couldn't move at all except breathing ultimately; I assume that was typical of cancer patients.

* * *

My parents never had a pet when I grew up. I remember that I read an article about having cats on a Korean website[35] one day; the writer said he had owned four cats one by one. He wrote how much he regretted letting his first cat go only because he had to move to another place. When he returned to the spot where he abandoned his cat, he actually came out from the basement of a building nearby and stuck to him; the guy removed him reluctantly since he was about to move away. He said he was still young and thought that it was the only way. When he came back to the place again, he could not find the cat any more.

After ruminate the story for weeks, I finally visited Erie county SPCA[36] in a Buffalo suburb; it was a big and clean facility; a small pet store was inside the building, too. The first thing I noticed was a bit of discrimination against a male adopter; I didn't find it offensive, though. I guess it's reasonable that SPCA staff can be suspicious of male visitors; some may be Samaritans, but some can be psychos, too. Once they handed over an animal, there was no way they could track it afterwards; they had too many ferals to take care of.

I could not find much hospitality from the shelter volunteers or a cat I felt right with in the first two visits. They seemed to do the right things apparently. I could see that they did not euthanize animals directly; they tried to

[35] Ddanzi.com
[36] Society for the Prevention of Cruelty to Animals

promote adoption as much as they could after neutering. I tried to see my situation logically. I was a money oriented guy and didn't do things unless they were profitable (I am not proud of this). I tried to figure out where this strong feeling of adoption came from. In the end, I concluded that this could be the only good thing I could do before I die: **Saving one animal;** *I was not wrong after spending 17 years with my cat.* What I did not expect was that I learned things from an animal who I adopted.

* * *

After having thought about it weeks more, I returned to the SPCA with my classmate Ricky. He was a Korean, who was 9 years younger than me; he said he had a cat before and knew a lot of things. Suddenly, I realized that the attitudes of staff toward me changed to welcoming; I guess that two torturers coming to SPCA together are rare. I still remember that there was a small striped cat trying to clean his face right in front of his cage; the cages were made of silver metal and stacked for three stories. Oscar was on the second floor right in front of me. Since they asked me not to touch a cat, I dangled my keys in front of him; he did not see me, but saw the keys and tried to touch it. I always knew that I would have a tabby cat. I said to a staff lady, "I will adopt him."
"Are you sure?"
"Yes."

They processed the adoption immediately; the fee was $65 in 2003. They put him in a brand new cardboard box. Right before they put him in the box, he jumped up resisting getting in, but the lady managed to put him in nicely. Then, they gave me extra stuff: dry cat food of a French brand, coupons from animal hospitals, etc. For some reason, I felt very excited as if I won a lottery; I felt like I found a stack of cash or something; the same feeling when I bought my house. The same when my daughter was born.

Sangrok (Ricky), the Korean guy and I went to PetSmart right after that. I bought a brand new cat cage which I still have in 2023 and other stuff: cat litter, a litter box, scoop, extra food, etc. The cashier lady asked if I adopted a cat; she said she has two dogs and one cat and they made her busy. I don't know how I remember all these as if they happened yesterday.

* * *

Yang (Oscar) was only three-months-old when my wife met him for the first time in Buffalo in 2003; we had countless good memories for 17 years afterward. One day, we noticed that he got very slow, so we visited the animal hospital in 2020; the doctor said he had blood cancer and only a couple of months to live. We tried to spend the best two months before he passed away. I brought him out in the garden every night and let him spend hours on the fresh grass; he couldn't walk or run around any more, and was easily caught. On the last day, I visited a pond for the last time with him. My wife, daughter and I brought him to the hospital together that afternoon; everyone helped him sleep in peace in my arms.

I bought a shovel at Home Depot and found a warm and quiet spot in a wild area near my home the next day. He taught me good lessons and spent countless hours snuggling, which helped my blood pressure down. Finally, he came back to where he was from: He is resting in peace now.

Summary

1. I think it is noble to adopt feral animals and take care of them.
2. Some go beyond crazy about spending on pets.
3. Some excessive spending are actually cruel on animals.

22

Being Unnecessarily Busy

Working for money more than we need
can bring us financial gain, but life loss.
-Brad Kong

The poor are busier than the rich by nature. They often cannot buy a bulk of staples or other stuff all at once; buying things little by little takes more time and money. The impoverished parents tend to have more children, which makes them busier. They may have to spend more time with bankers to borrow money for their houses or cars; those actions cost *more money* to pay interest later on; which means more work, too. Some poor people disguise themselves with luxury items: **If someone looks oddly busy despite looking lavish, he or she may be under debt now.**

Being slow can be a weapon itself when others are all busy. That is how sloths have survived; turtles address fishes to catch slowly. **Con artists usually depend their successes on quick and impulsive decisions made by victims**; if we act unhurriedly and process things step by step in an extended period, less likely we will be a scheme victim. The most common tactic of con-men is *hit and run*; they need to escape before everyone else figures out what's going on.

If things do not go *right*, we can go *left*: Whenever things go wrong, I think the first thing we need to do is to stop and have some time to think. See if you can have 30 minutes to think alone everyday: Not checking a smartphone, but just closing eyes and meditating. **Sometimes, "not doing anything" is the most productive action**; I read that our brains function to the maximum when we stop moving; people finally start thinking when they don't move.

* * *

I think rich people are *slower* for reasons. The virtue we need the most when we are poor could be diligence: *Hard working,* in other words; this means moving fast or being busy. **But I think that "not being greedy" is more important after we become affluent**: Self-control or abstinence; these cause spending less and having enough time not to do anything.

People often get confused that making money and saving money are the same things: Actually, these are two different things, if not opposite things in my opinion. Some people may be good at making money, but waste a lot and have nothing left (e.g., some former NBA or NFL superstars); some people don't make a lot, but keep money forever (e.g., me, some heirs of big corporation founders in Korea, etc); most people do not know how to make or save money; only a few are good at making and saving money (e.g., my father, Warren Buffett, etc); I guess this is why we hardly see rich people nowadays.

* * *

In my opinion, there are only two reasons why some people are busy: They get busy because they are either poor or greedy. **Greed is the thing making our life unnecessarily busy and painful.** I believe only a fraction of people are actually busy making more money, but the majority of us are busy spending more. Greedy spenders waste more since there are things they just want more: Actually, it doesn't even matter what that thing is; as long as it is something that provides them an opportunity to spend money, that should be enough.

Imagine there is one greedy man eating an extraordinary amount of food. He could be busier than people eating only one meal a day (e.g., me). Eating more food requires people to spend more time and money naturally; he will be busier than a frugal man.

Being greedy can be one reason why people go to a place like Hotel Atlantis in Bahama. I think visiting there will only make people's lives get busier without having much gain. **Greedy people are weaker at temptation in general**; they just want more by nature, so if someone suggests anything tempting, they will fall for it more easily. All they get from the Bahama trip is basically more stress: waiting in line at the airport, suffering in the airplane, wasting time on registration in front of the hotel desk, etc. When they actually calculate, they will realize they spent a surprising amount of time only on mere transportation. I am sure there would be a bit of difference between North America and Bahama, but I doubt it will be that huge: More likely a total waste considering the vacation costs. One day, they may be wondering why they get more tired even after vacation and where all their money is gone.

* * *

While greedy people are generally fatter, they tend to have more kids as well. Maybe they had intercourses more or plainly wanted more children as they want more of everything. I assume they try to have more partners for physical relationships or tend to have more marriages or divorces during their lifetime as well.

And here is one thing for sure: **These people will be busier than others as a result**; they may be short of time or money than others. They might feel they are important since they are busy getting requests all the time from everywhere, including their children, partners, court, lawyers, etc. While they are busy with more spending, their financial situation may start sinking down slowly.

* * *

We can see those unnecessarily busy people all the time: in real life, on TV, in magazines, etc. They may be proud of it, but here is my question: Is their state of being busy productive or profitable? **Not necessarily.** Let me explain this to you a little bit more with one example.

There was a Chinese woman writer named Amy. I found her book titled *Tiger Mother* in the Korean section of our local library. I am a father myself as you know. But, to me, the book was nothing but an unpleasant manuscript to show off how her children were great and why all the parents should extremely control their children even in minor detail: **It is total nonsense in my opinion**; There are a few reasons.

First of all, I like to mention that I will never talk about my child or post my family photos that way. My wife always strongly suggested not to do it online or even in books. I think she is right in this case and I believe that is what a responsible parent should do: Protecting my child including her identification and privacy to begin with. I believe there are people who do not know what shame is any more. Showing my child photos to make some book sales? Hell, no. **Unbelievable assholes and criminals do exist**: Posting simply will not happen with me.

Apparently, this Amy woman is a lecturer, lawyer, writer, wife and mother of two kids who looked uglier than her. Here is her *second* mistake: **Being busy and doing many things for nothing.** This is one of the most common misconceptions: Working more is good. Nothing can be *farther* and *farther* from the truth. **Actually, working less is good.**

Whether we work more or not, we will eventually all die within the next 100 years. **Do we get awarded by God since we worked more while we were alive after we die?** No. Do we get paid more by God in heaven since we worked more while we were alive? No. Or do we get paid less by God since we worked less when we were alive? Of course not. Probably, no one gets paid anything in heaven after we die. **If nothing happens or all the results are the same, working more is actually a loss.**

I found out that Amy's two kids eventually went to law schools, too. I am just curious, but does everyone in that family need to be a lawyer? Can anyone be a medical doctor, Silicon Valley app developer or something? A lot of smartphone app developers are young millionaires nowadays. In my opinion, the mother blocked her kids from getting other jobs by over-controlling them. **That is not only suffocating, but also less profitable.** Lawyers used to make some money: Not really any more. I felt the mother blocked better opportunities for her children. Her kids can settle in relatively low income jobs from now.

I guess I don't like this Amy woman very much since she reminded me of my over-controlling mother in Korea. Mother has been super-wealthy, but also super controlling. I guess I prefer to keep some space from others desperately.

* * *

Let me give you one more comparison regarding this case. My wife has one child and this Amy woman has two daughters. A lot of people believe that a two-kid family is ideal, but raising two children is way harder than one (most people do not realize this). **I don't think any single person understands how much taking care of two is harder than one financially or physically.** I know this since I have taken care of my daughter myself for years, especially when she was a baby.

Do we get a medal of honor from governments since we have two children instead of one? No. Do people respect us more if we have two children instead of one? No. Do people admit or comfort us if we are having a harder time with two children? Not necessarily. Are our parents much happier if we bring them two grandchildren instead of one? More or less likely.

Do we get a lot of money from governments if we have two children instead of one? The simple answer is *no*. Unless we are extremely poor, we virtually get no better advantage from the governments. We get a bit of tax deduction for one more child portion, but I do not think it is worth that much since there are also people not really paying any tax at all. **In conclusion, we are being busy for nothing if we have one more child:** We work more for nothing. Actually, it is worse than nothing since humans have destroyed the Earth gradually. Producing less humans can be good for everyone as I explained in Chapter 2.

* * *

I am just trying to say that there are a lot of people busy for nothing. **They are getting poorer and poorer while getting busier for nothing.** Let me take an instance of obesity.

Getting fat is another word for having been busy eating: Being busy for nothing again. In fact, it is also worse than nothing. People can lose vision, limbs, kidney, etc as a result of diabetes. **They get worse as a result of being busy.** When you are busy, I think there should be a beneficial reason for being busy: There should be a good reason, at least better than nothing.

* * *

That Amy woman above also reminded me of one lady I had conflict with when I had my own business in 2012. I originally opened my game store right next to an internet gaming cafe in 2006. Unfortunately, they had to close their business out since eventually no customers were coming in after fast internet started becoming available at home by 2012. After that, to my surprise, one aerobics company for elderly ladies took the space. I believe that the young generation of girls don't do loud and violent aerobics any more. I notice that they usually go for quieter meditation, yoga and Pilates. In my opinion, it was a mistake that they chose the space to start an exercise business to begin with.

In my opinion, a smart business owner usually chooses a space where a similar business was

occupied before. For example, often a new restaurant opens in an old restaurant location. By that way, they can use all the facilities the previous owner already built in. It costs a lot of money to reconstruct and connect a new gas line for cooking, for instance. If there was an old restaurant before in that space, the gas pipe must be there already, so we do not have to spend money for that. Also, we do not have to build a new spring cooler system, customer's restroom, etc. Previous owners can even leave refrigerators or fryers for new owners. It takes some time and effort to sell all that equipment before closing out a business. Depending on the situation, the previous owner can just leave them. We can use all those things and save tons of money.

I Just don't see anything in common between a computer cafe and aerobics, then. They spent a lot of money demolishing and reconstructing the whole aerobic exercise business. I still wonder why they chose that spot particularly. It was really out of the blue since the lease of the cafe was not even over completely.

And I did not like these three old female owners from the aerobics since they made huge noises from the day one they moved in. They did not spend any money on soundproofing for neighbors. **I had a lot of conflict with them for months and the plaza owner gave me a rental discount as a result.** My store rent started at $1,200 a month in 2006 and went up to $1,500 a month by 2011. And, then, it went down to $1,100 in 2012 after the loud neighbor business moved in.

I still remember one strange thing, though. When the property owner asked me to talk to the head owner of the exercise business, that woman sent me an email saying that, "My schedule is empty between 10:00 AM to 11:00

AM. So, I can talk with you during that hour." What is this? We all know that she is nobody; the business had barely any customers. Why did she act as if she was super busy? **Being busy is nothing but a sign of poor time management.** Or we can be busy if we are broke and desperate for a few bucks, so we need to work for an extra part time job, for example.

* * *

I think we can be busy when there is a right reason for that. When I checked her Facebook later on (head of the exercise business), I found out that this selfish lady was a divorced woman with three kids. It also showed that she remarried with a man with his own three kids, so it seems they have totally six children together in their new household. This is another example of being busy for nothing in my opinion: Being busy supporting double the amount of kids by failing the previous marriages somehow. Personally, I am exhausted already and I don't think I will ever do what they did even with a *miss universe*: Marrying a woman who already has three children.

Here is a different type of problem regarding this topic I noticed lately, though. **Some people are busy since they are nervous about not working.** For example, my wife cooks and cleans our house a lot. I appreciate that, but I feel she is nervous since she has not had a real job for a few years now. She can take it easy for a while as we can afford her unemployment without any problem. I think I am busy writing since I do not go to work outside any more as well. This writing can bring me some money, so I guess it is better than not doing anything, at least. When we are busy, I still think there should be a good reason. **Being busy itself will not make us important or better**

people. As Karl Marx once said, "Free time is the space for personal development," after all.

* * *

Summary

1. Being busy can make us poorer.
2. When we are busy, there should be at least one good reason.
3. Being too busy is nothing but a sign of poor time management.

23

Eating Too Much

Savings money starts from eating less.
Coincidentally, eating less is good for our health as well.
-Brad Kong

Ben Franklin once said, "A Penny Saved Is a Penny Earned." Actually, this is wrong in my calculation: It's more likely, "A Penny Saved Is Two Penny Earned." In other words, **"$3,000 saved is like $4,000 earned."** Why? After making some money, we have to deduct tax to pay governments and other expenses we have spent to make that amount of money: commute costs to work, car maintenance, newer clothing, shoes, haircut, etc. I tried to avoid the issue of saving in this series since it's too obvious. But let me just mention one time in this chapter.

When we try to save money, I think the best strategy is to **address the biggest expenses first**: The example is housing. I heard that some rents of one-bedroom apartments in CA are over $3,000 a month. I am paying an association fee of $350 a month in IL in 2022 as I have owned a one-bedroom *condo* in the past nine years. The quality of life we can experience in a one-bedroom apartment and condo are similar: Actually, a condo is better, according to my experiences; I have been in 9 rental apartments in America for 14 years (1999-2013). But people living in apartments pay almost 10 times more for housing a month than people living in condos. This is why I keep suggesting buying out even a small home with full cash.

The second thing we need to address to save money is repeating charges: I think eating is something we do *repeat* every day. Eating too much causes all sorts of diseases nowadays (e.g., Diabetes). A lot of people eat too much as if the food is free in this country: Absolutely, *not not not* true. Eating is actually more expensive in America than many other countries. I think that controlling eating amounts is inversely proportional to being wealthy if not getting out of poverty at least: **This means the less we eat, the more we get wealthier.**

* * *

It has been five times that I could not eat anything in Chinatown Chicago. I occasionally go there (a couple of times a year) as I live near Chicago. And what I mean is that I couldn't choose one place out of over 100 restaurants there and ended up eating some pizzas, fish fries or salads right outside the town.

One of the main reasons is that most menus they push to sell are very meat-oriented; I am close to a vegetarian. I saw that some foods they advertise on the wall are boiled poultries in water, which smell yucky (to me). If not, 30% of eateries there are some sort of dessert cafes including bakeries; these types of foods include too much sugars in common, so I quit eating those years ago for my tooth decay.

Besides, I don't see any self-serving places there (like Noodle Company or McDonald's). I don't want to pay an extra 20% tip on my bill only because someone brought food to the table. I saw a couple of places similar to our local takeouts not requiring tips; still these were more expensive; there is no reason to eat the same food for a higher price than in my hometown. Furthermore, the town has been in a dirty environment in general: This is the biggest reason, in fact; not very stimulating for appetite.

On the contrary, I notice that I always eat something in India town Chicago whenever I go there; I go there probably 4 to 5 times a year. There is one Indian Pakistani concentration area near Devon and Western and it has nearly 50 restaurants. First of all, I found that all the menus in that town are pretty much, if not all, vegetarian oriented. I guess it's hard to make vegetable food disgusting; it is safe to eat as well; I am sure most food poisonings happen with meats or seafood everywhere.

Secondly, I like their Chai tea; the ingredients are cinnamon, cloves and ginger; all of these are known to kill tooth bacteria specifically. Most importantly, they have plenty of self-serving places. I pay, get food myself and save 20% tips on waitresses. Some owners may think that customers don't have to pay 20% tip to their servers, but that's not what we diners think. In the movie titled *Reservoir Dogs,* some gangsters talked about tips and said, "Throw a buck." It's not a buck or quarter any more. It would easily be $15 to 20 tips for meals of a few people and people want to save on that. **Some restaurant owners never get it and go bankrupt** (Chapter 66). Lastly, almost always Indian restaurants provide free water in a visible space. Not only is it free, water is way healthier than other drinks.

From the point of *profit,* I am sure Indian restaurants make way more than Chinese ones. **Food costs for vegetables are much cheaper than those for meats while menu prices for both restaurants are similar.** Indeed, Indian foods are more expensive than Chinese sometimes because of rarity. Neehee and Annapurna are new self-serving Indian vegetarian-specific franchises and are getting more popular now. I saw the owner of Neehee once and he was really happy to smile to the maximum; I thought it's because of a lot of customers, but that was not it: It could have their higher profit margin than other types of restaurants.

* * *

People just eat too much nowadays; these may include you, me and everyone else. I was shocked when I learned that it's common for Korean households to have more than one refrigerator nowadays. The size of a Korean family is typically small. **My wife said my mom also has three fridges at home:** She lives "*alone*" although my brother used to live with her for a while. I lived with her until I became 26 years old by 1999 and we had one fridge in our house back then: our family of four people lived in a nice luxury condo, so I do not know what happened.

It shows that overeating causes all sorts of diseases from toothache to heart attack these days; that only brings us more hospital bills. The number of diseases caused by eating too much are literally millions: **I heard obesity even can cause mental disease as well like depression.** It shows that people used to eat occasionally just like wild animals do now. Still some people do that by controlling their eating habits (e.g., intermittent fasting). And they end up saving tons of money as well although that may not be their primary intention.

I personally have tried to eat only one meal a day since 2018; this means eating dinner only to me. I have lost a good amount of weight (30 lbs.) in the last three years; still, my target weight is 120 Lbs. or 55 Kg (my height is 5' 6" or 172 cm); I was 125 Lbs. when I measured it in Dec, 2022.

I feel better for myself since I look better than years before. **I have always felt bad after eating too much since I was born.** I like to keep insisting on eating less as long as I can.

As I mentioned in Chapter 1, our body is the most valuable asset we have and taking care of it starts with eating less I believe; we have to see if we can make our bodies attractive than just keeping them healthy. I believe this is certainly achievable by eating less. This may be off topic for now, but studies show that people's income can be proportional to their attractions; in other words, a handsome guy makes more money than others. **There is no way we cannot try this since eating less does not cost any money.**

* * *

There used to be a restaurant called "My Sweet Kake: Cupcakes and coffee" near my home; it was a hand-made cake shop for birthdays and closed permanently in early 2019; I think it was in business for about six years. I always thought that I would try the place at least once in my life: Not that much, but at least one cupcake and a cup of coffee. I am not interested in those types of foods in general, but **I thought that I could help out our local business once.** But I was lazy and the trial never happened until on the day the business was closed out.

Subsequently, what I learned was that it was beneficial for me not to try the place at all. I had a huge tooth problem in late 2019; I spent a fortune ($2,500) to have my molar crown on. Naturally, chefs use large amounts of sugar and sweets to make cupcakes and it is pretty bad for teeth; also, coffee is bad for oral health, too. It was good not to spend extra money to make my teeth worse; not that much, but having one less cupcake and coffee must have helped my body a little bit. When I think about it, everything in our life is something like this: **Having a little less food during our lifetimes helps**; 70% of diseases are caused by eating too much anyway.

* * *

I do not really go to an upscale restaurant; maybe I do not have much money, but also I just feel uncomfortable, regardless. And I know that there is nothing much we can expect: **Most likely, we will only get the same food on fancy plates.** I know this since I had worked in upscale kitchens for almost seven years; I think I observed how foods are prepared in those places too well.

Nowadays, everyone just eats too much; rich people eat too much; poor people eat too much; hospitals are getting crowded. I was admitted to hospitals twice and spent a lot of money in the last 15 years. **When I think about it now, the reasons for both admissions were eating too much.**

I was in the emergency room of Saint Edward hospital for a kidney stone in 2008 and it cost me over $5,000 without having insurance. The reason was drinking too much soda (particularly, Coca cola). I was in dentistry for severe tooth pain and it cost me close to $3,000 for a crown procedure on my lower left molar in 2018. I had eaten too much sugary stuff by then. **I learned that drinking a lot of water is important both for kidney and teeth health.** Nowadays, I strictly drink only water for my choice of drinks on any occasion. Although I have changed my eating habits greatly thanks to these incidents, I have to admit that I used to eat a lot and was fatter as a consequence.

* * *

I think that there are few signs of being greedy. Eating too much and being fat is one of them. We can hurt other plants and animals on Earth by consuming them a lot; we can hurt yourself as well as a result.

There is a book titled *Food Governs Your Destiny* written by Namboku Mizuno, the famous Japanese philosopher. It has been a super-seller in Korea even though the Japanese book was written 200 years ago. The book does not seem to be popular in America, but I notice that still we can find it on Amazon. The author tries to focus on being humble and modest by eating less: **Small eating can change our destinies to be better ones in his opinion.** He said it is hard to achieve success in an uncontrolled greedy life, but it is also easy to lose everything in that sort of life, too. Always being humble and modest is the key: that starts with eating less and small, according to the philosopher.

I have always wondered how my father made a lot of money while both of his sons have not made that much. He drinks and smokes and had caused a lot of trouble in the family by the 1990s: He got divorced as a result about fifteen years ago. He is not supposed to be wealthy, according to my theories. **One thing I know is that he eats really small.** He has been skinny for life. I wonder if this could be the reason why he has been super-rich just as described in that book.

* * *

Another book that affected me greatly is a book titled *One day one meal*[37] written by Nagumo Yoshinori. I know there are similar books on the market, but this guy is the original: He is a surgeon and research doctor in Japan who wrote that book in 2012. His father was a doctor as well as there is a tradition where a lot of sons take over their fathers' professions in Japan. He said his father was obese and passed away from a heart attack and got a similar symptom as he became a middle aged man himself. He said that was the reason why he started researching food science: He had to survive.

Anyway, the book concludes that humans have lived with hunger for over six million years, but we eat too much nowadays and it causes all sorts of health problems. When we stop eating foods for a few days, it shows that our bodies start eating fat inside our body: That is why we are "losing weight". **But, when our bodies eat our own cells, more importantly, they selectively eat tumor and cancer cells first.**

It is possible that we have some cancer cells in our body all the time since we have seven trillions of cells and mutations occur in our bodies every day. Simply, if we do not give our body a chance to eat out some of the tumor cells, we are actually accumulating cancer cells in our body. Obviously, we can have cancer someday. **No machine can detect the cancer cells and eliminate them at a microscopic level as our bodies do.** I found all this information from the book above.

* * *

[37] I can see that his book title is "1 Day 1 expression" on Amazon. But, that is the wrong translation; I do not know where it comes from.

I had lost a lot of weight in 2018. I used to be up to 160 pounds in 2006, but I am about 125 pounds now (172 cm height) as of Dec, 2022. I think I had lost 20 pounds only in 2018 and lost more little by little after that. I read "One day one meal" at that time, but also read various books about fasting from the library: "The Complete Guide to Fasting" written by Jason Fung was particularly helpful.

I learned that people do not die only because of skipping some meals. **Theatrically, we can live without food for at least 90 days and that is what Buddhist monks do during religious fasting period in Korea.** When I think about it, I do not really remember the last time I saw a news report that anyone died of hunger in America or Korea. Certainly, people die from all sorts of reasons everyday: it shows that gunshot wounds and car accidents are the biggest two among young adults in the U.S. But there is no hunger on the list. I guess people usually end up eating anything before the hungry 90 days are over: Indeed, I believe most people eat too much nowadays.

* * *

I think my weight loss started seriously with a root canal infection in 2018. Shamefully, my lower left molar had severe decay, so I had to spend close to $3,000 to get a crown on it at the dentist.

I used to be stupid to eat anything, but my diet has changed drastically after 2018. I have cut off a large amount of processed foods, carbohydrates and all of the sugar. **I cut off all the drinks except water,** and still water is the only liquid I put in my mouth since then. And I chew Epic gums (sugarless and aspartame-less) all the time since xylitol is good for teeth.

I started trying to eat one meal a day for weight loss reasons from 2018. I found that skipping breakfast and lunch has been much easier for me than dinner. I still carry tooth floss all the time, so I can floss whenever I feel like. I do oil pulling frequently: Swishing olive oil in my mouth for 10 minutes. I usually spit oil on the grass in case I am outside, so spit would not be visible. You would not believe how much money I invested in quality toothbrushes and pastes these days.

Unfortunately, the root canal infection problems remained on that tooth for about three years. And I tried to cure it with natural holistic methods. The drug I was taking was Padma Basic from EcoNugenics; it is a Swiss company and this herb drug had good reviews on Amazon. It helped, but didn't work out my tooth infection completely. The medicine was invented originally for the heart, but people said that it works greatly on root canal infection.

* * *

I remember that the book titled *Holistic Dental Care: The Complete Guide to Healthy Teeth and Gums* written by Nadine Artemis was greatly helpful then in 2018. We can see this book has 430 perfect reviews (5 out of 5) on Amazon as of 2022. **This book strongly suggests Japanese Natto and Miso soup for tooth infection cure**: I tried those foods and found out that these foods have been shockingly helpful. I know a lot of Americans may not be familiar with Japanese foods very much. I have to confess that I never had tried Natto before reading this book myself, too.

The science behind is that the enzyme of Natto (NattoKinase) helps blood get into the infected tooth. Our tooth is actually a living organ having long capillary vessels inside. Our blood includes an immune system fighting any type of infection. But, once the root part of the tooth swells due to infection, blood cannot get into the tooth smoothly. Blood entry to the tooth itself can be pretty much blocked and the tooth starts dying due to suffocation as a result.

Natto is very slippery food and helps blood get in the infected tooth. **I could see my swelling on the gum disappear as soon as I ate Natto.** I have never felt it is extremely tasty, but still I was able to see all I have bought. Nattos definitely work well on my teeth and expensive brands taste better (there are hundreds of Japanese brands).

Luckily, Chicagoland has some Japanese supermarkets and restaurants, so I usually buy from them occasionally: Mitsuwa or Tensuke Marketplace in Arlington Heights. Or I saw some Korean supermarkets have them in stock (H-Mart). It is usually under $4 for three packs in 2022, so these won't be that expensive. When I tried it with Miso soup, it was even better. Instant miso soups are $12 for 30 packs and we can have it instantly with boiled water within 2 minutes.

* * *

I did not like the Indian lady dentist very much since she suggested pulling the tooth out in 2018: She suggested it right after I spent close to $3,000 on a crown procedure on my molar. She could not find any crack on the tooth with x-ray in the beginning, so we proceeded for the crown, originally. I believe there are more frauds in dentistry than other medical fields: Too much competition makes each business desperate. It was my mistake to have my tooth rot by 2018. **I am restricting my sugar consumption more than ever:** I guess it will be like this until I die.

* * *

Summary

1. Eating a lot of foods naturally makes us poor.
2. We should not act as if groceries or foods are free: These are actually more expensive in America than a lot of other countries.
3. Intermittent fasting has been helpful for my finances and health.

24

Approaching too Many Women

Chasing women is like digging our own grave yards.
-Brad Kong

In my opinion, there are only two types of men chasing women after they become 50: The greedy and the stupid. Having good, fine or OK relationships with women is not chasing: What I mean by chasing is approaching women too much until making them (or everyone else around) uncomfortable. **Smart men already know that there is no fantastic woman existing**; they already know that there is no real difference between men and women physically. There is no reason to desire anyone desperately if some of us have done that for more than five decades: At least, not up to the point that it can cause trouble or a money loss.

I think fantastic women do exist only because some women try so hard to be like one. For example, I don't really remember the last time I heard my wife fart or saw her go to the bathroom and poop. Probably, I noticed those less than 5 times in the last 23 years. Does this mean she doesn't do those? No way: I think she tries very hard to be a fantastic surreal female. Probably, she docs those while I am not at home. This is why she gets upset sometimes if I stay in the house too long: She needs some time to do something she doesn't want to show to others, especially to me I guess. What most women do are things like those; they also spend hours to have make-up on or spend weeks having plastic surgeries. If we know what's going on in reality, there is no reason to desire anyone. Smart men usually know this from their diverse experiences by the time they become 50 I believe.

On the contrary, the greedy men may or may not know a lot of things about women. I think they just want more physical relationships no matter what. There was an old fat Mexican dishwasher in the nursing home I used to work at. He had been a dishwasher for 35 years by 2022 and didn't even own a house even though he was 60 years old back then. He told me that he had rented a two-bedroom townhouse for $1,200 a month for decades. He had three adult children and two grandkids: I would say that probably seven people, including his wife, had lived there; his adult son passed away suddenly by a sort of accident in 2019, so I assume still six people had shared two bedrooms after that misfortune.

Despite that unfortunate event, everyone, including me, didn't really like him all along. He was particularly notorious for approaching young girls (usually servers) regardless of others' eyes. He had many flirting conversations with mild touching with them in the middle of public.

By the way, I think I should mention one Mexican girl named Ari (she said her father is Mexican and mother is white). I noticed that some girls, especially Mexican girls in case of that nursing home, had a lot of flirtations with old men. **These girls are equally disgusting or even more losers than old men in my opinion** (at least, she was). Think about it: What can those old men really lose? Nothing except getting free physical relationships. On the contrary, these young girls do not gain anything out of their actions: They only get a bad reputation and disappoint young boys around. What this Ari girl (20) did was keep flirting with him although everyone knew that the old Mexican dishwasher was married. Even his daughter was a server working there as well, but she didn't seem to care. I mentioned her briefly in Chapter 8 of *UnBrokable* I*: I ended up getting a very bad impression from her. She made me uncomfortable on many occasions until I resigned that job by 2022.

* * *

This is what one Korean Buddhist monk (Pomnyun) said once: "**There is no desire lasting *forever*.**" This may be true for a lot of things in our lives, but I believe it is particularly true for women. Have you seen a photo of the girl you used to like 10 years ago? How about a celebrity? Most likely old celebrities turn into someone we do not particularly favor now. This is especially true for women than men since people care less about men's appearances. It is natural that we can get attracted to anyone. But, if we believe this is not it or doesn't make much sense, I think we should let the person go.

* * *

Did you know that the legendary womanizer Giacomo Casanova had been in prison for 14 months for a sexual charge (originally sentenced 5 years) and almost went to prison a few times more for having so much debts in his life[38]? He was a prodigy by birth and made a fortune a couple of times for the state lottery ticket salesman in

[38] It had been common to go to prison because of financial debt in Europe even decades ago. The father of Charles Dickens went to the debt prison many times.

France, but basically had spent all on woman addiction. He eventually died broke and penniless in Duchcov Castle, Czech Republic in 1798. Let me not go deep right now, but it seems Casanova had lived quite a miserable troublesome life and died with syphilis, according to Wikipedia. **Let me just say that being obsessed with women and saving money do not go well together.**

* * *

Is marriage *profitable* in a financial sense? By the time my daughter was born in 2010, I heard the following sentence from a radio show by chance: "The typical fifty-something married man has three times more assets than his unmarried peer. If you are married and stay in marriage, you will end up having way more money than a single or divorced guy." It was a brief talk, but a sort of an eye opening for me back then.

Honestly, I had never been interested in marriage for life before hearing it although I have been married all along since 2010 (I met my wife in 1999). I had always considered marriage as an extra spending, which is true in many cases: It is nothing but a sort of ceremony some adults go through, right? But, can it really be a kind of money generating tool for men somehow? I did some research about it for years continually and concluded that it is not true all the time. And here is the real reason I guess why a married man can end up being more wealthy (if the sentence from that radio show was true): Women choose men with better futures to begin with; in other words, women often choose richer men from the start. **Or women will choose men who will possibly make a lot of money later on they believe.**

Before blaming all the women as gold diggers, let me give you an explanation this way. Let's suppose that someone said, “Married women in their 40s tend to be thinner than single women in their 40s.” Does this mean a marriage makes a woman lose weight? Not really. More likely, men may choose skinnier women to get married to begin with: **At least, men never choose a super obese woman as a partner.** Overweight women can be more likely to stay single since most men do not prefer them.

All the married men are people who passed some sorts of tests from women somehow; one of the ladies’ top priority concerns could be money making or self-supporting capability of men. **I do not think marriage makes a man wealthier automatically.** Actually, men can have more expenses if a child comes along. I guarantee you that approaching a lot of women will never be profitable, and it is better for men not to go crazy about it.

* * *

As I mentioned before, I used to know one Mexican dishwasher who kept approaching women in an offensive way; again, this guy had never been out of a rental apartment in the last 35 years even though he was almost 60 years old in 2022. **I feel he made his life this way**. In fact, the wage those dishwashers get paid is not that significantly small after working double shifts (15 hours) everyday. For the comparison, Omar, who is the young Mexican boy living at his parents’ house, had saved over $70,000 cash after working there for 8 years by 2022.

As I told you before, I bought my condo 9 years ago even though I am much younger than that old dishwasher. Since condo association fees ($350) are four times smaller than apartment rents ($1,200) in our area, **it is possible he actually gets poorer every month.**

If he gets an extra child after repeatedly approaching more and more women, he won't be out of poverty for good (probably he won't be in any case). I understand it's a hard job to endure for hours without that kind of joy or fun (e.g., talking a little bit or flirting with coworkers). Then, I guess I would rather just change my job seriously: **There are millions of jobs better than dishwashers.** I originally started that job for weekend part time only in 2015, but I have moved to different jobs gradually as you see.

* * *

Today, I read a news article in *The Wall Street Journal* that Elon Musk had committed adultery with the ex-wife of the Google CEO, Sergey Brin and it caused the divorce of the family (Brin's family); the Brin's ex-wife name is Nicole Shanahan and it shows that she is a Chinese descendent. This is honestly stupid and disgusting for Musk regardless of the truth (probably, it is true). I will never buy Tesla stock since I don't want to get involved in any kind of bad thing; I cannot put my money at risk. **I believe wrong doing eventually can bring profit loss to a corporation.**

I do not like the face of this woman named Nicole, by the way; she looks like a Chinese gold digger after having plastic surgery. This woman strangely reminds me of the Korean woman singer Park as they both look similar. Park also had suspicions of having adultery with one married IT CEO in Korea as I discussed extensively in Chapter 8. After getting shocked twice, I do not think I can finish my meal well with women with those faces. I don't know why, but both women (Nicole and Park) necessarily chose married men with two kids respectively: The Korean IT CEO Jo had two kids before meeting Park; Brin had two children before meeting Shanahan as well. This is a very strange coincidence.

I understand that this Elon guy may have some money, but I am sure no one wants to be in his position: Wiki shows that he divorced three times and has *ten* kids now. **No man wants to be in this kind of situation with gigantic responsibilities**: I am sure I will not enjoy changing one more diaper myself or spending money to have someone do so.

* * *

This may be controversial, but let me just say what I am thinking: **I think men tend to get the maximum happiness when they become half-monks after marriage;** I am not saying that we need to be the total Buddha. I am just saying that our lives tend to get way more easy and optimal when we let go of some of our desires. Surprisingly, it's not that extremely hard in my age, according to my experience: I am not in my 20s anymore.

I conclude that I would get fed up with whoever I get married to, after all; I would feel bored after seeing the same person for years and it does not matter whoever that is. It does not mean I hate my wife, but I am sure I would not get excited forever regardless of whoever I chose; I won't be happy with whoever woman I chose eventually.
Quite frankly, we do not have to get married from the start: We can be singles forever. But I would say that it costs a lot if something goes wrong, especially after marriage. The fact is that it is ok not to have a lot of partners: Those pressures are only coming from DNAs. **I believe we get much happier when we relieve those pressures somehow;** maybe having a child once or religion can help. And I know there are things we would better not do even if we want it badly (Chapter 13).

As I wrote in Chapter 13, there was a two story house I badly wanted in Roselle, IL in 2012; I remember I woke up in the middle of the night once since I wanted it so much and it was in my dream. That was more than 10 years ago and **I am really glad I did not go for that then when I think about it now.** The house is in a poor Mexican neighborhood called Roselle and the area is known to have frequent blackouts from electricity. The area has the smallest, yet poorest library in Chicagoland I have ever seen and it was not even close to that house. I would say that my current condo is like 500% better than that house.

* * *

Sometimes, perfectly smart men make irrevocable mistakes only because of women: **I think humans are built that way**; we can see millions of examples everywhere. Maybe this unreasonable sexual desire is how the human race has survived for millions of years, somehow.

Some people think having high standards for partners is a bad thing. Often, they complain that, "I do not have a girlfriend because I have too high standards. I don't feel any girl is pretty enough for me anymore." This happens especially more to many men since we have watched too much media full of beautiful women every day for decades. Still, let me tell you one thing, though: **This is not really a bad thing.** In fact, the other way around is worse.

When a man has a too high standard, I think he won't be deceived by gold diggers easily; he will disregard these types of women in a second. He has turned himself into a *Zen master* overcoming all the desires without practicing for years. Since no girl is good enough, he can make a rational choice among all those "*average*" looking women even when he gets married. Chasing too many women is a bad thing:

Those guys must have low standards. **On the contrary, getting disappointed by so-so looking women will never cause trouble.** In real life, there are men who think every woman is good enough; they are the ones who will get into trouble; they approach virtually anyone and may make their wives angry; often they stay poor for life due to this type of reason.

* * *

I think having too much sexual desire is a curse: **Particularly, this is a curse for a man.** Some people think there are some super sophisticated mysteries about women. Particularly, a single guy who has not had much experience with a woman or was born and raised without a sister in his family tends to think like this. He is just being idiotic: As I explained, women are also the same creatures pooping and farting like men all the time.

It took almost fifty years for me to realize this completely: **women are like men**. We will naturally know if we have a wife and a daughter for more than a decade; without them, I would have still thought women are mythical creatures, which is unrealistic and stupid. This fantasy will not help us much in real life particularly when we have to choose a partner. We all know that getting involved with a wrong woman costs a lot of money or even a life in some cases.

* * *

Again, when I worked at the nursing home, there was an old, fat Mexican dishwasher everyone did not like; I just don't see a worse "*real life*" example than him. No offense since I liked most Mexicans there in general. But I did not like that one: Everyone did not like him. He was a sort of betrayer and gave me a headache until the last day I worked. Again, he was the one who gave me inspiration to write this series; **often he worked 15 hours a day throughout the seven years.** Or, more correctly, I would say he had stayed 15 hours a day at work while assigning his job to coworkers in a sneaky way.

But he had always been poor for his entire life. He was not frugal or broke: He was purely poor. He said that he had paid $1,200 a month for rent and spent a total of $1,800 a month including utilities, cell phones, etc for his whole family (six people). His adult daughter was working part time there as well, so I was not sure of the exact reason for poverty. As I will discuss in Chapter 33, **some dishwashers even own a house completely without a mortgage (fully paid off).**

One thing I noticed was that he always approached women excessively: **This guy never missed a chance.** There had been a large number of female coworkers in the nursing home all the time: servers, managers, CNAs, nurses, cleaners, securities, etc. The place hired over 1,000 people. His raider had been always on for women and an approaching plan started as soon as he detected one. He did it in an open, slow and disgusting manner: Addressing a woman with friendly talk out of nowhere.

His attitude had changed quickly to be hostile towards male workers if he needed to talk to one. He had a bad reputation since he helped only women while taking advantage of men. I honestly do not have specific answers with mathematical analysis for all those poverty questions in the prologue. But I strongly guess this could be why he had been dirt poor for life in spite of hard working.

I noticed that he approached a lot of young girls, too. **What is the point even if I get married to a new young one?** I do not want to spend time wondering if she was married to me because of my money or not. I do not want to be in suspicion that she might poison me to get my money early or not. Home should be the most comfortable place in the world: I do not want to waste my energy and live uncomfortably in my own place.

Men are not cautious about women instinctively. They think women are weak and safe creatures. Nothing can be further from the truth. **In real life, men can go down easily because of women**: One well-known example can be the musical *Carmen*. As you see in the Trump case, only stupid men are getting married more than once or twice.

* * *

There are three types of women I strongly recommend for men not to get close to in any case.

1. Smokers and drinkers
2. Women having plastic surgery including a tattoo and piercing
3. Women with no solid income.

I am not sure I will talk about the J exercise business right next door when I had the video game shop. Three women owned it and they all pretended they made a lot of money: One of those three drove an unnecessarily expensive luxury car. I know they actually had lost a lot of money: These types of women are "huge *no no*" (bigger than big no no) in my opinion.

I know not everyone will agree with me for the above three types I mentioned. But, personally, I just had bad experiences with those three types I mentioned above. Although it is subtle, there are plenty of women trying to utilize a man as I explained in Chapter 8. Usually greedy men approach women more, so they fall into their own traps more frequently in those cases.

When we think about it, sexual desire is definitely a sort of curse for men. It always does more harm than good throughout a man's life. In the best scenario, we can end up having a lot of kids who can bring us lifetime drudgeries and money drains. In the worst scenario, we can be one of those men committing suicide because of "Me Too movement" recently. Or a man can be strangled to death in a prison like Jeffrey Epstein: I know some said he committed suicide, but I think it is highly possible he got murdered in prison; he knew too much unpleasant secrets of other political figures. **I am not saying that these men should have lived innocently, but I am just saying that they shouldn't have dug their own graves "unnecessarily".** We just need to handle it with care and reason.

* * *

In my opinion, it is not really worth getting married more than once in our lifetime. My mother had been married only once and she has me and my brother. We can try marriage for our experience once. And, probably, most people will have good marriages at first try. But, I think it is stupid to keep repeating it only because the first one did not work out very well.

Everyone has his or her own good and bad points in characteristics. In my view, I don't think there is a woman way better than others or having good points only. Sometimes, it takes 10 years to find out bad points about our partners (at least, that was true in my case). In some senses, single life is better than married life, so there is no reason to try hard to get into a relationship. If that happens, that's fine. But it is nonsense trying hard to get into a prison named marriage to spend more money.

It's pointless to crowd our life with a wedding debt, a bigger mortgage debt, bigger car debts or more kids to feed. There is no need for these, especially when the population is growing fast nowadays. As I wrote in Chapter 2, the human population will be 9 billion soon by 2040. We can all die together at this speed of growth since the Earth has limited space and resources.

If you are a man with a partner, you can remember this: **There is no fantastic woman having advantages only.** If you want to live single, that is fine. But we do not have to go for another one. There is no woman way better than our current or previous wives. If anyone thinks there is, I would say the person just does not have much understanding about human nature. Statistics clearly show that second marriages fail much more than the first.

The least we can do is to see the lady's character when we get married. For example, I do not like loud noises[39]

---

[39] There was a loud business named J exercise next door when I had the video game store. It was a sort of aerobic exercise for grandmothers and I have trauma from loud noise even now because of that business. While new generations go for quiet businesses like Yoga or meditation, it has been the stupidest business I have ever seen. Those three female owners made only noise pollution to hurt my ears instead of money. I confirmed that two of them were divorced women for sure. The business was slow, lost money and moved out eventually after spending a fortune to build facilities in that location. Dance club moved in that location in 2016 and the facilities are used by it now. That loud business wasted money for nothing. I am glad that my wife is a quiet person.

nor does my wife: She is a very quiet person. It is crazy if we don't even check this kind of major discrepancy before the wedding.

I believe only greedy or stupid men approach women again and again up to the point they get hurt. As a result, they never get out of poverty or stay above minimum wealth level just like the dishwasher. Let's not be like Trump. I think he is still a poor old man among the super-riches. I think people can try to be like me, at least. I am living without much worry, at least.

* * *

Summary

1. It is pointless to keep chasing women.
2. Enough is enough.
3. Smart men know there are no true fantastic women existing.

25

Not Living Long Enough

We need to be alive until we gather the harvest.
-Brad Kong

I think people perceive thin and skinny women attractive and beautiful automatically (at least, this is true for me): That is why those American supermodels or Korean idols are super-skinny. And, personally, I think this is a *great* thing. Why? This makes us humans eat less overall on Earth. Therefore, I think a little less animals (including livestock and fishes) or plants are killed and consumed as a result. Have you seen photos of surprisingly old people celebrating their 100th birthday? No one is fat among them: I strongly believe that being skinny is being healthy, after all. **And being able to live longer and keeping money for long matters wealth wise.**

* * *

I had thought about this question seriously a year ago: If I have only six months left to live, what should I do? Definitely, I will not work a second more. Maybe that is why I resigned from the nursing home job finally in April, 2022; on top of it, things had been getting worse and worse there every year compared with in 2015 when I was hired. There was no reason for me to endure unfairness, especially from one short and disrespectful Mexican sous chef, while I have more than enough money. **I didn't want to play the nice guy role forever**, who still helps elderly people in spite of unfairness even though I have a lot of money: Having one mean boss was such a misery.

Some people may think they will live at least 40 years more since they are in their 20s. Then, let me ask another question: Is 40 years a long time while 6 months is a short one? When we think about it, 40 years may not be that long as we expect: Human life is short, basically. **In a sense, we are all having only six months left in our lives.**

* * *

I remember the husband of my wife's girlfriend died at 38 from liver failure at the hospital in 2007; he was a Mongolian and super-heavy alcohol drinker. I heard that he was the youngest child for his parents and his two *older* brothers visited his funeral: Certainly, there is no predetermined order for who's going to pass away first while there was an order for who was born first. If he is alive, he would be about 53 years old by 2022. I believe his wife has three kids and the man was an auto mechanic; I heard that he had worked double for decades: a regular mechanic job for a company garage and his own auto repairing business at home (he renovated his home garage for a business, then). Some people drink crazily after working for long hours: **Still, he would have not worked that long if he knew his life would be over that soon.**

People can be dead any time; we will observe that someone we know dies, especially if the person is over 50. A lot of people start dying from lung cancer in their 50s in Korea. I believe there are more smokers in the country and many start the habit as soon as they get into a college; it would be three decades of smoking by 50 and some already die. The same goes for drinking; alcohol is a known carcinogen, which causes cancers. If anyone dies at the hospital by 50, one of the most predominant reasons is any type of cancer, according to my observance. Otherwise, it's usually any disease related to drinking, smoking or obesity like stroke or heart attack.

Since a lot of people die in the hospital everyday while we do not notice, I think being alive after 50 can be success in a sense. I think we should be proud if we are old enough and alive now: I am not exaggerating; I really do mean it. **If anyone has never lost any tooth by 50, it is more than a great success in my opinion**; I am "*almost*" in that situation and plan to not to lose any more of my tooth until I die; that has been my new goal since 2022 and I think it's really possible since it's happening to a lot of people. I have been drinking strictly only water for the last four years now: Only water is healthy and safe for our teeth. Better yet, I notice that drinking water is good for my kidneys and weight loss as well.

* * *

I know it's possible for us to die early, but many of us will be able to live until 100 as well with medicine and medical technology advances sooner or later. If that is the case, I think it's important to start four things as early as possible to get wealthy: education; travel; house purchase; getting interests and dividends. Let's say that there is one boy learning how to speak English at the age of 10; he can use the skill in the next 90 years if we live until 100. Imagine I try to master how to speak Spanish by next year; I can use the knowledge only in the next 50 years. **Clearly, starting early has an advantage in education:** I can use the same knowledge longer. The same goes for travels. People get good memory and knowledge out of them. The earlier we travel, the longer we can use the knowledge.

This is absolutely true for house purchase as well. If we do not have enough money for a small house or condo, that is fine; we just need to try more. But I think buying a big house with a mortgage debt even when people have enough money for a little smaller house is *stupid.* If we free ourselves from a rent or mortgage at an early age, we can start to build wealth earlier than others: It is proven that time is more valuable than money in wealth building. Having debt for long will only bring us more debt in the form of interest, so getting out of that early is crucial. Also, the same goes for getting interests and dividends early; **getting dividends for 70 years is better than for 30 years.**

* * *

It sounds ridiculous, but I think some people are broke because they do not live long enough. Occasionally, it takes some time to harvest our wealth out of hard work. **If we die too early, we just miss chances to get paid.** In that case, after we die, people in the future may conclude that we had a poor life and died broke: The truth is that we die before getting outcomes. Let me explain this with four examples.

A lot of people say that Vincent van Gogh was an unfortunate artist. He had lived a poor life, but a lot of his paintings have been sold at high prices after his death. **Still, not many people know that he died only at the age of 37.**

What could have happened if he died at 60? I think it is possible that he could have made more sales and enjoyed some money for the last 23 years of his life after 37. It takes some time to get recognized and famous. And what if he died at 100? I like to imagine that he would have made a lot of sales for the later 63 years of his life after 37 and died as a millionaire.

On the contrary, Pablo Picasso has been considered a wealthy artist. **Did you know that he died at 91?** Or more importantly, was he wealthy at the age of 37? I do not think he was. Wikipedia shows that Picasso was poor in his earlier life, which is pretty common for artists. We need to live longer to get wealthy; that is the general rule, at least.

I can take Lucia Berlin as an example for writers. She never really got famous during her lifetime. She had been married three times and had been a poor single mother with four sons. She was a smoker for her whole life and died in poverty at the age of 68 in 2004.

But suddenly she got an award and became famous in 2015 after one publisher (Straus & Giroux) released a collection of her short stories: Manual for cleaning women. **She would have been 79 years old if she was still alive by 2015.** She died of lung disease, but if she lived until 100, she could have enjoyed some wealth for the last 21 years of her life.

Warren Buffett is 92 years old now (2022). Was he extremely rich at the age of 37? Not really. **I think it is important to survive through the brokeness period until we get to the next level.** That is the reason why I mentioned "no smoking and drinking" first in Chapter 1.

* * *

I don't think we should be frustrated because of money problems, especially when we are young: Do not commit suicide for that. According to my experience, money does not come evenly throughout our life. **People usually spend, waste or lose more in their early lives.** Brokeness is common when we are young even when our parents are rich. And people usually make or save more later on. There are three mandatory reasons for this.

First of all, education costs a fortune and it is mostly concentrated early in people's lives. It usually starts with kindergartens or elementary schools. It can go all the way up to postdoc in our 30s. **And we cannot make a lot of money from jobs while we are in school.**

Secondly, people usually get curious about the world and travel more at early ages: **Travels cost money if not whole a lot of money.** As they get old, they usually settle in one place and do not move around as much; old people are not curious as much; they checked the world out already. No adventure means no accidental spending as well, so people tend to save more in their later age.

Thirdly, all of us will go through a trial and error period. Let's not blame ourselves too much because of the mistakes we made so far: In my opinion, this is merely a part of our lives. **But, unfortunately, errors may cost some money as well and happen more during the early stages of our lives.**

* * *

I lost more than $2,000 for nothing only during the time I was in Cornell University in 1999. I had to move out from a shared apartment before the contract was over since I had three horrible roommates. Except meeting my wife, who eventually earned a doctor's degree with scholarship in UIUC, nothing good happened to me in the city of Ithaca, NY. I do not know if it was the school, the city or me. Let me tell you more in detail.

First of all, the English language school at Cornell was not that great: Super expensive, but poorly managed compared with other schools. I hope it is better by now (2022), but it had poor classes, faculties and activities in 1999. When I was in R.I.T. in 1997, the school even helped every student get social security cards. One officer came to a class and issued one card for every single student of ours. I did not take it seriously at that time. But when I think about it now, it has been a great help up until this moment. I still appreciate Mrs. Cone and would like to mention that she did a fabulous job on classes over all.

Secondly, the city of Ithaca was small with a population of 50,000 then and did not have enough housing for students: Low quality housing at super high prices. When I studied at Cornell, I stayed in the dormitory during the summer semester in 1999. That was when I met my wife even though she had to leave for a Master's degree in Arkansas after summer. I had to move out of the dorm only after summer, but the language school did not give us any help. I had to find one crappy apartment unit shared with three other people on my own. The three roommates were horrible then: Ron from Grenada; Steve, an unfriendly Korean American from LA; one Japanese guy whose name I do not even remember now. I remember that this guy named Ron, the black American from the Caribbean, was *especially* hideous. Facebook shows that he is divorced now and I clearly knew this would happen (another reason we should not post personal info on social media).

Lastly, I didn't like the gloomy atmosphere in the city of Ithaca very much. It was a small, but suffocating city: Stressful for no apparent reason. The place was not a study promoting environment at all. I skipped school so many times, which is very unusual and had never really happened throughout my life. I escaped the city whenever I had chances like weekends, vacations or holidays. I did not necessarily enjoy trips: I just wanted to avoid the city. These all cost me more money, ultimately.

Anyway, I did not like that particular four-people-shared apartment and noticed that a lot of students moved out before finishing contracts. Therefore, I found a one-bedroom apartment outside the city myself as well and moved out, too. After that, I got a strange letter from them to pay all the money until the last day of the 1-year contract: $350 a month for the last 6 months (about $2,000). I don't know how they even found my new address since tracking like that was illegal. My info was not even on the Internet since I stayed barely 1 year totally in Ithaca. I felt they are familiar with runaways and there was a rumor that some dispute records can remain on our social security. I decided to pay up and get rid of the trouble for good. I really feel sorry for my parents who had to pay all those things while they didn't even realize (this happened 24 years ago, though).

* * *

In general, I don't think I had much luck when I was in NY State. Moreover, I found out that Illinois State is much cheaper and cleaner as I had visited my wife dozens of times in Champaign, IL. For example, the cost of living in Buffalo, NY is similar to Chicago, IL, but Chicago is much bigger and cleaner than Buffalo. As a result, I don't think anyone really moves into NY State any more.

I still thank the State University at Buffalo since it suggested the cheapest tuition in America, which was about $6,000 a semester without scholarship by 2005. The school did not have pretty campus landscapes, but had plenty of places to study alone; it had a lot of libraries and computer labs. I remember that all the exams were competitive. I loved the fifth floor of the Law library, then; no one was there all the time. In addition, I had a chance to work at a banquet in the school and the pay was helpful for my living (thank you, Michael Kusinski, fat friendly great Polish Banquet manager!).

I lost a lot of money until I became 35: rent, housing, moving, business failure, etc. You name it. Actually, money loss stopped a little bit only after I bought out my condo and settled at the age of 40. **I am frugal now since I obviously know I have wasted a lot in the past.** At least, I have never drunk or smoked, so money has been lost on experiences, not on health damage. In a sense, these include unique Ivy League memories after all. I will give you more examples of how I lost a chunk of money in Chapter 45. For now, I think we just need to live long enough to get our investment back.

* * *

Summary

1. We need to live long enough to get our money back.
2. Some people die too early before getting paid.
3. Dying earlier increases the chance of dying broke.

26

Not Having Strong Opinions

We need to trust our instincts:
Don't be fooled by experts.
-Brad Kong

The more we get wealthier, the more temptations we will get: I think that *not moving by temptation* is key to maintaining wealth. One way is that we need to be mature enough to know that there is no point to fulfill all the desires. **I think a lot of desires are vain, pointless and disadvantageous.**

* * *

Have you heard of the *Broccoli test*? One Korean lady said that it is one way to know if we are truly hungry or not: If we can eat broccoli, we are really hungry; otherwise, it's just brain hunger or habitual eating.

This gave me an idea: There is something I like to call the "*Mona Lisa test*". There is a well-known painting called Mona Lisa in the Louver Museum and a crazy amount of people are always waiting to see it. If you feel like seeing it as well or urge to wait for hours since others do, you may not have your own strong mind.

We are all subject to *crowd psychology* somehow and probably have done whatever others usually do a few times so far. For example, some of us have bought crypto currency before only because it *seems* popular. But, if you feel that, "I do not know why crypto is so popular," or "Mona Lisa looks just another painting to me," more likely you are a person who has your own strong opinions. I think it is important for us to have those, especially when we do stock trading. **Frauds always use crowd psychology to some extent and victims fall for this.**

* * *

I think writing about our own opinions is important. In fact, the only thing truly left after we die can be our own articles. The book titled *The Diary of a Young Girl* written by Anne Frank is one of the most sold books throughout human history: She died only when she was 15 in March, 1945. It shows that she had the typhus epidemic in a Nazi Jewish camp. **She could have been forgotten a long time ago like her sister without her own writings.**

Christopher Columbus was the one who found the "new continent" (America) in 1492. Yet it shows that he believed it was Asia until he died. The record says Amerigo Vespucci was merely a small merchant from Florence, Italy back then; still, he published a four-page book in 1503, which is 11 years after Columbus' finding: "This must be a new continent!" **Now the ample North and South American continents have been named after Amerigo Vespucci**: America. I think this is the power of writing; it is impossible to make a small street named after me, but he made two huge continents named after him.

* * *

Sometimes, I feel like I am a hotel manager; my ideas are like my guests. I cannot squeeze ideas out of my brain, but I can accept those ideas whenever they visit me. I can take care of my guests by writing them on the note. If I am lazy, they will go away and disappear often for good.

The Roman emperor, Marcus Aurelius Antonius once said, "You have power over your mind, not outside events." I think having our own sane mind is crucial: **"Being always awake" in Buddhism.** "Control is power," also Oscar Schindler put in the movie titled *Schindler's List*.

I think this is how it works in real life: Whoever has stronger control over his or her mind wins; whoever has control over money cannot be poor. **When I think about it, having power is all about control**; it exactly applies to building wealth as well.

* * *

As I mentioned before, there used to be one Korean community website I used to go to. Virtually, I was the only one who wrote some articles worth reading there; the site had a lot of nasty trolls, commenters and repliers: They all have debts and support their lavish lifestyle against my opinions. Strangely, in common, they never really wrote anything real or helpful; at least, not something worth reading or replying.

How can I avenge them? The best way is not to write there any more: Forever. It is Friday, so if I don't write anything until this Monday morning, I think that would be a great revenge; I know they will check the site millions of times to see if I write anything new or not over the weekend. They will waste the whole three days until Monday: **Making them wait and waste their time is a good revenge.** They would feel stupid in this Monday morning since I am going to write about just the contents of this book series and release date only, so they can buy these possibly someday: All they get is my book sales info.

Here is one question in this situation: How can I get revenge on internet trolls so efficiently without breaking any law now? The answer is that I am the one who has control; I have control over whether I will write more or not; they have never written any real articles; there is nothing they can do except wait for my article. **As long as I can control my urge to write, I will have total control over those losers.** Certainly, I am not that strong and cannot control my mind reliably if I stay at home or near any computer to write. I think I will walk around the whole day since the weather will be nice over this weekend. I will just bring my paper notebook and pen just in case any good idea comes to me. I guess I will do that until Monday morning. This chapter will include "Being too emotional" topics as well.

* * *

One of the most realistic examples of control over money is *not checking* the stock markets often: It is hard, but possible. When I think about it now, I should have put all the $90,000 in the Pfizer stocks in January, 2021. As I explained in Chapter 17, I ended up having $90,000 cash after selling all the Pitney Bowes shares with profit on 1/26/2021. PBI stock was $13.45 only on that day and the next; I made about $20,000 profit this time. So I got my original investment back from Pitney Bowes company as a result, so the total amount of cash I got was about $90,000.

I believe Pfizer stock was about $35 in Jan, 2021. And now it is $50 as of May, 2022, so I could have made a lot of profit along with a 3% dividend of Pfe stock. I should have put all my money in there. **It was a big mistake that I**

did not trust my own instinct. Actually, I am losing money because of that.

In January, 2021, I was looking for a company which could bring me a solid dividend; I was ready to reinvest that $90,000. As I explained in Chapter 17, I usually address dividend stocks as if these are bank accounts. Pfizer originally released COVID vaccines in 2020 and my wife and I got three shots respectively by 2021. I thought that it was a great company making great products that will save the entire human race someday. There were only two companies successfully able to produce COVID vaccines by 2020: Pfizer and Moderna.

I did not like Moderna stock very much since this *new* company never made anything other than Covid vaccine before in 2021. That is fine, but it was not very ideal in an investment sense since it did not have anything to back up their loss in case Covid vaccine goes wrong. We have to admit that both companies had produced Covid vaccines at fast paces due to the emergency. No one in my family had adverse symptoms for vaccines so far, though. **Also Moderna stock does not come with a dividend.** I thought Pfizer stock is a better investment and it has been fine so far. Only problem was that I did not have the strong courage to stick to my own opinion.

* * *

I have a stock account with Fidelity and its analysis part kept saying this in 2021: I have too much concentration in only Pfizer stock and it's no good. Even before getting the $90,000 in January, 2021, I think 6% of my total portfolio was Pfe (Ticker for Pfizer stock). I still have 98 company stocks and 42 company bonds in 2022. With this condition, Fidelity said they strongly do not recommend putting more than 5% of my fund only in one company. **When I had a hard time with PBI stocks in 2020, it occupied up to 25% of my portfolio**; my portfolio was down only because of one stock then: PBI. I thought I learned some lessons. I decided to listen to Fidelity this time and put only $30,000 out of $90,000 in Pfizer in 2021. However, it was a mistake when I think about it now in 2022: I should have put it all in pfe.

Since I still had $60,000 left after the Pfizer investment, I decided to put those in bonds of diverse companies: Alphabet (Google), Apple, Amazon, Microsoft, Berkshire Hathaway, etc. These are some of the biggest companies in the world. **Many of these do not come with dividends, but bonds of these companies always come with interests.**

More importantly, I thought that economic depression will come sooner or later in 2021. It was the third year after Covid broke out in 2019. **If a depression comes, stock prices generally go down, but bond prices generally go up.** So I set up a new strategy: "Let me not buy stocks any more except Pfizer. Stock prices will go down one way or another soon. Let me buy bonds from now, so the total portfolio will not crash."

In general, this is not supposed to be a terrible tactic, but the problem was the timing. Luckily, stock prices did go down a lot as time went on, including that of Pfizer, so I had to sell a lot of stocks when they were still high. But the problem was the massive amount of bonds I bought after selling those stocks.

* * *

For your information, the bond prices are always $1000 for 1,000 shares (face value) originally. Bonds are not like stocks. **Bonds keep $1,000 (face) value in 1,000 shares all the time and we can get $1,000 back when 1,000 shares of bonds mature in the end.** The maturation dates of bonds are all different. But since we are guaranteed to get our $1,000 back eventually, it is extremely important to buy them cheaper than $1,000 initially.

And the bond commission to buy and sell is only $1 per 1,000 shares; it's called mark-up fee. So there is no worry about losing a lot of money for commissions or not. **Also there is no fine to sell bonds earlier than maturation date**: This is the main difference between bonds and bank CDs. In the case of CDs, if we break it before maturation date, we will definitely get an early withdrawal penalty (usually 6 months' interest). But there is no fine or early withdrawal fee in bonds. Also we can buy them where we buy stocks like Fidelity, Charles Schwab, etc.

This $1,000 per 1,000 shares is also called par value, nominal value or the face value. For the reason above, bonds are considered a much safer investment than stocks: There is no guarantee for minimum value back in stocks. **For bonds, we always get our $1,000 back as long as we wait until the maturation date of our bonds.** It is up to us if we sell bonds when the price is more than $1,000: In that case, we can make a profit and lose only $1 out of a sales commission.

* * *

Fortunately, I managed to buy all my 42 company bonds for less than $1,000 face value in 2021: For example, I bought the Google bond for $800 instead of $1,000 par value. **This was supposed to be a *smart move*.**

Nonetheless, unfortunately, the bond prices went down way more in 2022. Why? Suddenly the Federal reserve bank started increasing interest rates crazily due to high inflation rate this year (2022). **High interest rate means people will put their money in the bank rather than stocks or bonds.** The bond market especially collapsed more than stocks; Google bonds went as low as $51: This is ridiculous since it is supposed to be $100 as I explained.

As a result, 56% of my money has been in bond markets and these bonds are still all down now as of 2022. I have never not lost money technically since I will not sell any bonds any time soon: I will keep getting interest until they mature. If I can keep them for the next 5-25 years, I will get my $1,000 back from each bond. **But if I put all my money ($90,000) in Pfizer stocks as I got a hunch in January, 2021, I would have been seeing way more profit in my portfolio now as of Dec, 2022.** At least, I would have not seen any loss by now.

* * *

Summary

1. Trust your own instinct.
2. Do not change your plan only because an expert says something.
3. Be aware of crowd psychology and stay awake.

27

Living Recklessly

We are the ones who decide our destinies.
-Brad Kong

The Brazilian soccer team "lost" to the Croatian in Qatar World Cup in 2022: It's shocking that the Brazilian couldn't pass the quarter finals (the strongest 8 team play), which is rare. This is a shame for Brazilians since the FIFA ranking of their national team was number one (#1) in the world by 2022; Brazil has been the world cup champion five times so far. **It's even more astonishing that the population of Brazil is over 214 million while that of Croatia is less than 4 million.**

This is what they did during the game

Here is something most do not know. In my opinion, Brazilians lost since they overly enjoyed their little success too early while offending Koreans. They had a game with the Korean team right before the one with the Croatian (it's called the first round, which means the strongest 16 teams). They beat the Koreans 4-to-1 in the end, but whenever they had a goal, they danced too much offensively; that included their old, but thoughtless head coach, too. A lot of people (especially Brazilians after their loss) found their acts disrespectful. Some people live like this for life and they never end up becoming successful forever: **Some cannot survive their small successes.**

* * *

I believe relaxing and doing things *step by step* can save us tons of money. I think we should never get emotional in any case. The tooth filling of my left lower molar came out a couple of months ago (October, 2022). Now I have to do fasting in the next couple of months (I cannot eat very well for minor pain, anyway) and start looking for a dentist who can fill it up without upselling root canal surgery or implants. Fasting itself is one way to cure tooth infection as well: When we fast, our bodies start eating bad cells inside our bodies first. As a result, we lose weight. Some doctors claimed that a 30-days fasting can cure any disease. I would like to try that before spending a fortune on my dental treatment.

I think *waiting* and *delaying* are good *life strategies* on many occasions: I think we can have everything or make our lives close to perfect if we use these methods properly. There are things we would better not do, but we want. See if you can wait until the urge goes away: It always goes away, after all. There was a house in Roselle I badly wanted in 2012 as I spoke in Chapter 13; I am glad I did not buy it, especially with a mortgage debt. It could have been a terrible choice when I think about it in 2022; my current condo is 1,000 times better than that house and 4 times cheaper.

There was a girl from Italian immigrant parents when I worked at the nursing home; she seemed to be popular among boys as many Italians are skinny and good looking. But I am glad I blocked my interest in her from forming; she was a smoker, marijuana smoker and drinker; she had low education (barely high school graduate); she was rude and her parents were poor enough to lose their house because of foreclosure during the mortgage bubble in 2010.

My feeling persisted for a while, but finally it went away; I didn't want her at all, eventually. Now I will call the police if she addresses me. Don't do anything stupid with women; stay away from them if you believe they won't be helpful for your future; being in love is nothing but a dopamine addiction in a physiological sense. Whoever we marry, we will get fed up with her and find someone more interesting: Block a woman unless she is a logically good choice. One way to let the urge go is by delaying. If you want something, see if you can wait and get it later or tomorrow; delay it a week if you can. Remember: **None of our desires last forever.**

* * *

Have you ever been in a situation where a bunch of problems broke out all at once before? In this case, I think that it is important to not worry too much or be overwhelmed. Here is one way I recommend to handle the situation: **See if you can solve the easiest problem first**; then, see what's going to happen next. It may not be much, but still it's one less thing to worry about after solving it.

Human minds are strange; sometimes, a good idea finally comes out only after we solve a problem or two; we just do not see it until the situation gets better or changed. The same thing goes for a math problem; sometimes, we have no clue to address the problem to begin with. Every so often, a clue finally comes only after we start solving it to an extent. **In real life, it's better for us to see what's left after we solve one easy matter since some issues can go away on their own.**

Personally, I have 98 company stocks and 42 company bonds in my portfolio as of December, 2022. Currently, I am losing money on two electric car company stocks: Lordstown (ticker: ride) and Workhorse (ticker: wkhs); I bought these at $4.00 and $6.50 each. Lordstown was $2.58 (8/2/2022), so it seems I may have to wait for a while to sell these completely out with profit; in other words, I have to wait until Lordstown stock goes above $4.00. I never sell stocks on loss, by the way; I always sell them with profit even though profit can be $0.01.

Workhorse does not update anything for their new electric car or truck, but Lordstown updates their YouTube channel for this new electric truck called *Endurance* regularly. Therefore, I believe "ride" stock will rise first as they release the vehicle in the near future. If so, I think it's better not to worry about "wkhs" stock at all now. I do not know what's going to happen with that company, but let me focus on just selling off Lordstown first: I do not know when that will happen, but it's pointless to worry about two problems altogether. Technically, I have more than enough money; I just want to get rid of two stocks not bringing me any profit or dividends. **I think it's better to focus on the easy one to sell and see what's going to happen next.** Relax as no one will be dead by a couple of small stocks. Please *realize* that all of us actually have enough money and have accomplished so many things in our lives. No one needs to rush for anything.

* * *

There is one novel titled *The Alchemist* written by Brazilian author Paulo Coelho. This is one excerpt from the book: "You will spend the rest of your days knowing that you didn't pursue your Personal Legend, and that now it's too late." This is one instruction the alchemist gave to the shepherd boy. The boy tried to give up finding his treasure and the alchemist urged him not to give up for now; he's basically saying that, "**If we miss the opportunity now, we will never be able to find the treasure again.**" I understand there is timing for everything, but there are things I do not agree with the writer in this book.

Quite frankly, the only reason I bought this book from a used store ($8) was because the author made a lot of money; it shows that his net worth is $500 M. This book was flat-out boring to me from the start till almost the end; it was just a story of a shepherd boy trying to go to the Pyramid in Egypt for treasures, but he found out that those were buried in his hometown; that was all.

And it seems this is what the author is trying to say from the excerpt: "Do something if you really want to do it. You won't be able to do it if you keep delaying." This is a totally wrong lesson in my opinion. I used to be like this writer in my 20s: Doing as many things as possible during my lifetime is good; accomplishing more goals, making more money, getting more degrees, etc. Now I think a little differently: "We have to leave everything when we die: **Everything we use in this life can be a rental.** We do not necessarily have to do many things. If we can do it, that is fine; if we cannot, that is fine, too. I think it is perfectly fine if we live our daily lives just as we do now. Unless we commit a crime, we have the right to live peacefully. We do not have to look for more gains or treasures all the time.

Nowadays, a lot of people, especially those people from advertisements, ask us to do more and more things; we have to go to Cancun for vacation, we need motorcycles and RVs to ride, we need a new girlfriend like Dua Lipa, so we have to check her music videos every day, etc. **None of these is necessary.** It is perfectly fine if we are only concerned about making ends meet every month. Don't worry about those people saying we need more. Just worry about your salary from jobs or living cost in your housing: We will actually get happier when we do not diversify our attention to a lot of things.

* * *

There are people living recklessly beyond a necessary level. I am not talking about taking some risks for investments. Some people just live flat-out dangerously; maybe they do skydiving or extreme sports as a hobby. Some may have dangerous jobs like cleaning windows of skyscrapers. **Still, surprisingly some just go across**

the line between life and death for no apparent reason. And such a reckless lifestyle costs money and these people stay poor despite working hard. I usually talk about my own story first, but let me give you an example of Dostoevsky in this chapter.

Lately, I checked Wikipedia for other writers like Leo Tolstoy, Fyodor Dostoevsky, Karl Marx, Charles Dickens, Victor Hugo, Herman Melville, etc. When I tried to change my job to a writer early in 2022, the first thing I was glad about was that I do not have a lot of kids to support. Probably, I will not have more than one child in my life (no beneficial need for anyone as well). Taking care of one child has already been hard for me, so my wife does most of the child care work including making some money now. I just do not know how others manage this issue, especially when they have big families. By the way, these are the number of children those writers had during their lifetimes: Tolstoy (13), Dostoevsky (4), Marx (7, but one died), Dickens (10), Hugo (5) and Melville (4).

To me, it is ironic that most of these writers had a lot of kids while they wrote books about poor people. Victor Hugo wrote *Les Miserable* and it is all about miserable poverty. Dickens wrote *Hard times* and *Bleak house*. In the case of Karl Marx, it shows that three of his children died when young and he wrote the *Das Kapital* criticizing the emerging selfish capitalism in England. The title of the first major novel written by Dostoevsky was *Poor people*. Melville did not write anything particularly about poverty, but he had to borrow large sums of money from relatives after *Moby-Dick* commercially failed. **As I explained in Chapter 2, things could have been a little easier for them if they did not produce a lot of kids from the start.** It must have been hard for those innocent children as well.

I assume these writers must have had a tough time squeezing income out of writing, especially when they were not famous. As a starter, I was just curious how those writers felt about their situations and handled those issues. And I learned that Dostoevsky lived his life in a little more dangerous way than other writers.

* * *

Fyodor Dostoevsky (1821-1881) was born in a poor family in Russia in the 19th century and died only when he was fifty-nine years old. He was the second child out of seven children his parents had. And unfortunately both of his parents passed away by the time he was 18. Just curious, but isn't it common sense that he needed to live a little more carefully as an orphan without a parent? Strangely, he did exactly the opposite: He had lived recklessly throughout his life after those funerals. I am not just talking about drinking, smoking or gambling which he had done continuously. He had a whole new level of problem than others; **this guy was *sentenced to death* for going against the Tsar (Russian King) when he was twenty-seven.**

It shows that Dostoevsky was involved in anti-government (tsar) activity and spent eight months in jail before being scheduled to be shot to death in December, 1849. **The penalty did not proceed luckily since he was forgiven at the very last moment** (mocking execution). He survived the penalty and wrote about this experience in his book titled *Idiots*. Still, he had to spend four years in Siberian prison and five years in extra army service instead of getting a longer prison term (totally nine years for that anti-tsar charge). Surprisingly, all these happened after he finished three years of mandatory army service as a lieutenant officer in his early 20s.

So when I calculated it, it seems he had spent more than twelve years out of fifty-nine years of his life in the army service or prison. According to my experience, army service was like a mild form of prison. I think that the 12-years was a long confinement considering being against the Tsar is not exactly an offensive crime (it may be a political crime, which is not a crime at all depending on situations).

On top of these, Dostoevsky had four kids with two or three women and two of them died at an early age. He was a heavy gambler, drinker and smoker throughout his life. So now I am not sure of the reason why he had lived a miserable life: Was he just unlucky or did he carry plenty of bad habits to be broke mandatorily? Obviously, he was a prolific writer, so if he had lived with a little more caution, I think that he could have lived a bit easier and probably longer.

* * *

I wonder if the opposite example of Dostoevsky can be Tolstoy (1828-1910); both of these are Russian writers born in the early 19th century in common. I know Tolstoy had thirteen kids with one wife, but I do not see any prison sentence, gambling or divorce record of Tolstoy on Wikipedia. He might have met a wife like an angel. Or he just managed his life and marriage very well, so he did not get a divorce. As soon as I saw the portrait of Tolstoy, honestly I felt much more peace from him than Dostoevsky. **Apparently, Tolstoy had lived a quiet life in the countryside and died at the age of eighty-two**: That was twenty three-years longer than that of Dostoevsky, regardless.

I believe we make our life ourselves and decide our destinies on our own: **This trend gets stronger as we get older.** When we are only ten years old, our parents' situation can decide our lives. But, when we are fifty, whether we drink tonight or not can decide our incomes two weeks later (I used to get paid every two weeks). It is a big misconception that someone else decides our fates somehow: This is a big misunderstanding; this is not going to happen even to sons of rich people.

My father is quite wealthy, but I have received a good amount of money from him only after I bought my condo with full cash in 2013. He was impressed with how I got this unit at such a low price. Maybe he felt I won't lose his money at least. We have to earn our trust and accumulate our credit even for our parents. I admit that it is a great opportunity to have a wealthy parent to begin with, but I don't think that inheritance happens automatically unless we are an only child. We have to work for it: We have to prove ourselves one way or another.

* * *

Summary

1. Being boisterous makes us unsuccessful.
2. Some people are financially poor since they live dangerously.
3. Being direct or daring is not always good.

28

Preventable Medical Problems

Smart people solve problems;
geniuses prevent them.
-Brad Kong

I personally think these people making and selling candies are true criminals against humanity: The companies making and selling chocolates, liquid candies (sodas), sweet fruits, cakes, cotton candies, etc. **Did you know that alcohol and sugar share very similar chemical structures?**

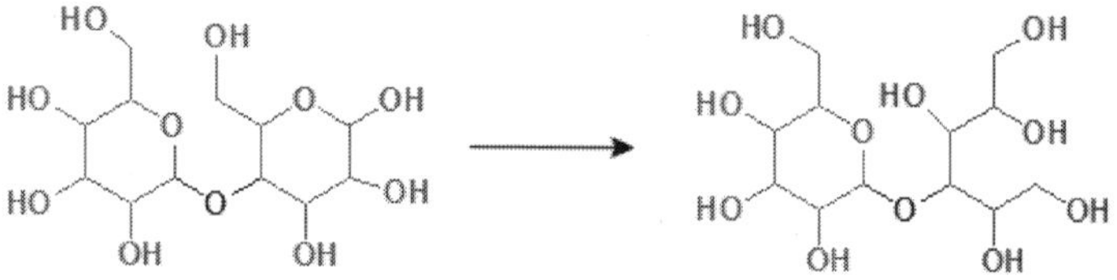

maltose (sugar) ⟶ maltitol (sugar-O-sugar alcohol)

Yet alcohol is restricted in a lot of communities; also people know that it is no good thing to our body by taste, instinctively. Personally, I have been a nondrinker purely because I do not like the bitter taste. But, in the case of *sugar*, most children do not know how *harmful* it is on our teeth and bodies: They just eat sweet stuff since it tastes good. **Mass productions of sugary stuff are the worst thing we can do for our children.**

I had my root canal infection when I was 45 years old in 2018. I had an unimaginable pain suddenly while I was eating my fruit lunch one day; most people describe that tooth infection is the biggest pain they have ever been through in their lives. My friend Frank also said, "It hurt like hell." If anyone saw me on that day, he or she might think I was crazy: **I just didn't know what to do to get out of the pain in my molar and jaw.** I went to the bathroom and kept squishing my mouth with warm water for 20 minutes and it went away finally.

Quite frankly, I have spent most of my life without knowing how painful a toothache can be really like. I thought a tooth is like a kind of stone (calcium deposits) without a nerve and it is ok to eat as many chocolate bars as I want as long as I brush my teeth everyday: This is why these sweets are sold everywhere, people eat them all the time. My parents also bought those for me when I was a kid; everyone has that, right? If manufacturers knew all about those pains and damages on bodies and still make them for money, they are definitely criminals: This is a shame. **Not eating sugar can save us tons of money out of medical bills.** For your information, I used to own Coca cola stock, but I sold all the shares long ago.

* * *

I think one of the most common wastes on dental issues could be the dental implants: these will be extremely useful for missing teeth in visible locations. But many dentists just recommend implants no matter what or even for trivial reasons since these are highly expensive and *profitable.*

Finally, I lost the molar tooth I had crowned on by extraction in September, 2022. I mentioned that many times in this series, but I had struggled to save it in the last four years. This is the only tooth I have lost out of 28 at the age of 49 by 2022; I will do my best to make sure this won't happen again; it was just too late to revive it to begin with. I was stupid to mistreat it for over the last 35 years. Yet, when I checked Quora to see if a molar dental implant is needed, this is what I found: **No medical reason at all to have the missing premolar replaced by implants.** It seems implants are pretty much for cosmetics.

I already mentioned this and I have lost two huge amounts of money on medical bills so far: Kidney stone (2008) and root canal infection (2019). I worked in my own business back then in 2008. After being in the emergency room for the stone, I removed all the soda from the store cooler and filled it up only with bottles of water. I would say that I have drunk only water for my liquid since 2008. I didn't think this way at that time, but it must have been helpful for my teeth as well: Water washes out sugars from teeth greatly. Still, I had a tooth infection in 2019 even after drinking water only for 11 years then. I think I should have cut out sugar and carbohydrates aggressively since only drinking water was not enough for decay prevention. I have taken care of my teeth more than a reasonable level in the last 49 years, but it has not been enough as well. **I believe controlling my diet is the only way and it may save me tons of money from now on.**

* * *

In real life, I think the surest way we can save tons of money from medical bills is done by taking care of our teeth. Let me give you a more specific example of how much with actual numbers.

As I mentioned, I had problems with only one tooth called "the left lower molar" in the past four years since 2018. I think I have spent at least $2,600 on that particular tooth from 2018 till 2022: X-ray twice ($200), Inlay crown ($2,200, 2018) and finally extraction ($200, 2022). Now I do not have the tooth any more. However, if I decide to have an implant on that gum space since my molar is gone, it will be another $3,000 at least (totally $5,600 only on one tooth): **The issue is that I still have 27 other teeth left in my mouth.**

Drinking only water for life and getting rid of sugary stuff completely are priceless life strategies: I know we may find we cannot eat 70% of the food we used to eat this way. Still, what's the point of eating unhealthy foods only to get fat? Only eating food good for teeth can save us not only from huge medical bills, but also from incredible amounts of pain. How can a dentist charge a huge bill? It's because customers are willing to pay. Why? **Root canal infections hurt like hell.**

Some may think daily brushing and flossing could be enough; they were not in my case. I have reached the conclusion that I have to get rid of sugars completely to save my other 27 teeth. I think being interested in health issues and reading health related books can save us tons of money literally. **I found out that many diseases are chronic nowadays and preventable.**

* * *

I think there are three things we need to do on a daily basis to be healthy: eating small, sleeping a lot and taking extra care of our teeth. When we focus on keeping our teeth clean, we will see that we get healthier throughout our bodies in general. There are three things we must do to keep our teeth clean everyday: brushing, flossing and oil pulling. **We should consider losing a tooth is like losing an arm.** I recommend doing intermittent fasting for our teeth on a weekly basis as well (no eating two days a week can be ideal). Regardless, I think that not eating anything 12 hours a day (including overnight) truly helps our health overall; this should be easy since 8 out of those 12 hours would be sleeping.

Food wise, I think the Thai are the worst for teeth (among the foods I am willing to eat). I heard some Middle Eastern desserts like Baklava have lots of sugar, but I just do not eat those. Thai put sugar directly in Pad Thai, for example, which is unusual for everyday meals in other countries.

Processed foods in Mexican supermarkets (e.g., Cermack) are terrible for teeth, too; they put too much sugar even in drinkable yogurt as well (some people choose kefir or drinkable yogurt to cure teeth, but it does work that way with Mexican yogurt brands like Lala). Have you been to a Mexican supermarket yourself before? Commonly, I notice that these have more sugary stuff than any other markets in the world; grocery shopping in Latin supermarkets must be avoided if that's possible. Korean and Chinese foods are not really beneficial as well. I think Indian foods are relatively safer for teeth. I learned that Chai tea especially has a lot of ingredients that kill tooth bacteria: cinnamon, ginger, clover, etc. **Japanese foods are not particularly good for teeth as well, but their nattō and miso soups are excellent for tooth cure.**

* * *

I think there are three guaranteed ways to live a happy life: Being satisfied with what we have, accepting who we are, and having easily achievable goals. **For example, can**

I just be happy with the fact that I am alive now? It doesn't matter how much money I have; I am tired of pushing myself to be a millionaire. Why do I need more money, anyway? Only to satisfy my ego? So I can feel that I am better than others? If I forget about keeping superior feelings today, maybe I can be a happy person at least today. There are plenty of people who pass away before they become 49 years old; some become disabled before reaching my age, too. Some can lose more than one tooth at least, which didn't happen to me luckily.

As far as goals go, I like to have something other than money as well: I think I can try to live until I become 100; preferably, I like to walk on my own until I die; I like to keep all my natural teeth in healthy condition as well. I used to have less than $500,000 in my stock portfolio. Now I have more than $560,000 including savings by 2022. But it hadn't made me excited for more than a few months. I still look for discounted sushi at the supermarket even with all that money. Will I be much happier if I have $ 1M? **Probably only for a few months.** I like to be satisfied with little different accomplishments I have made so far: For example, I have a wife and child. Some people have never been married or even dated for life. I have seen some Korean lady trolls lately, and I don't think these single women will ever have a chance to meet a decent guy (they are too old single women to begin with).

* * *

The dental mold in my molar came out when I chewed gum the other day in Sept, 2022; I immediately thought that the Indian lady dentist deceived me in 2019. I paid close to $3,000 in cash since she said it was a crown procedure on my tooth; it was supposed to be less than $1,000 if it was just a molding procedure. Regardless of the costs, she just did not do her job very well. The old mold on a different tooth I got from Korea came out after having it for over 25 years; it is supposed to go for a lifetime. This inlay crown I got from her only has stayed in the tooth for less than 3 years. **I believe a lot of overcharges happen particularly in the dental businesses out of all the hospitals.**

I read a few books and countless web articles regarding dentistry after spending $3,000 for diverse services in 2019. To be fair, I would say that the Indian lady's deep cleaning ($800) was good. Still, here is what I found: There is *no real cure* in dental offices; all they do is basically the cleaning and cosmetic changes. **I concluded that the only way to prevent decay is not eating sugars and carbohydrates to begin with**; that does not guarantee perfect teeth, but that is certainly the basic. My diet has changed greatly and the only liquid I am drinking is strictly water (H2O) since then; I check sugar contents first before buying any food and often not buy it if it has some sugar. Also I started eating omelets, kefirs, cheese and Nattos more than ever since these are good for teeth; I have never tried kefirs or Nattos before 2018. Coincidently, this habit has been great for weight loss and diabetes cure as well.

* * *

It is important to keep our health in good condition, so we do not have to spend extra money in hospitals; it shows that medical bills are the number one reason why people go bankrupt in America. **The most undervalued factor for good health is having enough sleep in my opinion.** People do not realize how crucial it is only because we do it every single day; it is the same way we do not recognize how important air is.

There are a few things that disturb good night sleep: Certainly, we may need a quiet house and a firm bed. Smartphones or physical pain can disturb sleep. **Above all, I think that it is important not to have anything to worry about**; people wake up in the middle of night for that. Just try not to have any type of debt including a mortgage. Also, I think we should not go greedy for anything if it can bring us something to worry about unnecessarily.

I suggest people sleep a lot instead of doing anything else; it is not wise trying other hobbies while we do not get more than enough sleep. **Some scientists suggest that less sleep can induce dementia or Alzheimer's disease later in our life**: They talk about complete memory loss including our names; I know a couple of examples.

Margaret Thatcher was the former Prime Minister of the United Kingdom. She was the most famous short sleeper as far as I know; the record shows that she slept about four hours a day. She suffered from dementia and stroke for about 10 years before she passed away at the age of 87 in 2013.

Johnny Yune must be the most successful Korean comedian in North America; his net worth was about $15 M by the time he passed away in 2020. I watched his show a few times (similar to the Tonight show in Korean version), and he often joked that he couldn't not sleep for many hours since he had to work to death in the beginning of his immigration. He said people often asked him "Johnny?", which means "sleeping?" in Korean. I thought it was just a joke since many old Koreans tend to exaggerate their hardships: It was not. He was diagnosed with dementia in 2017 and the news shows that he could not even remember his own name before he died; I believe this is a particularly severe case even among the patients. **I think sleeping a lot now is important since some consequences come decades later.**

Secondly, taking care of vision and teeth also saves a lot of money; Personally, I have wasted tons of money for glasses and contact lenses in the last thirty years. Lately, I spend a good amount of time taking care of my teeth every day.

* * *

Men like pretty women, but I don't think they ever like a woman who had cosmetic surgery: Men like naturally beautiful women and I believe women know it already. Therefore, when they get plastic surgeries, I heard that those Korean women preferentially look for surgeons who can perform the procedure without leaving any noticeable marks: **They want to look naturally pretty and pretend they never got it;** they also decline the fact that they had surgeries if someone asks about it. This is not only deceptive, but also pathetic: I would say it's just sad.

Having plastic surgery is dangerous for women by itself: Every surgery is dangerous, in fact. Some ladies not only spend a lot of money on surgeries and take the risks, but also they have to hide the fact that they had them. I mean, how low can they go? Why do they have to sacrifice that much? Because they are super ugly from birth? Or do they care for other people's eyes too much? Or they have never gotten any attention from men before? None of these seem to give me a positive feeling: If possible, just stay away from these women; don't get too close. I honestly do not like "super-incompetent" women (not this much). The top class of women I will never date would be the ones having cosmetic surgery before. **These types of women often have vain, too.** If a man marries one of these, he will be more likely a human ATM for her lavish lifestyle until he gets a divorce.

While plastic surgeries on the face are popular among Korean women, it seems those on the body are more popular among American and Mexican women. It shows that breast augmentation is the most popular procedure in America. **If a woman gets breasts by surgery, what is the difference between a man and woman?** I heard the silicones for those augmentations are pretty toxic; reports show that some women fainted for no apparent reason and found out that they had fungus on those silicones in their bodies. I would never try this kind of thing if I were a woman: for my body and money.

The most ridiculous plastic surgery I have witnessed was that of a Mexican young lady who got buttocks augmentation. I actually saw this on TV twenty years ago (probably in 2003) and still cannot forget. The doctor asked her to be careful whenever she sits since the silicones can *burst*. **I wondered why she got this since every woman will eventually have fat butts, anyway**; at least, my grandma had big butts. And, it is such a turn off for me: I do not think I get attracted to a fat woman to begin with. Why would I like a girl with fat butts? Are Latinos very different from me? After surgery, I saw that she ran to a bar with friends. I wondered why life seems to be so easy for some people though her family did not look that wealthy.

I included stories about cosmetic surgeries in this chapter since these look like the most unnecessary, but expensive medical procedures in my opinion. **More than half of plastic surgeries seem to be failures from my perspective:** I hardly see a woman who looks much prettier after those. Occasionally, they look worse than before; I am not talking about long term side effects. I believe many of the procedures are just wrongfully done to begin with.

* * *

Some people say that hospital bills are too expensive in America: They are wrong. These are actually expensive in every country in the world. I do not believe there is any country providing quality healthcare at low price; most likely it is not quality care if it is provided for free or at low costs. One example is free healthcare in Canada; I heard that old people die even in the hospital aisle while they are waiting for a doctor; some get only a couple of Tylenols after eight hours waiting. It seems it is the same as not having a hospital at all in Canada: **If it is free, it is never a quality one.**

I was in the emergency room at a big hospital in Naperville, IL in 2008: I did not know it was a kidney stone. The pain was incredible, so I thought it was something more serious. I stayed there only for five hours, had a couple of CT scans to detect a kidney stone and got Vicodin, a pain reliever and water: **These cost me $5,500 total after all, then.**

It was an unnecessary big spending, especially when I struggled for my business rents at that time. **I had to pay up to three different rents for six months at that time**: my store rent, apartment rent and my wife's apartment rent in 2008. Soon, she and I found one small one-bedroom apartment near my store and moved in together, so three rents became two in 2009: one apartment and one store rent. Still I had to pay these two rents for eight years and three months back then (from 2006 to 2014).

* * *

No wonder I still had trauma about paying rent. Although I had paid the big store rent for 8 years, **I had paid all sorts of rent from 1992 till 2013**: I moved out of my parents' home originally to go to college in 1992. But I have never moved back after that for diverse reasons: college, army service, immigration, universities, starting my business, getting hired, having my own family, etc. Luckily, I bought my condo out with full cash, so rent had been gone for good out of my life since 2013. So, basically, I had paid rent for 16 years in my 20s and 30s except for the army service. And this was my calculation:

"Let's suppose that I live until I become 100 years old. I have lived in my parents house for the first 20 years of my life rent free. And I paid rent for the next 20 years (except the military service). Then I bought my condo completely with full cash when I was forty in 2013. If I can live without a rent or mortgage for the next 60 years, that is not bad: **I only paid rent during the 20 years of my life out of 100.**"

I am glad that I did not go up to the point of paying a mortgage. Technically, there is nothing wrong with paying for it, but there is one Korean troll guy who does not know what shame is (he's always on a Korean website). He never wrote a constructive article, but always writes nasty comments on other people's postings: **Coincidentally, he has a *huge* mortgage.** My hatred about the mortgage has started and grown mainly because of him I believe. Maybe this is a good thing since a mortgage is not necessarily beneficial for personal finance.

Anyway, I had changed all my diet including quitting soda permanently after the emergency room visit in 2008; I did not know I could lose a surprising amount of weight only to cut out sweet drinks. As I described, I removed all the drinks in our store cooler and filled it with water only after that happened.

* * *

Summary

1. Medical bills are the number one reason for personal financial bankruptcy.
2. A lot of diseases are preventable nowadays.
3. Drink water only and eat small.

29

Unnecessary Legal Problems

Some lawyers just want to make money out of others' trouble.
-Brad Kong

O. J. Simpson is an American former football player, actor, and broadcaster: He was one of the top stars in America, especially during the 1970s; he had been my hero for a long time. It shows that his maximum net worth was over $10 Million in the 1990s (about $20 Million value in 2022), but it is estimated at just $3 Million as of Dec, 2022. Most of us probably have heard of his trial, but that was not all the cases he has been related to. Unfortunately, he was involved in tax fraud with the IRS and armed robbery in Las Vegas, subsequently. I cannot mention all, but it seems he has had diverse types of legal troubles with law enforcement every few years continually. I have to confess that he used to be my favorite football player, so it's sad for me to observe all these over the course of decades.

* * *

I concluded that we do not have to take revenge on anyone. Sometimes, we see people we really don't like. Occasionally, we cannot forget some of them and think about getting revenge on them. Trust me: We don't have to do that. **If anyone was very unpleasant to us, most likely the person lives a miserable life by now.** Why?

The person must be more than annoying to others, too. Let me give you some examples.

When I was in Cornell university in 1999, I didn't like one of my roommates in a shared apartment. All three were not that great, but one particular black guy named Ron from the Caribbean was the worst; I remember that he was more rude than the average African American I see in America. No race issue here, but I think he is a genuinely bad person regardless of his nationality. Lately, I checked his name on Facebook and learned that he was divorced. **I certainly did not like him and it seems his wife didn't, either.** Probably he's paying alimony pointlessly now. I didn't have to take revenge on him: he screwed himself. And he will keep doing that until he dies.

When I was working in that nursing home, I particularly didn't like a woman cook. She was half Mexican and Cuban or something, but very rude to all the dishwashers in the kitchen of the nursing home. As I described in Chapter 2, she was a single mom with three kids back then. She kept making a lot of troubles at work and eventually got fired from the work by 2019. When I checked her Facebook lately, I saw that she was taking care of two more babies who look similar to her. **To me, she has ruined her life big time**: Now she has five kids from three different men and no man is staying with her. This woman screwed herself completely. As a father myself, honestly, I don't want to support five kids since it will be very stressful. No need to get revenge on anyone, again: I am sure she will never stop ruining herself on her own until the moment she dies.

There are Korean internet trolls going against my frugal lifestyle on a website. The best revenge is letting them live as they have: These rent, mortgage, car loans or other debts they have will ruin their lives. I will keep living frugally and letting my overhead be small, so I don't have to get back to being offended in the working places again.

I think one of the biggest wastes in our lives is lawyer fees caused by any legal dispute. I still remember I paid a $3,500 lawyer fee around 2001 (this would be like $7,000 in 2022). I prefer not to talk about it in detail now, but it was definitely an unnecessary loss, especially when I was pretty much broke at that time.

* * *

I don't think smart people get into trouble; they know it costs money being in trouble, so they tend not to commit anything against the law from the start. Stupid people not only get into trouble, but tend to get caught easily, too. One of the examples was George Floyd, honestly. I know some people are trying to describe him as a scapegoat from judgmental society or even worship him as a hero: This is a sort of nonsense in my opinion. Did you know that he had been arrested 11 times, convicted of 8 crimes and spent more than 5 years in prison? He died right after using a fake bill, which is another federal crime. Some people said the police officers planted a fake bill to cover their crime in Quora, but I think these people are crazy. Why would officers choose an extremely tall (6′ 4″) black guy only to bully on. I am not saying that he deserved to be dead, but he was not completely innocent as protesters claimed, either. He ain't no Jesus Christ and it is nonsense to praise him beyond a reasonable level. **There are plenty of African Americans working hard in unfair conditions.** I would say my friend E (his name is Erskine, but everyone calls him E) is 10,000 times better than Floyd. Regardless, I would say that having frequent trouble with law enforcement will make us poor.

Another example of people who went bankrupt because of legal troubles could be Giacomo Casanova (1725 – 1798); as you may have heard of him already, he was a famous Venetian adventurer and author in Italy in the 18th century. Probably, I think most of us know him as a famous playboy back then. Yet, did you know that he was sentenced for 5 years in prison and spent 15 months in a dungeon for a sexual crime? He had kept having similar problems throughout his life and had to move from one country to another to escape charges until he died at the age of 73.

This guy must have been a genius to get a doctor's degree at University of Padua when he was only 17. He had made a good fortune a couple of times, but spent it all for women, prostitution, etc. He had been in jail a few times additionally since he was not able to pay some debts (debt prisons were common at that time). He got Syphilis, so he became sexually inactive after mid-40s. He died penniless without having a family in Duchcov, Czech. Getting involved in a legal problem does not really help anyone including the plaintiff, sometimes; still, it would be especially bad for the offender. Let me give you just one more example of a rich man who went down because of a crime.

* * *

There is a person named Bikram Choudhury, who is the founder of *Bikram* Yoga. It shows that Bikram Yoga is everywhere in America and most parts of the Western world, reaching a peak of 1,650 studios in more than 40 countries by 2006; Choudhury's net worth was estimated to be up to $75 Million because his highest salary was $10 M a year by 2006.

Unfortunately, it shows that this Bikram guy has not been in America since 2017; I would say that it is like he has lost his entire $75 M basically since his business foundation has been in America. By January, 2014, five women had sued him with allegations including sexual harassment and assault; he eventually lost $7 M for fine in the courts and decided to return to India forever to avoid more charges. In October 2016, Choudhury's attorney stated that he would not return to the United States to defend himself at the other pending court cases. **This is ridiculous to lose the entire life savings for little things**; maybe, these are not little, but he should have controlled his desire a little bit before being kicked out of America. One film shows that he used to live in Beverly Hills, CA; I hope he enjoys warm weather in Calcutta, India, where he was originally from; the city is one of the worst parts in India near Bangladesh, just for your information.

* * *

I think only stupid people commit a crime; smart people already know that there is no real way we can escape from it. **Often, the action of committing crime does not benefit us to begin with.** Let's take drug addiction for instance (let's not talk about painkiller addiction from hospitals for now). Taking drugs is a legal crime, but even if not, it will not benefit us much health wise. It is not even free. It is total nonsense for smart people if someone tries that from the start.

I think it was 2001 when I had a legal problem for the first time in my life. I hope it will be the last time since nothing has happened in the last twenty-two years after that. I was still a student at Buffalo, NY in 2001. Maybe I will talk about this later as time goes on.

* * *

You know what, though? **When I think about it, the most effective way to decrease the crime rate in a society is lowering the unemployment rate.** I had a job at the banquet on the college campus at that time. For some reason, they have never given me enough hours for months. Actually, they never gave me any hours at all during the whole winter vacation. I was still in my 20s and eager to make some money to support myself. I remember I tried to study over the winter. Still, I had too much time to kill while my bank account was getting empty. If I was busy with some jobs or lived with my family, nothing would have happened.

Now jobs are available everywhere due to the Pandemic in 2022: "Help wanted" signs everywhere for now. I am pretty sure the crime rate will go down as well: People do not have much time to think about committing a crime when they are busy with jobs. It sounds ridiculous, but people actually need some free time to do that. Besides, when they have enough money coming in as a wage, there is no reason to try anything else to make money: I think that crime usually happens when people have too much time to goof around, but no money in their pocket. **I believe nothing is more important than lowering the unemployment rate as far as social safety goes.**

* * *

Anyway, I ended up spending $3,500 for a lawyer fee and $125 for a court charge in 2001. This amount could be about $6,000 value in 2022 after inflation, which is a huge loss. The ridiculous thing was that the court did not give me any fine: **They disregarded the entire case only with a court fee ($125 then), but the lawyer fee was huge.** I guess it was a total waste of money. I know the lawyer we hired did not do much in this particular case. Not violating any law or even not getting close to the point to see whether we violate or not will save us a lot of money.

A lot of people assume that lawyers are good people and try to help innocent people accused wrongfully: Nothing can be further from the truth. In real life, probably those people who got charged may not necessarily be innocent from the start. And a lot of private lawyers try to take advantage of their situations as opportunities to make money. I am pretty sure some lawyers are good people, but I did not have a good experience myself with one. I would say this lawyer named Mark did not do anything and took my $3,500 for nothing. It was my fault to cause any trouble to begin with, but I will remember that this has been one of the most ridiculous ways to waste money for my whole life. Getting a lawyer is simply a financial punishment itself in a sense. Maybe that is how the legal system works: **We get punished financially for causing any trouble somehow**.

There are a lot of reasons why hard workers are broke in spite of working full-time. But, I could find so many examples that some people stay in the low income class because they keep causing legal troubles. I heard that OJ Simpson had lost almost $10 million only for lawyer fees in the case. In extreme cases, I heard some people lose most of their life savings for legal defenses. I feel sorry if a legal situation happens for inevitable reasons we cannot control. But, in my opinion, a lot of disputes or crimes happen because of greed. I believe a lot of conflicts can be resolved before they go up to a court if we are more considerate and less greedy. **And *not having a legal problem* is not just about money.** I think I visited the small town court three times in 2001 and I had felt nervous and stressed out all the way over the course of six months. Worrying about a case had been a waste of time and energy as well.

* * *

Today I suddenly got a letter from the State unemployment office saying that I have to pay them $1,200 back since my *unemployment case* cannot be qualified for "laid off". This is not exactly a legal case, but I guess people can go to jail if they don't pay the office quickly: **Which is the reason why I paid them immediately this afternoon.**

Initially, I applied for unemployment benefits only because the HR from the nursing home sent me the information package right after I resigned from that job. I didn't even know there was such a thing called unemployment benefit in the beginning. Anyway, the State approved it after my filing and I got $1,200 in the last month in May, 2022. Originally, I applied for a "laid off" case since a new company called Morrison came and took over our dining department. I was blocked from being transferred to the new job (which I am glad about, so I finally became a full time writer as I have a lot of investment incomes). But suddenly IDES sent me a letter that I am not qualified and have to recoup the money today; I sent them a $1,200 check right away. **If I delay repaying, the amount will only get bigger.**

Still when I think about the State benefits, I feel Illinois State is a little too stingy. I have paid Illinois State tax without any problem in the last sixteen years. They obviously know that I had worked at the nursing home for seven years and the stated job was dishwasher (a merger wage job in general). They cannot let a retired dishwasher keep $1,200 when the person is resigned by the condition he couldn't control? Should I really have to pay it back today? I already paid $1,500 State tax only for the last year (2021). **I think they are very stingy**; these people will never give anything for free.

* * *

In my opinion, one of the legal ways to fight high tax and government stinginess is living in a smaller house. The property tax rate in Illinois State is the second highest in the nation next to New Jersey. I know a lot of single family homes pay $10,000 property tax a year in and around my town. **But, strangely, when it goes to townhouses or condos, suddenly property taxes drop significantly.** I personally have paid $1,700 a year for a one-bedroom condo in the past few years: That is like I am saving $8,700 a year out of property taxes legally. It can be over $500,000 tax savings in the next fifty years.

I do not have a car now, but I think I had been in traffic courts about five times when I had them for eighteen years (1999-2017): three times for high speed, one time for a stop sign violation, etc. The total fines accumulated were probably over $500 by 2017. Besides, I had to pay for parking tickets at least 5 times if not more: The total might have been over $300. **All had been a waste of money**; I wish I had this $800 in my pocket now.

Some people get DUI violations or car accidents, so fines can be much higher in those cases: It shows that DUI violation penalties start up to $2,500 in Illinois. I think avoiding those legal issues can be one way to save money. We have plenty of things to talk about, so we can move onto the next reason that causes poverty for now.

* * *

Summary

1. Getting along with others and avoiding troubles saves a lot of money.
2. Committing a crime can be a reason to be poor.
3. Drug related crimes are more stupid than others in a financial sense. Drug addicts spend money on buying drugs first and pay more on legal fees after getting caught: Double whammy. Some thieves at least try to make some money, but those addicts don't make any profit out of anything.

30

Talking Too Much

Speaking one less word can save our lives.
-Brad Kong

Noise pollution is everywhere nowadays: I cannot find silence anywhere except my home. There is one girl talking continuously in the library: Brainless. I mean I usually go to the library in the morning since there aren't many people during that time, but one computer assistant girl keeps talking. She is not very loud, but her voice is very annoying. I really wonder how some people can keep moving their mouths nonstop for hours like this. Certainly, that's impossible for me.

And I am glad my wife and daughter don't do that: They talk only when there is a reason, which is fairly normal I thought in the beginning: **I just didn't know that it's such a blessing until I met some people, especially women, outside my own family.** I have never heard any man say that, "I love the girl since she is talkative." Quite the opposite is true in real life.

I quit the weekend nursing home job in April, 2022 since I did not like one *sous chef* there. He talked too much and interrupted others whenever he liked: **No one liked him.** He said his family had been on food stamps before he got that manager job (sous chef job is not a big deal in common sense, but still a manager in that kitchen). Stupidly, the first thing he did after getting that miserable job was leasing a Lexus with a car loan. I got a gut feeling that he will probably be poor for the rest of his life despite working day and night.

I think fasting from talking could be more important than fasting from eating. It will make our lives quieter and simpler: **A mute never creates an enemy.** When things do not go very well, I think we should live without speaking for a while.

* * *

It shows that the Sun King in France, Louis XIV (14th, 1638 - 1715) was a very quiet person: **A man of few words.** He was the most powerful king throughout French history ruling for 72 years; I think that this is the longest in any regime; he had the Palace of Versailles built for himself.

It shows that he usually listened to his officials completely, and often said only one word, "I shall see[40]." Then, he walked away; the ministers and courtiers would never hear a word from him after that, but only see a result by his action afterward. The author Greene suggests that not letting people know our intention or thought by speaking less gives us power in his book *The 48 Rules of Power*. **He mentioned that Louis's silence kept those around him terrified and under his thumb.** This book shows one more story about someone who died for not being silent in Russia.

* * *

When a new czar named Nicholas I ascended the throne of Russia in 1825, rebellion broke out immediately and they

[40] In modern English, this can be translated into "Let me think about it."

demanded modernization of Russia in the 19th century. The leader of the rebellion is a poet named Ryleyev; sorrowfully, he was caught by the Russian army and sentenced to death in 1826. On the day of execution, it shows that Ryleyev was hanged, but fortunately, the rope around his neck broke, so he saved his life (actually, it says three out of five prisoners saved their lives due to broken ropes on that day). And this is what he said: "The czar doesn't even know how to make a rope properly."

At that time, it was a common practice to pardon a prisoner who saved his life somehow only because execution went wrong; they believe it's a sign from heaven to save this person. Before signing the pardon paper, the czar asked one question.

> Nicholas I: Did Ryleyev say anything after this miracle?
> The messenger: He said, "People in Russia don't even know how to make a rope properly nowadays."
> Nicholas I: In that case, let us prove the country.

Ryleyev was hanged again and died the next day. This is just one example, but I had countless moments myself saying something unnecessary, making things awkward and regretting it. When I think about it, surprisingly, there is almost no moment to regret not saying a thing in the past 49 years. **If we feel wondering whether we have to say a thing or not, I concluded that it's *always* better for us not to say.** Unless you are sure, just don't say it.

* * *

I notice that speaking less and eating less are the common traits among the monarchs staying in the position for long. I already mentioned that Louis XIV was known as a silent man who had reigned France for 72 years (this is the longest).

There was a king named Youngjo in the Joseon dynasty in Korea in the 17th century: **the king was well-known for eating small and not eating meat**; he reigned the country for 52 years (the longest in Korea). He also died when he was 82 years old; he was considered a person living surprisingly for a long time in 1776 (about 110 in 2022) since Louis XIV died only when he was 76. In a sense, living longer means hurting more animals; we eat more lives as a result. I wonder if we tend to live longer when we don't hurt other animals; this includes becoming a vegetarian.

Queen Elizabeth II has also been in position for 70 years since she passed away at the age of 96 in 2022; she had been well-known for frugal spending and lifestyle. **It seems to me that all those things like speaking too much, eating too much or spending too much are from greed.** I conclude that we should not be greedy to maintain our wealth for long.

* * *

I noticed that there is one common characteristic among those people who have worked only for dishwashing over 30 years: **They talk *unnecessarily* a lot.** I had always felt that they talk way more than cooks or chefs.

As I mentioned, I had been a weekend dishwasher close to 7 years and that's what I had observed. Also, one of them used a cell phone to talk more; just killing time on excessive talking seems to be their daily routine. **I eventually concluded that moving their mouths without having a point is a lifelong habit for losers.** I saw one poor old Mexican guy sitting in the middle of the library the other day; he talked on the phone and it was bothering everyone. These types of people never look for a book to get better even in the middle of a library; talking, talking and talking only while surrounded by plenty of books. In a way, his life is already over and he will continue his low income job until he dies.

All religions, including Buddhism, Christianity and Catholicism, have a fasting and silence period on each own; they do not talk or eat for a while. I am not a religious person, but I always try to get those habits; I am relatively skinny, but I am trying to lose weight even more. **Taking too much is often a waste, and words can cause trouble.** If we are serious about getting out of our current hardship, I think the first thing we should do is talk only when it is necessary; this is especially true for men. When people talk, they stop thinking and moving. **Words are tools, not toys, especially when we are at work.**

Only a few people know how to control their mouths; most people just make noise with their voices. **Moving mouths without thinking not only can make people poor, but also can put them in danger.** Knowing how to close our mouths could be the most important skill in our lives.

* * *

There used to be a time when being careful with our mouths was enough. If we did not talk, nothing would cause trouble. At least, that happened before the invention of a letter, which is about 4,000 years ago.

But now it is the digital age. We have to be careful with our fingers as well. **Not only speaking, we have to be careful with our writing and photos.** Luckily, I have never posted my bare face photo in public, including this book (I have posted only one photo with a mask on by 2022). My wife and daughter do not have social media accounts, thankfully. But I used to write a lot of articles online and something happened to me in 2009. *Let me tell you about my story*. This may be long, so bear with me for a while.

* * *

There is one popular web community site called "Dcinside" in South Korea: Digital Camera Inside. It is very similar to "Reddit" in America except that everyone should post one photo first to write an article. The popularity of the site is so big that it has 200 Million visits a day. It is considered an underground site with hundreds of message boards divided by topics. They call the message boards "galleries" since it started out as a digital photo posting site.

I used to go to "small business" gallery since I was a small business owner (2006-2014) in 2009: *Cyb Knight* video game store. I wrote a lot of articles regarding how to improve the small business success rate. When I think about it now, I have been interested in "how to improve money situations" for a long time. And I had been stupid since I wrote precious articles for free for too long. If I knew more about self-publishing in 2009, I would have published ten books by now in 2022.

The biggest problem was low quality young people gathering on that site. High unemployment rate was a serious problem in Korea by 2009. Still, the same problem persists, but relieved a little bit only because of tragedies that happened due to Coronavirus. In particular, I remember that a lot of young people could not get a job around 2009. Basically, they gave up finding a job, getting married or buying a house: "Giving up the big three" was the major keyword in that society, then. They were frustrated and angry. Not everyone was like that, but a large number of those people were like that.

* * *

I think South Korea is a hellish country to live in by nature. The territory size is as small as Indiana State in America. It is like an island since the whole country is blocked by seas and North Korea. And 70% of the region are high mountains, so the space people can live on is very limited. Conclusively, 52 million South Koreans are trapped in a very small space. **There is no single family house in South Korea any more.** The space is so limited that everyone lives in sky scraping condos or any type of multi-units regardless if people are wealthy or poor. It has been a very stressful and crowded environment from the beginning.

On top of that, the country does not have many natural resources like oil. To make things worse, the political situation is bad. The country is surrounded by big and aggressive neighbors: China, Japan, Russia and North Korea. I was raised on the 13th floor of a tall condo while I was a teenager and never liked it. I learned that I have acrophobia later on.

* * *

I started to write about my business and what we can do to improve a small business from 2008. That was about two years after I started my business in May, 2006. And I realized some of the readers were people who used to own small businesses and a lot of them failed them. Small business failure rate is notoriously higher in Korea than America for at least four reasons in my opinion.

First of all, real estate costs (store rent) are much higher for business owners in Korea than America: **Business rents are expensive mainly because too many people are crammed in a small space in the country.** The most popular business locations are on the first floor of buildings and they cannot build properties forever in a limited space.

Secondly, I believe that lack of diversity is the reason for the higher business failure rate in Korea. America has more diversity in ethnicities, languages, religions, foods, etc. While we do not notice, **American businesses are also more diverse than Korean ones.** For example, Korea does not have Taco made by Mexican or Falafel made by Turkish in the country while America *does have* Kimchi made by Koreans (99% of the Korea's population is Korean as Mexicans or Turkish people do not really live in the country). Diversities make business owners avoid direct competition from similar businesses somehow: I think avoiding direct competitions makes our businesses unique and stable to survive.

Let's suppose that there are two Mexican twin boys building exactly the same two Burrito restaurants, respectively. One built it in a Mexican neighborhood having dozens of taco stands. The other built it in a Japanese neighborhood having no Mexican restaurant at all. Whose business can survive better? The situation of the first guy happens in Korea nation-wide all the time.

Thirdly, the lack of creativity among Koreans is the reason for failures in my opinion. Actually, the Korean education systems have been blamed and criticized for depressing the creativity of students for decades; they said these students are only good at memorizing things. There are not many high school dropouts in Korea: Ironically, this has not necessarily been good news in the country. In consequence, people can see a lot of factory-manufactured dull adults there. **As a result, we can see too many of the same businesses in Korea.** I am not talking about franchises. Korean businesses are mostly independent, but many of them look pretty much alike.

I think that I am the only Korean who has owned a GameStop type of business in America ever; most Koreans own restaurants, laundromats, hair salons or groceries here. I am the only one who married a foreign woman among my high school friends (they all marry only Korean women somehow). This trend causes another reason why Koreans are not good at starting businesses.

Fourthly, Korea has a strange culture that people can be blamed for if they try something different: **Koreans are *afraid* to be different.** They all start Ramen houses together when the food is on trend. They all start coffee shops together when coffee gets popular. Then, they all go bankrupt and close out businesses together as well. They will complain that, "It is how it goes in the world as everyone is in the same situation": This is simply not true; their complaints are not based on reality. I am not sure if they feel comfort from the fact that everyone does the same things. It is surprising no one tries anything different or even gives a little variation in his or her own business.

* * *

Anyway, those failed business owners started to leave nasty comments on my articles on "dcinside" site anonymously; I assume they were jealous. I should have quit writing there by that time in early 2009. But I was pretty happy that a lot of people read my articles, then; 10,000 clicks on my articles were common. I think I was born with a strong desire to write. Only issue was that I did not forgive those nasty commenters all the time. So I *counter attack* them occasionally with my replies. And then, what they did was mean.

Those loser trolls found the address of my business and started ordering food to the business. They made prank calls for delivery to the store location. I had to let a lot of delivery people go without paying them. The great internet cafe customer guys helped me to take care of those foods, though. They were so generous: They said they were hungry anyway, so paid for those deliveries and ate many of those foods. I still truly appreciate Lance, the second owner of the DMZ internet cafe next door; he always said, "We can take those foods instead of ordering somewhere else." That was too generous of him; I truly wish my best luck to him; I will remember him as one of the best people I have ever met.

At that time, my wife called restaurants around my business to warn them about the prank calls. But, in the end, one Korean troll called 911 and falsely reported that there was an oven fire in my store. A fire truck came in once briefly and found there was no fire. The police said they will try to find out who the caller was with their IT team. I never wrote anything on dcinside after that even though my articles could have helped a lot of people. I am not sure if the caller was caught eventually. All I know is that this kind of prank call crimes are increasing throughout nations and fines are not small. Above all, I will never understand people wasting time on something not bringing them profit.

* * *

I guess I will start writing books instead of writing online from 2022. If I write four pages a day, it would be six hundred pages only after five months out of a year. I guess I can write a six-hundred-page book every year. I will write about the poverty solution for a while, but eventually I may end up writing a sort of diary.

Most people don't know that diary is a surprisingly popular genre; for example, my daughter reads *Diaries of wimpy kids* and *Dork diaries* all the time. Still, every article I write will have points and a conclusion. And I will add a three sentence summary at the end of every article. I know everyone is too busy to read the whole article all the time.

* * *

Summary

1. If we are not sure, it's better not to say a thing.
2. A lot of people generate noise pollution while they do not realize it.
3. It's a serious disease to talk continuously without having a point.

31

Expensive Hobbies

Not only can a hobby be inexpensive,
it can generate income, too.
-Brad Kong

I think writing is a great hobby to help us survive through a recession. COVID pandemic is not completely over yet as of Jan, 2023; Google just laid off 12,000 employees the other day; people expect that we are getting into a long depression slowly. I quit my job 8 months ago and live without a car now. You know the cruel Chicago winter; everyone is locked inside somehow: What can I do in the next 3 years?

While most hobbies cost money, I don't think writing does; it helps me kill some time and save money; in the best case, my books can be sellers, too. I have already published 24 books so far and the number will increase every month. Besides, I don't think it's psychologically healthy that we cannot say what we want to say and bite our tongues all the time. Alternatively, we can write instead of saying.

Sometimes, I wonder why I keep writing; I have written millions of articles on so many websites over the past two decades. I had problems with internet trolls, but I couldn't stop writing. There was one time an offended troll called a fire truck to my business as a revenge in 2009; police said someone called 911 and said there was an oven fire in my video game store.

Maybe I am lonely; I do not have many friends; maybe I am an internet addict. Or maybe I do not want to let good ideas slip away for good. **Regardless, I think that it is a good idea to keep writing as a hobby**; this can be better than riding a motorbike, which can even cause death.

In my financial situation, writing is profitable *even if* it does not bring any income. I have good savings and may be able to lose a lot if I have different hobbies. Being obsessed with writing prevents me from visiting sports car dealerships or casinos. Some people lose fortunes since they are into cash-burning hobbies: Audio upgrading, photography with DSLR, Golf, etc. I will be more than happy if my books sell, though.

* * *

What makes a person decent? These were moments when I felt some people are attractive:

- When a rich person still eat at cheaper restaurants (Michael Bambang Hartono, Warren Buffet, etc)
- When a super rich lives without a car (Chow Yun-fat, Takashi Kotegawa, etc)
- Minimalists
- When a rich still works a little (e.g. writing)
- When a person has a easy job (Me working as a "weekend" dishwasher)
- When a person does not eat or talk much
- When a person still read a lot despite having a fortune (Nicolas Berggruen, Bill Gates, etc)
- When a person completely owns a house without a loan (25% of Americans)
- When a person does not work much
- When a person marries only once and has one child

In my opinion, when a person is missing out on childbirth, he or she may not understand half of the social phenomena; they may not understand how the world works truly; singles may be crippled in getting broad experiences. At the same time, I believe it is pointless to go crazy for more children since overpopulation is coming soon. In my opinion, the father of one child is a sort of winner in the modern day marriage system; he can live like a half single and married.

I think I have felt attraction from people living simply despite having enough money; these people do not exaggerate, but spend money if necessary without desperation; **I believe that is where *decency* comes from.** Being greedy or suffering financially will *never* look good; some get poorer from that point since they will push out appeals even more.

* * *

I observed that some people are poor simply because they waste all their passion and talents only on hobbies or other things; they fail to connect their flairs with opportunities to make money productively. When these hobbies do not bring them money back, they tend to be broke all the time. One of the examples is me, unfortunately.

When I think about it now, I have written zillions of articles on myriads of web sites for nothing in the last 23 years. No one paid me, rewarded me or even appreciated me. This brought me a little bit of fame only online since people remember my ID, "brad". I realize too late that I have always had so much passion for writing; I just wasted a chunk of my life only because I did not know much about self-publishing. All I knew was some rejection stories of famous writers; Harry Potter was rejected forty times or something like that.

To make things worse, I often made a lot of enemies instead of friends since I did not forgive those nasty commenters all the time; I often offended them back. As a result, I have wasted the first forty years of my life for nothing in writing. However, I may be lucky, relatively; I still have 51 years left if I die at 100. Some people really waste their whole life for reasons. I guess I can publish 30 books before I die if I can write one book a year or so from now; if I can write 4 pages a day, I can write 600 pages in 5 months, which is enough for a book. I can take a break for the rest of the year after publishing a book; this means a 7 month break a year; Writing a 600 page book every year can be possible.

Some people just have unproductive, expensive hobbies. Have you heard of "Ferrari beggars" in Japan? There is a group of people in Japan spending all their salaries on Ferrari cars. Alternatively, I think they could have used their passion to work for Ferrari dealerships or other sports car sales; I am pretty sure some of those people can use their passion and knowledge (I hardly know anything about cars). Let's suppose that there is one girl who likes to dance. She can waste her desire to dance at a nightclub. Or she can use it to work as an instructor at a dancing school. Nevertheless, losers always waste time and never use things in a constructive way.

* * *

After quitting my job in March, 2022, writing has been my full time profession. So I wondered how I could increase my book sales to support my family. I cannot imagine how Herman Melville would have felt since he had four kids by the time he started writing "Moby-Dick"; I cannot imagine how Charles Dickens took care of a family including 10 children; Regardless, I do not think I can even produce that many kids to begin with. I feel lucky that I have only one child; I feel even luckier that the world is crowded with 8 billion people now, so I can relieve myself from the pressure to produce more children.

I do have a bit of income from investment and savings, but writing will be my major income from now. Here are three things I will try to increase book sales after analyzing Amazon bestsellers. This may be off topic a little bit, but I hope this info will be helpful for you in case you want to write something for your side income.

First of all, I concluded that I have to write as many pages as possible to increase book sales. I originally planned to write only 300 pages for this book, but increased my target volume to over 800 pages. I think this is merely human psychology: People can read anything; when they buy a book, they prefer a thicker one. It is natural for customers to go for more information for the same amount of money. I noticed that a lot of top 10 bestsellers are at least 400 pages and the book, "Life force" written by Tony Robinson was even 720 pages. My wife reads a lot of books written by John Grisham and James Patterson and these are usually up to 600 pages. It seems many readers tend to prefer thicker books.

It shows that the book, "Alchemist" written by Paulo Coelho, eventually sold over 1500 million copies. But he confessed that only two copies were sold in the first six months after release in 1985; when I checked the volume, it was only 170 pages. It was the second book for Coelho, so he was a pretty much nameless author at that time. No one will buy a thin book at a high price from a nameless writer. "The Old Man and the Sea" by Hemingway has sold millions of copies even though it is just 120 pages, but the novel won the Nobel Prize in 1954. I am talking about strategies for ordinary writers like you and me.

Another advantage for a thick book is extra library purchases in my opinion. When patrons borrow thick books at the library, it usually takes longer for them to return it. So it is possible there are more waiting for those books somehow. It is possible for a library to buy an extra copy for that book since there are too many people waiting. America has 140,000 libraries. If one library buys one extra copy, we can make extra sales of 100,000 books. Kindle Direct Publishing at Amazon shows that I can make about $7 profit whenever my final collection book (#9 in *UnBrokable** series) sells. Then, it could be $700,000 extra profit for the author. Less likely that is not going to happen to me. But it is possible I can sell 20,000 books instead of 10,000 if I write a thick book.

Secondly, I assumed that a book should be written in English to sell more (Korean is more comfortable to me). I did not realize that the Korean population is only 0.05% of the world population (I mistakenly believed it is 5% of the world). Only the USA population is 6 times bigger than that of South Korea. And there are 67 countries whose primary language is English: the UK, Canada, Australia, New Zealand, Guam, Singapore, South Africa, etc. Also some countries like India or China have huge populations and these people know how to read English (certainly, not Koreans). Nevertheless, there are some great Korean authors having sold over 1 million copies of their books only in South Korea. Again, I am talking about plans for ordinary writers like me.

Thirdly, **I think it is important to include certain numbers in book titles**: How many points will an author cover in his book? I know this since I have written millions of articles online. The number included in titles always attracts more people to click my articles. I strongly believe "10 Reasons Why" is a good one.

I can give you an example of two titles from Amazon top bestsellers in 2022: "The 48 Laws of Power" and "12 Rules for Life". Another example can be "The 7 Habits of Highly Effective People". It seems readers love to know how many points authors will cover exactly in advance. I like Rolf Dobelli, but his book, "Art of thinking clearly" was not a big hit. If he wrote the title as "99 ways to think clearly", I believe the sales could have been twice better.

Lastly, I think uniqueness matters. I do not know if this book will be a success or failure. But I like to make people say, "I have never seen a book like this." There are over 2 million new books published only in America every year. But I feel like too many books have contents that I have seen somewhere else before. Most do not include unique ideas or experience, not to mention style.

For example, I think that "Art of thinking clearly" written by Dobelli failed because it does not have much personal unique experience. It includes only theses and experiments from other books. Simply, the author read a lot of books and collected them in line: I do not see much of his own ideas out of those. Any book can be boring as hell without writers' own story and I could not finish that book within the past six months. I think we have to put our own unique ideas or what's really in our minds to make a book vivid.

There are a lot of books written in a rushed way (usually from paid-in-advance authors); a lot of these are less than 250 pages. Maybe they have jobs other than a writer or do not have much savings to win some time to write in a calmer way. I feel very lucky in that sense; yet I feel sorry for them, too.

Coco Chanel once said, "The best things in life are free." Writing may not be exactly free, but it is a great hobby to relieve stress and arrange our thoughts. When I say what I really want to say, it relieves my stress a little bit. And, sometimes, we can get some money or fame that way.

* * *

Currently, my favorite hobbies are walking, riding a scooter and reading books. None of them costs a lot of money. I try to walk for a long distance one day a week; I learned that the total distance is up to 30 miles a day. I usually walk to the big bus terminal behind the Woodfield mall which is three miles away from my home. There used to be a local bus to get there every hour, but the village canceled it two years ago after COVID came in 2020. I hope they will reschedule it soon, but now I just have to walk or use a scooter to get to the terminal first. Once I get there, it has millions of buses going everywhere. Probably, it has 20 gates for buses having different routes and many of them go in the east direction to Chicago.

I got this long distance walking habit when I was a teenager thanks to my younger brother; he used to walk surprisingly long distances. He made me realize that a human can walk that long. I think the city of Seoul is different from any cities I've seen in America; it is well designed and ideal for walking. The population including the vicinity is almost 25 millions and the entire area is packed with 300 subway stations and countless bus lines; this city is hell of hell for car owners, but heaven for walkers.

The streets in Seoul are like never ending shopping malls to me: these are endless miles of coffee shops, restaurants, stores, entertainments, etc. If we can combine 1,000 shopping malls in America and align them in line, that could be the streets in Seoul: A never ending walker's paradise. I remember the streets with shops never ending; we can walk the whole week and these will still never end. In fact, I had walked for twenty years like a crazy man, yet I was not able to cover the city much.

If we check the streets of Seoul on YouTube, we will see that many people are skinny. Believe me that it is not because of their food: They just walk a lot (walk too much). Plus, it has a world class subway system. My wife said it is ten times cleaner than that of Chicago. Plus, the weather is mild, so walking has always been pleasant there.

On the contrary, I do not see any long enough streets in American cities. According to my experience, the longest fun street on the west coast was Hollywood Boulevard in LA (you know Mann's Chinese Theater). I have been there probably three times since I had visited my brother who used to live in San Diego. It was long, but I remember that just four hours were more than enough to cover it all. Downtown San Diego was nice, but I think three days were enough to go everywhere. In the Midwest, Downtown Dells, Wisconsin was pretty similar to the Niagara area including the "Ripley's Believe It or Not! museum", but the *walking everywhere* was over in just two hours. I read that one Norwegian guy visited Seoul 18 times only to walk around on the street in Seoul: I guess it is healthy fun for the residents without costing much money.

* * *

Depending on the situation, a hobby costs a fortune. I saw a sports car accident on the news the other day. The guy must have blown $240,000 for nothing and got a criminal record. We can live like that or we do not have to.

Bond prices have dropped significantly in America as in 2022. A lot of my CDs are getting matured this year and I will probably have $150,000 cash in my hands soon. Personally, I plan to put all that money in bond ETFs as "getting more interest brings me pleasure". There was one person who said that exact comment two hundred years ago: John D. Rockefeller. I guess it is really up to us how we spend our money.

* * *

Summary

1. We don't have to have an expensive hobby.
2. Some recreations don't cost money.
3. Some even make money out of their hobbies.

32

Not Doing Things Yourself

If you cannot fix it, see if you can live without it.
-Brad Kong

I don't think being successful in personal finance is about living diligently; we don't have to be busy to be rich. I think success is more likely about reducing the time we waste. This can be achieved by making our lives more efficient overall.

When I was at the Forest park blueline subway station the other day (the last station of that line), I saw several people hanging around there for no apparent reason; I hate to say this, but most of them were black, unfortunately. I do not know what they wanted exactly, but they made people waiting for the bus from the subway very uncomfortable. I was dying to hope that my bus would come quickly before anyone addressed me. Security cameras are everywhere, so I don't think they can do anything illegal much, but they were just smoking and approaching people for no apparent reason while making them feel really awkward.

There are people calling for a professional for every little thing all the time. Unfortunately, not everyone is really a professional; many of them are not honest, too. I saw a couple of programs on TV regarding this issue. They showed how some HVAC (heating, ventilation and air conditioning) or garage door technician guys can deceive customers. One way not to become a victim of deceptions is living without a lot of stuff in my opinion. For example, I do not own a garage since I live in a condo; garage door deception will never ever happen to me. I don't own a car any more as well; the biggest reason is that I had had decades of bad experiences with deceptions and overcharges by auto mechanics.

* * *

In the book titled *12 Rules for Life*, Peterson mentioned that "Achieving a hard goal is more related to personality and quality growth than making money or getting power." I agree with him since I can see that some people are still cheesy even after they made some money. I concluded that decency is not just from just owning money; certainly money helps people get it, but that is not all. As I have gotten some money as I get older, I find myself to be more interested in decency, personality or quality, which I didn't care about before. I just do not want to give bad feelings to others by overspending; I prefer to be remembered as a high quality person to others.

Sometimes, I truly wonder why I have a strong desire to write. I think virtually everyone has a desire to leave something before he or she dies; still, I feel people obsessed with photos on Instagram are a little superficial. People with profound minds want to leave some record of their mental status. One of the most efficient ways to record ideas, thoughts or mental analysis is writing. I think that is the reason why I prefer writing to putting my face on Youtube. Regardless, I noticed that self-publishing has been more popular these days.

* * *

Doing things ourselves can give us a reasonable challenge; we will learn some skills and can grow ourselves a little after a project. Regardless, hiring people is getting more expensive nowadays: it can cost. With the help of YouTube videos, Home Depot, Autozone, Advance Auto Parts, other IT technologies, etc, we can do a lot of things ourselves nowadays. Doing things on our own has at least three practical advantages in my opinion.

First of all, we can save some money. Secondly, we may face some hardships and start using some parts of our brains we never used. I heard that humans can use different genes we have never used before depending on the situation. I guess challenges can help brain development or dementia prevention in similar ways. I tried knitting next to my wife a couple of years ago. In conclusion, I failed, got frustrated and gave up. I tried to guess how it works, but I was not able to knit even a simple thing. Even my nine year old daughter then did a better job than me at that time. It was a challenge I have never had and I found a different type of brain is needed for this. We are all familiar only with what we have done so far and have lost the chance to try something new. We can realize what skill we miss, try to learn something new; it can increase our survival rate in a given situation.

Thirdly, in the opposite way, we can find some unexpected talent we did not notice we have so far. For example, I did not know I had a huge desire to write articles before publishing a book in 2022. Before then, internet addiction has been a big problem for me and I wasted ten hours a day only on browsing and writing on sites for decades. Actually, it was worse than waste since I made a lot of enemies online along the way. My browsing habit suddenly stopped in the last four months after I started writing this series. Now I am spending ten hours a day on writing without checking the internet much. I think this is more productive than browsing until my brain gets hurt. The best part of doing things ourselves is getting a chance to try something new.

* * *

These are some of the things I have done on my own for years. I hope you can learn something from these examples, so you can save some money, too.

1. I have always filed taxes myself in the last twenty three years. Recently, I started using the web site, "eztaxreturn.com" and I am happy with it so far. It should be free for you unless you have a huge income to report. It was free for me three years ago, but I am paying $29.99 only for federal return as my income has been up. Before using this site, I made a mistake, so I did not get a $1,000 refund for my child credit a year for many years. The first year I used the site was 2019; I got a $1,000 direct deposit for child credit for the first time in that year. I decided to stick with this site after that happened. For Illinois State tax, I just use this government site: "https://mytax.illinois.gov". This site is not perfect, but fine since it's totally free of charge. I heard that H&R Block charges $200 for simple filing with their "accountants". I think $29.95 is a cheaper choice even if you need to pay since you can be qualified for free filing.

2. I did some plumbing work in my condo myself: New bathtub wall construction, kitchen and bathroom faucet changes. I was able to do these with help from Youtube videos, Home depot, Ace Hardware and Enterprise rental cars nearby. I had to rent a van only for one day to bring Durock wall supplies. Renting a

van cost me $50 a day in 2019. I learned a lot of new skills along the way.

3. I used to change the air filters, spark plugs and engine oil of a car myself (when I had a car). I checked some Youtube videos.

4. I have published eight books myself in the past four months by Jan, 2023. I have done editing with help of Google Doc and Grammarly. I do book cover design with Edit.org ($69 a year); I do publishing with Kindle Direct Publishing on Amazon. And I do marketing with free social media including Facebook. If I hire people for all these, it could have cost me $10,000 or so. Worst part is that the final product could have been something I did not expect. I am the best reader for my own book and will try to make something I would buy.

5. While I owned the video game store, I had not been able to hire anyone. Basically, I did everything myself starting from cleaning the carpet (I hired Miguel for window washing a few times, though). I was an online sales agent and a security guard for my store as well. I did everything although my wife helped me, occasionally (I *appreciate* her help).

6. I have never hired a financial advisor for my investment in the last twelve years. I started stock investing in 2011, did just fine and even made a small fortune in 2021. **I don't think hiring a professional guarantees anything, especially in stock investment.** In fact, it is possible I could have lost money since I had been on a loss with PBI stock for five years. I just did not sell it until 1/26/2022 and made $20,000 out of selling all my

PBI shares on that day. **In this case, actually hiring someone could hurt our long term profits.** It is possible that an advisor could have pushed me to sell before 1/25/2021 (check chapter 17 to see what happened on that particular day). Then, I could have lost double: The financial advisor fee and stock loss.

7. This is not me, but my wife teaches how to play violin to my daughter. She usually charges up to $100 an hour to others since she has a Doctorate degree in violin.

We will talk more about these later on. Let's move on to the next chapter for now.

* * *

Summary

1. We can save money by *doing things on our own.*
2. It can bring us a new opportunity via trying something new.
3. It can help us find new talents we don't know we have.

33

Being a Taker

All we have is what we give.
-Brad Kong

It seems a lot of people do not have sympathy for livestocks nowadays. I understand we raise them to eat; still they are animals with their own precious lives. It's not like we have a right to kill them. I think that attitude can be the biggest threat to the entire human race in the long run. No taker can survive, not to mention "thrive."

Marie Antoinette was the last Queen of France before the French Revolution in the 18th century. She was executed in guillotine for depletion of the national treasury in October, 1793; the record says she was only 37 years old. In other words, she died because she spent too much government money for parties without caring about starvation of French people. It shows that no one came to her defense or visited her during her prison term: Not even her brother who was the King of Austria, then. I thought this could be an example of the consequence of takers: We cannot be selfish, arrogant or keep taking from others forever. Those could be the reasons for poverty as well if not for death.

* * *

We meet people all the time, but we may not know who we are dealing with always; some people believe they do, but they don't. Our reasons and instincts are not as immaculate as we think. For example, not many people know that I have a good size of stock portfolio. We can miss opportunities when we act based on assumptions. Even worse is that we can make a formidable enemy unexpectedly that way; some enemies may not seem to be strong, but we will never know. This could be a reason why some people stay poor forever. The stories about Ghengis Khan may be well known, but the writer Greene describes one with details in his book, *The 48 Laws of Power*. Let me summarize that here with supplementary info from Wikipedia.

Ala ad-Din Muhammad II was the king of the Khwarezmian Empire in the beginning of the 13th century; it was a huge empire covering the territory of Turkey, Iran and Afghanistan back then and the capital was Samarkand[41]. This king received a visitor with plenty of gifts from the Mongol empire one day in 1219. Ghengis Khan was a smaller king at that time; he only invaded and conquered a part of China. What this "small king" wanted was to open up the Silk Road again and share the profit from trades together with Mongols. Muhammad lightly disregarded this offer.

Ghengis Khan tried again. He sent hundreds of camels filled with treasures this time. Unfortunately, one Islamic governor named Inalchik captured this group before it even arrived at Samarkand; he killed the leader of the group and took all the treasures himself. Ghengis Khan was a patient man; he thought this could be just a mistake.

Uncomplainingly, he decided to send one more group of caravans filled with treasures one more time. This time, Muhammad II himself killed the leader, took all the treasures and sent back the other people after shaving their

[41] Samarkand is the Valley of Zarafshan River, Uzbekistan now.

heads. Ghengis Khan considered it as an insult and whispered quietly, “Kill them all.” **These stupid people from Samarkand did not know who they were dealing with.**

The Khan from Mongolia attacked Inalchik’s province first in 1220; he captured him instantly and killed him by pouring molten silver into his eyes and ears. While Khan’s armies were smaller, they attacked efficiently and surrounded Samarkand quickly. Muhammad fled, but died while running away on an island near Caspian Sea in 1220; it shows that he was only 51 years old. Samarkand was fully destroyed and a large portion of its residents were massacred within 11 days. What is the lesson here? Sometimes, we have to think we may deal with another Khan. We will never know who we are dealing with by his or her appearance.

* * *

Depending on where we go, international travel could be a total waste of money; this is true especially when we go to underdeveloped countries like Vietnam. I just read the Korean travel writer Park’s blog and he said street food sellers in Vietnam often do not give him his change back after selling food. Maybe I am writing this since I have been tricked a lot; I just don’t see there is a point in visiting these countries after spending a huge amount of money on air fares; we do not travel to feel deceived and ripped off, or get close to low lives. Americans often forget how safe and fair a country we live in; some countries are literally corrupted from top to bottom. I don’t think it's a mandatorily good idea to visit a poor country only because it’s cheaper to stay; we may not learn anything positive from the experience.

In 2003, my girlfriend and I visited one small grocery store north of downtown Chicago (she is my wife now in 2023); I remember it was near the Michigan lake, so I believe it's close to Edgewater. I bought a couple of ice creams with cash and the change was $0.05 or something. Unhappily, the Indian or Pakistani owner, not a very old guy, suddenly winked at me and put the nickel back into the cash register: I felt disgusted. If that happens now, I would get my change back for sure, but I didn't know what to do at that time. He may be a taker, but it was the most ugly thing a human could do for $0.05; the best thing he could do was having a tip jar I guess, which is common in a grocery store. Personally, I am not interested in taking someone else's changes: **How many more years would I live in this life?** Besides, there are plenty of chances to make money in fair ways.

I frankly doubt if these types of people will ever get wealthy; it is nonsense to go to a country full of these people with air tickets. I admit that I envy free travelers who go all over the world sometimes. But, when I spend money, I prefer having a cherishable experience.

* * *

It is said that there are three types of people in the world: takers, matchers and givers. Takers are people taking advantage of others mostly. The problem is that other people are not fools, too; I suspect that many takers usually end up being poor with a low ranked job, according to my experience with dishwashers. Matchers are the people giving and getting help equally; I think I am a matcher. Givers are these people giving more than taking; I think my wife is definitely a giver.

Some people have been nothing but unpleasant takers from me. I have seen most of these people at working places; they have been poor and probably will be poor for life. While this could be just my imprudent assumption, let me tell you what exactly happened to me at the weekend dishwashing job in the nursing home for 7 years.

* * *

The nursing home I worked at had about 1,000 senior residents and 1,000 employees; probably 100 employees of them were in the dining department. Throughout the 7 years of the career, I had chances to speak closely with roughly 15 dishwashers.

First of all, I think it is just a misconception that all the dishwashers are poor. Surprisingly, many of them actually had more than decent living. I learned that 4 guys paid off mortgages on their houses though they were in their early 50s. They had multiple bedroom houses, not like a one-bedroom condo I have. **I even found out that one Filipino dishwasher lived in a five bedroom upscale house.** He had worked for two dishwashing jobs and his wife was a nurse; they had one daughter like us.

Technically, considering the dishwasher job, I myself have not been in that bad shape as well; I bought my condo with full cash at the age of 40 in 2013. Not many people do that regardless of professions in America or Korea; only 25% of citizens in this country own houses free and clear without mortgage debts (75% of people live in apartments or have mortgages not paid fully); even among those 25%, not many of them pay off their mortgages before 40 like me (to be fair, their houses are bigger than mine). All I can say is it's wrong to assume others' financial situations by their jobs.

Among those 15 employees, there were only two dishwashers who had lived in only rental apartments for life: Let me call them E and F. They had never been able to reach a point to consider getting mortgages from the bank though both were about 60. And I realized that these two worked in a particularly unfair way.

* * *

I was able to work in the morning shifts two years after the start of that job. Everyone preferred the morning hours, so he could go home early; senior employees had priority for the schedule. The morning shift had two different positions for the dishwashers: Pots and the dishroom. Whenever I worked with E or F in the morning, they pushed their job to me in a rude way. Both acted similar; I had so much problem with this in the beginning, but I gave up eventually. I still do not know why they were not afraid of my anger and resistance.

When we switched positions the next day, they were still rude to push their jobs to me the other way around. How do you feel that you gave them a forced favor, but they do not do the same thing right next day? I felt ignored foolishly and had burst my anger countless times. They acted as if nothing happened the day before.

What I could not understand especially was so-called "half washing." There were about ten cooks and two dishwashers in the kitchen every morning. There was not a single day the kitchen was closed in the nursing home. If pot position washes pots and the dishroom washes dishes, everyone's job could have been much easier.

But, strangely, whenever these E and F were in pot position, they cleaned pots only half way through and brought all to the dishroom, so the other dishwasher could finish cleaning. Probably, it could have saved them some effort to rinse all the pots and stack them.[42] They might have had an easier time in the pot position momentarily. But that made the dishroom job double, which made everyone's work double eventually. I think these two were just cunning, stupid and selfish.

The opposite example was a Mexican boy named Omar. I detected that he always helped people too much. I always felt sorry for him since he and F are mostly scheduled together during weekdays.[43] I saw F crazily took advantage of him one day.

Strange thing is Omar had been much wealthier than this old cunning F. He was a 28 years old boy who lived in his parents' house then. He was the first child out of five in his family. I learned that he had saved over $80,000 cash out of the 8 years of work though a good amount out of his income had gone to aid his parents.

Another similar example was Hector. He had been a great helping hand to me and had only one child like me. He was about 50 years old and owned a three bedroom house outright with his mortgage paid off perfectly. Interestingly, all of these four people were Mexicans (E, F, Omar, Hector); they all spoke Spanish fluently.

After all, these E and F continuously had betrayed mutual help rules all the way up until the last day I worked: Getting help, demanding help, but not helping others unless it is a woman who they can approach with sexual intention.

---

[42] Pot cleaning steps are washing, rinsing and stacking. They brought pots to the dish room only after washing.
[43] I had been scheduled with F only every weekend.

I had complained about this to management many times, but nothing ever changed. I even tried to change my job to a waiter, but it did not work out for any visible ground. Yet I still believe this could be the reason why E and F were broke as hell for life compared with the other two Mexican dishwashers.

* * *

Summary

1. Being a taker only makes us poor.
2. Others are not fools.
3. We don't have to be givers, but I think we must be matchers at least to get wealthy.

34

Not Being Persistent

Being persistent is the only superpower in the real world.
-Brad Kong

Little things are not little; small things are not small. I decided to change the line space of this manuscript to 1.3 from 1.5 the other day. This means I can write up to 32 lines on each page instead of 27. A small change, right? Wrong! Since KDP allows the maximum number of pages on paperback to 828 pages, I was going to make my book less than 800 pages at the maximum, originally. Now I can insert 125 more pages in the same 800 page book: 800 pages x 5 more lines = 4,000 more lines to write; 4,000 lines ÷ 32 lines per page = 125 pages. It would be the same 800 page book, but 125 more pages of articles will be added in the final book.

* * *

I saw a novel titled *The Hotel Nantucket* in the bestseller section in the library yesterday; the story was only about 300 pages since the 100 pages in the end seemed to be another novella out of the 400 page book. I was a little surprised since I believed thicker books usually sell more; a lot of fantasy novels by Armentrout are over 600 pages. I saw that *The Game of Thrones* series is 5,200 pages for 5 books; which means 1,040 pages for each book; that series is in the super thick category. I detected that all of these are the steady bestsellers. And that was the reason why I tried to write a thick book myself, too.

At home, I found out that this lady Elin Hilderbrand, who wrote the hotel novel, has written over 32 novels, particularly about summer vacation in the Nantucket area since 2000 (summer beach read series). Now it makes sense: She has accumulated enough fandom in the last 23 years. If I keep writing, I can be famous like her after 32 books (hopefully before). Then, the question is how can I write that many books?

First of all, I think I should forget about sales for a while if not forever. I need to find something I like to write about passionately and continuously. I don't think there is no right or wrong field in this case: Art is not exactly mathematics; there are no right or wrong manuscripts to get a better grade. I still assume that a very little amount of people are interested in romance in Nantucket town compared with the total population in America. I believe choosing a specific field I am particularly interested in and going deeper is the key. For now, I decided to write things about people in financial desperation or hardship. After all, we all need to fight against harsh environments, take care of money problems and survive.

* * *

Making a fortune suddenly is not important; I think getting out of poverty is more important. Also, increasing our net worth little by little continuously may improve our happiness; even after having a lot of money, we may feel bad if our savings decrease somehow.

Every writer has experience with failure. I am reading *The Alchemist* written by Paulo Coelho now; he said he wrote it when he was 41 years old in 1988 and only 2 copies were sold in the first six months; he said he was old enough to be desperate; he made a new contract with another publisher and it started selling in massive quantities a couple of years later; just let you know that Coelho's net worth is over $500 millions USD as of 2023.

There is a book titled *A Time to Kill* written by John Grisham. He was a successful lawyer and politician holding a position in the Mississippi House of Representatives. Naturally, I assumed that this white elite guy never had a hardship for his whole life; I was wrong. It shows that he had 1,000 copies of this novel in the trunk of his car when it was first published in 1989; he said he tried to give out those copies for free to the libraries, coffee shops or whoever wants it, but had an extremely hard time getting rid of these; he said one friend helped him clear those out; still the novel eventually became successful and a movie based on this book has made as well; the net worth of Grisham is over $400 millions USD in 2023.

The German philosopher, Arthur Schopenhauer was a well known genius in the 19th century. When his masterpiece titled *The World as Will and Representation* was first published in 1844, it shows that only 200 copies were sold in the first year; which made this successful young professor frustrated.

When the famous American writer, Henry David Thoreau published his first book titled *A Week on the Concord and Merrimack Rivers* in 1849, record says that less than 300 copies were sold out of 1,000 copies already printed out. Over 700 copies were returned to Thoreau after years and this is what he wrote: "I have a library of 900 books at home and 700 are written by myself." Even though *Walden* was much more commercially successful later on, only 2,200 copies were sold during his lifetime: Now the book is considered one of five greatest books ever written by Americans in this country.

I think being persistent is the key: It makes a normal person exceptional. No one seems to get really successful at the first try. I notice that poor people often don't do things all the way up to the end. And many of them end up not achieving anything for life as a result.

* * *

When I read a book titled *Nomadland,* I learned it starts with a story about one generous, but poor lady named Linda; she has been poor for life and ended up living in a cheap camper at her age of 66. This book ended with explaining her ultimate dream; she had a dream to find land without having many building code restrictions and tried to build an eco-friendly house called Earthship. In the last Chapter of that book, it reads that she actually bought a barren four acre land near the Mexican border in Arizona with $2,500 payment ($200 down payment and $200 every month pay). I was curious to see what happened after this, so I checked the internet all over.

You know what? It seems she ultimately gave up again. I understand she must have gotten into a lot of difficulties; it is not very cool during the summer in Arizona. Still, I suspect that this could be the reason why she had been poor. Only news I found was that she donated the land to a van dwelling organization. After all, her friends and she did not even start the ambitious building project. What a waste of all those plans and research taking up the last 100 pages of the book. **I think that actually doing it and doing it all the way up to the end are the real superpower: the only superpower in the real world.**

* * *

I usually do not go to the novel section in our library. There is one huge room having tons of only novels on the first floor. Still, I don't really read novels. But lately I went there every day only to check what the best sellers look like.

What I found surprising was that there were a lot of authors who are not very famous, but have written a lot of books. Have you ever heard of "Eric Gerome Dickey" or "David Sedaris?" Personally, I have not until recently. I just checked their books out mainly because each writer has at least fifteen books on the shelves in our library. Eric wrote types of black couple romances until 2021 as he passed away because of cancer that year; David has written diary type essays.

No offense, but I did not perceive that their books were anything astonishing. I felt like most people could have written just that much if provided with a pen and paper. There is a reason why I have never heard of them. But, at the same time, I learned that their books have a surprising amount of reviews on Amazon. This means commercial success of books and, in fact, I found out that both had or have been actually millionaires. And here was my final conclusion: They got famous mainly because they have *persistently* written large numbers of books; some writers are rich since they wrote excellent books; others are still wealthy since they published so many books in *one field* continuously even though their articles are not mandatorily unquestionable masterpieces.

* * *

When we see a large quantity of books written by one author, we automatically assume that this writer is talented and successful, so he or she must have written so many books. But I think the other way around is also viable; the writer keeps writing a lot of books, so he or she ends up being well-known and wealthy. In fact, I believe the second case is much more common than the first. No one really gets famous as soon as he or she writes only one book. Think of one author you like and check Wikipedia for bibliography of that person. Chances are we'll see the writer has written many books before. This can be true in other fields also.

Have you ever seen an amusing video on Youtube, clicked the channel of the video and got surprised by the number of videos in that channel? For example, there is a YouTube channel called "Alux.com" and it has 1,500 videos in it. For some reasons, YouTube makes it impossible to count the exact number of videos in a channel. But I can say that those YouTubers have made efforts persistently for a long time. Now I decided to watch all of the videos in Alux for my English exercise. **Book sales could be the same: Qualities come from quantities.**

When I searched "Best-selling fiction authors" in Wikipedia, William Shakespeare came out as the number one. It shows that he sold two billion copies of his books. But did you know that he wrote forty two different books of poems and plays? Not many authors write that many books; not even for professionals. For example, the Harry Potter author, Joan Rowling has written 15 books so far by Jan, 2023. I assume most writers have less than 20 books published during their lifetimes. I can see that plenty of novelists have only one book on the library shelves.

* * *

Being persistent does not necessarily mean being painful. *UnBrokable** would be my first series and I thought I could write six hundred pages if I write four pages a day for five months. I planned to make all my final books have at least six hundred pages; I thought thick books may beat the sales competition since anyone can write a thin book. Also, I supposed that readers would not feel ripped off when they buy a thick book at a reasonable price. No one wants to spend tons of money on thin materials.

And I thought that five months is a reasonable time frame since some people take years to complete writing one book. I imagined that I could write one book a year: Probably spending five months on writing and seven months on taking a break every year. **We do not have to kill ourselves to be persistent, but we just need to do the same thing everyday.** I usually start writing from 8:00 AM till 2:00 PM and found that it is much easier than the weekend dishwashing job at the nursing home; I am free in the afternoon these days. If this career goes well, I believe writing would be a better job than owning a business or being employed.

* * *

When I worked at the nursing home over the weekends, they used to hire temporary people occasionally since laborers were consistently short in the kitchen. I heard that some temp people even quit their job within 30 minutes after starting their work. In general, the food distribution part was much easier than my dishwashing. I still remember I saw one fat youngish Latina lady working very reluctantly and slowly in the food distribution. I recall her since she had the biggest butt I have ever seen; surprisingly, she disappeared in the middle of work that day I saw her;

shockingly, she didn't complete that easy 4 hours of morning shift. I guess she must be busy eating though she couldn't work. I don't think there is any hope for people quitting a job even before the first day is over.

When people talk about salaries, they tend to talk about the amount of salary a year: Not many people talk about how long they can work to get it. Again, "persistence" matters and I believe that "how long" is a more important question than "how much" as people start to live longer nowadays. Forced early retirement is a social problem in Korea and people lose jobs from huge companies at early ages (lay off in their early 50s). In that case, making $100,000 for 10 years is much worse than making $80,000 for 30 years.

Again, I just would like to focus on the fact that being persistent doesn't have to be necessarily painful. For the same concept, I usually invest my money in dividend stocks and interest bonds. Once I buy a stock or bond for that purpose, I hardly sell them. I value that getting $30,000 interest and dividends every year is more important than "buy and sell for quick gain" as the lifespan of people gets longer. Besides, "Buying a stock and selling for profit" does not work well frequently; no one really predicts which direction the stock price will move, after all.

* * *

Summary

1. Being persevering is the only *superpower* in the real world; it's one way to be a superhuman.
2. Poor people tend to give up easily.
3. Some people persistently eat a lot, but abandon their jobs quickly.

35

Stuck in a Low Paying Job

Too much comfort might kill us.
-Brad Kong

There is a book titled *The Four Agreements* written by Miguel Ruiz. This author explained that our education can be a sort of domestication:

"Human domestication is so strong that, at a certain point in our lives, we no longer need anyone to domesticate us. We don't need Mom or Dad, the school or the church to domesticate us. We are so well trained that we are our *own* domesticators; we are auto-domesticated animals."

Do you know what I tried to say? **These old people willing to continue *lower*-paying but harder jobs are *overly* domesticated people.**

* * *

Being *lazy continuously* is not being persistent. Some people just work for the same job for too long even though they know it's not a good one: They just do not want to change things. Often, they make all sorts of excuses just to themselves about why they should keep their current job. Occasionally, they are just too tired to make a change as well. **I think it is important not to put ourselves in a situation where we must accept a bad job to begin with.** I feel bad for some Mexicans who do dishwashing for

30 years since they have five kids to feed; having too many kids is not mandatory for anyone, though. This is just one example, but I think no one should give such an obligation to anyone.

When we make such a life decision, first of all, I think we have to see if that's what we really want. Then, we need to check if that's good for us. If it's bad, at least, we have to estimate how bad it is. I know some men running away from their own family after having 8 kids with their wives; one of them was the father of president Lula in Brazil. **Ultimately, I believe caring about ourselves benefits others the most.**

* * *

"Humans are not interested in minimizing risks. Unless there is a limitation, people tend to choose an adventurous life." The Canadian psychologist Peterson mentioned this point in his bestseller titled *12 Rules for Life*. People do not like to be in too much danger; they do not like to have too much boredom, either. The author took an example of skateboarding; it is not as dangerous as skydiving; still, it is not as safe as riding a bicycle. People tend to *enjoy* a bit of *risk*; that is why casinos and stock markets are so popular and crowded.

As soon as I read this, I was able to realize why I had bought PBI stock a few times after the big sell-off and sold them immediately with trivial profits; I assume I had been enjoying risks. I already explained this extensively in Chapter 17 of *UnBrokable* II*, and there is a publicly traded company named Pitney Bowes (ticker: PBI). The stock used to give me a headache for over four years, but I was able to sell all my 6,500 shares with $20,000 profit on 1/26/2021; I still appreciate the Wall Street Bet group on Reddit for pumping up the price temporarily for a couple of days.

Before 2021, I had all the 6,500 shares of PBI for $10 average purchase price; the price jumped up to $13 only for a couple of days in January, 2021; I sold all mine and made some profit. Even after that, I had traded the company stock on and off when it was under $4 before 2023. One time, I bought 250 shares of PBI with $3.40 average purchase price in August, 2022. I must have thought this was an affordable risk and I probably enjoyed the trading; $3 was a much better purchase price than $10. The stock gave out over 5% annual dividends as well, so I did not think I would lose money much.

* * *

When I think about it, the same thing goes for the tourism industry as well. When I checked the world tourism rankings on Wikipedia, I noticed that way more people visit the United States than Mexico or Canada. To a lot of people, Mexico can be too dangerous a country to visit; I had seen so many photos of deceased people killed by mafias; some were hanged by highway signs or something; Personally, there is no way I can visit there. On the contrary, Canada seems to be too boring. I think the United States is not extremely dangerous or too boring.

There are millions of adults working without meaning in their lives; these people tend to be old, who are married with their habits; they often work in the same job for decades. In a sense, they definitely live against human instinct. They may or may not be wealthy, but here is one thing for sure; they tend to get paid less than newcomers. **There are not many companies paying their *current* employees more than new ones voluntarily**; frequently, current employees need to ask, demand or fight for the same rate of newcomers. In general, it is less profitable for us to work for the same company for long even though we can stay in the same field; employers tend not to feed the fish they already caught.

* * *

Today I visited a huge Indian supermarket for the first time in my life. I had been to Indian markets before, but they were not ample. As soon as I entered the place, I heard Indian background music. Every single worker and customer was Indian; it seems they were all surprised to see me. They sold so many religious statues as well. Surprisingly, these were all elephants; I thought Krishna was in human shape; these could have been Jesus statues in Mexican supermarkets or Buddhas in Vietnamese ones. I did not know Indians make so many food products with their own brands (e.g., Swad). It was a unique experience for 30 minutes. I am just giving you this example since something new doesn't have to be expensive.

Some people get stuck in their old jobs since it's too comfortable for them; they will find some reasons to stay even though it's not necessarily beneficial for anyone. When I worked at the nursing home, I had seen a couple of dishwashers working there for over 30 years; these two did not even try to be a cook. **Eventually, I felt they turned themselves into people who do not know how to do anything else.** Coincidentally, I end up remembering these two were the most unfair and unpleasant human beings I have seen in my last 49 years.

* * *

To get out of this harmful habit or detrimental destiny, my suggestion is to have a habit of always trying something *new*. It doesn't have to be an expensive thing like visiting a foreign country we have never been to. Actually, international travels could bring us the same boring experiences: waiting at similar looking airports, riding the same airplanes from Boeing or Airbus factories, sleeping at the same Marriott hotels somewhere, etc.

I think we can start by eating at a different restaurant, for example. Today, I tried one Indian food (I cannot remember the name of) at a restaurant called Mumbai cafe; it cost me only $7. I will try the new Indian egg place next time. On the way back, I found a boat renting for $12 an hour in a lake next to a high school. Maybe I will try that with my daughter next time. Always try something new at least once if it doesn't cost a lot. This habit can get us out of our old jobs paying us less, but giving us more work. It is nonsense we get stuck there forever only because we feel comfortable.

* * *

Hardship does not always grow us. More often than not, it crushes us or makes us exhausted. The best way is not to create any hardship to begin with. The second best would be to remove all the reasons to be in a hard situation if we already created one.

Changing a career takes a lot of energy and courage. I have changed my job about six times in the last fifteen years: an eBay seller, game store owner, weekend dishwasher, medical coder, investor and writer. These have been extreme changes. I think this has been possible virtually because I have lived like a single guy; gratefully, my wife has taken care of my daughter mostly. My daughter and I have lived fantastic lives based on the wife's sacrifice, frankly. In my opinion, there are two reasons why people cannot change bad jobs: One is *being too comfortable with them*; the other is *being too tired to make a change.*

* * *

People may think being comfortable happens only in employment. But I have seen this happen a lot among small business owners, too. Even if a business loses money, some owners stay for long if not forever. **In this case, it is not even a low income like working for a job, but actually a loss.** Still, except for the money loss, the life of a small store owner is often fantastic. I believe that is the actual reason why they stay forever, according to my experience. Let me give you some examples.

In the prologue, I already said that I had about these three jobs in the last 15 years: A business owner, employee and investor. Among these, the only job I still keep is the investor: managing a $600,000 portfolio including stocks, bonds and ETFs. **In a cost sense, an investment job is totally different from the other two.**

Simply owning a store or even working at a nursing home had cost me money. I think it is easy to understand why owning a store costs us money: rent, utility, credit card machine charges, employee salary, etc. Surprisingly, working for someone else costs money, too: bus fare, a car to commute, gas, nice clothes, lunch, etc. But managing an investment really has not really cost me anything so far: **It does not cost money to own stocks to begin with**[44].

---

[44] If we sell stocks for profit, we have to pay tax. That is an option. We can just keep them without selling them.

When I had the video game store, I had to pay about $1,200 rent every month for 8 years by 2014; it was a 900 sf store in a Chicago suburb. The total rent had been about $120,000 for 8 years. Also I had to pay at least $100 electricity and $50 credit card terminal charges every month. I cannot remember all, but there were numerous other expenses: ADT security charge, license fee from village, tag fees for fire extinguishers, etc. So, I would say owning the business cost me at least $2,000 a month back then.

Business had been good sometimes, but bad mostly during the 8 years. Unluckily, I had so many bad months particularly after 2010. Serious economic depression came after the mortgage bubble burst in 2007. I clearly remember I had lost at least $1,000 a month in the last 6 months of the 8 years. Still, I am glad I closed it in 2014 as COVID came in 2019.

But I noticed that some business owners keep their businesses open forever despite losses. I do not believe they made money while I was in trouble. They just get money from somewhere (parents, relatives, credit card debt or wherever) and stay. The most common excuse would be something like this: "Well, more people will know us when we stay longer." They think they are survivors and I am a loser since my business was closed out: **The other way around is true.** I would have stayed if there was no ownership cost as I explained above.

* * *

There are a couple of real reasons when a business stays in spite of prolonged loss. One is attachment; they love the businesses they created. But the other more important reason is the cozy life of a business owner.

When we own a store, there is no boss there. In my store, customers did not come all the time, so my life was pretty comfortable. When I worked at a nursing home, I could not even take a break for 10 minutes peacefully except lunch hours[45]. There was one short sous chef notorious for over-concerning. Once, he was looking for me everywhere since I went for a break 5 minutes earlier. I guess he was one of the major reasons why I quit the nursing home job. Dishwashing jobs are exhausting by nature; most people do not have any room to think about career change at the end of the day.

Nonetheless, when I think about it, I think we can also use this laziness to work in our favor. As long as we are settled with good habits, we can kick out any new bad habit this way, too: "It's annoying; I am tired. I do not want to try new bad things."

Some people said they made a lot of money out of Bitcoins. In my opinion, it is new, but can be fraud, too. **I can simply disregard the temptation since I am too bothered to try new investments.** I saw some people drowning to death after they tried scuba diving in narrow caves. Some people die while skydiving. That will not happen to me since I am too tired to try new adventures already. I hope you are getting my point.

* * *

Summary

1. Some people lose money since they don't want to change things.

[45] Luckily, we had a one-hour lunch time. They removed two of the 15-minute breaks and combined them to lunch time.

2. We need some energy and courage to change careers.
3. We can use laziness not to try something dangerous.

36

Not Minding Your Own Business

Nosey people never do their jobs well.
-Brad Kong

One ironic thing in our life is that people who don't need to do a thing usually do it more. For example, it is possible that people who read this book are mostly those who don't have to worry about money. Fat people who don't have to eat more often eat more. Obese people having a heart problem go to steak houses more than skinny girls. A father with eight kids meets other women continually like Jon Gosselin. Yet a large number of single guys never really meet a woman. A mother with four kids got pregnant again like one of my ex-coworker. Yet women who never had a baby before never really have one for life (which is fine). Rich people save more and poor people spend more. I think the rich get richer and the poor get poorer as a result.

* * *

I strongly believe that spending time on being jealous is the biggest waste in our lives; sometimes, this happens nationwide. One French guy on a Korean TV show admitted that Frenchs tend to be more jealous than others in general. He said that Americans want to buy a nice car in the future when they see a rich man driving a luxury car. But he commented that Frenchs would want to get the rich out of the car and force him to walk together. I believe him since France seems to have had more revolutions led by people in her history; a lot of Kings and Queens died by guillotines including Louis XVI and Marie Antoinette.

But, at the same time, did you know that France has conquered much smaller territory compared with its neighbors during the age of colonialism? For example, England had built a huge empire once covering the USA, Canada, Australia, New Zealand, India, etc. The west neighbor of France is Spain; it was once the governor of oceans and Spanish is still spoken throughout South America. Then, what does France have now? No one really speaks French except a portion of African countries near France.

Why is this happening despite the fact that France has enough ocean sides? Is it possible that French people might have wasted more of their energy or time on being jealous than their neighbors? To be fair, Germany does not have much seaside and no oceanside at all. I am afraid that Koreans are closer to Frenchs than English or Spanish people; I am Korean and we are aware of our character of bigger jealousy. That could be why those smart people have been stuck in that tiny land in Asia for 5,000 years. **In a personal sense, this could be the reason why some people are poor while working hard.**

* * *

The famous Canadian psychologist, Jordan Peterson once said, "If you are not the leading actor in your own play, probably you are taking a role in others' plays." The role others let us take could be a trivial, mundane or miserable one; I know they will never give us the best roles in their own plays. This is why it's important to be the main actor in our own lives; we need to protect ourselves from being despairing.

He also mentioned a mental disease called *Paranoia*; he said the patients of this disease assume there are a group of observers thinking about them all the time and try to hurt these observers. Here is one piece of good news for you, though; I don't think there is anyone thinking about us all the time; everyone lives in his or her own body and needs to manage to survive. In a sense, concerning others' lives is like concerning others' driving while we drive our own cars. We all have mental problems of worrying about others' eyes to some extent, so I hope this helps.

* * *

Losers never get lives; their lives are often pointless and boring; commonly, they have nothing much exciting or profitable going on. **As a result, they tend to talk about others or concern other people's lives more.** Even on a message board online, they do not write and upload even a single post on their own; what they do mostly is write nasty comments on others' posts: meaningless negative comments. Keeping losers nearby is unprofitable and harmful. Don't make them part of your family by marriage or have a too close relationship anyhow.

Mind our own business is supposed to be the easiest thing in the world. But it seems this is the hardest thing in the world for some people (usually losers); this habit of focusing on ourselves humbly may require some discipline. But it's worth it since it can prevent divorce or other inharmonious discrepancies in our lives. Any conflict with other people, especially our own family, can cause financial damage, too; alternatively, we can have some distance from them. Regardless, when we shut up and do our jobs immaculately, everyone can be happy; everyone may like us, or he or she will not hate us, at least.

* * *

Sometimes, I go to downtown Chicago only to walk around. I do that on my scooter occasionally. I have a kick scooter from Razor company and it is about $80 from Amazon. Originally, my wife bought a small scooter for my daughter as a toy in 2015. Then, it broke somehow and she bought a bigger version for an adult (the spring under the handles has been broken almost every year). Still, you know what? I found that the scooter for adults has been more than just a toy. After riding it for 30 miles one day, I realize that it can be a practical form of transportation.

I tried to walk around for a long distance at least one day a week. This scooter is foldable, so it does not take up a lot of space on a bus or subway. I always put it in the shoe closet at home. Now it is May, 2022 and I know summer is not very long in Chicagoland.

I usually go to Chicago by bus called Pace 600. It is only $2 one way and I can pay it with a Ventra card; the card looks like a credit card. We can add money on it online or at a vending machine at a station and use it for both bus and subway everywhere in Chicagoland. It is about 3 miles from the bus terminal to my home. There used to be a bus called Pace 608 to my home, but that was suspended after COVID came in 2020. I usually walk or ride my kick scooter to home, which is more exercise after all. There is a Target store on the way, so I usually shop a little bit, put items in my backpack before coming home.

* * *

It was 8:00 PM when I came back from Chicago yesterday. Wife was at home checking her iPhone in the living room.

When I was eating the leftover Chipotle veggie bowl, she started talking about web news: UIUC civil engineering school ranked number one in the nation, UIUC is considered a public Ivy League, etc; it was annoying. She graduated from UIUC music school twelve years ago and does not have a *real* job for now. What is the point for all these? I wish she would listen to my problem instead, so she can get some money from me. My talking was easily cut off by her pointless news. **I hate these types of people concerning something else other than their own businesses.** As a result, they never do their own job very well.

In fact, I was waiting for a phone call from the Unemployment Benefit agency at that time. They sent me a letter saying that they want to interview me one more time for my benefit. I don't care what others do; I was just worrying about my own interview and trying to pass it nicely.

For your information, unemployment benefits are not necessarily for poor people. If we have a job for more than 18 months in a company and lose it for some unfortunate reason we cannot control, you are eligible only for 26 weeks; anyone can get it even if he or she is rich, theoretically. People usually get anywhere from $200 to $300 a week, but we cannot get more than $400 even if we have a large family to support. So the amount is not very big to begin with. And the period is 26 weeks at the longest only until we find a new job. It is not like Snap cards or other benefits we can get every year: a payment of 26-weeks once in our lifetimes and that is it. If the same thing happens again, we may get it again, but less likely that happens multiple times.

In my case, I was supposed to get $302 a week since I have one child to support. We still can get it even if we have some savings or investment incomes. The important thing is we should not be hired by any company during the 26 weeks period and the agency will check that thoroughly. And the reason for being unemployed should be beyond your control like getting laid off. Here is exactly what happened to me.

* * *

After closing my video game business in 2014, I took about a 13 month break. It was very nice: Probably one of the happiest times in my life. I bought my condo in 2013, so I have not had any rent to pay. I remember my association fee for my condo was $290 a month in 2014 to 2015, so I did not have much obligation. My daughter was 4 to 5 years old at that time, but she and my wife were in a foreign country to take care of her ill mother. I admit that it was a great rest solely based on my wife's sacrifice.

And then, one day, my wife suggested that I should get a job. I was a little bit bored after taking a rest over a year, too. She used to work for "home elderly care" service when she was in graduate school. She strongly suggested something similar since nursing home jobs are available all the time. Later, I happened to watch YouTube videos of a famous Bhuddist monk in Korea. One person asked what kind of job he has to get now and the monk suggested that he should get any job for now and move to a better one later. I filled out a job application online for a nursing home nearby; I had been a dishwasher before both in America and Korea by then. I had a job interview only for 5 minutes the next day and got the dishwasher job immediately.

It was pretty good in the beginning. I was happy to get a slightly higher rate ($11.04 an hour) than others in 2015. Everyone welcomed me, meals were free and they gave me a lot of food to take out after work; I remember I didn't even go to a supermarket for over three months. But the problem was the "transfer" to a better department.

I had worked for that nursing home for almost seven years. My original plan was working as a dishwasher for about two years and transfer to a little better job eventually. But all the managers blocked me from going to a better department somehow. These blockings were caused by a combination of bad luck, bad timing and selfishness of managers. But I think I did my best to try to get out of the situation: **Passing two exams of Medical Coder and Pharmacy Technician virtually by self-study.** I did *what I had to do*, so I don't have much to regret. Besides, I have been making more profits out of my investments since 2020. I could not hire any advisor, but have spent a lot of my time studying investments myself.

* * *

Finally, I decided to let go of that dining service job at the end of that nursing home career since a new company Morrison took over only the dining department in March, 2022; this new company took over only that dining department, but nothing else in the huge nursing home.

I had a letter from the CEO showing that the nursing home's management on dining service would be over on 3/31/2022 and I did not have the right to argue about it. And, then, I got information about unemployment benefits from the human resources. That is how I processed the steps to get $602 in benefits by April, 2022.

But the issue was that IDES (Illinois Department of Employment Security) contacted the dining department and asked how I would stop working there: these stupid people answered that I quit the job *voluntarily* (voluntary quitting is not the ground for getting benefits). I did not quit the job on my own; **I was pushed out while I was not against it** (this is supposed to be the ground).

Before I stopped working, I suggested transferring myself to this new company Morrison twice, but my suggestions were declined for no apparent reasons. Maybe the managers knew that I was not happy with the dining department for a long time. When I suggested the second time, they said the transfer period was already over and I had to fill out a new application and start my career as a newcomer; they said they had to suggest a lower newcomer hourly rate; I thought this was absurd since everyone knew I had been there for almost seven years. The last thing I did was applying for the transportation department in that nursing home. Even though I have an Illinois driver's license with a perfect record, they did not choose me in the final stage for no reason. I could not just do the dishwashing job forever; they acted as if they wanted me to do only the job for good. Especially at a lower rate.

* * *

There was a short Mexican sous chef everyone did not like in the kitchen of the nursing home. He was the major reason I tried to move out of the dining service originally. It seems he was not helpful to me even after I stopped working there since I believe he was the one who answered the IDES's question incorrectly. First of all, the nursing home did not have to answer IDES necessarily at all. The policy is if there is no answer from the previous employer for 10 days, IDES does not verify the reason for unemployment repeatedly. IDES had my seven years of employment record already and I believe they tried to help people in misfortune. That sous chef guy never helped me when I worked there and still was a pain in the butt for unemployment benefits.

Secondly, he should have answered IDES correctly at least. Most people did not save those letters from the CEO which arrived months ago. These chefs were all hired by Morrison years ago and started their careers in the nursing home as an outsourcer. As a result, they do not know what exactly happened to which member in the kitchen; there are over thirty people working in the kitchen. If someone disappeared, they seemed to think it was voluntary quitting, which had been common in that place. I am really glad I saved the letter from the CEO for proof of my forced resignation.

I wish my wife had a chance to talk about this with me. She checks the internet news too often and knows something we really do not have to know. We had heavy rain today and I got three Tornado warning messages via my smartphone which is pretty unusual. I was going to check the exact location of the Tornados, but my wife suddenly asked if I remembered the sports team mascot of my college while she was reading a novel. I do not know what is wrong with her, but I can see why she is unemployed. Employers need employees who focus on their job without concerning irrelevant things.

* * *

Have you ever been disgusted at yourself since you know too much about entertainment? I have. In the year of 2000, I studied at a language school in Cornell and tried to apply for graduate schools. When I was with my girlfriend, who is my wife now, suddenly music, "American woman" came out from a movie screen. She said, "It is music from *American Beauty*." I know it was music from *Austin Powers*. Then, suddenly, I got pretty upset at myself: 'Why do I even know this? Without getting accepted by any graduate school?' Both movies were released and popular in that year. **For your information, my unemployment benefit was**

canceled finally since IDES decided that I was not qualified.

* * *

Summary

1. Some people stay poor since they are concerned about someone else's business.
2. Minding only our own job needs some discipline.
3. Losers care about celebrities more.

37

Living in a too Big or Old House

Cars and houses are things that make us in pain only because we own them.
-Brad Kong

This chapter is all about jealousy; making others jealous can put us in poverty or danger. When people have more than enough money, the real qualities from each of us come out. Some may start a decent hobby like writing or traveling. Some may start spending money on new cars or bigger houses. The worst case can be that some people will spend all their money on something like drinking or even get into debt to buy expensive items; some people actually become poorer with debt only because they got some money in advance.

* * *

I do not think it's a good idea to make anyone jealous: Jealousy equals anger; The fact that *someone* is angry at us will not help us anyhow. More surprisingly, people can even go to prison or be dead if that *someone* is our boss.

Nowadays, I am reading a book titled *The 48 Laws of Power* written by Greene. This book starts with a topic titled "Never *outshine* your master." I like to understand this as "Do not make anyone jealous, especially our bosses."

In my opinion, one way to offend someone silently, but unnecessarily is to buy a big house or luxury car for ourselves; those not only cost us money, yet bring all sorts of problems. **Houses and cars are things that require constant care and expenses endlessly**; getting unnecessary attention, jealousy or anger from everywhere is a special bonus.

Greene's book starts with a story of Nicolas Fouquet, who was the Superintendent of Finances in France under the Sun King Louis XIV (14th) in the 1650s. Wiki shows that Fouquet had a glittering career initially and acquired enormous wealth in the beginning; he was also well known for having an extravagant lifestyle and frequently throwing lavish parties. At that time, he owned a magnificent castle named Vaux-le-Vicomte; it was so luxurious enough that King Louis XIV got an inspiration from it and had the same architects build the Palace of Versailles for himself later on.

It shows that Fouquet was expected to be a prime minister after the former prime minister, Jules Mazarin, passed away in 1661. Instead, King Louis XIV just eliminated the position of the prime minister itself for any reason. So Fouquet decided to throw a big party for the king with an excuse to celebrate the completion of his huge castle, Vaux-le-Vicomte. Fouquet invited 6,000 people to throw a housewarming party for his chateau, but his real intention was to show his royalty to the king and give him a wonderful time. All the famous people in France gathered at that party and everything seemed to be pleasant.

Then do you know what happened? Out of the blue, Fouquet was arrested two weeks later and got a life sentence for stealing money from the government treasury; history says that it was not really an honest or fair accusation for Fouquet. Nonetheless, Fouquet spent 15 years in solitary confinement before he died in the isolated Pyrenees mountain prison. Technically, I believe it's more than just jealousy in this case. **Fouquet just surprised this 22-year-old Louis XIV with all of his luxury and power and made the king worry that his power could look smaller than Fouquet.**

* * *

These are a couple of stories I found about jealousy online the other day: When cannibals, who eat the flesh of other humans, in a remote Pacific island need to kill someone in their village during famines, it says that they usually kill a guy with a beautiful wife first. During the emergence of communism in the beginning of the 20th century, poor peasants killed a lot of rich farmers in Russia and China; it was not all about the unfair systems only; it was about jealousy, too.

In my logic, I do not think it's a good idea to drive a luxury car, especially to work: **Do not show that to your bosses or customers if you need to get paid by them.** In fact, smart people never show their money to anyone and know how to live simply. I am honestly happy with my condo; 850 square feet is enough for a family of three. I feel comfortable when I don't spend a lot of money. **Furthermore, I believe that being frugal is one way to protect myself and my family.**

* * *

I usually focus on eliminating bad stocks from my investment portfolio. When we do stock investing, some focus on buying good stocks; that's what I used to do. Now I have 90 company stocks and 40 company bonds as of January, 2023; it has grown from $100 in 2011 to $560,000 in 2023. While a lot of my stocks are doing fine, I think about 20 company stocks and 1 bond have given me a headache. Experts said a recession may come soon; I think it's more wise to get rid of bad apples for now than look for any better companies to buy; all the stock prices may drop as if we get into a depression. The same thing goes for a house.

Some people feel more comfortable when they walk on quiet back streets rather than the bright shiny main streets; I feel more cozy when I sit in a nameless park than noisy crowded Disney World; people may feel more restful when they live in a small moderate house without debt than a luxurious big one with a mortgage. **People often do not realize how mental comfort is important**; they have forgotten to live lives for themselves instead of show off to others. Many people do not recognize the beauty of simple living; some just go for bigger, bigger and bigger houses even with a huge amount of debt.

* * *

When it comes to a real problem in the house, roof leaks always have made me crazy; I am serious that I get a panic attack or mental disease from it. It is supposed to be a very easy thing to fix since we are living in the 21st century now. But, for some reasons, I have never had luck with repairs on them. No matter how much I tried, roof leaks had kept happening to me for a long time. Now I have more than a phobia, so let me tell you my story.

I don't think I am really a complaining type of person to begin with. I notice that my wife complains a lot even about the weather. Now it is May, 2022 and the temperature is above 80 F in Chicagoland today; I was happy since I did not feel freezing. But she got upset since it was too hot this morning; she always turns up the thermometer up to 75 F when it is a bit cold even in the spring since it is freezing for her. All she does is complain, complain and complain. It is sad to see a girl (24 years ago) turn into an old complaining grandma. And who made her this way? Herself. No one asked her not to get a good job. Whenever I talk about a job, she always makes an excuse that she cannot do anything since she has a child. How many kids do we have? One. People cannot have less than one, for your information. I got a feeling that she will keep complaining, making excuses and being poor until her death: **There is no cure for these types of people.**

* * *

I started my business at a large stirp mall in 2006. It was a huge plaza, but I rented only 900 sf, so we occupied less than 1% of the property. We were located in the middle of the plaza and it had an ample parking lot. It was great that we had one stop sign right in front of the store, so people could see us whenever they stopped before passing by.

But I believe the management had the roof maintenance a long time ago. There was a store ceiling with tiles and grids under the main roof in my store. Having that ceiling was nice since it cut out the large amount of upper space from the roof; the ceiling blocked cold air and noise from the roof, too. I saved a lot of money for heating and cooling since we had to take care of the air space under the ceiling, not from the ceiling to the roof. But I noticed that the ceiling tiles got wet whenever it rained in 2006.

Actually, the very first roof leak started from the air-con duct in the middle of the store. I called the landlord and he sent us a couple of roof guys hired for that plaza and the issue seemed to be solved immediately. The guy mentioned that some storm seemed to move our air-con unit; I remember it was ok for the next three years.

* * *

The major roof leak all along was at the north east corner of my store: One major spot. I started repairing that by buying a lot of ceiling tiles from Home Depot and replacing them in the beginning. After doing that for a couple years, I bought a caulk gun and sealants one day. I used a ladder, opened the sealing tile and went up to the roof to seal up any leaking spots myself. When I think about it now, it was quite dangerous since the distance from ceiling to roof was 6 feet long. I barely stood on top of the ladder. Whenever I complained, they said they will do a major roof construction for the entire plaza soon.

I think they did a major roof construction in 2008, but, strangely, things did not get much better. **I think I started going crazy and having roof leak phobia from that point.** It took almost a year to finish the construction in 2009. There was one time they made a mistake pouring a bucket of water on the roof and I saw a new water leak coming at a totally new spot. How hard is it to fix a roof leak? It is America in the 21st century. I started to wonder how those hotels can have swimming pools on the rooftop or in the middle of buildings. They explained that they did not work on that spot yet.

After finally finishing the total construction, I thought that I would never see a roof leak again. How hard could it be since humans were on the Moon sixty years ago? It was just a matter of money for new construction, right? Wrong! Soon I started having different leak problems.

* * *

The landlord suddenly sent a new air-con guy to our store against my will and the roof around our air con duct started leaking; that was in the middle of the store, not the corner. Originally, the stupid landlord said so many different people touched the air-con units in our plaza, so that caused those leaks; so he said he found a "quality" technician somewhere and everyone should use him mandatorily. It was $65 for filter change and check up service, so I did not expect any trouble. It seems these recommended technicians also started hiring "not very reliable looking" subcontractors soon enough. And right after they touched the air-con, I started seeing water marks around the air con duct on the ceiling. **I went literally crazy:** How can I get out of these leaking problems? How hard is this to solve in the 21st century? They came to repair it and I asked them not to touch the unit ever again: Not just for money, it was psychologically aggravating.

I ended up solving the problem completely by not owning a business there any more. I didn't make a huge amount of profit there anyway. I made that decision in 2012 and our lease contract was over in 2014: I did not renew the lease. After closing out my store, I saw the big Polish supermarket in that very plaza had a big roof leak around their door area. I was more than glad that I did not have anything there any more.

* * *

And it seemed owning a nice looking condo solved my problem entirely. Still, unfortunately, I had a couple of leak problems around the chimney area in my condo in 2015. I called the association office and they sent technicians a couple of times and everything looks fine after that. I live on the top floor of our residential building. But I still could not believe the roof leak problem persisted this much wherever I had been.

Then, a *severe* hail storm came to our village in 2017: Very severe like Hurricane for 20 minutes. All the trees collapsed, cars were crushed by big hail and, of course, roofs were damaged, too. I had roof problems again and spent a painful one year on roof reconstruction by association. I had to stay in a motel twice in the middle of winter for their construction: 10 days each stay. They removed the old ceiling before winter and reconstructed a new one in May, 2018. This means I had to live without a ceiling over the winter in 2017: it was exceptionally painful and freezing; I had the worst cold symptom in my life during that winter.

After they built the new ceiling in my unit, they started the roof job. They completed the job 90% and stopped the construction to come back the next day. Then, you know what? Suddenly it rained out of the blue and I had a good amount of water stains on the brand new ceiling again. They sealed up the new roof right next day and apparently all the roofs and ceilings are fine after that. **I don't know what went wrong, but these roof leak problems had harassed me aggressively for more than two decades.**

In a sense, I am glad that I live in a small condo now. When we live in bigger and older houses, we can go through hellish lives for all sorts of repairs. These are some of the problems I had even though I live in a 850 sf condo. My recommendation is buying a newish small house or condo. It can save you a lot of money and headaches.

* * *

Summary

1. Do not make others jealous, especially when you do not have enough money yourself.
2. People can pay double the amount of cars or houses with debt. They get nothing out of vanity.
3. Smaller houses could be better for peace of mind.

38

Not Fighting Against Platforms

We may have to get out of where we are
only not to lose money.
-Brad Kong

I think it is important to forget everything sometimes: **Do not trust anyone or anything.** We can be the only ones who are truly on our side. Lately, I found out that sugar and carbohydrates are the ones causing diabetes and subsequent kidney malfunction. I have believed rice is the healthiest food in the world for decades (most Koreans do). I assume some people go broke since they fail to accept new info. It is important for us to see if we are in a system which puts us in the wrong direction or utilizes us in a malicious way.

* * *

I guess some people are just smart at doing business. I saw a restaurant called Rosario the other day and noticed that the owner is super clever. First of all, the founder built a new property to start the pizzeria; they may pay a mortgage for the new building, but I think it's better than paying rent endlessly; they will completely own the building outright someday. Secondly, I saw that they divided the building in half and made some part (30% of the building) for a casino slot machine cafe. I see more and more small gambling places like that in Illinois; I never go to those, so I am not perfectly sure how they make profit out of it, but I feel it would be an additional income for them. Thirdly, I saw that they made the front part of the gambling place for a colorful ice cream parlor (Italian Bon Gelato thing) neatly. So this is how they set up the entire floor plan: pizzeria (50%), gaming cafe (40%) and ice cream shop (10%).

I will explain about a Chinese restaurant that closed out sadly later on; it was near my home and they expanded *rental* space double pointlessly in my opinion. It was a take-out place originally, but having an extra remodeled dining area didn't bring them any money, especially after Covid. **When it comes to an offline business, I believe rent is the biggest *headache*.** I have a good friend paying over $10,000 a month for rent for his restaurant. I admit that he made great plans to have a full alcohol liquor bar in his place and join the school lunch program. I had more ideas like taking orders like the Noodle company instead of having servers requiring tips, but I was not sure if he would listen to me.

As I mentioned in Chapter 35, I think the habit of "trying something new at least once" is important; it is ok even if it's just a new restaurant or dish; see if you can meet a totally new person once a month as well. I know these are bothersome. But these can help us find out there is a *better* option. Getting stuck in a wrong system may not be a typical problem for young people. But, as I get older, I can see myself trying new things less and less every year.

* * *

The definition of *platform* in a dictionary is "a standard for the hardware of a computer system running softwares." What I try to mean by *platform* is "a huge system trying to make money out of visitors." And those visitors can be us.

Since the word, platform, originated from a train station, let me give an example with it.

Let's suppose that there is a train station and you are a passenger on a train. Millions of trains pass through the station everyday. The owner of the train station will make money whenever a train passes. Maybe he or she charges toll fees on trains; if you are on a train, basically you are the one who pays for it; the owner is the one making money out of us. Let me give you a couple of real life examples.

I think one of the good examples for a platform is a site like Facebook; it shows that over one billion people visit Facebook everyday. Who is the one making money out of this? Mark Zuckerberg. No visitor at Facebook makes money; mostly, they just get addicted to the site and lose time and mental energy called attention. He is the train station owner and some employees work for him at his station. And let's imagine that all the visitors are the passengers on the trains; maybe these are free trains since Facebook is free.

But we have to see millions of advertisements while on the wall of trains. Also we may have to use lots of facilities the train station provides if we pay some money: snack bars; restrooms requiring payments; cash ATM service; shopping malls or flea markets in the station; news stands; magazine counters; etc. And maybe some companies want to post advertisements on the wall of the station; still, these companies make money, not us.

Another example of a platform could be KDP (Kindle Direct Publishing) at Amazon. Amazon has built a huge online bookstore selling worldwide. And, more smartly, the management also built an easy book publishing system and connected it with the book sales site; now people can publish books easily with KDP at Amazon.

Authors don't have to go door to door of publishers asking to publish their manuscripts any more thanks to Amazon. Nonetheless, here is a little bit of a catch: KDP will take out 40% of our book sale profit whenever our book is sold. In other words, millions of writers will go through a train station named "KDP" and the station will make money out of authors. For your information, I am *not* against Amazon. I actually appreciate the company since I had no idea about how to publish my book: I believe most people do not know it, either.

* * *

In this point of view, I think the biggest platform in this country is the U.S. Federal Government. People can come in legally and make money in this country. But we have to pay taxes if we make any money somehow. If we cannot get a job or fail a business, it is our problem. But, if we make any profit, we have to pay tax. If we make a huge amount of money, we have to pay more tax at a higher rate: **This is smart as the platform owners will never really lose.** They will help us make as much money as possible; we just have to pay tax, if not a lot of tax.

I am still not against the federal government since they helped me a lot, personally. I know the Federal tax rate is higher than the State ones in general; they have more deductions, too. Also, my family received a good amount of stimulus checks when the COVID Pandemic was everywhere in 2020; those were helpful. I think I did my best to help society since a nursing home is also a health care place; I helped senior citizens get assistance for seven years.

* * *

The platform I am not very happy about is Illinois State. It is not just me: Illinois loses a good amount of residents every single year, according to the statistics. This is surprising since the total population in the U.S. is increasing. **It is even shocking since the housing prices and living costs in Illinois are up to three times cheaper than the East and West coastal States.** Large portion of the Illinois population is Latin Americans who give out a lot of babies. Still, Illinois is losing a noticeable amount of population every year.

Why is this happening? In my opinion, Illinois State is quite stingy to its residents while trying to take more taxes from them than others. There are seven States not charging State income tax as of 2023: Wyoming, Washington, Texas, South Dakota, Nevada, Florida and Alaska. A crazy amount of people move into Texas every year these days; that includes the world richest man, Elon Musk; Tesla factory also permanently moved into Austin, Texas in 2021. Florida gets tons of retirees as well while Illinois loses them.

Not only does Illinois have State income tax, but it is higher than many States (4.95% in 2023). However, this is something I like to point out: When a State has higher State tax, usually it has lower property tax. That is not what's happening in Illinois: **While it has high State income tax, the property tax of Illinois is the second highest in the nation only next to New Jersey**: the 2nd highest out of 50 States in America. I would say that Chicagoland out of Illinois is *the highest* property tax region in America (e.g., Lake and Cook county); half of Illinois residents are living in Chicagoland. Having two high taxes is a double blow by itself, but here is one more thing not to ignore.

Is the Illinois government reasonably generous to its residents since it takes more money than others? **Absolutely not.** According to my experience, all they do is take money diligently. All I have done is pay a large amount of taxes every year and I have never gotten anything back in the last seventeen years: no stimulus check from the States, no unemployment benefit or any type of help whatsoever.

* * *

Recently, I resigned from the weekend dishwashing job since a new company took over only the dining part in the nursing home. I filed an application for unemployment benefits as the HR sent a letter to suggest that; the process was long and complicated, but they decided to give me $300 a week for 26 weeks, originally I thought finally I got a little bit of help from the State after all those taxes I have paid for two decades; the amount of State income taxes has always been much more than that of the federal ones for me.

But, a month later, they suddenly contacted me again and said "Not being able to transfer to a new department" does not qualify for unemployment benefits (even if it was beyond my control). I thought that, at least, they would let me keep the $1,200 they already sent by April, 2022. Apparently, the situation looked like a poor dishwasher just lost a job after seven years of employment due to the company outsourcing issue, which is not his fault: They answered, "No." They asked me to pay $1,200 back, so I sent a check of $1,200 right next day. I paid $1,500 States tax only for the year before (2021). **They could not even let me keep the $1,200 once in my life since I lost a job?** I thought this was too much. It is an extremely stingy State government: I felt no wonder why everyone is leaving here.

* * *

Another thing I do not like about Illinois is the tax filing website in 2022. I understand the government made a new site, so they can collect tax efficiently. Since I made some capital gain out of stock trade in 2021, I paid about $250 estimated tax for the State that year. Having estimated tax means paying income tax one year earlier (2021) since I may have to pay too much in 2022. You would not believe how much they tried to hide information about my estimated tax already paid; I was not able to find the estimated tax info. Finally, I did, but had to try so hard. Unless I made a separate note at home, I could have forgotten that. **I almost feel like they made it that way, so they can collect more tax thanks to forgetfulness by residents.** Yet they have tried so hard not to give out any benefit even though I had a low income job.

Also, by rule, when we invest in stocks of a company headquartered in Illinois, we are not supposed to pay tax on the dividend of that company; it is called "High Impact Business Program in Illinois" and currently four companies are listed in the program in 2022: Walgreen, Abbvie, Abbott Laboratory and Caterpillar. I could not believe how much the governments tried to hide this information. Type "High Impact Business Illinois" in Google and see what results come out; **I found out that, at least, no government related site showed this info;** they tried super, super, super hard to hide this simple listing of four companies. I guess they want investors to pay more tax on dividends for not being aware of information.

* * *

Honestly, I seriously considered moving to Texas three years ago in 2019. I already bought my house in 2013, so it was hard; all the houses in America were cheap in 2013 because of the mortgage bubble burst. **I could not find a house of the same price anywhere in 2019.** If I still lived in an apartment, I could be in Texas by now in 2022. I thought I would move to Texas and forget about State tax for good in 2019. Unfortunately, it did not work out.

Still, Illinois has some advantages over others, though. It has a relatively good transportation system, so I can live without a car now. Also everything is cheaper than coastal areas in America. It has top ranked public universities, according to the U.S. News and Report magazine (e.g., public Ivy League like UIUC). It has a lot of quality libraries (the 2nd highest number of libraries in the nation next to NY). Also the weather is cool while the Earth is getting hotter due to global warming. And I am originally from Seoul, Korea and have always missed a big city. Chicago is the third largest city in the U.S. and I have enjoyed working around; the big city atmosphere and endless streets to walk are important to me.

I just hope the Illinois government will get close to the one in Texas, someday; there are reasons why it loses residents and Texas gains a lot. People are not fools and know which one is better exactly.

* * *

Summary

1. We have to check if the system we are in is the best one, once in a while.
2. Some people lose money all along since the platform they are in takes more advantages from them.
3. One excellent legal way to save on property tax is living in a small condo.

39

Lack of Financial Knowledge

What we do not know can kill us.
-Brad Kong

I think we should never disregard our intuitions: This can be the most formidable logic from our sub-consciousness. We cannot explain this visibly in a word, but this can be more important than mere knowledge. I think we should walk away if we do not feel good about anything: Never ignore the first impression or just a bad feeling out of nowhere. It's possible there are trillions of logic behind these gut feelings; we get bad feelings from people out of the blue, too. This sixth sense can help us improve profits, avoid losses or even save our lives.

While intuitions matter, knowledge is more powerful than ever nowadays. A little bit of health knowledge can save us literally millions of dollars if not our lives. We can get a lot of knowledge from YouTube or Netflix as well. Knowledge and information are two major tools that make you survive and possibly thrive. It does not necessarily cost to get more of these.

* * *

Piketty is a French economist and professor of Economics at the School for Advanced Studies in the

Social Sciences (EHESS) in France. He suggested a controversial theory in his book titled *Capital in the Twenty-First Century*: The rate of return on capital is greater than the rate of economic growth over the long term. **In other words, it reads that people make more money out of investment than salary at work.** According to his theory, investors will get richer than ever while those who do not invest will never get out of poverty no matter how much they work. I am not sure if this truly happens, but I think it's worth listening to.

Personally, I have been fully living on dividend and interest income since 2022. My life is far from luxury, though; probably, the biggest luxury I can have is dining at Thai or Indian restaurants; nonetheless, I feel blessed that I don't have to go to work.

* * *

I believe what's important in personal finance is getting rid of debts, first. I suggest people not to jump into an investment even if they are sure; I know it's extremely hard to make actual profit out of it, according to my 11 years of experience. In fact, I decided to stop buying stocks after 2021 although I will keep my current $600,000 portfolio; it gives me about $30,000 in dividends and interest every year.

There were some Korean trolls who talked about leverage *loans*, but never understood a simple thing: No point in investing if we have a debt already; the chance to lose money out of debt interest is 100%; the amount is not small. On the contrary, the chance to make some money out of investment is less than 30% (probably close to 0% for some trolls). It would be like going to the gym to lose weight while having a tumor. I believe we need to extinguish fire first before remodeling a house.

* * *

People often make the mistake that making money is the most important thing to be rich; this is true to some extent. But, if we are in the top 10% of the wealth pyramid, not making a mistake could be more prime: **Most financial mistakes are caused by greed.** Personally, I own my small condo outright and have a portfolio of 90 company stocks, 40 company bonds and some savings; probably I will make more money with book sales and eventually inherit a small fortune from my parents. In this case, not losing money by a big mistake could matter more.

My father has been wealthy for life and currently lives in Korea; he owns a few condos and one commercial tall building; we believe his net worth is over $20 M in USD (No one knows how much exactly). He is a clearly self-made man as he lost his parents when he was young. Here is one thing he has always made sure of for life: "No debt."

What he means by "no debt" is no "business" debt; he does not mean a mortgage, car loans or other consumption related debts. Buying a house or car with debt has never been his concern; he always has bought those in full with cash. I know there was one Korean troll borrowing a chunk of money for his house debt called a mortgage to live in luxury houses to show off; he said he bought a $4 M house with a huge debt in 2022. I am sure my oldman will look at him like an animal.

Technically, there is nothing wrong with borrowing money for houses since they are naturally expensive. I think I started hating mortgage payers only because of the troll I just mentioned above; this one always showed off as nasty as possible even though all he had was an incredible amount of debt.

* * *

The first finance book I read was *Rich Dad and Poor Dad* written by Robert Kyosaki in 2007. I know it was written a long time ago, but my wife strongly suggested that book to me when we were at a Borders bookstore one day. I was not interested in the beginning, so she started to read the book to me. By the time she finished reading the first paragraph in the prologue, I decided to buy it. I think I ordered it online for a used copy, though.

Here are the key points in the book I understood: **An asset is something putting money in our pockets**; bank interest is an example. We get the bank interest automatically only because we have some money in the bank. If we can live only on interests without touching the original money, our wealth will last forever.

This has actually been an important principle for me in the last fifteen years. When we have a small amount of money, it does not matter much. But let's say that we have $1,000,000 in AT&T stock. I know it's a lot of money, but some people have it. AT&T stock give 6% dividend a year just like bank interest (check chapter 17 in *UnBrokable* II*). Then we can get a $60,000 dividend every year. **If we can live on less than $60,000 a year, $1,000,000 can last forever.** A considerable amount of people have more than $1,000,000 nowadays; they can get $60,000 a year forever unless they touch the original $1 M. This is why there are people living without a job everywhere nowadays; honestly, this includes me even though I am getting only $30,000 a year from 130 companies.

I had a chance to get some money from my parents after my daughter was born. I put all the $90,000 in my bank CDs in 2011 and started getting 3% interest a year, then. It was a nice side income since I had struggled to make money from my business at that time. Then, suddenly the mortgage bubble burst and all the house prices dropped crazily. I was able to buy my condo at $60,000 in 2013, which is almost one third of the current price in 2022.

Without that book, I would have not known what to do with that $90,000 to begin with. Maybe I could have bought a racing car since holding only cash is no good? What if I would have lost the money at the casino? Thanks to the book, I have my concept about assets established and kept saving money in CDs, stocks and bonds for interest and dividends since 2011. I can see that the book is still a top seller at Amazon and helped tons of people not waste their capitals.

* * *

Summary

1. Financial instinct and knowledge are both important.
2. Not having a debt is priceless.
3. Reading one book helped me greatly.

40

Not Being Unique

Unless we are unique, we can be replaceable.
-Brad Kong

Sungwoo Lee used to be an average Joe working at a department store in Seoul, Korea. But he became a local hero who made several headlines and has his own Namu Wiki page now since 2014. He has been a hard core fan of the baseball team Kansas City Royals. The team members were shocked that they have a serious fan in South Korea and invited him with air tickets. After that, the team has won a good number of important games for years. Would people care if he was a fan of the Yankees? That team has a million fans worldwide: **He could have been just one of many.**

I go to Subway for only one menu item: Veggie patty sandwich; it's better than the "impossible meat" in my opinion. This veggie patty is made of green beans and tastes just like fish cake in Korea. No one else is selling this. And the day they get rid of this from their menu would be the last time I go there since I don't eat anything else. Likewise, the reason why I go to Zupas kitchen is because of their crab avocado sandwich: **Again, no one else is selling it.** Subway used to have a similar one called "seafood sensation," but they dropped it. I have no choice but to go to these two whenever I miss them.

I still remember I visited Ribfest Chicago in Lincoln Park in 2007. It was only one year after I opened my video game store in 2006 and the festival had a PlayStation Mobile Truck; people were able to play *Uncharted 2* for free in the trailer. It had about 20 restaurant vendor tents selling ribs: But do you know which vendor sold the largest amount of food? Grilled corn. I still remember that there was only one vendor selling them on the cob; which is a favorite side dish for barbecue. The vendor did not sell ribs at all, but people were waiting in a long line while others didn't seem to have crowds.

* * *

Author Greene mentions that a lot of hired soldiers were killed by the States which hired them originally in the Middle Ages; those soldiers were fired, imprisoned or even executed after winning battles for the States. Those soldiers were readily replaceable after all; it shows that they tried to take more power or salary from employers after winning battles; they did not realize that there are others who can do the same jobs. When I think about it, even Jeanne d'Arc (Joan of Arc) was burnt to death after saving the State of France. Greene wrote one interesting story about an indispensable astrologer in his book, *The 48 Laws of Power*, so let me summarize that here.

Louis XI (1423-1483) was a king in France and he had one astrologer in his palace. One day, the astrologer predicted that one lady of the court would die within 8 days and it came true. Louis XI started to worry that it's either this astrologer killed the woman or he has too strong *sorcery* power; the king finally decided to kill him.

When he arrived in the king's room full of soldiers, Louis XI asked him one last question: "When do you think you will die, sorcerer?" Then he answered, "I will die three days before you die, Sire." The King asked soldiers not to kill the astrologer; actually he provided him with the finest doctors in the country until the king himself passed away, first. History shows that the astrologer actually had lived several years longer than the king. By wisdom, he made himself indispensable for the king and saved his life.

* * *

Thai foods are always a little bit more expensive than Chinese; usually Chinese lunch specials are close to $8, but Thais are close to $10 in 2022. Why? Thai restaurants are rarer than Chinese; I don't see other reasons as a Korean. When I think about ingredients, those should cost about the same for both types of restaurants. **In this logic, the best way for us to make more money is by being the only one.** It does not matter for whatever field we work in; I just need to be someone people cannot find anywhere else. In the case of my books, I hope people must say that I have never seen a book like this before. I think that is a success itself by my definition: Being different.

In the book titled 12 *Rules for Life,* Peterson mentioned that there are about 1.5 million new titles of books published in North America every year, but only 500 books sell more than 100,000 copies. Here is one question: What do I have to do to make my book outstanding? If my book gets a big award, that would be the best-case scenario, but we all know that it won't happen, especially as soon as I release it.

I concluded that I can write more at least. I notice that almost 100% of self help books are less than 600 pages. I can make my book close to 800 pages as Amazon publishing allows a maximum 825 pages for paperbacks. It is possible for a reader to look for the thickest self-help book as a lot of novels are over 1,000 pages; for example, *The Game of Thrones* novel is over 5,200 pages for 5 volumes in a collective box. This is the sign that there are readers who prefer choosing thick books; when they search for a self-help book having over 800 pages, only my book should come out. **I thought that is something I can try to make happen at least.**

* * *

There is a comedian and actor named *Hong* in Korea; he is well known that he is a gay. In fact, he is the only one coming out as a homosexual in the country as the Korean society is conservative. I watched one radio show and this is what he said: "It is painful to be the only gay in this country. Still there is one great advantage. **No one can replace my role.**" He is pretty wealthy and has managed his career well in the last 29 years.

I think another example of uniqueness is the actor Peter Dinklage in America; he is famous for his role as "the dwarf" in *Game of Thrones* dramas. I admire his courage as a man; it must be so hard for him to apply for an actor job to begin with. Google shows that his net worth is $25 M; I think that he deserves more than that, but let me ask one question: Would he be that wealthy now if his height is 170 cm (5.5 feet)? **Possibly not**; I think it's probable that most people would not even remember there is such an actor since he could have been one of billions. Here is one thing we should not ignore: he may be short, yet he cannot be replaceable in some particular roles. It shows that he is casted for the new *The Hunger Games* movie coming in 2023. I am pretty sure he will keep getting good roles without time off until he passes away; this is important since a lot of Hollywood performers do not get enough roles.

* * *

In my opinion, being unique matters to writers, too. When I publish this book, I can choose 10 categories to list this book in. **Marketing experts recommend listing my book in as rare a category as possible**; they said it is important to make the book the number one seller in a small sub-category in Amazon; otherwise, readers do not even notice there is such a book. The two categories I may choose are Asian study and Asian American writers; this book can be considered an autobiographical story. Asian numbers are less than 5% in this country. People cannot list in those categories no matter how hard they try unless they are Asians.

I think the most important feature of an art is uniqueness: The originality is the one everyone just imitates from. I know this book is not exactly literature, but it is also a sort of art made by a human. I want it to be different from all the others in the world. I like to hear that, "I have never seen a book like this." I would like to include some distinctive ideas people never can find anywhere else. As long as that is achieved, I would consider my books a success.

I believe the same thing goes for our lives. In my point of view, a lot of people (especially, Korean trolls) live too boringly in the traditional way: finishing school; getting a job; getting married and having two kids; mortgage for 30 years; retirement in Florida; death. I like to have a little bit of variation if that is better for me.

I did not want to live in Korea forever or marry a Korean woman only because I was born there. I stopped having more children after having one since I did not want to spend most of my life working like a donkey only to support a bigger family; the world is bursting anyway. I bought a decent condo in full instead of buying a two story house with 30 years of mortgage debt. **I will not try very hard to be different, but I do not follow a conventional schedule set by others blindly.**

* * *

There are a few things unique about this book in case you didn't notice. The first thing is three sentence summaries at the end of each chapter; this is a common practice when someone writes a long article *online* in Korea. People are busy and get easily impatient nowadays; I notice that a surprising portion of people buying books are young people; I have been in a lot of bookstores lately and witnessed this myself. Besides, I do not want to waste time for anyone including myself.

The second thing is bold sentences. The reason is the same as the first; I want readers to get points and move on. I have seen that only three books do the same so far: "Life force" written by Tony Robbins, "Humor, Seriously" written by Naomi Bagdona and "How to Fail at Almost Everything and Still Win Big" by Scott Adams; in the case of Adams' book, only the Korean version did it. I am not copying them; I thought this is one way to finish this book efficiently; the final will be a thick book. Honestly, some books are nothing but torture without this methods.

The third thing is a lot of examples related to Korean news and culture. Not many books published in America deal with those, especially in self-help books. I think I can list this book in Korean American literature or Korean American memoir as well if there is such a category.

The fourth thing is the spaces between paragraphs. I feel suffocating when paragraphs go on endlessly without having a break. Not many people use one-line space and indentation together between paragraphs just like me. Some people may like this and find it breathable. Frankly, it does not matter whatever it is; **I think it is more important to be different than others.**

It is all or nothing. Being unique may not guarantee success; being the same as others must guarantee failure. I would not say being normal is a failure, necessarily. But, when we are unique, we gain some control; we can put ourselves in an advantageous position. Let me explain with examples.

* * *

When I was at the library about five years ago, I read one travel diary. It was on the shelves in the new release section; a lot of new books were placed there first and moved to the right section as they became old. The female author wrote a journal while taking some trips including cruise ship travel.

What was very unique about that book was she wrote the entire book by cursive handwriting font. And she took photos even including a porter boy moving their luggages on the cruise ship; the Caribbean boy wore a red uniform looking like a marching band. She wrote a lot of explanations on photos by hand as well. The lady writer seemed to be passionate about her life and travel; the book had hundreds of photos people usually do not post on blogs; I truly felt I was on the trip.

The only problem is I cannot find the book ever again in the last five years; unfortunately, I do not remember the exact title of the book; I only picked that up at the new release section then. And probably it has not been a mega hit, so not many people know about what that is. I checked amazon for "cruise travelog", "Caribbean travels" or "a travel book written by hand" so many times, I could not find it. I even checked the entire travel writing section in our library. The section has about four hundred books and I checked one by one the other day. It was not that super hard actually since I could tell a book without a color photo easily from the spines. Also, I recall the approximate size of the book, so I eliminated too small or giant books.

Here is one question: Why am I trying so hard to find that book? **It was unique.** I have never seen any book written in *handwriting* with that vividness and warmth. I see a lot of travel guide books with photos, but even the photos were different in that book: insignificant ones for official tour guides, but cherishable for personal memories.

In a sense, this is important for other fields, too. We may not have to be distinctive to survive, but we have to be unique to be successful. We can make our living somehow even if we are mundane; it is possible we won't make much money that way, though. **We should be irreplaceable somehow to be successful**. I am not talking about being excellent; we just need to be a little different in a positive way.

* * *

Summary

1. Societies often think being different is bad.
2. I think being unique is essential to get rid of a chunk of similar competitors.
3. If anyone knows about the travel book I mentioned, I would greatly appreciate it if you let me know the title along with the Amazon review on this book.

41

Living for Harmful Satisfactions

Satisfaction and happiness are two different things.
-Brad Kong

There is an American romance writer named Danielle Steel; she has been divorced five times and has nine children (one died of suicide, unfortunately). Seemingly, she has lived a very productive life, publishing over 500 novels, career-wise. Oddly, I found out that her second husband was a prison inmate who she interviewed once in Lompoc, CA; she married him in 1975 even after he returned to jail on robbery and rape charges in 1974; it shows that she eventually divorced him in 1978 after having multiple miscarriages.

I don't think that we should get addicted to love: Love can be everything. Or it is merely a hormone interaction, forcing us to keep producing offspring. Simultaneously, I don't think we should let our successes blind us to try something too wild; we should not let our wealths crash our lives.

One Korean Buddhist monk[46] once said, "There is no desire lasting forever." Even though we want something badly, if we believe it doesn't help, I think we should pass some time; maybe we won't long for it soon. I used to eat a lot of Chicago dogs in different joints in 2021; I don't

---

[46] Pomnyun

want any of those any more; personally, once a craving is gone, I found that I do not want a specific menu forever. I guess that the similar thing goes for dating. Let a person go if things do not work out well; it is possible that the person may not be as fantastic as we are imagining now.

I often feel that poor people may be disrespected not because of lack of money, but because of being bothersome. Humans are not like plants; it's not that we don't move only because they don't have a job. By nature, people always act, regardless of making money or not. If we move in a constructive way, we can end up having sufficient one way or another; at least, we may be above the poverty line. Being broke despite all those movements means some live in unfruitful ways; these people usually bother others; they lower the productivity of a society over all; rarely, they become a cancer of a community, too. We never get paid for annoying others; this can be why some never get respect.

* * *

I don't think we can buy decency; having some money helps us not downgrade our quality of lives, though. Personally, I have never really felt a huge amount of decency from Trump; I feel more materialistic greed from him. **In a sense, going for more money always is the attitude of a slave**; some are rich slaves, but they are still slaves. I think that we can give a decent feeling only when we do not show off wealths; maturity should come in together to give decency.

I was passing by Chinatown Chicago the other day; there were an array of massage parlors, so I opened one door only to check out the prices. Weirdly, a Chinese old man was standing virtually naked in the middle of the store and hid quickly as soon as he saw me. I felt suddenly disgusted; I felt yucky and left the town quickly; the town didn't look the same after the incident. I am sure that not every Chinese gentleman is like that, but I guess I learned some lessons.

I think buying fake luxury goods or getting plastic surgery only makes us look cheap even after spending money; talking about TV soaps or celebrities puts a low price tag on us. Talking about books, speaking, reading or writing a foreign language always puts pricey tags on us. Wearing a thong in the public pool or Chicago riverwalk didn't look decent this summer (some women); catcalling women or having too low standards on them is not decent. We will never buy decency with money.

* * *

***Not* reading a book is one guaranteed way to get poor;** we can absorb other people's life lessons within a day only by reading; we can advance more; it might take twenty years for those writers to get lessons, but we can get them immediately. I just finished the book *Nomadland* the other day; shamelessly I think this is my first time that I finished a book in English *completely*. I actually found it for $2 at the clearance section of a Half priced book store; it was boring, but I thought I would finish at least a book completely *once* in my life. I have a habit to read some parts of books and move on to another; one Korean professor said it is ok, though; this is the reason why there are *contents* and *indexes* in books.

The book made me realize there are a lot of *houseless* people in America. As the author admitted at the end, a *houseless* is practically a "homeless"; I know some try to describe van life as "a cool life with so much freedom."

But no one can sleep comfortably in a vehicle; a car can go too hot or freezing fast; the van dwellers have to worry which restroom they can use this time. For some reason, almost all the people living full-time in a van or RV are white Americans; many of them are old but it shows that one third of them had been wealthy when they were younger. **I also learned that virtually all of them had mortgage problems.**

* * *

My next book to read would be "Body" by Bill Bryson; it looks thick, but I found it is *easier* than *Nomadland.* Personally, I hate people trying to write in a *hard* way; some do not give clear meaning *intentionally*, which is horrible. Also there are writers using rare words on purpose or twist grammar for artistic value; I *detest* them. I like Schopenhauer since his books are clear and easy to read. There was a Korean professor named Ma; he was well-known for easy writing. He was the youngest professor of Yonsei University, which is one of "Ivy league" schools in Korea; it shows that his motto had been "*writing as easy as possible.*" I can see that he suffered from snobs enjoying hiding meanings arrogantly; some may think it is a way of showing off philosophical knowledge, but I think it is stupid and wasteful. Languages were invented for communication 150,000 years ago; it was not created to torture people.

Schopenhauer was the professor at the University of Berlin and Bryson is a former Chancellor of Durham University as well. I love those extremely educated ones writing in easy fashions. I am nobody, but this would be my principle in writing, too: easy, simple and clear. Besides, I believe this is the only way I can sell books since I expect non-native English speakers to buy those.

I have been a full-time writer since 2022 and wondered how I can be a better one. Here was my conclusion: Reading is the critical prerequisite to be a good one; I may read 8 hours a day. When I read other books, it brings me more ideas; I can summarize other books, translate hard meanings and add my opinion; readers can get two books this way. I guess that my book will be thicker as I read more books. As a result, I hope this series will be full of quality points from my brain and other masterpieces.

* * *

Some say that we are living in the age of YOLO[47]; others say "Be here now." These are fine but, weirdly, I feel that our society is changing to focus on *instant yet harmful satisfactions*. In a sense, the more we focus *on* now, the farther we may stay away from wealth; saving is not necessarily the best thing we can do for today.

I bought a brand new Dell desktop package in 2022. It was a $550 deal with everything included: a new monitor, PC with Windows 11, keyboard, mouth, etc. I bought the same deal from Dell sixteen years ago in 2006 and had used it well for decades. So I did not expect any trouble: What can be wrong with a brand new PC, anyway? And, technically, I guess that Dell did not do anything wrong this time, too; they made a mint PC combo at a low price and delivered it quickly with free shipping. I was pretty amazed at the order processing speed and happy on the day it arrived.

Then, my itching eye problem started about three weeks after I started using it. I had used only an old flat screen

---

[47] You only live once

15" monitor in the past 17 years. But there must have been some technological advancements; Dell shipped a wide 24" high definition monitor with HD cable this time. I have lived without a TV for a couple of decades now for my mental peace and meditation; I have avoided movie theaters and Blu-ray players as well. I noticed that this high definition monitor killed my eyes seriously. This may not be exactly Dell's fault; I assume that they developed new tech, accordingly. Here are 11 ways I figured out how to save our eyes from frying by sharp monitors.

1. If you own a Dell brand monitor, you will see five buttons right below the screen; usually these are the same for other monitors, too. The first button from the left is preset modes. Choose "Comfort view."

2. Raise the contrast to 80%; letters would be more visible from far distances. We can place ourselves farther from the screen this way.

3. Make the brightness a little bit darker than your surroundings. I have an LG smartphone and it has an automatic brightness function under display. When I turn it on in my computer room, it shows that the recommended brightness is 51%; I set the brightness of the desktop monitor to 50%. I had thought that a very dark screen was good by mistake. It is like when we get into a dark room, we tend to put some pressure in our eyeballs to search for things: **Pressuring our eyes for long can give us headaches.**

4. I feel better with my old VGA cable than the new HDMI one. Both are 1080p; still my eyes feel better with VGA.

5. Make the sharpness up to 40%; the preset was 50%, but I lowered it a little bit.

6. Avoid the blue background on the Windows start screen; I notice that any blue color hurts my eyes more.

7. Download free Magic eye 3D images and use one of them as a background image (screensavers). They actually improve vision by changing focus inside our eyes; we can watch frequently if it is on the start screen.

8. Buy a blue light prevention glass, which is only $5 on Amazon.

9. Take a look around every twenty minutes.

10. Buy a matte screen monitor instead of glossy if you have an option; I did not have a choice for a combo package deal. I found out that the previous Dell monitor was way more matte than the new one. I suspect Dell added glossy on the monitor for gamers as I found a lot of Xbox gaming features in Windows 11. I turned all those off as they made my computer slow.

11. Get rid of other HDTV or Gaming monitors from home; do not bring a smartphone outside the house to watch *more* screens. TVs are designed for maximum visual effects; these will fry our eyes off in the end.

Finally, I switched two monitors and have used my old Dell monitor, which I bought in 2006, for about 2 years now.

* * *

Summary

1. Too many people waste money on instant but harmful satisfaction these days.

2. Those will hurt our eyes and health one way or another.
3. Cut them out of your life: Enough is enough.

42

Smartphone Addiction

"Cell" phones: Some users are prisoners.
-Brad Kong

Checking smartphones pointlessly is one way to make ourselves exhausted for nothing. Chronic fatigue from endless browsing can make us stop moving forward. First of all, let me talk about internet addiction briefly.

I believe that one of the best ways to get out of internet addiction is "delaying" or "deterring." See if you can live without the internet at home; some people use it only at work, libraries, etc. If you have to keep it at home, see if you can choose the minimum option with the slowest speed; that should be enough for business use (may or may not be enough for entertainment). Personally, our village library offers 5 hours of free internet a day with their newish computers. If we bring our own laptops, we can use them there for up to 11 hours a day.

* * *

For smartphones, see if you can leave it at home whenever you are out; this can cut our internet times virtually in half; it may sound weird to some, but, personally, I always leave my phone at home.

I have lost a lot of things outside in the past five years: an umbrella, four winter gloves, even a backpack once, etc. But I have never lost my smartphone; it's 6 years old, yet still in mint condition since I use it solely at home. See if you can choose only a *free* phone coming with an annual plan. Sometimes, I stop browsing the internet since my smartphone battery is out quickly. I think expensive phones with longer batteries can make us more addicted.

* * *

There is a Korean entertainer named Yu; strangely, he has been married 9 times and 2 of them were Mongolian women; oddly, he has only 5 wives out of 9 marriages since he had been married to the same women two or three times. He said that he must marry if he is in love, so the ladies can get some benefits out of him legally. I disagree with his lifestyle since I have been married only once and she is the mother of my daughter now. Still, here is something I remember from his interview. When the reporter asked him to give the last advice to his fans, he answered, "Just go out. You will go crazy if you stay in front of a computer too long." I agreed with him; suddenly, I felt he was a sane man.

Wasting time on browsing online is an issue all of us need to deal with in the 21st century; smartphones extend the time to waste; they cause physical accidents, too; it can cause death while the internet itself can be a mere mental problem. Control is the key in this case. Alternatively, we can downsize it, at least. I decided to stick to the basic smartphone provided for free, so my usage can be limited.

* * *

I personally have a strange habit of keeping writing online; one example of the places I write is a message board in *Reddit*; still, there are so many similar sites in Korea. It may be a little better than social media addictions; I always write my own articles with some ideas; maybe I have improved my writing skills a little bit that way in the last twenty years. But I have suffered enough from troll attacks and waste so much time arguing with them; there is absolutely no point for those. Writing articles *for free* online did not bring me any monetary gain, anyway.

I always leave my smart phone at home. Rarely, I bring it out only when I need it for double authentication for specific sites when I use a newer computer at the library: stock brokerages or banking. After entering my user ID and passcode, they usually send a security text to my phone and want me to type that in (double authentication). Other than that, I always leave my smart phone at home and use it as if it is a landline home phone even though it is wireless.

I had had only one landline phone by 2018. I had a mobile phone before only until 2009, but I canceled it since I had never really used it. Besides, I did not want to get bothered all the time; my wife used to call me all the time when I had it and we had arguments about it. I thought it was unnecessary fighting on top of spending extra on phone bills. There was no urgency to call each other every 4 to 5 hours. I still had a video game shop by 2014 and the store had a landline phone.

* * *

There are a few critical advantages if we leave our smartphones at home. First of all, we do not have to worry about losing it outside. I lost one very expensive umbrella in 2020. I think I left it at a Korean restaurant in a poor area and somebody took it before I returned there; it was a restaurant located inside a Korean supermarket near Belmont Ave in Chicago. And I had lost my gloves three times in the past two years; I left them once in a bus, but I do not even remember what happened to the other two pairs. Secondly, I can keep my phone in mint condition since I use it only at home: No crack on screen or anything.

My phone is a free LG smartphone; I got it when I started a one year contract with Tracfone. I recommend this Mexican company since it has never raised the monthly fee for the last 4 years: AT&T hiked the price every single year, which is the reason why I canceled my home phone with them. Regardless of costs, things will get complicated if I lose it. Probably, I have to get a new phone with a new number, so I may have to let everyone know my new number: An extreme hassle.

People often use smartphones to check social media. In my opinion, the damage caused by a smartphone has three categories: physical damage including death, lowering vision and mental distraction, which eventually causes exhaustion. I see some people carry smartphones to work all the time and they check while they work. **They act as if they get paid when they check webs more:** That is extremely dangerous behavior. Let me tell you what happened to my ex-coworker in 2019.

* * *

There used to be a young openly-gay guy working in the dietary care department in the nursing home. For your information, I have nothing against gay; if I have anything, I feel sorry for them; I have been discriminated against before as a minority in America in the last two decades. Still, regardless, that boy was a little bit of an asshole.

What I did not like about him was using his gayness as a tool to offend straight men. I do not know where this came from to begin with. He had been close to a lot of female coworkers as a friend. Then, when a male coworker was interested in a girl, he pretended to flirt with the girl in front of him intentionally. Most people did not know if he was gay or not. Who cares? He was a nobody, anyway. But those straight men usually got offended for no reason or even got heart broken. There was one girl close to him and she and he offended a lot of people until they both quitted the job. As I said, I have nothing against gay as I read Sapiens written by Harari all the time (Mr. Bell, who wrote the foreword of this book, may be gay and I don't care as he helped me more than anyone else). But I believe that these two were no good people by nature.

And, coincidentally, he was a dishonest worker, too. He checked smartphone all the time during his working hours. I believe he had an expensive new phone; he had driven a brand new Corolla his mother bought for him, too; it was less than 6 months old. I know some people drop cell phones and screens get cracked sometimes; something much bigger happened to him.

When I checked Facebook one day, I saw one photo that showed he had bad bloody scratches on his entire arm. He wrote that he got in a big accident on I-290; his car rolled over several times till it totaled: It was damaged beyond repair, so he had to abandon it.

In my view, it was almost impossible for anyone to have an accident in that spot in the middle of summer; it was a wide highway near Woodfield mall and I have never seen any accident around there in the last 16 years. **I assume he probably checked his phone while he was driving.** He could have been dead at the age of 22; at least, he blew out a $25,000 brand new car completely, which is an unnecessary money loss, nonetheless. I think smartphone damage is much bigger than home internet addiction. I do not know any more stories after this since he quitted his job after all.

* * *

Secondly, I like to talk about vision damage caused by smartphones. As a 49 years old man, I hardly ever got any vision check up in the last 15 years. My vision had never really changed, which is normal for an adult of my age; at least, I did not notice any change.

As AT&T kept raising phone bill every year, finally my landline phone got more expensive than mobile phone in 2018: AT&T home phone was $29 a month while Tracfone mobile was $16 a month including 500 MB data for internet (Tracfone has never changed the price last 4 years). So I switched to Tracfone in 2018.

But, suddenly, my vision has become more and more near-sighted noticeably. I think one reason is the distance between my eyes and the internet screen has gotten much nearer. When I had checked the internet with a computer only, the distance to screen from my eyes would have been about 30 inches (80 cm). Now it has become like 10 inches (25 cm) since I have the phone in my hand and the screen is very small. Besides, the screen keeps shedding lights on my eyes, so they get tired and itching more. I changed the brightness of the screen to the lowest and downloaded Gabor eye training app on my smartphone (this eye exercise game is supposed to improve my vision).

* * *

Thirdly, using more internet via smartphone has made me more impatient somehow; attention span has been getting shorter and shorter. In a sense, checking the internet is like giving ourselves more work; our body never takes a break.

When I close my eyes and meditate, I feel so much boredom. **But it truly gives me rest.**

I am glad I have a strict policy to leave my phone in my house. Who knows how many times I would have lost my phone. I may be an internet addict, but luckily not a phone addict. Do not give yourself one more thing to carry. You have lots of burden already. Do not give yourself extra work to do. If you cannot control it, just throw it out. Cut the subscription out and save money. And use the internet at your work or library only. It will give you more freedom.

* * *

Summary

1. Smartphones can cause physical damages including death.
2. Having the internet at home may not be necessary for everyone.
3. If you cannot eliminate those, make your lifestyle hard to access them.

43

Lack of Alone Time

Time to be alone is time to grow.
-Brad Kong

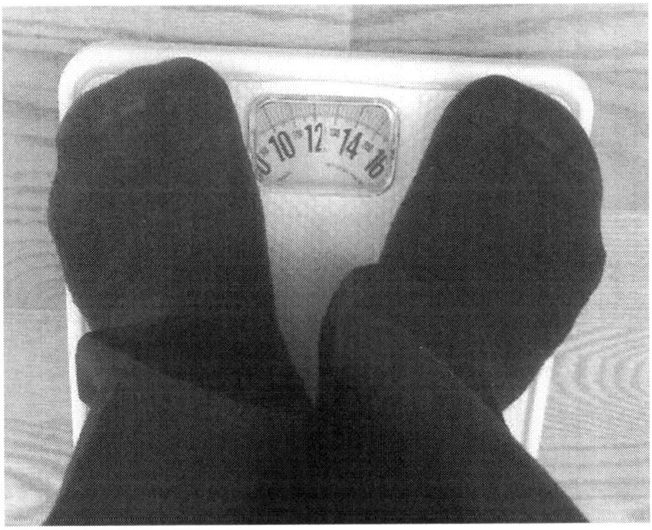

I am 123 pounds as of March, 2023.

I think that time to "fast (not eating food)" is the true time to take a break. Surprisingly, we can even take some breaks from our eating instinct. When I think about it, eating is a lot of work, especially when we need to cook. I have been 125 Lbs. in the last few years, but try to make my weight down to 120 Lbs. I have a minor jaw infection caused by a rotten molar tooth. Now the tooth is finally gone in September, 2022 after four years of cure attempt; now I am trying to cure my jaw completely. I do take antibiotics, but I believe one way to cure my disease is fasting. Losing weight means our bodies eat some of our own bodies: **It shows that they eat diseased cells first.**

* * *

Today I saw a news article about a Thai man having two wives and nine kids; his name is Manop Nuttayothin who is 42-years-old living in Bangkok; it shows that he originally had one wife having three kids, but she passed away, unfortunately. He married twice more after that and all three women wound up having three kids respectively, so he has nine children total as of 2022.

I will be honest with you: I have never envied a person having a lot of kids, personally; I have envied a person having a lot of money or a writer who has written many books; occasionally, I envy a person working for a less painful job. But I have never been jealous of people having multiple divorce or marriage history records, not to mention a lot of kids.

Raising a child is a huge obligation in a sense; I cannot even take care of my daughter properly, so my wife does most of that job now. For the same obligation reason, I will never envy a person getting a prison sentence or having many years left to complete his or her Army service. This Thai guy seems to be merely an auto parts salesman in Bangkok, which is a hellish hot city with air pollution; he looked poor and painful in the photos on the news. The worst part of his life would be being occupied all the time; he won't get time to be alone: I believe a time being *alone* is necessary for both happiness and growth.

* * *

What I do not like about my mother is she never respects my boundaries; I am 49 years old already, but she always violates it. I don't even know why she keeps calling me while I never call her; every relationship should be mutual even for mother and son. It's an old story, but I do not think I had a pleasant childhood with my parents in general. I understand they did their best to raise two kids (me and my younger brother) in hellish conditions; I get it since I am a father myself. But that does not mean I want to get close to them now.

This is what I want to say to my mother: Do not contact me unless I contact you; as grown ups, the communication should be mutual; at least, it should be something like I contact her once, so she can contact me two times. If I do not contact her forever, she should accept it as a result of her misbehavior (or abuse) when I was young.

I did not have a good time when I was in the Army or the nursing home career as well: The major difference is that these places never contacted me again. I had bad customers before when I had my business; the good thing is that I do not have to see them ever again. All those may not be interested in seeing me again, but at the same time, they happen to respect my privacy and boundaries. Or they may not have my contacts or whatever.

Whenever I hear the voice of my mother, I feel like I am revisiting some bad memories from my childhood or young adulthood I wish I would forget forever. She thinks she's doing me a favor when she contacts me first, but that is absolutely not true; it is plainly a rude act. I am not a shy person who cannot contact someone first if I need to.

There is a Thai restaurant waitress who I will mention in Chapter 56. No big deal; I found a Thai restaurant by accident and ate lunch there; there was a waitress. That's all. She was not outstandingly beautiful or anything; it was not an upscale restaurant. But I thought she looked interesting talking, so I left her my name and phone number. I do not know if she will contact me or not, but here is one thing for sure, though: I will never contact her unless she does it first (more likely, I do not know her contact in this case). It is not like I do not know how to approach others. It seemed she worked hard to make a living; certainly, she seemed to get bothered when I talked to her in the restaurant. I assume that she has her own situation there; I need to respect others boundaries.

* * *

It shows that Schopenhauer was single for all his life. The first woman president in Korea, Park has been single for her life, too. A lot of great minds and over-achievers have been singles, in fact. Time to be alone is time to advance and grow; I believe being able to acquire plenty of alone time is the key to success.

There are people *too busy* all the time. Some people automatically think being busy is good; this is simply not true. **Often being busy is just being busy;** nothing more than that. Actually, being busy for no reason is a total waste of time in that sense. Let me tell you one story.

I watched my favorite advice channel on YouTube the other day. One lady asked a Korean Bhuddist monk why people are still busy in 2022 despite all those technological developments. The monk answered that probably working two hours a day should be enough for basic needs nowadays. He continued that, "Koreans were busy when

GNP[48] was $3,000 in 1970. They are busy now even though GNP is over $30,000 a year in 2022; they will be busy even if GNP will be $100,000 a year someday." **He said people will keep inventing things to make themselves busy.**

I understood that people are wired that way: Doing something all the time whether it is necessary or not; they will do things by instinct even though these are not necessary. I think it is important to understand our instincts and not to waste time only for being busy.

* * *

Summary

1. Being busy doesn't automatically mean being productive.
2. Doing something all the time is merely an animal instinct.
3. Poor people often do not acquire enough time to be alone for personal growth.

[48] Gross national product

44

Not Simplifying

Having less makes our heads clear.
-Brad Kong

Do you have any know-how to finish a lot of work in a short time? My personal secret is simplification. Pyon-Pyon-Sha is a successful Korean restaurant with a strange name in Japan; it shows that this business gets about 800 customers a day on average; still they manage everything fine with a small number of staff. How? The eatery has only one menu called *Morioka Reimen* (cold noodle). Usually, poor restaurants have dozens of dishes on their menus: As a result, things are getting harder in their kitchens while profits are getting smaller.

* * *

I always order only one food and try to finish it completely at a restaurant. I notice that some people order three to four dishes and do not really finish them all, thoroughly. That's not my lifestyle; it's a waste of money, too.

Also I have not really carried any cash in my wallet at all for a long time; I have used only my credit card everywhere for years now. I can track where I spend money exactly on my bank website that way; I pay the balance off and get reward cashback at the end of every month. I can get cash from ATMs only when it's really necessary; I have never lost cash since I do not carry it from the start. Having one type of payment has made my life simpler.

Some people say that we tend to spend more when we use credit cards instead of cash. That's true, but I honestly don't think that type of issue has ever happened to me. I spend probably $1,000 a month excluding my condo association fee ($367 a month in 2023). I have never paid any type of late charges, fees or interest; I do "get" interests and dividends from my savings and portfolio every month, though. I assume I am frugal and have control over money.

* * *

Whenever things do not go very well, what I do foremost is *simplify*; it clears things out. **Usually not spending money for a while works out the best, according to my experience**; it makes my life simpler fast. On top of it, I usually stop checking websites I usually go to; use my smartphone less; eat or talk less. I just have to wait until bad things pass away. I usually focus on basic things (e.g., paying bills) for a while without eating out or traveling around much.

Now it's at the end of February, 2023 and the Dow Index dropped 3,000 points in the last month; I guess we may get into a recession. Don't try to make more money, compete more with others or move to a bigger house when things are getting bad. We can complicate or expand things little by little only when things are great. Maybe this is why I have only one child and decided not to expand my family, which I am happy about; things have not been that great personally, publicly or even globally in the past decade. After all, I realize that a minimal life makes me the most content and comfortable.

* * *

Writing an article is an odd way to connect our minds to our sub-consciousness in my opinion. If I get some ideas, I only know what to write in the first couple of sentences; then, I am often surprised at how the paragraph or entire article ends. I mostly end up finishing with something I did not expect in the beginning. Psychologists suggest that our subconsciousness determines 95% percent of our behaviors; everything I wanted to write has been in there all along. Additionally, I think writing is a good way to relax and simplify my life.

Some people think doing more is a way to be happier or at least more productive; nothing can be further from the truth. Some people keep doing something unnecessarily and even create troubles only to get out of boredom. For example, they may play a lot of video games, which is not necessary to survive; their eyes may get hurt eventually, so they visit an eye doctor; all of those cost money, so they have to work longer; hence, their children do not see parents often; the family become strangers and the parents divorce. Vicious cycles.

While they have been through all those, their homes can be more and more crowded with video games, consoles, toys, prescription eye medicines, divorce papers from lawyers, etc. They could have just not done anything to begin with and spent some time with their children.

Do you have any other solution whenever things go bad? Again, I usually stop spending money for a while. It could be a week, month or quarter[49]. For sure, it makes things simpler and better after all. I just do not spend money other than APT rent (which is the condo association fee for me now) if I start that *period*; I pay utility bills online, too, but that is about it. With no spending, we may have to skip some meals for a while, which is good for weight loss. We will eventually feel better and have more money in our pockets as a result. According to my experience, this solves problems other than money-related as well in the end.

* * *

I think it was 2008 when I had a conversation with an old man named Lester. I was a single guy back then. Strangely, he was really successful in persuading me to get married and have a baby; as a result of the conversation, I would say that my daughter was born in 2010. Ironically, he was a single old man for life himself.

I was 35 in 2008 and had a lot of pressure to have a baby from my parents (a grandchild for them). I guess that sort of pressure started coming to me after I became 30. In fact, my parents have always insisted on something in my life. It was just baby pressure at that time. Conclusively, as a 49 years old man, I do not speak with them any more.

---

[49] Three months

I had always thought that it was not reasonable to pressure myself to have a baby before I met Lester; I was single and broke. I would have at least understood my parents if they pushed me to make more money to support myself; for your information, I will never do that to my daughter. But I have always thought my parents do not have common sense; they have never known what they can or cannot ask from others; I recall that they were demanding unpleasant people regardless of money.

Despite the fact that I do not remember Lester was a good customer, he had visited my video game store (CybKnight) for a long time. Accidentally, one day I found out that he does not have a kid; he said he could not have one. I was surprised and asked, "What do you mean you couldn't?"

On that day, he told me a lot of things that I had not known by 2008. Until then, I thought only being pregnant could be a problem. I realized that not getting pregnant can also be a problem for the first time that day; I didn't know some people have a hard time getting pregnant or adopting a child. He said that he and his wife tried everything, but finally gave up completely after they became 40. My age was approaching 40 fast in 2008. Store did not make much profit, either.

I thought I needed a huge change to get out of the bad destiny I was in then: being solo and poor, no money from the business, etc. Having a child truly changed my life conclusively, but it was an unexpected sudden addition of a family member at the same time. I had to go through some hell after my daughter was born in 2010; it must have been very hard for her, too. All I can say now is that there is a reason I decided not to have any more children. I learned that simplification always made my life easier while addition or complication did it harder.

* * *

Summary

1. Simplification is essential to be wealthy.
2. Stop spending money for a while makes our lives simpler fast.
3. I learned that addition and expansion always makes my life harder.

45

Being Impulsive

I do not write stories; I have to wait until ideas come and entangle them slowly.
-Brad Kong

It shows that the richest person ever alive on Earth was John D Rockefeller Sr. (1839 – 1937); surprisingly, he had lived for 97 years. It is said that not only had he a calm temper, but his heart beat was actually slow. I can say that the longer we stay calm and the less we become impulsive, the more money we will make, according to my experience.

I think calm people are true winners in real lives; from my observation, they tend to be more successful than others. Koreans are known for their hot tempers in general and some people falsely believe it's a good thing: **No, it's not.** In fact, I believe that the more we get calm, the more money we make in the end. The good news is that I believe we can promote our calmness by repeating exercises including meditation.

* * *

It is true that a lot of men do not know how to attract women. The famous relationship expert, Bobby Rio, emphasized that uncertainty is the key. For example, as he suggested, sports games will not be fun if we know the final scores already; people are thrilled since they do not know the ultimate result in the end. It could be the same for dates: Rio tipped that women tend to think of a man all the time when she is not sure of what he is thinking.

A lot of guys give out his intentions too early; Rio suggested that men should stop *confessing* their feelings to anyone easily; **I think maybe they shouldn't do it at all.** The girl a man is interested in is not a father in a catholic church or shrink: Stop confessing!

Theoretically, these guys must be honest people; they may be straightforward businessmen who hate wasting time in general. The only problem is that they never get a girl they want; they usually get girls they have never been interested in. An uninterested girl naturally does not know anything in his mind since he has nothing on her in his mind to begin with; ironically, that is the reason why the girl thinks of him continuously once she is into him. These straightforward types of guys don't play with other girls' minds in general; they tend to be *impulsive* in dating and lose.

* * *

I can give you millions of examples regarding this issue, but let me start with the one mentioned in *The 48 Laws of Power* written by Greene. It shows that there was a woman named "Ninon de l'Enclos (Lenclos)" in France in the 17th century; she had been a courtesan for life, so she must have known a lot about women's psychology than anyone else; she was already 62 years old when she was consulting an aristocrat named Marquis Sévigné having struggle to pursuit a young countess.

Lenclos suggested that Sévigné should keep some distance from the lady countess, first of all; she asked him to have a conversation with her: "We will be friends for now." Then, Lenclos planned ahead to make the girl jealous. She had Marquis surrounded by other young women at the parties;

Lenclos explained that women are interested in a man who is popular among girls. Next, she instructed Marquis to be unpredictable; sometimes he went to a party and sometimes he missed it out of the blue. Everything seemed to go right smoothly.

Then, suddenly, without informing Madam Lenclos, Marquis visited the countess' house one day. He decided to wrap things up his way; he did straight talk with the countess impulsively; he told her how much he is in love. After that day, unfortunately, the countess had not been available all the time whenever Marquis tried to visit her. She allowed him to come in long later, but Marquis did not want it any more himself, by then. Sounds familiar? They ended up becoming total strangers, after all.

* * *

Personally, I like *straightforward* types of people. Still, here is something all of these people above didn't know: *Waiting* is the key for attraction. I think all the methods Lenclos used were necessary only to make things quicker. **But I assure you that all women tend to be in love with the man who is genuinely interested in her eventually**; that is how human generations have continued over 6 million years; if it did not work that way, humans would have gone extinct long ago. Women's minds have adapted that way evolutionarily since it's impossible for every woman to get the *exact* man she wants statistically; that probability is like winning the lottery. From the DNA point of view, generations need to continue somehow despite this discrepancy; I believe that nature has changed her mind to work flexibly.

The only problem is that a woman's mind changes very slowly; it takes up to years. She can be in deep trouble for the rest of her life if she chooses a wrong man; the trouble can be her own death. By instinct, she needs time to watch and think; it's a life and death matter for a woman since so many male partners have killed females throughout animal history of 4 billion years (almost all the males are bigger and stronger than females); police investigations and court sentences were created less than 200 years ago. She may still marry a man with flaws, but she wants to know if these are affordable. I just gave you examples with some relationship issues so far. Nonetheless, being impulsive can make us lose diverse games in our lives other than dating.

* * *

Being calm always brings us more money. Calming character will be something I have to try to get all the time until I die. My father was a pretty impulsive person; he got divorced and made his two sons enemies. I have to always try to go against my own temper inherited from my parents.

In my opinion, the job of an investor is all about waiting; it is called timing, too. If we cannot wait, we just do not make money: The right moment will be available, occasionally. Rarely, we have to know how to kill years if not decades wisely; I decided to write while waiting instead of doing anything else. Writing only requires me to read and think, which does not cost me any money.

Lately, I notice that I cannot write whenever I try to write a masterpiece; I just have to write lightly as I talk with a friend. I cannot squeeze good ideas out of my brain; I have to wait until one comes to me. I think it is important not to miss small ideas. **In the same sense, the job of a writer is waiting as well;** in many senses, being successful is all about waiting. I suppose people who can wait and do things little by little can have everything.

* * *

I lost about $3,500 for one deal when I was impulsive in 2005; I was 32 years old. As I wrote in Chapter 25, I don't think we make money evenly throughout our lives; we usually lose more money early and make more later in life. It seems it took almost 17 years to learn my lesson: staying calm.

I was an old college student in Buffalo, NY in 2005. eBay was big at that time and I was making an income out of selling used items on that site: some small used stuff I do not need at home any more, initially. Subsequently, I sold used video games I bought from a wholesaler; by the way, that wholesaler was a little bit of a fraud; he was either an Indian or Arab named Hassem and gave me mostly unpopular sports titles; I was able to sell them all with a very slim margin, though. It was before I made up my mind to sell only video games and open the video game store in 2006.

* * *

Then, I saw a car with a sale sign in front of a house in Buffalo one day: $3,000. It was a Mercury Cougar 2001 model in white; it looked fine outside. When I checked the price on eBay, it was listed at about $6,000. Suddenly, I got excited, which was stupid.

When I think about it now, the car had been in the same spot for a few months; there must have been reasons why no one bought it. Also, there must have been a reason why the trashy young owner, Justin, could not sell it on eBay on his own, either. But I wasn't thinking straight. I was obsessed with the idea that I could make $3,000 profit out of one transaction. I think $3,000 in 2005 was like $6,000 in 2023. It was a big profit for a young and broke student who I exactly was.

When I stopped at the house, the boy's mother came out. She took my phone number as her son was not there. I recall that she was a nurse and single mother with two sons; her first son was the owner of the vehicle and I remember he was trashy; he was about 22 years old, a community college dropout and went out of the town frequently for any reason. Later, I learned that he was waiting to join the Army in a few months. **I was too eager to make money and waited to close the deal no matter what, impulsively.** I got a phone call from him about three days later and he said he can make it for $2,500. I met and handed him $2,500 cash without suspicion; it was a huge mistake.

* * *

First of all, I found out that the used car did not have any license plates; I was stupid not to even check it. I think I was really out of my mind for a possible $3,000 profit. But what made me crazy was the boy kept not being available to apply for the plate together (both old and new owners were needed). He got paid full already, anyway. I believe it took about a week to get a hold of him and we went to the DMV together to get the license plate for the car, finally. I still remember he kept smoking a cigar and said, "Life cannot be better than this," or something outside the DMV (WTF?).

Secondly, the condition of the car was way worse than I expected. Strangely, the outside looked close to new (that was what my potential buyers said later on, too). It did not have a super high mileage, so the boy must have driven it very roughly. I remember he said he made a round trip to California on it; if I had a test driving, I would have walked away immediately. I spent an extra $500 on repairing it at a Meineke; that did not improve the condition of the car very much.

Thirdly, I made a mistake not to tell the difference between "listing price" and "sold price" on eBay. We can list this Cougar for $6,000. But that is not the final sales price, but merely a suggestion. Later, I learned that a lot of cars sold much less than listing prices on eBay. Eventually, it was sold about $4,000 twice even though both buyers decided to walk away without paying me. The driving condition of the car was bad. I learned countless lessons during that era.

* * *

All of these above happened in 2005. I was about to graduate from the college in Buffalo, NY in March, 2006, so decided to donate the car to a Kidney Foundation before graduation. When I think about it now, it was the last mistake I made since I could have sold the car for $500 at the junkyard. I needed some money to move out, anyway. For some reasons, nothing worked out and no one helped me in NY State and I am glad I moved to Illinois as soon as I graduated.

A similar thing could have happened when I tried to buy a house in 2012. For some reason, I was obsessed with one three-bedroom house in Roselle, IL. Luckily, my wife blocked me at that time, "Will you buy a house even without a home inspection?" She had a serious face. It quickly reminded me of what happened in Buffalo.

* * *

I don't like all those people involved in the auto sales in 2005: the boy, the mother and a stupid babysitter for the younger son in the family who wrote a strange contract for the transaction, which was bad for me. The mother even paid for a babysitter since Justin did not want to take care of his younger brother while he didn't seem to do anything all day. I should have not missed all the negative signs and gotten involved with these types of people from the start. But, in the end, it was my greed that played a major role in getting into the trap.

Never get impulsive if you want to win. We are living in a strange society promoting rushing. We do not have to make ourselves too busy, either. Some people get into a "squeezing-time-out" pattern since they are too lonely. We will talk more about this later on.

* * *

Summary

1. The more we get calmer, the more money we make.
2. Greed inside us is the most formidable enemy.
3. Waiting patiently can get us everything in the end.

46

Not Being a Good Spouse or Parent

It costs a lot to be rude; being selfish is expensive.
-Brad Kong

As a head of household, I think that it's important to have a personal policy to leave my daughter and wife alone. If I don't say a thing, they do not concern my life, anyway (at least, not the way my parents did). If I keep concerning their lives, all of us may not end up living under the same roof in the end: Living *separately* means paying more than one rent in a family; that will be a great loss in the long run. Some people drain more money by being assholes to their own families.

* * *

From my perspective, the best thing I have done for my wife was letting her get pregnant only once; that is our daughter. Not only did I make her less painful physically, I think I let her psychologically feel comfortable as well. She seemed to have a strong mind to have two children originally; I gave her more than enough reason that she doesn't have to do that. I already explained a lot in Chapter 2; I still believe no one gets benefit out of me only because I have two children instead of one; let me elaborate this.

First of all, I myself would have been more exhausted physically to take care of an extra child if having another happened to us. Secondly, I might have spent twice more money than I do now; I don't really have enough money nowadays. I might have been in the situation to teach two children face to face; frankly, I do not want any of these. I could have been in the situation to move out to a bigger house for a little bigger family, which might have brought me a mortgage debt; this sounds horrible to me.

In short, I am glad I did not try something I didn't feel like doing only because of social stigma: "Having two kids in a family is the most ideal!" Besides, having one less child is good for farm chickens, too. If a child is a meat eater, he or she can eat at least 100 more birds during his or her lifetime; that is pointless 100 more killing of other lives while humans are getting overpopulated fastly these days.

* * *

I believe that the best thing I can do for my daughter is just being myself and staying in the family as I am nowadays. I do not think a child can grow better with more education or concerns from parents (regardless, I am too tired to do so). **Statistics show that the chance a child without a father becomes a poor adult is *four times* higher than a child with a father.** I can see why whenever I see what my wife is doing with money; for example, she has never bought a stock for life. I will try to stay alive and pass my financial knowledge and little fortune to her. I guess that letting her stay much far from the poverty line would be my best gift to her.

* * *

I don't think that there will be any woman who will completely satisfy me in the end; we can be fed up with a woman, regardless of whoever we are married to; this can be bad news especially for men, but simply true. Please accept this if you are about to get married; whoever you get married, she will not be enough; there will always be a better woman; there will be continually a new girl you may find interesting in the future.

In fact, this will be true for foods, TV channels, movies or everything else in the world. Only difference is that the marriage system will push us to stick to one woman for life; people may learn that marriage is a sort of house arrest or home confinement in the end. Still, if you accept this before marriage, you will be fine. So there is no joy in married lives at all? There will be some; it is just not like a chunk of happiness happening everyday as in the popular belief: Far from it.

* * *

Do you know what kind of person divorce more? Rude people and assholes probably divorce more in my opinion. Have you ever seen an unpleasant person at your work? It is highly possible that the person has been divorced already or before, according to my experience.

There was a Cuban Mexican woman cook I never liked in my previous culinary job; she was plainly rude to dishwashers. I learned that she was divorced three times; she had five kids with three different men, but no one stayed with her for long. Personally, I don't even understand why those men made a baby with that kind of woman originally. **All I can say is that it costs a lot to be rude, impolite and unpleasant to our own families.** No one can know more about us than our own families; we can end up making our spouse or children complete enemies, too.

* * *

Lately, I learned that it costs about $13,000 for a woman to have her eggs frozen at a fertility clinic in 2022. It's a free country, but personally, I do not understand why some ladies stick to leaving their own DNAs this much; technically, they leave only half of their DNAs to an offspring since the baby will have the other half from a sperm; it seems doctors put so many needles on women's abdomens during the multi-step process.

If a pregnancy can happen naturally, that is fine with me and I will take care of the baby. But I will never try super hard to go through multiple surgeries only to leave half of my DNAs with a chunk of money; Earth has millions of orphans, so adopting one would be more beneficial for society if singles really want to be a child.

Still, sadly, I may have to suggest they should be a little bit careful even for adopting; we will never know where those children are exactly from. These are too long, but I heard a lot of horror stories including murders after adoptions. Even after we adopt one good kid, being a parent is a neverending hard job; **I admit that these people adopting kids and raising them well are real-life angels.**

I read an article titled "IVF and Single Girl" written by Dionne, a black lady writer who won three awards. I did not expect that the entire IVF process is a sort of major surgery and she said it will cost over $26,000 to make the eggs to be a baby on top of freezing costs ($13,000). Of course, it costs way more to raise the baby in the next 20 years after birth.

I feel that spending this much money and going through pains only to be a parent of my own DNAs is like spending money to get into prison. I know that my wife cannot get out of the house or do what she needs to do only because she has one daughter; a lot of women gave up her careers; motherhood is at least a kind of home detention as far as I can see. If this happens naturally, I will do it, but I will never try an extremely hard way to make it happen.

For the record, our daughter was born naturally in 2010. My wife and I could have had more kids biologically. But I decided not to since it has been so hard for me financially in the last 13 years; Earth has been getting crowded and overpopulated as well.

* * *

Wikipedia shows that Cameron Duglas had been in prison for seven years; he is the son of the American actor, Michael Douglas; Cameron was convicted for drug dealing. Michael said he wishes he would have spent more time with his son in an interview. Being a parent may be expensive and time consuming: **I assume not being a good parent can cost more than a fortune.**

By the way, just in my opinion, I wondered if Michael Duglas marrying the young actress, Catherine Zeta-Jones and producing two more kids was necessary. Apparently, he wounds up having more things to worry about, after all.

This is something I have to be careful of; it seems there are girls (especially Latina girls) particularly getting attracted to old men at work; they don't seem to care if he has a family already or not. People may think I am crazy if I say this, but let me be honest with you just for once: I am glad I am not super-rich or handsome enough to attract those females; they may be younger now, but will eventually get older and ugly. These successful men just wound up having messy marital records, divorce costs, and a bunch of additional kids they do not necessarily enjoy raising.

Some think these rich men who have been married multiple times are stupid, but those young girls know how to persuade them to get married again in a wicked way; those females' lives and incomes depend on it; they have professional skill to make men insane and let them sign a deal that is absolutely disadvantageous for old men. I am glad I am not a desirable target for them to begin with. Please check my book titled *How to get rid of ladies* for more information.

* * *

Greed can make our own child an enemy. Sadly, I have not spoken with my parents for more than a decade. Their unreasonable demands, which do not benefit anyone apparently, never stopped, so I decided to cut them off despite their wealths.

This issue is especially true in Korea. For example, there are a lot of *education fanatic parents* in the country; these people spend a fortune on their children's education, which is an obvious waste, and push them crazily to study. They do not do that to make their children happy or mature; they just want their children to get some good grades and better jobs eventually. It is disgusting for those parents to consider the future income even when they see their children; these are unhealthy relationships and I know many cases end up being tragedies. It's not always about money. Yet, I strongly believe having a pleasant relationship with my own family is a way to get wealthy as well.

* * *

Summary

1. We do not have to try super hard to create our own offspring.
2. Being a good person in the family is important in every sense. Coincidentally, it saves a ton of money, too.
3. Being an asshole costs money.

47

Pressure to Spend Money

We need to be comfortable sitting on money.
-Brad Kong

Jack Whittaker was a construction businessman in Putnam County, WV; he was known as the winner of a lottery jackpot of $315 Millions USD in the Powerball in 2002. It shows that he was a millionaire already with a net worth of $17 M even before winning; in a word, a millionaire won a huge lottery. He must be the luckiest guy on Earth, right? Wrong!

Strangely, a series of unfortunate events happened to him for no apparent reason after winning. First of all, a boy named Jesse Tribble, who was the boyfriend of Whittaker's granddaughter Brandi Bragg, was found dead from drug overdose in Whittaker's home in September, 2004; three months later, Brandi Bragg herself was also found dead on the property of a male friend in December, 2004; it shows that cocaine and methadone were found in her body; she was only 17 at the time of death.

Subsequently, Ginger Bragg, who was the mother of Brandi Bragg and Whittaker's daughter (42), was also found dead in Daniels, WV in 2009; the police suspected that the cause could be drug overdose again. Then, Whittaker's home in Bland County, VA, was reported to be on fire in December, 2016. Finally, Jack Whittaker himself passed away following a long illness in June, 2020. It shows that he had frequently visited casinos and strip clubs when he was alive; I guess lack of sleep and disorganized lifestyle could have brought him an illness.

Apparently, it shows that Whittaker was generous and gave a lot of money to the lottery ticket seller, his family members and others; I think that's how some of his family bought a large quantity of drugs, originally. **I think there are people who just cannot sit on their money in the bank comfortably.** Could they just live off the interests for decades and pass the fortune to children when they die? At least, that's what I am doing right now.

* * *

Just hold your spending for one year in case you get a fortune. Just put the money in the bank CDs or Treasury bond ETFs and get some interest for a while (up to 7% a year). In this case, most people have strong urges to waste the fortune particularly in the beginning. Sooner or later, you may be angry if you do not have that full initial amount in your hands; your point of view on your own net worth can change. Reasonable spendings will start only after that point.

I think decency matters since it attracts people by making them feel good; it makes people lose less money; it matters more for wealthy people since they have more things to lose. When we choose and insist on living a decent lifestyle, we will waste less money. For example, some rich people choose to spend time in the library instead of the red light district in Vegas. We can get true respect while we stay in wealth for a long time.

There is a difference between decency and snobbery; decency gives a good feeling, but snobbery does not. I believe that decency is from self control; I notice that snobbery often comes from the low quality people.

It shows that Mukesh Ambani, who is chairman of Reliance Industries, built a $1 B house called Antilia in Mumbai, India; the house looks like a square tall skyscraper to me; I simply do not like the design to begin with. And I had been raised in a rectangular condo like that and felt I was standing in front of people uncomfortably. Regardless, this is not a decent action when half of Indians do not even have proper toilets in the country; there is no way he can live happily alone; I would donate some money for infrastructure if I were him. Stupidly, he only makes other Indians feel bad now.

* * *

Michael Bambang Hartono is a Chinese Indonesian billionaire living in Kudus, Indonesia; his net worth is $20 B in 2022; he has been the richest man in Indonesia in the last 11 years, according to *Forbes*. Strangely, one photo showing him eating alone at a poor restaurant went viral on social media in 2019. The restaurant owner said Hartono has been a regular customer for a long time from the time he sold foods on the street. He said this billionaire is a simple guy who does not mind eating on the street.

I am not particularly respecting him, but I felt a bit of decency. Good feelings. Modesty. And a sort of attraction. I believe that this is why Gorat's, which is Warren Buffett's favorite restaurant, is so popular in America. **Being decent does not cost any money**; it often saves money in fact; still, it is one of the most important assets rich people carry. And I like to believe that I am a decent person as well since I decided to be a writer instead of buying a sports car with all my money; it is nice to spend some time thinking and studying freely when I do not have to worry about money: Maturity and decency make our wealth last longer.

* * *

There was the *Lollapalooza* music festival in downtown Chicago the other day; I just went downtown to walk for exercise, so it was a surprise for me. I saw a lot of girls in bikini tops and jean shorts, which were uniforms for female audiences I assume. I saw some black market sellers selling wristbands, which were admission ticket to Grant park; they said these were $300 each, but I found out that the original price was $125; I saw some men selling T-shirts having obscene phrases for $20 each; they shouted to pedestrians, but I did not see anyone buying it.

Frankly, for some reason, I could not really detect any pretty looking girls among the crowds for hours. No offense, but mostly they looked cheezy or poor; their clothes all looked cheap, too. I did not like the blasting sounds from speakers even from a distance or enjoyed the blazing hot sun that day; I did not have money for the ticket, but also did not feel that I could enjoy the festival; it could have been nothing but a painful situation for me.

* * *

I went to Chinatown on my kick scooter after Lollapalooza that day. The condition was even worse. They had a sort of summer festival in town as well, and I am still not sure where all these *cheap feelings* came from. I know I was supposed to feel blessed to catch two festivals in a day, but that was not what I felt. Just cheap feelings that I had never felt from Midsommarfest in Andersonville or Septemberfest in Schaumburg. I have been to plenty of art festivals (e.g., Arlington Heights, Oak Brook mall, etc), but this was the first time I felt something like this. Most fairs had brought me reasonably decent feelings, but I felt like I am the only human among monkeys that day.

After thinking about why overnight, I conclude that decency may be from something beyond wealth. One example is education; we just have to read books and think enough to give high quality feelings to others. There is a word called "pariah capitalism" in Korea; I can translate it to "bum capitalism" in English. Some people may be rich, but they spend all the money for drinking, gambling, shopping or prostitution; they just do not give a good feeling to others. I think the recent economic boom has produced a lot of these in China; I hope they will change and get mature instead of mainly satisfying the basic instincts.

* * *

In my opinion, the most stupid desire in the world is *consumption* desire: The pressure to spend money out of nowhere. Do you know how we can make a $1 M mansion into a slum? Buy 1,000 items from the Dollar Tree and bring them to the house. It will certainly look like a cheap slum even after spending money.

Weirdly, I had so much of this *consumption desire* when I used to live in Ithaca, NY in 1999. It was a small college town with a population of 50,000 then. The city was surrounded by layers of mountains and no major highway went through the city. I always felt suffocated and stressed out; I felt I was locked in a broom closet or something.

I think I spent more money than ever in my life during that one year when I stayed in Cornell university in 1999; I received so much complaint about spending too much money from my father; his complaint stopped immediately as soon as I moved into Buffalo in 2000; part of the reason is the living cost in the city was much cheaper than that of Ithaca; in fact, it is cheaper than any city in the U.S. And my suffocation was virtually all gone after I moved into the big city, Chicago; the living cost of Windy city is not that bad even compared with that of Buffalo.

* * *

Some people may not believe this truth: We do not really have to do anything for our whole lives. Maybe we need to breathe, eat or make some money to support ourselves; still, these are pretty much all when I think about it. There is no animal born with ambition, greed or personal agenda; in a sense, these are the things making us painful. Everyone dies in the end: **No one will get reward in heaven since he or she worked harder than others.**

We have the right to live freely unless we bother others. We do not have to pursue Personal Legend as the book *The Alchemist* suggested. **It is the problem that others keep pressuring us to have an idea that we have to do something.** We really do not have to do anything; we do not have to go on a blind date since most people get married. We do not have to go to India to see the world and broaden our knowledge; some people wound up being dead by crime or contaminated food there. Please trust me that we do not have to do anything. So stop checking Facebook or watching TV and take some breaks.

* * *

When we get a large amount of money suddenly, we may feel pressure to spend money; sometimes, people win the lotteries or inherit fortunes. According to my experience, usually the heavy pressure comes in the beginning. If we can pass one year without spending much, we may keep the fortune forever.

Please trust me that we will need some money later on; we are in a society where we need money everyday. After that one year, we may not *feel* that we have fortune any more; we have it, but having a fortune will be a natural part of our lives. I am not saying that we need to be greedy; **I am saying that we will not have strong pressure to spend any more.**

* * *

Summary

1. If you happen to get a fortune, do not spend it right away; hold it just for one year.
2. A year later, you may be angry if you don't have that money any more.
3. Spending pressure is temporary. Pass that time wisely.

48

Not Getting up Early

If you want to make your life better instantly,
sleep one hour early tonight.
-Brad Kong

I think keeping early hours is one way to make our life efficient instantly without spending extra money. Staying late *usually* means wasting more time. Probably less than half of people stay late to work or study more. A lot of people stay late to do something unnecessary or even not recommendable.

* * *

How do we know if we live our lives fine or not? I think the direct way is checking our weights. See if you can check if you are fat or not; this is an easy, but the most important visual indicator in my opinion. We are living in an era to get fat easily; foods are available at low prices everywhere. If you are skinny by chance, I would say you are living just fine; probably you do not live as social pressures push you blindly; most likely you are living with your own ideas. Also, you are probably intelligent enough to be conscious about being healthy from a medical point. Practically, we will not waste a lot of money on medical bills in that case in the future.

Being skinny by some harmful methods (for example, smoking) does not count, though. When I used to work at the nursing home, there was an Italian smoker girl who was skinny. When I checked her Facebook, both of her parents were super fat (Facebook will never help you as I explained in Chapter 7). She was the only white among food distributors (mostly Mexicans and Indians) and poorer than anyone working there; her parents lost their house by foreclosure in 2010 and her family had lived in a rental APT for over a decade. I felt like the smoking habit of everyone in that family (parents and two daughters) had brought them misery.

It may not be my concern any more, but there is only one strict rule if I consider dating again: I will never be with a fat or talkative woman. This sounds offensive, but I like to be honest in my own book. Talkative ladies will continuously distract me until I break up with them. I do not like chatty people by nature, regardless of gender.

The other indicators are to see if you sleep early or have some money in your bank account. If we sleep early everyday, we are more likely to live our lives fine. This is one efficient way to *lose weight*, too; people tend to eat more late at night. I assume we can use these types of biorhythm patterns the other way around. If you want to get wealthier, sleeping early may be a good and costless way to start.

* * *

For some reasons, I notice that the world is built easier for early risers; when we check the public transportation schedules in Chicago, we can realize that immediately. For example, there is a bus called "Pace 600 express" directly connecting the Blue Line subway to Northwestern suburb near Woodfield mall; the schedule for this starts at 5:00 AM everyday, but finishes as early as 7:00 PM on weekends; there is no bus at all in that huge terminal after 10:00 PM. I am not just talking about public facilities. When we actually check the open hours of anything, we can find that everything is easier for early birds, but harder for night owls.

Surprisingly, sleeping early is the fastest way to lose weight; at least, it worked out very well for me. Physiologically, it shows that a hormone called "Ghrelin" comes out in human bodies after 10:00 PM every night; this hormone is known to cause extreme hunger in the middle of night. That is why those late night restaurants are unexpectedly crowded. **I think it's better for us to sleep before hunger strikes us.** Wikipedia also says that, "The level of ghrelin increases from midnight to dawn in thinner people." Just sleep early, so we cannot devour any food unnecessarily overnight. Also, it confirmed that our body burns fat while we are sleeping.

Physiologists say that a hormone that does the opposite function of ghrelin is "leptin"; leptin makes us feel full, but it shows it only comes out 20 minutes after every meal in our body. Since it does not have any specific time of the day to release, theoretically it may be a good idea to skip dinner and sleep early (I don't do this as I usually eat dinner). I believe there is not much calorie consumption overnight as we do not move much, physically.

Sleeping early helps us cut out any bad habits as well from my perspective. For example, if you want to quit drinking, see if you can start it by sleeping early. Not many people start drinking during the day time. When it's dark outside, just sleep, so you can save electricity in the worst case. Personally, I tried to decrease the internet hours. I notice that I often do pointless browsing during the night. I guess I will sleep by 9:00 PM, so I can write more early in the morning.

* * *

Keeping early hours makes people wealthier in general; if you are not sure what to do exactly to get out of poverty, I propose this is a good point to start. Frankly, I have not been an early riser by nature, but I found out that I can do way more things in those few hours early in the morning.

I happened to watch a documentary regarding "Angola Three" in 2005; this film was about three African American prison inmates held for decades in solitary confinement. One Jewish lady interviewed one of the members, and he said he was falsely accused of murder at 1:00 AM when he was outside. As soon as I heard that, one crazy idea striked me: "**If he was sleeping at that time, would he have not been involved in that crime at all?**" Occasionally, a chain of unfortunate events starts from one little bad thing. I was relatively young and used to go out any time I wanted at night in 2005; I remember that I started sleeping much earlier after watching that interview.

By the way, I had a minor car accident in 2011; one taxi driven by a young Indian man, who looked exhausted by overworking, hit my butt hard while I crossed a road in Downtown Chicago. It happened about 10:00 PM on a Saturday night. Walking downtown at that hour was not necessary. Maybe I am alive now since I don't do that any more.

* * *

It sounds ridiculous, but I think most people can save more money only by changing their life cycles. Imagine there are two identical twins; let's call them A and B. Let's suppose A wakes up at 5:00 AM and sleeps at 9:00 PM; B wakes up at 10:00 AM and sleeps at 2:00 AM. Both are awake the same 16 hours a day.

Let's say that both make exactly $100,000 a year and it has been like this in the last twenty years. They both sleep eight hours a day this way, too. Who do you believe has saved more money? I think A saved five times more money than B. Let me explain why.

First of all, there are less places to spend money when you wake up and sleep too early. Where can you really go at 5:00 AM? Not that many businesses are open to begin with. Maybe we can go to the gym, but probably we can end up saving more money from medical bills by doing exercise.

On the contrary, when you sleep at 2:00 AM, there are so many bars open till late night. We can also go to late night restaurants or strip clubs. These all cost money. Also, drinking can bring us DUI ticket problems, legal disputes, violences, harassment and more hospital bills. I still believe that people can stay out of trouble only by sleeping early.

* * *

Summary

1. When we are not sure what to do to get out of poverty, I think sleeping early is a good point to start.
2. Sleeping early makes us lose weight naturally.

3. A lot of troubles happen overnight while we do not notice. We can avoid them by sleeping at home.

49

Too Thirsty for Cash

Cash makes us blind.
-Brad Kong

Baron Rothschild was a German Jewish banker, who was the founder of the French branch of the richest Rothschild family in the 19th century. Originally, it shows that he was looking for a way to get accepted by French upper classes to stabilize his banking business. He learned that those people were bored to death then. So he hired the best architects to redesign his mansion and chefs to prepare great banquets; he threw some cash to hold lavish parties for Frenchs on a weekly basis; eventually, it shows that he was able to settle his businesses well.

The similar thing happened for Lorenzo Medici in Florence, Italy in the 15th century. History says that the Medici family was the absolute billionaire banker at that time. To relieve anger from poor people, he built a lot of art schools; even Michelangelo and Leonardo Da Vincci were students who attended those once. He let some cash go to people and it eventually introduced the boom of the Renaissance era later on. This has brought so much money from travelers to Italy even nowadays.

* * *

Some people make less money only because they go crazy for "cash" instead of anything else: stocks, royalty or other assets; some lose money or even their lives because they stick to cash too much. Let me give you one more example from the book, *The 48 Laws of Power*.

There was a fraud named Count Lustig in America in the beginning of 20th century. He visited Al Capone, who was the kingpin of gangsters, in Chicago one day in 1926. He said, “Mr. Capone. If you give me $50,000, I will make it double for you in 2 months.” Capone had too much cash surplus at that time, so he gave that to Lustig.

Lustig put the money in a security deposit box in a bank and did not do anything for two months. He just got it out and visited Capone again two months later. Then, he said, “I am sorry, Mr. Capone. I was not able to double it. Here is your money back.” He returned the money back politely.

Surprisingly, it shows that Capone said, “Wait a minute. You could have run away with this money? You are an honest man; we cannot find a person like you any more. Here is a 10% reward for you; don’t insult me for not accepting my appreciation.” Lustig humbly accepted the $5,000 gift money from Capone.

You know what, though? That $5,000 was the profit Lustig was running after, originally; $5,000 in the 1920s must have been $50,000 in 2022; it’s still a large amount of money. Lustig could have lost his life if he really ran away with $50,000 belonging to Capone. He became a happy man with the perfect crime since he was not crazy about cash; he was aiming for a small amount of gain.

* * *

I decided not to be stingy any more one day in July, 2022. I read this in a book by accident: "Today is the moment we are truly living: **It is the life of life.**" I decided not to save money blindly only for later as I have done in the last four decades. It is just crazy if I go for more cash forever; this desire for cash will be endless.

There is a Korean American artist named David Choe; he is known for his wall graffiti and mural arts. In 2005, one of Facebook founders, Sean Parker, asked him to paint graphic murals in the interior of Facebook's Silicon Valley office. Subsequently, in 2007, the current Facebook CEO Mark Zuckerberg commissioned him to paint more murals for their next office.

After finishing all the artwork, it shows that Zuckerberg asked Choe one question: "Would you get paid $60,000 cash or Facebook stocks of that amount?" Oddly, Choe chose Facebook stocks even though the company was virtually nameless in 2007. Here goes the biggest shock: **When Facebook was listed at the stock exchange in May 2012, the value of Choe's shares was close to $200 Million.** Google results shows that the net worth of David Choe was about $300 Million as of 2022.

Choe could have ended up with 60,000 cash. I learned some lessons from the example; this was what I decided to do for the rest of my life: "**I will choose something other than cash from now on as long as I have enough money.**" I learned that there are a lot of chances out there, but I have not had much luck with most of them since I have pursued cash too much; Iguess that I have been poor since I have been too obsessed with money. Let me give you one more example.

* * *

You probably all know McDonald's Burgers since these are everywhere. It was 1954 when the American businessman, Ray Kroc first met Richard and Maurice McDonald brothers who founded the McDonald's Burgers originally in 1940. I actually watched the movie titled *Founder* and it shows that Kroc was initially a milkshake-mixer salesman. He did not make much sales in the beginning, but he was impressed that McDonald's ordered eight blenders all at once, so he decided to visit the burger restaurant himself.

To make it short, Kroc decided to buy out the whole restaurant from the brothers later on. The two McDonald brothers asked $2.7 Million from Ray ($1 M profit for each after tax); it was paid full by Kroc since he was able to raise that fund successfully in 1961.

What is the surprise here, though? I watched a CBS TV program showing that Jason McDonald, who is the grandson of Dick McDonald, visited one old location in 2017. This is what he said on TV: "There was a deal on the contract that was never delivered. Kroc was supposed to pay us 0.5% royalty from the company profit every year; that would have been worth $100 M a year now. Our grandfathers focused on and enjoyed the $1 M cash and forgot about it; that was crazy."

Do you see what I am trying to say? Those brothers decided to stick to cash in 1961, so they are losing $100 M every year now. **If they chose something other than cash like stocks or loyalties, they would have been much wealthier by now.** We all make this kind of mistake; cash makes our eyesight narrower; it makes us blind.

* * *

I have been interested in money for my whole life. But I have not made very much. But, strangely, I have never been interested in marriage; ironically, I met a good wife and my family life is fine now. **I feel I have not made much money since I have been interested in that too much**; in fact, this happens in every field.

In the case of stock investment, watching financial news too much can be the reason for failure; some are so eager to make money, so they do not see a bait; it is secretly known that frauds use the media to take advantage of stupid investors.

Occasionally, women, who are too keen to get married, do not see the true face of male gold diggers: A quality man does not approach a lot of women; when things are too good to be true, it probably is. People just do not see the real value, especially when they are obsessed with money; I think those end up making less or losing after all.

* * *

Summary

1. Unless you have money trouble, see if you can choose something other than cash if there is a choice.
2. Don't think about money all the time; some people lose it for that reason.
3. Don't put yourself in a financially desperate situation by getting into debt from the start; debtors lose the most in any case.

50

Not Realizing Money Drain

What makes a castle collapse is not a missile:
It's a mouse hole.
-Brad Kong

I finally got my molar tooth extracted the other day in Sept, 2022. It has been the only tooth I have lost until the age of 49. I tried to save it for the last 4 years, but I couldn't. After losing it, I found out that leaving an infected tooth in my mouth had been quite a dangerous thing. It shows that up to 40% of people used to die because of an abscessed tooth before the invention of antibiotics in 1928. Even nowadays, so many people end up in the emergency room because of infections caused by periapical tooth abscess.

Pulling a tooth out was *not* very painful for me after getting *four* shots of anesthesia; besides, an infected tooth tends to come out easily since our bodies do *not* want it. The entire process cost me only $208 (2022). If you have a severe or chronic pain because of a tooth, my suggestion is just remove it. Subsequently, we can decide whether we live without it or have a dental implant. Still, I triple assure that it's never a good idea to keep a source of incurable infection in our heads; it shows that some people die because that moves to their brain.

Little things are not little; these can kill us! We have to watch out for any little damage or leakage in our finances as well.

* * *

I read a Korean doctor claimed that fasting 12 hours a day is critically important; he explained that eating continuously makes our hormones less potent and lower metabolisms; we gain weight as a result. Some hormones have a function to burn out foods (e.g., leptin); these don't work effectively when we keep being full. Skipping a meal for 12 hours sounds hard, but it's not; many of us sleep 8 hours a day overnight, so actual time to fast consciously is 4 hours.

I think lots of people do not realize that it actually costs a *fortune* to eat. When I was on a diet in 2019, I was surprised that my money kept accumulating without having higher incomes. I am trying to establish a habit of eating one meal a day for life. **It's for health reasons, but I still can see that I will end up saving millions of dollars in the next 50 years.** Eating less is one wise way to save money while making ourselves healthier; personally, I have never dated a fat woman not only because she does not look good, but she does not make a sensible choice for her body.

* * *

The electricity bills were the problem when I had my video game store in 2009. It was ok in the beginning in 2006, but I was able to see a loss after three years in 2009. I used to pay up to $300 for electricity every month for that small store (900 square feet); I used to turn on lights and aircon all night even though no one was working there; I thought it would be a visible ad since people can see my store more during the nights.

I was wrong. When I actually checked it, those electricity bills of $3,600 a year were 3 months rent in the space in 2009. **Little leak of waste was not little**; a tiny hole in a huge water tank can drain all the water out within a week. We always have to look out for any little drain or waste; I know it can make a huge difference in the end by experience.

* * *

I think the biggest money drain in America could be lawn care for most houses. California has severe drought now in June, 2022; it could be more intensifying since summer just started. I saw that Lake Mead is drying up fast on the news; people can get up to a $1,200 fine for watering their own lawn during the daytime in California.

I live in Illinois, and saw some people watering their lawn this evening. Suddenly, one question hit me: What do all those lawns do for houses, exactly? Here is my answer: *Nothing much,* really. These do not produce more oxygen; I do not think it has any significant function except covering the grounds.

Sometimes, I have wondered what would happen if every house planted corn in the front and back yards. Apparently, it looks a much better choice than growing just lawns. Corns are tall plants, so these can cover our windows for privacy; we can harvest corn to eat; also they will provide way more biodiversity than lawns for other lives; more ants, spiders, insects, etc; Earth will have more lives. I think this is more productive than wasting water for lawns.

* * *

There was a nasty troll in a Korean online community. Actually, there is such crap on every web site: someone who never contributes any article, but always leaves bad comments on others' postings. For no apparent reason, that garbage had done those things there for years. The web site was about job related information, by the way.

One thing I noticed was that he had a huge amount of mortgage. I believe he bought a $600,000 house with a thirty-year mortgage. So the total amount of money he will spend would be about $1,000,000; the additional $400,000 would be purely mortgage debt. And he said that he had a couple of luxury cars with car loans. Also, he had HDTVs and other items with credit card debts. As a result, he had all sorts of debts: mortgages, car loans, card debts, etc. He said his wife is not working (no professional woman would marry such a man), so I assumed he must have been in deep financial trouble. I believe nasty comments showed his miserable situation.

Here is my question to him, though: "You will not be OK if you see a $5 suspicious charge on the supermarket receipt. **But why are you OK with a $400,000 extra charge on the same house?**" I am sure that some of his neighbors must have bought a house in full; the numbers are as high as 50% in 2022. How come is he OK with this? Or vice versa? He lived in a trashy way, so he ended up being like that?

The troll's logic was that he could use some of the money for investing instead of putting all in the mortgage. He said anyone can make 7% a year only by putting some money in the S&P 500 index fund: Nonsense.

First of all, the $400,000 loss caused by the mortgage debt is a "confirmed" loss; making money out of investment is merely "hope." **Hope is not a profit.** When you make a profit, it is a profit; it should come with a "confirmed" x amount of dollars.

Secondly, no one makes money out of S&P funds all the time. The S&P 500 index dropped greatly this year in 2022. Anyone who invested in those funds in 2020 must have lost 30% by now.

* * *

Personally, I do not see anything very wrong with purchasing a moderate house with a mortgage. That's not necessarily a gain, but an acceptable loss. I just do not like the troll's attitude. It is reasonable if he shuts up and tries to pay up the mortgage debt as fast as he can. Who knows if he loses only $100,000 instead of $400,000 that way? **It is never a good idea to be in debt for too long.**

If you see $30 more on the electricity bill this month, you will try to figure out why this is happening. If you see a $5 extra charge you do not understand on a grocery bill, you will ask the cashier. But, strangely, a lot of people seem to be OK with $400,000 extra charge on their houses.

Some people may think it is fine since others are doing it, too. When you think about it, it is not really the matter of percentage of population. Even if 99% of people in the world have mortgages, it could be an incredible saving if you do not have one. This is a personal issue; it does not matter whether others have it or not.

Again, I cannot blame people only because they have mortgages. I just think that it is sinful that someone does not admit his big loss and acts nastily to others. I learned that nasty repliers always do that regardless of articles. Maybe pointing out their massive debts was one way I could attack them back. If I were them, I would never be in the mood to write anything online; I just do not know what went wrong with those.

* * *

Summary

1. Little loss is not little: Check how much you lose a year instead of a month.
2. It is OK to have a mortgage. Don't insist it's a better deal than full cash payment for a house; some trolls are stupid.
3. Using money for investment instead of paying off a house is risky: Hope is not profit!

51

Too Interested in Politics

Being poor is not a fixed state;
it triggers chain reactions of misfortunes.
-Brad Kong

Sun-il Kim (1970 – 2004) was a Korean interpreter and Christian missionary who was kidnapped and murdered in Iraq; he was 34 years old when he passed away. Admittedly, part of it was his fault for entering a dangerous country where the Korean government seriously warned against traveling repeatedly. In 2004, Jihad, which became IS later, released the *decapitation video* of him; it shocked the nation, especially minors. Young students said that they thought it was a fake video in the beginning since everyone was too calm for the most part: It was not. I heard that he screamed to death at the end, particularly because their machete was not sharp enough.

Maybe he did the right thing to help Arabic interpretation for a trading company, or spread Christianity in his point of view. Or maybe it was wrong to enter the country during the height of the Iraq war. Regardless, I would say that there are people acting unnecessarily dangerous without getting an obvious benefit. Coincidentally, Namu-wiki shows that Kim had been poor for life despite his rare mastery of Arabic in South Korea.

* * *

After reading some books about histories, I learned that a lot of people used to be executed after they got politically involved. Maybe I am not much of a diplomacy guy, but this sounded close to nonsense to me. **I believe politics was created to help a community originally**; at least, it shouldn't cause its people to be dead. Now politics has turned into a sort of power game to decide which side gets more benefits.

It was the same nonsense I felt when I heard that some travel to dangerous areas; they say that it helps them get new experiences and expand their views. **What is the point of getting broader views after being murdered?** Who the hell cares if they have a wide range of experiences or not after they die? New experiences may (or may not) help us as long as we are alive. I think it can be a waste if we know too much about politics. It is the same as some guys know too much about sports; some girls know too much about celebrities. Just like the case of pro-wrestling, often TVs do not show the truth.

One example of political waste could be PETA[50]'s performance in my opinion; some women do it naked trying to get some attention to be sorts of celebrities. I think they should seriously work on developing meat substitutes, instead. I am close to being a perfect vegan, so I support their goals, though. I saw a girl demonstrating in front of Whole Foods near DePaul college the other day: "Security at the market should not carry a gun!" Do you see any point? No one has used armament there as far as I know. My gut feeling was that she picked out an issue only to put herself in public attention for a different reason.

---

[50] People for the Ethical Treatment of Animals

* * *

There are countries unstable politically in 2023: Somalia, Venezuela, Myanmar, etc; it is unfortunate to be born in those; they do not have a healthy government; as a result, even currencies are useless in a few places. However, there are people involved in political misery, occasionally in wrongful ways, even under stable governments. Some spend their lives in brokeness as a result: Shin in Korea; Mandela in South Africa; Thoreau and Ali in America; Marx in Germany; Dostoevsky and Solzhenitsyn in Russia. I know we cannot blame them blindly: **It's true that we live better thanks to some of them.**

Sadly, many of these had to be in prison for a long time; Mandela had been in jail for 27 years; Shin had been locked up for 20 years. Technically, they did not commit a crime; they were just against some political discrimination or tyrants. They probably have done the right things; we all benefit from them. Nonetheless, their own families must have suffered since those actions didn't generate immediate outcomes. On the contrary, I saw that some people became miserable or even lost lives when they tried to be too dominant in politics.

* * *

Shinzo Abe, the former prime minister of Japan, was assassinated while speaking at an election event in Nara, Japan in 2022; he was 67 years old. This was big news on CNN and I saw that people talked about some political crap regarding this. But I had a different question: Would he be alive now if he had been completely retired after 2020?

He initially resigned his PM position for a health reason in August, 2020: Ulcerative colitis. He was at the retirement age (65), anyway. Eventually, he got a couple of gunshots from an angry Japanese, while he was in the campaign to be a senator again. I passionately suggested this already; I think too much greed and desire are the one killing us; they make us poor, too. **Giving up when it is enough is a great strategy to save wealths, if not our lives, in myriad cases.** I think we need to be diligent *selectively*: We need to be industrious only when there is a need at least, not all the time, including when we *spend* money; some are busy shopping and losing money as well.

* * *

There are people talking about politics by habit all the time; I believe these tend to be old. They talk and write about politics out of the blue on any message board online. They always watch CNN or C-Span, and know everything they do not really have to. Famous politicians become celebrities and subjects of gossip.

My wife is not a hard core “political fanatic” yet; unfortunately, she showed a talent to be it, though. There was one time when I was shocked at how much she knew about Trump. Then, he finished his presidency two years ago: **Why do I have to know anything about him now?** There was no way I could hear the name unless she kept mentioning: Unproductive waste of time and energy; I thought that she gossiped about politicians instead of Justin Beaver. You know what, though? She is not wealthy as far as I know despite her doctorate degree.

* * *

I used to go to one Korean message board online. There were always several old men writing about Korean politics out of nowhere. The site is about American jobs, so the moderators always delete those postings. **But those political zombies kept writing.** And their knowledge about Korean politicians was *surprisingly extensive*; I think most people probably never have heard of those names. Who the hell cares about the candidates for department of education secretary in South Korea? I thought that those fanatics ought to be in intensive care for mental disease; these people are often over 60 and have nothing much going on with their lives: Not shockingly, they[51] tend to be in the bottom economy class.

I assume that political obsession might be an elderly form of reality TV craze. If someone knows the exact names of all the members in the Kadashian family, the person must not have gotten a life: Would he or she make a lot of money? Probably not. Ironically, those who seem to be far from poverty read more books about finances.

* * *

Summary

1. We only need to know what we have to know.
2. Political gossiping can be a form of celebrity buzz.
3. We don't have to be ambitious after getting more than enough.

---

[51] Koreans call them "flag division" as they carry national flags in gathering.

52

Not Recognizing Opportunities

It is important to be aware that we do not know everything yet.
-Brad Kong

Joshua Bell is one of the richest violinists in the world; it shows that his net worth was about $15 millions in USD in 2022; he made almost $1,000 per minute during his concerts. The Washington Post did an interesting experiment with him in 2007: *Stop and Hear the Music* metro experiment. He was playing violin on the street for free and the newspaper company checked how many people stop and listen to it; his violin was a multimillion-dollar Stradivarius; he played for 43 minutes. Result? **Almost no one stopped**; this is what the Post wrote exactly: "Out of 1,097 people that passed by Bell, 27 gave him money; only *seven* actually stopped and listened for any length of time."

We are all blind to some extent. I was actually surprised that he made $32.17 for 43 minutes; I think those buskers make more money than I expected since I have never given them anything other than food; unfortunately, many street performers are known to be drug addicts in Chicago. The only reason why I ended up not even giving them food was that I saw a huge disappointment in their eyes one day; obviously, they were not there since they were hungry.

Anyway, we may miss opportunities like this on a daily basis; this could be the reason why some of us are not wealthy in the richest country in the world.

* * *

Isaac Asimov was a Russian American writer and professor of biochemistry at Boston University; he was known to be a claustrophile who enjoyed being in small spaces; he wrote more than 500 books during his lifetime. It could be a coincidence, but I often can get ideas to write when I stay in a walk-in closet in my house for a while. I originally converted the closet space to a bedroom to save money; it seems that space has become a quieter place to think. Without staying in that space, writing a series of six books might not have been possible. Getting a new opportunity may be important. **Yet we still do not know that we already have one in hand, sometimes.**

I have observed that some people found chances even in impossible situations; we call them winners, occasionally. On the contrary, losers lose obvious chances which were given to them. Some teenagers get admitted to colleges while studying in homeless shelters; some children of billionaires have drug problems.

Do you know what's one common point among all the losers in the world? Keep passing opportunities: chances to buy a house cheaper, invest in a stock at lower cost or meet a nice woman, etc; they keep losing those. I don't think that rich people are particularly super-smart or diligent; I do believe that they repeatedly recognize good chances and take them.

* * *

Have you ever had a restaurant you always wanted to try, but couldn't since it was permanently closed out while you delayed? I think opportunities are something like that; sometimes, it's available all the time just like McDonald's; in other times, it's available only once in our lives. If we miss it, that is all: nothing more for the rest of our lives.

I recall that I visited Las Vegas in 2003; I went to Los Angeles and San Francisco from there during the 10-day trip. I was 30 years old and thought it was a total waste of money; I was living on my mother's money then, but I was too eager to go to western parts of America at least once; the movie *Leaving Las Vegas* played a great role for that desire.

In the long run, I think I am glad I was there 20 years ago as it is 2023 now. It was a unique experience; I have used the knowledge well in the last 20 years; I will probably use that in the next 50 years, too. Whenever I see others' photos taken in Vegas, I know where they were or what those looked like in reality. I have no desire to visit the city again, though**: When you really want to do it, I suggest you just do it;** after your urge is gone, you may not want it forever.

* * *

In that sense, I am glad I started my business in 2006. I made some money in the end; it brought me over 7,000 eBay feedbacks with $300,000 sales revenue only online. There were more important things: I have learned plenty of real knowledge about small business for 8 years; sometimes, we just do not know what it is unless we actually go through it. **It was a great opportunity just for once in my lifetime**, particularly considering that I do not want to rent a space any more as it was the biggest waste in my life. Now I do not have any passion left for a retail business, but I can use the knowledge in the next 50 years.

I guess the same thing goes for writing, too. I notice that I have written over 700 pages in the last ten months for *UnBrokable**; I would like to make the final book over 800 pages if I can. I heard that thicker books sell more in general. But, more importantly, it is possible that the final book can be my only super-thick book; I like to remember that I wrote a very thick book once in my life. Even if I can publish more books, I am not sure I can make other books over 800 pages. **It is important to do it when we can do it.** Chances do not come often or easily; often, we do not even recognize if we got one.

* * *

We pass millions of opportunities everyday while we do not even notice. I was at the Renegade Craft Fair in Andersonville the other day; Andersonville in Chicago is a nice neighborhood to walk around. I saw about three hundred shops displayed under small tents along the main street; small business owners were showing their own brands: clothings, accessories, drinks, foods, jewelry, etc. What I was interested in was a soap company.

As soon as I was in the tent, I smelled a decent scent from organic soaps. One girl tried to sell the soaps for $9 each, but I saw boxes of small leftover soaps for $5 each, too. When I thought about it, these boxed soaps were twice as big as regular soaps. I just needed to attach those small soaps with a little bit of water. I know most soaps do not attach well. But, these were organic soaps, including a little bit of honey; these attached pretty well to each other as I expected.

What I did not like was the sales girl's attitude. I guess men are not her target customers. She was just sitting at the corner and sipping a free drink given by one participant. She probably also knew that customers can save some money with boxed soap that way. Actually, I figured that we save almost four times since half of the box soap ($2.50) is the same size as the real soap ($9). She acted as if I was an intruder. The soap turned out to be good, regardless.

And here is something she did not know. I could have gone back to the fair the next day and bought all the box soap she had in the tent. After using one overnight, I felt cleaner and did not need lotion for dry skin. I don't assume that she made a lot of sales at the fair since most people just walked around. I believe she probably sold like 20 soaps the whole day. I could have bought about 20 boxes if she was a type to accept reasonable negotiation; "I can buy 20 boxes. Can you include one real soap for free?" Although it was organic, half of the box of broken soap ($2.50) was the same price of any regular soap; there was no reason for me not to buy that many since I have a family to share. I did not go back there since I did not want another unpleasant encounter. Instead, I went to Whole foods and bought similar soaps.

* * *

When I saw my wife twenty four years ago in 1999, I knew she was a good person. It was extremely hard for me to find one woman I could trust. How many men who have only bachelor degrees marry a woman with a doctor degree as in my case? Most males are blind to choosing a good partner and 40% of them get divorce. Not only do most people not recognize opportunities, but also they do not tell the bad ones: **Most people do not acknowledge frauds and lost money that way, too.**

There was a Korean fraud and murderer named Young-hak Lee. He actually had been to prison several times even before committing murder of a young girl. Strangely, it says that a lot of Koreans knew him from online donations in the past twenty years.

Coincidently, he has a daughter who has severe genetic illness and that caused unbelievable face modification on her. She didn't look normal, unfortunately, but the man kept showing his daughter's face everywhere online for donations. I saw it once, too; I personally didn't feel right and thought this man seemed to have some intentions behind this. But those generous Koreans ended up donating almost $1 Million to him and found that he spent most on new sports cars, etc. Now he is serving life in prison for two murders: his wife and one teenage girl.

I think it is important to have good intuition for success, too; it may be necessary for survival. I love to say that everyone in the world is good, so we can live laid-back. But, regrettably, it doesn't seem that everything happens that way.

* * *

Summary

1. Some of us may be poor since we fail to recognize opportunities.
2. Some people do not realize that they have a chance in hand already.
3. The chance we face now could be the only one in our lives.

53

Believing a Loss as a Gain Mistakenly

Some people fail to update themselves.
-Brad Kong

Henry VIII was the King of England in the 16th century; it shows that he had married 6 times after getting divorced 5 times. Shockingly, two of his ex-wives were executed to death at their young ages: Anne Boleyn (2nd) was 29 and Catherine Howard (5th) was only 21 when they passed away. The irony is that all those ladies seemed to try hard to be queens their ways; they all must have believed that becoming a queen would be a great honor with privilege. Nonetheless, it shows that Henry VIII executed up to 57,000 people during his lifetime. Maybe it wasn't a good idea to get close to a dangerous person from the start.

This can be true for me, too, in a perspective. I am writing this book partly because I believe I can make some money out of publishing. That would be great, but it can bring me troubles as well. It's important not to get too excited by small successes.

* * *

Some people are poor because they stick to a little thing and try to make it right; they can end up spending way more energy or money than originally expected; it's better to let go of little things and focus only on important things. Greene took "Pancho Villa" as an example in his book *The 48 Laws of Power*.

Pancho Villa was a general in the Mexican Revolution in the early 20th century. Originally, he was a sort of bandit helping poor people; he robbed trains and gave money to the poor in Mexico. Greene described that he had a character of Robin Hood and Casanova combined; I believe the motive of the film *Zorro* came from him.

He attacked Columbus, New Mexico once in 1916. America supported the Carranza regime in Mexico which Pancho was against, then; he lost a battle because of defective ammos purchased from the U.S. It shows 17 Americans died from the attack as a result.

President Wilson sent 123,000 forces in total to capture him, subsequently, but failed. All the Mexican farmers liked him and gave the U.S. soldiers false information. It cost the American government $130 million for nothing in the aftermath of the expedition.

* * *

A hardship can make a person a saint or evil; it really depends on how the person can translate it; he or she can take it as a lesson or regret; it is also up to which direction the person can choose to go when the hardship is over. In his book *12 Rules for Life*, Peterson compared two people for extreme examples after hardships: Carl Panzram and Aleksandr Solzhenitsyn.

Carl Panzram was an American serial killer born in the 19th century. Wiki shows that he confessed to killing 21 people, but was suspected to have killed over 100 in total in the United

States alone, as well as several other murders overseas. He was originally sentenced to life in prison, but eventually hanged for killing a warden in prison in 1930; he was 39 when he got executed.

He definitely seemed to have a hard time when he was young. Panzram's parents were not happy to lose their children to school during the day, so forced them to work in the farm fields throughout the night, instead; Panzram later reported that he used to get just two hours of sleep before getting up for school; punishments for children in the family ranged from being chained to being starved.

Carl started committing petite crimes early; it shows that his parents sent him to the Minnesota Training School to get rid of him. According to his autobiography, while there, he was repeatedly beaten, tortured and raped by staff members in what the children dubbed "the paint shop"; youngsters left the room "painted" with bruises and blood. Some people may think all those misfortunes turn him into a monster: I still believe that he *chose* to be that way; he might have thought that killing others was good for him while it did not bring him any real gain.

On the contrary, Solzhenitsyn seemed to take his hardship differently. He was a Russian Army officer and his letter to a colleague brought him imprisonment; he blamed the Russian tyrant Stalin in that letter. Solzhenitsyn spent eight years in Soviet prison Gulag, but took this as a chance to think about and observe human nature deeply. He started writing after his sentence was over in 1953 and eventually won the *Nobel Prize in Literature* in 1970 after publishing a few books. I think this is a great example of how a person could use his hardship to accomplish more; he died at the age of 89 in 2008.

Regardless, when I read Solzhenitsyn's story, I felt that Russia is a country related to pain, hardship or death all the time: I would say that she could be a sort of *cursed* country. This is probably the last country I want to be born in; it has extremely cold weather to begin with. A lot of Russians died when the Mongols invaded her in the 13th century; wars have never stopped there ever since. Besides, many Russians were massacred by their own governments throughout the 20th century. Even now in 2023, they are having battles against Ukraine. I feel Russia has failed to change her own destiny even a bit.

* * *

In February 2022, Russia invaded Ukraine again in a major escalation of the Russo-Ukrainian War that began in 2014. These Russians are plainly stupid in my opinion; their dictator Putin is obsessed with old ideas: getting more land is a crucial thing; killing people of other countries is beneficial to us.

Things have changed greatly after World War II: **We are living in the economic war era now.** Getting more territories doesn't mean much in the profit sense; people do not live merely on agriculture any more; both countries have more than enough land, anyway. I think it is nonsense for Russia to spend $900 Million a Day to fight for borderline issues.

Nevertheless, humans are the most valuable capital assets on Earth these days. One human can generate a mountainous amount of wealth during his or her lifetime; this means one person can pay large taxes to the government, too. Spending money to destroy capital assets of other countries does not bring gain to us any more; killing Ukrainian people does not bring Russians any money; it only brings a bad reputation. Russians got stuck with this medieval idea: Every human in the world is a soldier and we have to destroy it.

As a result, Russia is making more enemies and losing more money than ever in 2023. **They have wasted fortunes to give a bad impression to the world**; they have been trying so hard everyday to be singled out and get into the poor class of nations.

Putin is the leader making all those brainless decisions: **In a sense, he is the true enemy for Russia;** one idiotic insider is more dangerous than groups of evil outsiders. I believe that he thinks those losses are profits; this kind of thing happens the most frequently when people fail to educate themself; I think that it is important for Russians to stop drinking and start reading. I believe that self-education fails principally due to laziness; Alcohol has provided too much indulgence to Russian comrades.

* * *

I found a black lady named Jessica when I watched Youtube the other day. The CNBC channel shows that she bought a one-bedroom condo for $44,000 in full in Detroit, Michigan. It was impressive to me in the beginning since I have never seen anyone who paid for a home less than I did ($60,000).

But soon I learned that she is paying $660 a month for association fees a month; I thought it was too much as I am paying $367 a month in 2023. She renovated the place fully as she planned to live for the rest of her life. I know those fees accumulate over time, so in her case, I think that the low condo price was nothing but a bait and would not bring her much benefit overall. I think she mistakenly thought that the cheaper condo was profitable despite the larger association fee.

The last example for this chapter topic is the Koreans obsessed with real estate investment in America. The property tax of real estate in Korea is about ten times cheaper than that of America; it makes more sense to invest in real estate in Korea since carrying costs is much cheaper. Some Koreans in America never understand this. They habitually go for bigger houses no matter what and regret higher taxes and upkeeps later on.

* * *

Summary

1. What we believe as a gain can be a loss in fact.
2. What used to be a gain to us can be a loss now.
3. Failing to educate ourselves can be a reason to be poor.

54

Being Too Nomadic

There is no better place than where we are now.
-Brad Kong

Stephen "Otto" Olshansky was a veteran thru-hiker; he was known as "triple crown" holder because of his many completions of the long-distance trails; he had hiked the Pacific Crest (2600 miles), the Appalachian (2,189 miles) and the Continental Divide Trail (3,100 miles) multiple times. Olshansky had hiked into the northern New Mexico wilderness again in November, 2015, looking for more solitude. Unexpectedly, the temperature was too cold; he had been snowbound and stuck in a camp latrine for over a month. Later, police found that he tried to end his life by blocking the vent of the building and pumping carbon dioxide into the space. Eventually, he passed away due to starvation and hypothermia near Chama, NM in 2016; he was only 56 years old.

* * *

Humans are not that strong: No one can survive alone in the middle of frosty mountains in January. Lately, I read some books regarding "van life" and personally don't even think it's possible to live sanely in a van. Above all, I believe that we need a constant supply of water to live a *healthy* life: drinking, brushing teeth, washing, cleaning, etc. Having plenty of water is no problem at most houses in America, but a huge hassle even in a luxury RV. I read a book titled *Nomadland* written by

Bruder the other day; I felt that she described *van life* too idealistically. I don't think anyone can sleep well in the metal can; it's psychologically bothersome, too, as sleeping on streets is technically illegal. I think it is better to accept reality and try to own even a tiny condo as many seemed to choose van life due to financial hardships.

Wanderlust can be nothing but a basic instinct in my opinion; human ancestors have traveled from Africa to Siberia by walking in the first 6 million years. World traveling can be a productive way to expand our views to some extent. But it can easily turn into a waste if we do it more than enough. Some people waste their whole life with savings after getting addicted to wandering. At least, I think that we can try to go to as many different destinations as possible to minimize being wasteful.

* * *

There is a travel writer named *Park* in Korea; he has been to myriad countries and written five books so far. He was born in 1973 as I was. He said he was diagnosed to have hepatitis-B 20 years ago; he said he has a 35% chance of developing liver cancer and one of his friends died of that before turning 30. So he said that he retired early and decided to enjoy his life, especially in Thailand. Apparently, he attends alcohol drinking parties continually, according to his YouTube channel, so I wonder how serious he is about his liver condition.

Anyway, he has lived in Thailand for the last 15 years and this seems to be his current situation: no money, family or language; he said that he cannot speak Thai even though he is trying to learn. He never met a Thai girl to marry or have a child together; he never had any savings of a meaningful amount.

On the contrary, I bought my house in full in America 10 years ago. I had owned my business for 8 years before; I have a healthy stock portfolio and a good amount of savings. Besides, I am married with my wife who received a doctorate degree and have a daughter; I am fluent in English. I have been to only seven foreign countries in my whole life: Korea, America, Denmark, Finland, Netherland, Canada and Japan; Netherland and Japan were only flight layovers; Korea is where I was born; therefore, I am not sure if I have to include those three in destinations. Maybe he is happier than me; we do not know. Still, I would say that being nomadic may not bring us much money and can put us in poverty.

* * *

It shows that the countries having the largest amounts of tourists were France and Spain in 2019. I understand France, but I don't know why people visit Spain; at least, I do not desire to. And it says that Thailand made the largest revenue out of tourism among Asian countries: $60 Billions in USD in 2019; this is big considering it is not very expensive in the country. Only the USA, France and Spain have bigger tourism revenues than Thailand, but these three are wealthier countries; everything is more expensive and tourists naturally spend more money.

I see that more Koreans stay in Thailand for a long time these days; they say that it is like heaven. Seriously? Then, why do a lot of Thai people come to Korea and stay illegally to make money? The massage industry has been dominated by Thais for the last decade. I do not want to waste my life on envying people from tropical countries or indulging myself with little money for a long period in South Asia. Current wealthy Korea has not built that way; I have an obligation to pass my parents' wealth to my daughter's generation. The USA has the biggest tourism revenue, statistically. I prefer to enjoy where I am now; I feel comfortable when I don't waste a chunk of money.

* * *

Wanderlust is a curse in a sense; it can be at least a sort of addiction in my opinion. Traveling costs money, so it can make us save less money; it can make us go bankrupt; it can put us in jeopardy depending on where we go; it can make us disappear or even die. We need to travel if there is a reason. Many just travel long distances for nothing; some waste their whole life without getting a job or having a family; they can have nothing left in the end.

If you are dying to travel, I suggest you do it early in your life, at least. We certainly learn new things from travels. We can use this knowledge for the next 80 years when we travel at 20. We learn less and less from travels as we get old: Why? All the travels are too similar, after all: **It is getting closer to be a waste as we get older.** For some reason, I usually regret it after eating or traveling too much. Being nomadic is nothing but a human instinct, but it can cause problems.

* * *

Moving in and out itself costs a lot as well. There used to be a townhouse I was interested in near the library in our town. I had a chance to speak with the owner on the day he moved out in 2021. He said he was moving back to Dallas, TX from Chicago, IL and it cost him $8,000 for the trailer service; I saw one big trailer and two movers in front of his house that day. Honestly, I thought that I would sell everything and move by car myself if I were him (they had two cars); he could have saved $8,000 this way. In addition, he could have made some money out of selling stuff; he looked old enough to consider downsizing, anyway.

Moving from one place to another is not just about money; it takes a lot of effort to pack things and move them: a month's amount of physical work. Besides, it can scratch my furniture or break items; I can lose them, too. I still remember someone stole my daughter's violin when I moved from my old apartment to this condo alone in 2013. It was a low income apartment; I chose it only because it was right in front of my business and they suggested lower rent. The thief must have thought that the instrument was expensive; it was a $30 baby violin from Amazon.

* * *

I read a book titled *Nomadland* written by Bruder recently; a movie was made based on the book; it won Academy Awards for Best Pictures in 2021. It shows that they spent $5 Million to make the film and the box office sales was $35 Million, so I would say that it was a big commercial hit, too.

The book explains that tens of thousands of Americans live in vans full time instead of a house these days; they set up vans or RVs just like rooms in a house. The author explained that they do it to avoid housing costs like a rent or mortgage. It sounded rational in the beginning, but I found it kind of nonsense in the end.

I have been living in a condo without a car for the last 6 years. I feel lucky to live near a library and four supermarkets within walking distance; I think these two facilities are the most essential when living without a car as a writer. Maybe some should be able to go to work by walking; that was what happened to me when I used to work for the nursing home. These days, I plan to walk around Chicagoland a lot as it is April, 2023; I check carefully whenever I run into clean, decent and walkable neighborhoods. Sadly, most places do not have a library or supermarket nearby.

If we live in a van, we can certainly save money out of rent, mortgage or property tax. But we have to pay for gas constantly, which is expensive. The car-related costs are diverse and these are not cheap: gas, car wash, parking, insurance, license, registration, regular inspections, repairs, maintenance, etc.

There are so many places that prohibit overnight parking: **Staying in a van is not rent-free if we have to pay for a long term or short term parking.** In fact, these could be more expensive than $367 a month, which is my condo association fee in 2023; I pay $367 HOA instead of $1,200 apartment rent a month because I bought my condo ten years ago; this $367 includes heating and water, so it can be actually cheaper than van life.

* * *

Have you been on a road trip before? I live near Chicago and I have been to the Mall *of America* in Minneapolis, MN three times. I have not been particularly interested in the mall; this mall has a theme park in the middle and has a lot of things to ride (e.g., rollercoaster). I have never tried those things; all I did was just eat at food courts and walk around there.

Minneapolis is about 400 miles from Chicago suburb; I can stop by Madison and Dells, WI, on the way. These two cities are fun to walk around. There are plenty of hotels around Dells since it has dozens of massive water parks. Dells seems to be the Vegas in water park version; it has everything from Casinos to Torture museum. Once I am in Minneapolis, I can go to St. Paul and other vicinities as well, so I can visit many places without a huge amount of driving. Besides, the roads are not very crowded even during summer since they are in the middle of America.

But did you notice that we spend a lot of money as soon as we are out of houses? Regardless of hotel costs, I still spend way more than staying at home even when I sleep in my car: **Once we are out of home, we leak money constantly;** whatever we do, it costs money; even when we do not do anything, it still may require expenses like parking.

In my opinion, being nomadic or living in a van is not just for money saving. There are bigger reasons behind those: Some people have a bigger desire to travel around. A wanderlust; some just cannot stay in one place; they just like to hit the road for any excuse.

* * *

According to the book titled *Sapience* written by Harari, humans only settled 12,000 years ago when the agricultural revolution started. Humans have been on the Earth as long as 6 million years if we include the last common ancestors with chimpanzees (Hominini): We have been walking around without permanent settlement from Africa to Asia, America and Australia for millions of years; then, we settled down in one place a moment ago. I guess this is why I walk around all the time.

Regardless of instincts, does it cost more or less to move around? In my opinion, it definitely costs more to be nomadic. That is why countries like Kazakhstan or Mongolia can be considered as low income countries. Spending all our energy and time on moving around may be good for health, but not very good for profit. I am just pointing this out since people in the *Nomadland* book keep saying, "I do not know why I am poor despite working for life."

And do you know which countries are the most nomadic yet poor in the world? Many countries in Southern Africa. Traditionally, Africa never had agriculture, at least not for a meaningful level: There were even no borderlines in the continent until the 20th century. A certain size of land did not matter much for cattle farmers looking for grasses everywhere. And did you know that Africans are good at learning languages? I believe this is the proof that they have been nomadic for a long time (up to six million years): **Nomads meet new people all the time and need to learn their languages fast.** That is great, but if we have to concern ourselves with poverty issues, being nomadic may not be very cost efficient in economics.

* * *

The *Nomadland* author interviewed one lady named Linda in her book, repeatedly; she smoked Marlboro all the time and said, "I do not know where all my money is gone? Soon I will be 65 and get my social security check. It will be only $500 a month and does not cover my trailer park parking fee of $600." Really? Seriously, you do not know where all the money's gone? Did you get the cigarette for free? **It is obvious for some people; others never get it until they die.** Shamefully, I have never been able to learn how to knit from my wife; budgeting could be like that to some people.

I am not saying that we have to suppress our wanderlusts crazily. I walk all the time instead of driving a car (I do not own one). I like this Chicagoland since it is one of few cities where I can walk comfortably with public transportation.

* * *

Summary

1. Wanderlust is an addictive instinct.
2. Being too nomadic can be expensive or dangerous.
3. There are better ways to relieve wanderlust than luxury travels.

55

Being Unable to Grow

Growth may need time and effort, but not necessarily money.
-Brad Kong

I read a book titled *Talking to Strangers* written by Gladwell the other day. It starts with the Hernan Cortez story which happened in central Mexico about 500 years ago. The emperor Montezuma and his people in Tenochtitlan were massacred by the Spanish army mainly because they had no contact outside before; 20 million Aztecs died by European armors, guns, horses and, most importantly, germs carried by Spanish soldiers. The lesson is clear: **It is better to know what's outside.** Do not separate yourself from it, voluntarily.

I do not like those Koreans who have only Korean friends in America; they meet their Korean families and relatives frequently, eat only Korean foods or go to Korean supermarkets; they watch Korean TV channels and news all the time for an extra fee, and talk about Korean politics out of the blue. This is stupid in my opinion: **They just fail to adaptate in America**; many cannot speak English even after a decade of staying in the U.S.

* * *

I think there are two types of people in the world: People who can change after learning lessons and people who cannot.

I quit all the sugary drinks including juices or coffees on the day I had a severe root canal pain in my molar tooth in 2019; the only liquid I drink has been strictly water since then. I quit drinking cola on the date I had kidney stone pain in 2008; I did not know soda can make severe pain in my abdomen. I can see that some people never change their diets even after having multiple teeth extractions (e.g., my mother) or even a kidney transplant (e.g., my friend Bob). I think that it's natural to make some changes after detrimental things happen; I guess that some do not, and stay poor.

Learning English is more likely an education than cultural effects in my opinion: **What makes me upset is these parents do not study themselves for English while pushing their children to study in unpleasant ways**; they tend to unnecessarily spend a lot of money on private education, too, which happened to me. If an animal fails to adaptate in an environment, the result can be deadly; the same goes for humans. These no-English Koreans usually stay in low income classes unless they take others' money. This is horrible: Toxic family members; I know too many examples. For sure, I will try not to be one.

* * *

I don't have to cut myself off from outsiders, and stick to Koreans, especially when there is no proof that Koreans are better than others. Often, the fraud schemes targeting Koreans are committed by Koreans in America; some kidnap other Koreans for money in the Philippines; these crimes are frequent on the news in that island nation. I think smart ones know how to keep some distance from other Koreans and try to accept others as much as they can. I believe this is the right way to adaptate in America.

I found one Youtube channel the other day; the comedian was a Korean girl living in LA (the city is the Mecca of the Korean population in America); I clicked it without knowing her identity. The channel seems to be popular with millions of clicks on her videos. I understand she has a Korean husband although I did not marry a Korean wife. But when I watched her video showing a ramen house, I found all of her friends are Korean girls (fat and not pretty, honestly); the ramen house was exactly in Koreatown as well. I mean, what's wrong with those people? She seems to be young; she didn't have to start restricting herself at such an early age.

Frankly, I see similar things happen everywhere; some white girls meet only whites; some black girls take photos only with blacks. Do you know why this is a problem? Some girls choose abusive men since they are familiar with these types of guys; maybe they are from families having violent fathers. Some people choose a poor lifestyle since they are comfortable with it. This is why some criminals commit the same crimes repeatedly; rapists don't usually commit arson. Also dividend investors like me don't really buy Tesla stocks: **What's comfortable can kill us.** See if you can try something new to expand your sights. This is the only way to survive; this will protect us, at least.

* * *

As one Malaysian comedian said, only an Asian can be a neutral judge between whites and blacks in America. I have nothing particular against both blacks and whites; I feel more sorry for blacks. So hear me out.

I saw a book titled *His Name Is George Floyd* written by two black columnists from *The Washington Post* the other day: Do you know why this book was not well sold? The main reason was that Floyd was not really a Jesus. First of all, he was not manly enough, so he abandoned his wife and five kids living in Houston; he had been convicted of 8 different crimes and spent at least 4 years in prison; he was a fentanyl addict; he got arrested again for using a fake $20 bill to buy cigarettes in 2020. He was a big guy and crazily resisted while being apprehended. I feel sorry that the guy died of suffocation; I do appreciate what black people have done for civil rights as an Asian. But blacks cannot be on a black's side all the time for no matter what. We have to go reasonable; we know he was not Rosa Parks. The same goes for Koreans; I am not going to be on their side all the time.

I feel sorry for those police officers as well; they always do things I don't want to do. Police job is not like something in a movie. Regardless of race, I believe that all the officers deserve to get paid more than now; I strongly believe more tax should go to police stations and libraries.

* * *

There is a Japanese travel writer named Takano. Apparently, he has written over 10 books about traveling as of 2022. I read one of his books regarding Thailand; he said he had stayed as a Japanese language teacher in the country for over 15 years. He worked for a Japanese newspaper for Thai people after that; he said there are a lot of Thais living in Japan. Surprisingly, he said he does not know how to speak Thai after all those years; he said his Thai language skill is below conversational level.

There is also a Korean travel writer named Park; he also has written about ten travel books by 2023. Although he had lived in Thailand for over twelve years as well, he said he virtually does not know how to speak, read or write Thai, either. I love their laid back lifestyles. Yet, I assume that this is just too much.

Personally, I feel that language teachers in a foreign country are too easy jobs. No offense, but think about it: **What did they do to get that mother tongue?** Being born in America or Canada; even a homeless person knows how to speak English here. So these people chose the easiest way to live a life, originally. Whichever country they go, many fail to learn native language in that country: Why? They didn't choose a challenging lifestyle from the start: **They fail to grow and incline to stay in the low income class as a result.**

* * *

There have been a lot of Americans and Candians going to Korea to teach English these days. Some caused troubles at places like a nightclub; the language institute often does not require anything from them except being whites; they do not pay a lot to those teachers, either. Personally, I think choosing that kind of job is hopeless to begin with. For example, I am not writing this book in Korean though the language is easier for me. I know that the book market in Korea is very small and limited; the Korean population is only 0.5% of the world. Besides, not reading books is a trending problem in Korea, so I won't be able to sell my books there: **I am not going to choose a tiny market only because English is harder for me.** I have been in America for 24 years, so writing a book in English is not supposed to be an immense hardship for me.

I like to be laid-back. But there should be a bottom limit: If we do not challenge even a bit, we will stay in poverty; this can be a sign of going extinct. Why do girls like rich men? That's not only because they can spend the men's money. Even independent girls prefer rich men: Why? Self-made men might have had some qualities to be rich, initially; no one can be rich without trying anything; there are reasons. These are what these girls love about and chase at.

* * *

Personally, I strongly believe people grow more when they are poor. Life gets simpler when we go broke; the condition will bring us more time to think. I am not saying that we actually need to be poor: **See if you can act as if you do not have money.** We can acquire more time when we free ourselves from all those spendings; please trust me that 50% of our spending does not have any point. When we imagine we do not have any money; we may find more free time left for the day. If we decide not to spend money for a week, it can be a week of free time to stay at home to reflect on ourselves; it will not necessarily cost any money; it will mature, grow or educate our inner-self a little bit.

Have you ever felt bad after spending money? Have you felt ripped off after watching movies or playing video games for hours? Not spending money can block us from having all those bad feelings. **Consumerism not only steals our time, but also intercepts mental growth;** some people speak like idiots since they never had time to grow themselves.

* * *

I already told you that there are Koreans who cannot speak English even after staying in America for decades; I think that almost a quarter of Koreans are like that in this country. They usually live in Korean towns or similar concentration in a big city like LA or NYC. They are often surrounded only by Koreans and work in Korean restaurants. They rarely get out of the neighborhood alone, must take Korean airlines and usually get married with other Koreans. It is unimaginable to write a book in English for them.

The similar case is Mexicans living in Mexican areas like Little Village in Chicago. Most Mexicans in America speak English fine or at a certain level, somehow. But I have seen some Mexicans having no English at all in those areas as well.

And these are not only cases for Koreans or Mexicans. Do you know how to speak a foreign language yourself? How about a foreign language not spoken by your parents? Most Americans speak only English, too; many have not grown beyond their mother tongue. I made examples with languages, but actually this is happening in every field. If we cannot expand our language skill, it is possible we are behind in other fields as well: **This is why plenty of immigrants are wealthier than Americans.**

* * *

Let me give you an extreme example of not being able to grow with a Korean writer named "K"; coincidentally, he was good at lying and deceiving as well. When I found his book in Harold Washington library in 2017, I actually thought that the book was well written. The writer is about 55 years old in 2022, has lived in America for over twenty years and has three sons. He said he failed several businesses, but finally got successful with a sushi business; he calls himself "a CEO selling Sushi." The book was self-help; he said that he wrote it to leave his entire life lessons for his sons.

The part that I do not like is that he has kept exaggerating his success in America and it seems it is accepted without suspicion in Korea. He said he made over $400 Millions profit with a sushi franchise named "SF", which I have never heard of; I checked it in depth and could not find such a brand in America at all. There was such a brand only in Korea since he lied to Koreans that it is a famous brand from America;

some Koreans opened those stores with him in Korea. It seems there were about ten SF locations only in South Korea and that is it; not thousands of locations in the U.S. as he claimed.

I do not know how this kind of scheme works out. The Korean community is so small in America that he could be famous if he really made $400 M after immigration; he could have been on Time magazine cover if that's true. Of course, his name is not found on Wikipedia, Korean Wiki, Namu Wiki or anywhere.

And, mysteriously, no one seems to ask for any verification in Korea. He published three books in Korea, had many interviews with newspapers and had lectures with minor TV stations. But no one seems to be in suspicion. I believe his real job is just a writer and the copyrights from books are main income. I believe he is one of those Koreans who cannot speak English and had to go back to Korea to do anything: That is why all of his books are written in Korean. Here is something I really would like to point out: **He failed to grow up speaking English, so he is wasting time on deceiving Koreans now.**

* * *

First of all, it does not make sense to go back to Korea to do any business in a profit sense. South Korea is a small country whose size is similar to Indiana State in America; the U.S.A. is 98 times bigger than South Korea. And the population of the USA is about 7 times bigger than that of Korea; the GDP of the USA is 21 times larger. Does this make sense if you have to go back to a smaller country to do business because of the language barrier? Inevitably, the market for anything is smaller there. It is sad that the major skill he has is pretending to be somebody in a bigger country.

Secondly, it is even more absurd for writers to go back to Korea for her book market. How many people speak and understand Korean in the world? The world population is over 8 billion while the South Korean population is about 52 million (no book sales to the north): **This means only 0.6% of the world population is South Korean**. Does it make sense to lose 99% of world readers only because an author cannot write in English even after staying in America for 20 years?

English is not just a language; it has been the universal language and sixty seven countries speak it as their primary language: the USA, UK, Canada, Australia, New Zealand, etc. Since Koreans learn how to speak English as well, I can increase the number of potential readers to 100 times only by writing in English. Let's not talk about which country was bad for now: I am not necessarily admiring English speaking countries. But, in a business sense, I would rather write in English than lying about my American achievements to Koreans.

Thirdly, I think it is important to be aware that Koreans have a reputation for not reading books. Most Americans do not know this, but there have been some concerns regarding this topic in the country for decades; by a simple Google search, I found a result like this: "48% of adults do not read even one book in Korea." I also found another article that said "Korea ranked 30th out of 30 countries for reading time a year." It is nonsense to write a book for this country only because someone didn't learn English.

Do Americans read a lot of books? I am not sure, but probably way more than Koreans: How do I know? That could be why Amazon became the biggest company in America and Bezos became the richest billionaire here. Amazon originally started out as a bookseller in the 1990s. Since many people order books, it has become stronger and could be able to expand to other areas; many orders in the early stage means that many people read books. Conclusively, when I write a book in English, not only would I have more readers, but I can have more avid ones as well: Growing myself to be good at English is the only way.

* * *

Summary

1. Some people fail to grow and stay poor.
2. Some get stuck only in their own races or languages.
3. It's crucial to grow out of our comfort zones to get wealthier.

56

Getting Married By Pressure

Most people live lives predetermined by society.
-Brad Kong

Before getting married, I think it's important to check the finances of *significant others* (e.g., brides), at least once. The advantage you believe she has could be only your imagination; if she has been poor so far or has not achieved much, the chances are she will be like that from now on, too. You may be happy to pay everything only in the beginning; it won't be acceptable, eventually. That is why half of marriages end up being in divorces, which causes even more troubles.

Always remember that no one has to get married. If you still see a person approaching you, see if you can accept him or her. Personally, I cannot accept a woman talking nonstop; there was a middle aged Filipina speaking in Tagalog in the middle of the library the other day; she was more annoying than two young Latinas nearby. Being talkative is like being odorous; I would not be surprised if she got divorced; it was unbearable to me, at least. Always keep in mind that there is no fantastic woman on Earth; every woman farts and poops; she just does not show it to you yet. If you are still not convinced, meet the girl's mother or grandma; they are the future of the young lady; if you can accept them, go ahead to get married.

* * *

A lot of men do not know how to attract a woman: The principle is that women's minds change *slowly*. Most men violate this ultimate truth and cannot give enough time to girls. As a result, men cause bustles in the beginning and even be called stokers. Playboys are geniuses of *waiting*; they know there is no fantastic woman in the world and it's not worth rushing; they know how to give a girl huge amounts of time and waiting is a must. Their patience is based on their own confidence and thoughtfulness; they know a woman has her own life and schedule, so she cannot change everything for a man, suddenly.

Women are not interested in their partners at the first sight in general: Being suspicious of men is a survival skill. If a girl is interested in a man right away, it's not the man who gave the reason; she must have known someone like him before. This does not mean that a man does not have a chance, though: **Women's minds change just like shaking reeds in the middle of winds;** it usually takes a few months to years to be their ideal type; a man can see a sudden attitude change from a girl one day. If we keep pushing a girl before she is ready, we must fail.

* * *

I stopped by one Thai restaurant in a small village a year ago; I was surprised that the waitress was good looking. What I mean by a small village is a small town in Chicagoland. I try to walk or scoot around one day a week for exercise; I just have a kick scooter I bought from Amazon (not electric); I see that more people ride scooters instead of bicycles these days. I ran into the downtown of the village while I was riding the scooter from the old Orchard mall. From there, I was going to go south to Skokie for Zad Middle Eastern restaurant. But I thought that I could try the northern area this time.

I have not worn contact lenses in the last a couple of months for vision training. Initially, I decided not to wear those for my cat allergy. But I thought I could live without it longer since I am not doing anything special except writing books. I am nearsighted, but I could feel that my vision got a bit better. I did not wear my lenses when I visited the Thai place; I thought that every girl looked pretty without my lenses.

I checked the Facebook page of the restaurant; the receipt from the restaurant showed the waitress's Thai name; when I typed it on Facebook, her page came out. She looked fine, but far from pretty in photos. I thought I could visit the place one more time with my *contacts on*. On the second visit, I found she looked OK; I was surprised that she looked much older; her skin looked damaged, probably from heavy alcohol drinking or harmful skin cosmetics. I did not want to bother her job, so I introduced myself, gave my name and phone number and left.

It has been about a year passed; now I don't know why I did that; her attitude was not welcoming. Apparently, her face has changed greatly since 2019, according to her Facebook; she might have got plastic surgery, but she seems to have lost her smile from that moment; it looks like she used to be a plain looking, but smiling girl. I used to think that it would be nice if I could stay in France or Thailand for one year each. Now I do not have that strong desire any more; I am happy with where I am, especially because I can save more money this way.

* * *

Personally, I do not think Thai foods are good for teeth; those dishes are unnecessarily sugary starting from Pad Thai. I do not think they created healthy meals even though the country has plenty of food ingredients in nature compared with those in Korea. Whenever I eat Bibim Naengmyeon (Korean cold noodle), I feel Koreans are hidden geniuses for food creation; I do not see any food in the world close to this mastery; it is more surprising considering the country is cold and does not have much food materials.

Men cannot do much when they have a wife and daughter: Still, isn't it sad that we cannot meet a new person only because the person can be a female? It is like we are living in a jail for the rest of our lives. I still believe the human population is growing fast and having another child does not have a huge point; I get less and less interested in *physical* relationships every year, too. Married men cannot meet anyone because it is an emotional affair nowadays. I don't know why people spend big money on weddings to get into this much restriction; I guess men should get paid to be at weddings, at least.

Getting into marriage is somewhat like becoming a prisoner or monk in my opinion; I prefer to be a monk than the other, but unless we accept this, marriages just won't survive; this rule is the same regardless of whoever we marry. It requires an incredible amount of patience, especially after our child is born. Once we decide to get married, we just have to give up a lot of things. In a sense, it is similar to getting a job; every job brings money somehow, but will be hard, boring and disappointing after years. When a marriage is hard without benefits, I think divorce happens.

There are diverse types of pressure for adults to get married from society. **When you get married while you do not necessarily want to, it can cause immense mental and financial damage:** Seriously, you are digging your own grave in this case.

* * *

When I was in my 30s, I had received huge pressure to get married from my parents: rude and direct pressures. My daughter is thirteen-years-old now, but I will never understand why they pushed me like that. I could have understood if they pushed me to get a job or make money; that is the maximum understandable level. I just did not see what profit my parents could get out of my marriage.

My parents have been stupid enough to get divorced themselves, after all: As a parent, I just do not see any obvious profit I could get only because my daughter gets married. In fact, this can be the other way around: If she gets married, it will bring me some spendings, a ceremony I do not want to attend, some clothes I do not want to wear and numerous other headaches. If this happens, that is fine; I will try to deal with them. **But there is no way I will ask or even insist her to do this:** Even if there is a profit, I do not want it if that requires some sacrifices from my daughter.

I can say that my parents must have acted somewhat like animals; they never really have acted logically based on reason for life. That is why there always had been a lot of quarrels in the family before they divorced; this is surprising since they made fortunes despite all those. They might have had strong instincts to get offspring, which I do not necessarily have; they gave me a good amount of money after my daughter was born, though. In conclusion, as a parent, I do not understand these pushy parents (especially, mothers); I have no desire to spend money on my child's wedding while I can make her uncomfortable.

* * *

Another type of pressure for marriage is social pressure. There are industries making money only when people get married and have a child: wedding bride and bridesmaid shops; tuxedo rentals; jewelries; wedding halls (a big industry in Korea); wedding makeup, photos, flowers, singers and limousine rental; daycares; baby foods (e.g., Gerber), diapers (e.g., Huggies), strollers (e.g., Newell); toys and video Games (e.g., Nintendo); theme parks (e.g., Universal Studio and Six Flags); animations (e.g. Disney, Pixar, etc); school supplies (e.g., Staples); education industries including private tutoring; divorce lawyers; infertility clinics, etc. Some of these truly survive only when people get married; their advertisements come in diverse sneaky ways; they will never show the hard, boring and miserable part of married lives.

Ironically, I do not see that many industries particularly benefiting from single people now. Maybe nightclubs? Personally, I have never really been there when I was single. Maybe a take out restaurant for men who do not want to cook at home? Still, restaurants can get more profit from a large group of family customers. When there are equal numbers of industries making strong profits out of single people, we will get less pressure from the wedding industries: Finally, we will make sane decisions, then.

I think that still one more pressure may be from our friends or neighbors in environments; I would call it peer pressure. When I walked around different areas in Chicagoland, I saw some areas have more families and some have more singles. Sometimes, I really wonder if 100% of Latin American women have a child without exception. Still, I believe that it is our choice whether we will get married or not, regardless of what village we are living in now.

* * *

Summary

1. As a parent, I will never understand those parents pushing their child to get married.
2. I just don't see any profit out of my daughter's marriage.
3. Even if there is a benefit, I do not want it if it requires my child's sacrifice.

57

No Plan B

Only preparation can assure survival.
-Brad Kong

My old mother (75) had lost 9 teeth by 2022; she has been wealthy and taken care of her teeth reasonably well for life. I have never seen her eating anything particularly sweet; she has been a non-drinker and smoker. I think that Korean foods themselves are sugary and carbohydrate-oriented: Complete change of her diet did not happen: She always says, "How can I live without rice?" I do not think she will ever change her diet even if she can lose all her teeth.

I finally lost my molar tooth by decay in Sept, 2022; I was 49. I had been stupid to eat sugary stuff blindly for my whole life; nothing really significant happened until I became 45; a serious pain came one day in 2018. Luckily, I have not been a drinker, smoker or coffee drinker while I have changed my diet completely since then. **Quitting eating rice was a revolutionary change for me as a Korean**; I didn't see other choices left; I knew that there are foreigners who never try rice for life; I didn't think just brushing teeth or going to the dentist were enough. Unless I change meals completely, I thought that it is possible I can follow in my mother's footsteps.

* * *

Do you know what the biggest mystery in the world is? Rich people tend to work harder while poor people waste more time. According to my observation, this is almost true, regardless of age or nationality; neither side will change. People who bought this book are usually those far from poverty; some of them might have thought that they can protect themselves from being in worse situations, just in case.

There is a Korean autobiography titled "*Army of Two*" written by Lee; this author was originally a lead singer of a rock band *Sister's Barbershop;* he was successful in the music industry; he had published six albums before *quitting* music in 2017. Also he wrote five books and one of them was listed in 100 bestsellers ever published in South Korea.

In the book, he confessed that it was a bad decision to stop playing music and go only for writing; he was both musician and writer by 2017. He said whenever he couldn't compose a song, writing gave him comfort; when he couldn't write well, music was his exit to try something different. He said that he has been more stressed out after becoming a full time author since book sales has been his sole income; **he used to feel more relaxed when his income depended on two things: the band and writing.**

In the book titled "Let's go to a better place", Jung describes a similar thing. In the book, there is an article named "I am not doing only this job"; she emphasized that it was important for her to have two identities. She said she often got upset during the daytime while she worked at a magazine company; writing a couple of hours after work relieved her stress; it gave her hope to get out of her hellish job then. Eventually, one of her books became a hit and she has been a full time mom and author now.

* * *

Personally, I have been an investor in the last 12 years; my portfolio has been up from $100 in 2011 to $560,000 in 2022. I have been reasonably successful and this gave me a chance to try writing as a career; I did not realize I had so much desire to write until recently.

Currently, I am reading a Brazilian novel *The Alchemist;* it shows that this book has sold over 100 M copies. Almost at the end of the story, the alchemist gave some extra gold to a monk for the shepherd boy Santiago. The boy asked why and he told one arabic proverb: "Everything that happened once may never happen again. **But everything that happens twice will surely happen a third time.**" The boy had lost his entire fortune twice before; the alchemist implied that the monk would save some extra money for the boy.

* * *

I have experienced big recessions twice in my life: the Foreign Currency Crisis in Korea in 1997 and the Subprime Mortgage Crisis in America in 2008; the 1997 recession is also known as the "IMF[52] Crisis" to Koreans. During these eras, so many companies filed bankruptcies and people committed suicides.

I found out that there are millions of Koreans going to fortune tellers, especially around New Year; I feel that these are stupid. I can see hundreds of those fortune tellers on Youtube, too; in my opinion, they may be good psychologists, but certainly not prophets; most of them seem to be normal people trying to make some money out of sessions. I have never visited a fortune teller for life mainly because I did not want to waste a $100 "consultation" fee; I do not read "the

[52] International Monetary Fund

zodiac of this month" in newspapers, either. **I believe that the only way to guarantee a better future is preparation.**

There are people living without any preparation for emergencies; some preparations can look like a waste at glance. But, without these, our life can go downhill fast. Let me give you some examples.

* * *

As I wrote, I have two licenses acquired in America: Medical coder and Pharmacy Technician. Why did I get these? Maybe I was bored while I was working as a dishwasher for a part time job. But, more importantly, I thought I could use these just in case something happens like a stock market collapse. The exams for these licenses turned out to be super hard, so I had to study way more than I expected in the beginning. But I had studied by myself with textbooks I ordered from Amazon, so I did not spend much money, after all; I just had spent countless hours at the libraries.

The same went for writing, too. I already had a good amount of money in my stock portfolio and CDs; I have lived purely on my dividends and interests for a while; I bought my house in full ten years ago; besides, I have wealthy parents. Maybe some people live like this forever; I decided to write books, instead. Maybe killing time did not bring me much meaning. At the same time, in case something goes wrong, I can live on my book royalty, too. Plan B: **One more safety net.**

* * *

There is a writer named Michael Crichton; he is well known for the Jurassic Park series. Did you know that he had a Medical Doctor degree from Harvard? Some may think that it was a waste since it cost money and time to get it. But the situation could have been much different if he was not successful in writing; still, he could have lived as a wealthy doctor, alternatively.

Preparation is a survival skill. In a sense, 90% of our life is a sort of waste; we waste 90% on something other than essential activities like eating. If we have to waste our life anyhow, I think that it is better to waste time on preparation. While we do it, we can find unexpected ways to make money, too.

A similar rule applies to spending in my opinion; basically 90% of our spending has nothing to do with indispensable these days. As one Bhuddist monk suggested, working two hours a day should be enough if we strictly spend money on essentials like food. Houses are vital, but many go for more than comfortable shelters. For example, I do not believe seven bathrooms were needed for nine people as in Kate Gosselin's old house before her bankruptcy.

After winning a lottery, some people buy sports cars first, while others pay off their mortgages faster. Paying off the debts makes more sense; if we do not take care of it quickly, it tends to get bigger; the longer we hold it, the more it costs. I think it is important to get rid of problems first in any case. The two actions above will affect future finances differently; one can be poor later while the other are not. This is why some people work crazily, but are still poor: No preparation.

* * *

I borrowed six books about poverty from the library the other day. I am trying to read them all, but I was initially surprised that most books point out the issues to governments and society: Are they all crazy? There is no fucking way governments can solve our money problem unless they was built by our grandmas: No one gives any money to anyone for free. That is the rule ever since the Earth was formed 4.5 billion years ago. There must have been a wealthy or poor person one million years ago, too; some primates had enough food or some did not. That is why some *Homos* like Neanderthal went extinct, ultimately.

Do you know how the Dodo bird went extinct? They got too comfortable on their island and lost capability to fly. That's exactly what can happen in the personal finances now. Modern governments will not change the rule of the Earth which has existed for billions of years. Even if it is the society's fault, it is more reasonable to take care of some issues personally, instead of demanding help from outside.

* * *

Summary

1. Only preparation can guarantee a better future.
2. Preparing can look wasteful until something bad happens.
3. Wasting time on preparation is better than on anything else.

58

Concerning Other Eyes Too Much

We are all slaves to the trends to some extent.
-Brad Kong

Simplicity makes people look decent; I think that this is why Ikea furniture is popular. We do not have to buy luxury goods to cover ourselves up; people already know if we are wealthy or poor. Surprisingly, it is totally visible when someone is low-life, but trying hard to look rich.

Our society has all sorts of strange pressures. One of my latest concerns was the pressure to have "two children" in a family; many people seem to believe that it's ideal; in my opinion, this is simply the wrong pressure, unless you are comfortable with it. Having one more kid after the first child can cause more troubles than not: The foremost reason is that the second child can be born when parents are old; ages of parents are getting older as people get married late these days. The children from old parents have more chances to get down syndromes, autisms or other genetic diseases; natural born diseases are rare, but do exist; these can devastate an entire family; obviously, the biggest curses are still on the children themselves, though.

Secondly, parents will be more stressed out to take care of two children instead of one in the best case scenario: Possibly, more shouting and fighting in a family. It is probable that the second children can be more troublesome; this was true in my family when I grew up; regardless, second children usually get less attention than the first or only child. I don't think any of these is necessary since the human population grows fast nowadays.

I have suspected that this "two children pressure" is pretty much an American thing. When I checked on Facebook the other day, I actually found out that several Thai people have only one child in their families. Google shows that the birth rate in Thailand is 1.51 in 2019; this means half of all the Thai ladies have only 1 child while the other half have 2 kids, theoretically. China used to have the one child policy by force; "one child a family" phenomenon is getting popular in Korea as my brother has one son in the country, too.

Conclusively, I am glad that I didn't move by pressure or surrender myself to that. I knew how many kids I could afford, financially or physically. I know that taking care of multiple kids will not make me happier; it is not mandatorily good for Earth as humans become overpopulated, too. Sometimes, we just need to grab some control while disregarding others; we need to defend ourselves from noises. Otherwise, no one will get benefit out of anything; especially, we will be guaranteed to live miserably.

* * *

Another example of pressure is getting french fries and sugary drinks together when we order a meal at the fast food joints. I often ordered only a burger and ate it with free water; a lot of quality restaurants provide that option; for example, Shake Shack always has free cups next to the water valve ready; many Indian restaurants have those, too. Is taking fries and soda together blindly good for us? Not only is it more expensive, it's extremely bad for our health. This is one example showing that we should not move by suggestions.

I think that one more example for this topic is eating three meals a day; I do not know how the tradition was formed originally; it is not only unnecessary, but actually bad for our well-being. I have tried to eat only dinner a day in the last five years although I often ended up eating way more than that. Nonetheless, it has worked out somehow; I have lost about 40 pounds in the past few years. The same thing may go for car ownership, car loan or mortgage: **"Others do it" is never a good excuse**; it can be merely a social pressure.

* * *

In his book titled *12 Rules for Life*, Peterson keeps pointing out how it is important to focus on current moments. This is not the first time I have heard of this somewhere, so I decided to try this time. I assume that we all worry too much, so we cannot focus on the present; mostly people focus more on the future by nature. At the same time, I guess some people worry about other people's eyes too much.

I have observed that a few people were total slaves for others' eyes; all they were concerned about is what others would think about them. Some people buy a big luxury house not because they need it, but because they can show it to others; many of them start inviting people soon after moving into the house; they do not even own their houses, technically; the banks own them with mortgages; these people only have the right to move in there to live since they are paying mortgages every month. I saw that some people even insisted their children have a sleepover party with friends; such a thing is usually bothersome for parents; they don't mind that as long as they have one more chance to show off.

Here is one thing these people will never tell others: They often pay double their house prices with massive mortgage interests. **It is disgusting that some people show off while getting into debts secretly behind.**

* * *

Smart people never show off: What can we really get by showing off? What benefit do we get after offending people, financially? The nasty reality is that some people spend money or even get into debt to make others feel bad: Do you know what can happen after making others feel deprived?

There is a Korean movie titled *Secret Sunshine*. A young single mother moved to a new village in the countryside; she pretended to have a lot of money to invest in that area; her only son was kidnapped and murdered; it turned out that she didn't have a fortune to pay the kidnapper. This story is not just about a movie plot. Similar thing happened in Korea only because her child always wore nice clothes. Then, I asked my wife not to buy too good clothes for my daughter.

* * *

Most Americans do not know this, but Koreans have a reputation for caring about others' eyes too much. There is a community college where a lot of Koreans study near my home; many of them are directly from Korea and there is a big supermarket next to their residences. When I was in the market one night, I saw one Korean girl wearing full makeup in an impressively nice white dress; it was weird since no American does it only to go to a market. I heard that Korean women do that whenever they go outside. In that sense, living in Korea could be almost like living in a jail; I do not think that anyone lives happily that way despite having some money.

The territory size of South Korea is small, so the size of condos are smaller in the country, too (most live in a condo regardless of wealth due to the lack of space). We usually mention a house size by the number of bedrooms in America; people mention house sizes by unit called "pyung" in Korea (1 Pyung = 35 square feet). It is common that some celebrities buy a large condo and release the info to the public on purpose; maybe it is similar in America, too. Nowadays, even average people act as if they are celebrities. Here is one thing I can say: "Wake the fuck up: No one cares who you are." Most of these are nobody; often, they live in a fantasy land called Instagram with debt.

I used to have a strange habit of showing off on one not-very-famous Korean website. I think I started going there since they let me write anything without ID registration; I ended up becoming a celebrity there after writing for a few years. Still, I believe that I have been better than other vain people; I did not spend money to show off, at least. To me, it always looked cool for guys to show off something other than money. I guess I will show off how many books I have written from now.

* * *

Summary

1. Slaves care more about their master's opinion.
2. If you care for other eyes too much, you may be a slave.
3. Don't have one more child only because our society pressures us to do so.

59

Too Much Gaps Between Jobs

Life is full of unemployment: infancy, adolescence or retirement; the period we work is limited.
-Brad Kong

The nursing home kitchen I used to work at had about 25 employees: a head chef, sous chefs, cooks and dishwashers. Strangely, the position having the most frequent change was the head chef. I have seen six different head chefs during my employment of seven years: Walter, Rob, Phil, Kurt, Adam and Robert; I didn't like most of them since they were arrogant to dishwashers. On the contrary, many other guys had kept their jobs without a problem for 7 years; that included myself.

Initially, I thought that being the head chef would be great since he would get paid the highest: Not particularly. It's never really good since they can lose it only after a one-year contract unless they bring exceptional sales to the nursing home. After losing it, there is no guarantee that they can find similar jobs soon; even if they do, they have to go through hell of a hiring process again. This kind of thing never happened for cooks or dishwashers; some had worked continuously for decades. Making a lot of money a year may matter: **Making money continuously or longer matters, too.**

* * *

Jeju is the largest island in Korea, which is 60 miles south from the mainland. For some reason, a lot of Koreans moved there to start hospitality businesses, lately: cafes, restaurants, hotels, etc; they chose locations with nice ocean views. I saw on the news that most of those closed out in 2022 since they had not received enough customers in the last few years. One cafe lady said, “We are making money only three months a year during summers.” I thought we can learn three things from her interview.

First of all, I don’t think it's a good idea to start a vacation related business in a place having severe winters. For example, Disney world is located in Florida since it can get visitors all year long. Secondly, many of our careers are seasonal, which is similar to those hospitality businesses in Jeju. Some people think that they work five days a week, but we probably work less than 50 years during our lifetime (100); no one starts working before 16 and most retire at 65. Thirdly, it’s safer for us to get a job that brings us income continuously throughout our lives. I think writers make money after 65 if they are reasonably successful; I think I will try to publish 500 books by then; I hope that I can accumulate some fans and royalties.

* * *

There is a documentary titled *American Winter* released in 2013; it is about the poverty over the 2008 recession caused by the subprime mortgage crisis. It showed five families struggling, but I still remember one particular guy; he was a black Hispanic man with a wife and four children living in a trailer park. With pressure, he was constantly looking for a job, and got hired occasionally, too. But he bluntly said this a few times on the film: “I just got fired.” I had been through my business and employment before, so I was not sure of his reason: What did he do exactly to get fired on the first day of work, repeatedly?

I know that many low income jobs do not ask employees for exceptional performances, especially on the first day. Maybe he did not want to work since he was tired from taking care of four kids in the small trailer; I guess that he should have been a little lazy to make multiple babies.

Another family I remember was a mother and her son; they were crying out loud since "pay as you want" Panera bread was closed early on Sunday. They said they cannot afford to go to McDonald's: **What is this, seriously?** The two-cheeseburger meal at McDonald's was only $5 by 2019; people can share one meal for two people, too. I felt that a lot of those documentaries do not show everything; they just want to focus on how our social system is wrong. To me, this was possible when the mother wasted a lot of money on something else than food: Drugs, for example.

There are plenty of kitchen helper jobs paying $16 an hour plus meals as of 2023. If you do not believe me, go to any restaurant and ask if a dishwashing job is available: The dishwashers had been painfully short throughout the 7 years while I was employed for the nursing home.

* * *

I had never really enjoyed the nursing home job, by the way. Maybe I learned some lessons there; I've never liked anyone except some Mexican guys. The work had brought me good money; that was pretty much it. In the end, I was sick of persuading myself to work there one more year. I am glad that I happened to walk away though it was not solely my decision; I am glad that some changes they made provided me a good excuse to resign.

In my case, I didn't really take some time off after work. First of all, I have been an investor all along since 2011; this has brought me about $2,000 a month as interests and dividends. And I started writing intensively a month before quitting; I do not remember how I got into self-publishing seriously. I didn't have a mortgage, rent or car, so interest incomes have been enough for me.

* * *

There are people jumping from one job to another throughout their lives: These tend not to save a lot even when they seem to get paid a lot. On the contrary, there are people sticking to a job longer; they usually end up saving more and stay away from poverty. Let me give you some examples.

I already told you that the head chefs changed every year in the kitchen of my previous work; often they were not employed until they found a new job. I assume the gap could be six months or longer only after one year of employment. Is a chef considered a high paying job? Not really; this is one of strange jobs with a lot of authority but low pay.

People often check the annual salary of a job, but forget to see how long they can work there continuously; we can end up being poor this way. I mentioned the book, *Nomadland,* previously: I think one of the reasons why those American nomads are indigent is that most get seasonal jobs; they don't seem to get paid half of the year.

Conversely, I found an opposite example, too. There is a movie titled *I, Tonya* released in 2017; it is about Tonya Harding, the American figure skater. I knew something bad had happened, so she has not been skating since 1994. But, when I checked her recent photo, surprisingly, I could not detect any sign of poverty from her face; I am good at finding those, but actually she looked better than before to me. I wondered why.

For one thing, she has only one child to support. But, more importantly, I found out that she has worked all sorts of physical jobs continuously regardless of her fame in the past twenty five years: a boxer, waitress, landscaper, deck builder, hardware sales clerk, etc. **This is respectable since some people never get over their fame from the past;** some never try other jobs. From her photos, I had an impression that she never really had a money problem since she has been paid constantly.

* * *

Again, when people talk about salary, many focus only on the annual amount: How much can we make a year? **But how long we can keep the job is equally or more important.** For example, some Korean corporations (i.e., Samsung) are notorious for "forced early retirement" of employees; this happens mainly because the population of South Korea is a lot (52 millions), but it has only a handful of large corporations. As a result, those companies push old people out early to get young people in. When you see the pay stubs of a Samsung employee, you may be surprised that the annual amount is quite high in general. But almost no one works there for more than 25 years; no one gets wealthy with that career.

I heard that many of those middle-aged early-retirees open franchise chicken joints, which are oddly growing in Korea now. These restaurants are different from KFC because they use diverse recipes and sauces; therefore, Koreans often joke that the final destination of engineers is chicken delivery.

There are a lot of jobs and businesses inevitably having many non-working gaps: movie actors and directors; wedding gig players; Halloween costume store clerks; firework sellers; New year calendar shops; Christmas decoration businesses, etc. I think it's important to keep a job having fewer income-less periods.

* * *

Summary

1. Salary amount for one year may matter.
2. Making the salary continuously or longer matters, too.
3. Some jobs have too many off-seasons.

60

Not Knowing "Enough"

Everyone makes money:
Those who believe "enough is enough" keep it.
-Brad Kong

I remember I bought a blu-ray player in 2011; I returned it a couple of weeks later and got a regular DVD player, instead. The blu-ray movies were too sharp for my eyes and kept giving me headaches (even when I played regular DVDs on it). It shows that blu-ray was introduced in 2006, but I still can see that new regular DVD movies are releasing in 2023: Why? I guess I am not the only one having painful migraines: Enough is enough; newer, bigger or better is not always good. I think that it's a waste to spend more money on more than what we need.

* * *

There is a book titled *Stillness is the Key* written by Holiday; it reads an episode regarding the golfer Tiger Woods. It shows that his father Earl was a sort of mean person to his son and annoyed him on a regular basis until he shouted, "Enough." The author reasonably deduced that it's where Tiger's troubled personal life might come from: Pent-up anger.

I am a father myself and it's hard to imagine doing that kind of thing to my daughter: I think that she is a different individual on her own even before I can address a family relationship issue. I may not mention anything in detail, but it didn't seem that this guy Earl was a role model to anyone in an average standard. **I don't think it's right to be mean to a weaker creature including a kid.** Besides, my daughter will be a grown-up soon; it's not a good plan to give a bad impression to a possibly strong creature in the near future. I do not think that this old man Earl had been good at stock investing. Some people are poor because they are mean by nature or narrow-sighted in planning.

* * *

Our society tends to promote greed out of any reason; **it is stupid to fall for that.** People usually say that not giving up is a great thing; *giving up is an equally good thing* on many occasions, according to my experience. Knowing that we have enough, taking breaks, retiring early, sharing, letting others work and giving up eating more are all good life strategies.

* * *

I eventually realized that having less desire truly made my life happier; I am not trying to be a moral instructor; it actually has made my life better. Honestly, I still hope that I will have a little more money than now; I have not been much interested in donating. I just felt more peaceful when I stopped asking for more everywhere; there are subtle signs that some people ask too much: traveling a lot, eating too much, having too many kids, etc.

While we do not notice, a lot of these desires are triggered by others. The results are always the same: *Regrets*; all the desires go to this sole final destination one way or another. It is time for us to give up spending more: More specifically, it's time to stop being busy for nothing. To me, it only makes sense to be busy making money. We do not have to make our lives complicated or exhausted by spending more.

* * *

There is a big Polish supermarket not far from my home; Chicagoland has a big Polish population; they even have their own supermarkets and food brands. It used to have a sushi bar inside just like Mariano's market or Whole Foods. They gave a 50% discount after 7:00 PM as the market is closed at 8:00 PM everyday.

I often went there and picked up three boxes of sushi, so my wife didn't have to cook dinner; these were all less than $5 each after the discount in 2022; these actually tasted pretty good. I know that one fat Japanese guy makes all those alone; he must have been a trained chef from Japan. I always told this to my wife and daughter: "I can try to find better sushi than these with more money. But that won't be necessary; that would be overkill." What I tried to say was that it is pointless to spend more money to get a better one; I have eaten all kinds of sushi for the last thirty years as a Korean and know which one is good; this is more than good enough for me.

When I think about it, people make this mistake all the time: **Some just over-spend on something more than they need and go broke;** some never get out of poverty due to this. Imagine I bought a $2,000 gaming computer just to write this article: Does it make sense? I bought a $500 Dell desktop set last year; it has worked just fine for what I need. In the worst case, I can play game on this PC as well since it is brand new, anyway; I found Windows 11 on this computer has a lot of gaming features; I turned it all off to make this computer run faster.

* * *

I heard that one Mongolian grandma ordered a cable TV and got ripped off by the company big time. I believe that Mongolia is not a cruel capitalist country yet; people do not seem to deceive each other this way. She ended up having a $110 a month package with thousands of channels in 2012. They gave her a big extra remote also; I heard she complained that she could not even figure out how to use it. Although she got deceived in this particular case, many Americans voluntarily order that kind of package; many end up not even watching half of the channels, but pay huge subscription fees every months; people just go crazy for more these days.

* * *

So far, these were all tiny mistakes. Once this happens with a house, people can actually lose a humongous amount of money. We all know there is a debt called a *mortgage*: some people get a huge amount of debt to get a house bigger than they need. This is fine since the house prices may go up.

Or that may not be fine exactly since there is one crazy shameless dog barking all the time on a Korean web community; as I mentioned before, there is one Korean website I used to go to; one troll always tried to argue with people and leave nasty comments on frugality articles. I can live with debt, which I do not necessarily prefer. But I will never be proud of it or insist that it is the best way of life. Anyway, I decided not to care further since it is not my loss.

I personally do not think a family of three needs a bigger home than 850 sf, which is the size of my condo. I can try to move into a bigger house; this can be a lifetime mistake. Although three people live in my place currently, my wife may visit her home country frequently; my daughter can leave for college within 6 years; I might travel a lot later in life.

It is possible that this home can be empty, continually; it may be a small house, but it may not even be full. It is pointless for me to spend more on housing, especially now; I am more than happy that I bought this condo in full 10 years ago and solved the housing problems for good. It will only cost more if I do anything. Some people just go for 3,000 sf single family homes with debt, no matter what. Please trust me on this one: No one really needs that much space; at least, it will be an overkill for a small family like mine, which will be the dominant population from now on.

* * *

Summary

1. Enough is enough.
2. Something more than what we need can make us painful.
3. Do not go for more expensive items brainlessly; these items can be worse than cheaper ones.

61

Living in a Disastrous Area

Poverty brings troubles.
-Brad Kong

Have you heard of *Pattaya Plunge*? I think that this can be the most extreme example of moving into a dangerous area and ruining lives; I know this does not happen to every expatriate in Thailand; it still happens a lot, especially to white foreigners, including Americans. Pattaya is a recreation city located about 60 miles southeast of Bangkok, which is the capital city of this Siam country.

Thailand has a high HIV infection rate; it has much larger numbers of AIDS patients and prostitutes than neighbors. Pattaya is especially notorious and named as "the red light district of the world"; the city is fully covered with clubs, go-go bars, freelancers and drugs. And a lot of white retirees from Europe and America, also called *farang* in Thai, move into the city with life savings. They enjoy pleasures for a while, then they go bankrupt within years, occasionally. After bankruptcies, some commit suicide by jumping out of tall buildings. **This phenomenon is so common that Australians put a name on it: *Pattaya Plunge.***

I heard that local news in Pattaya report a new suicide of expats once a week on average. I guess debauchery is as dangerous as a natural disaster, particularly to single men; it is similar to moving into a Hawaiian island near a volcanic mountain. Some think Siam is a country of smiles and these young Thais are kind to old Westerners by nature. Here is only one condition, though: **They will be like angels as long as the men have money;** once their funds are out, these girls are out.

Life is hard for everyone, especially for those who are poor in an impoverished country. By the time tourists realize this, it might be too late; they may find out that their pockets are empty already and their livers got damaged by alcohol. What if they got HIV+ positive? Their sweet girlfriends who give that will be nowhere to be seen; some might think there is only one way out in the foreign land where they don't know anyone personally. **As a result, Pattaya has highest suicide rate surpassing anywhere in the world;** it shows that some even jump out of airport windows before exiting the country.

* * *

There is a travel writer named "P" in Korea; he was known for his series titled *10,000 Hours in Latin America* and the three volumes were published in 2007. There are a group of Koreans traveling cheaper and poorer countries all the time, living solidly in the low income class in South Korea; they spend their entire lives that way.

When we travel to a foreign country, maybe we want to see something different. Simultaneously, maybe we can learn things to improve our finances, especially when we travel to a wealthier country. I am not saying that wealthier countries are good ones; it is true that a wealthy country did bad things to make more money; I am just saying that there could be something we can learn.

But it seems those Koreans who visit India or Thailand all the time have a different mindset: "We are rich enough compared to them, so it is OK to waste our lives a little bit." There is nothing wrong with enjoying our lives; travel does not always have to be productive, either. **But some only look downward;** it is like we play soccer with little children and are happy about scores. P wrote the three books 16 years ago in 2007. He is fifty years old now without getting married and having a house: He has drained all the money in Thailand in the last 15 years. I know that I am not in a position to judge others. But I believe that he could have used his early talent a little differently.

Millions of westerners live like him without learning Thai in the country. Only advantage they take is that their home countries are richer than those in South Asia; another can be being an American or white. **I mean, how low can a human go?** They never get a job in south Asia since pay is extremely low. This is a pointless lifestyle from my perspective; no one gets anything out of this.

* * *

I don't recommend foreigners to settle in Thailand or the Philippines for different reasons. First of all, all the foods are sugar-oriented there: Have you ever eaten Pad Thai before? This Thai tradition is extremely sweet: **Siam is almost the only country in the world putting sugar directly in its main dishes;** Americans never throw sugar on steaks or burgers. I am particularly fearful of torment caused by tooth decay. Besides, I spent over $3,000 on my molar tooth years ago, but I failed to revive it: I concluded that it's better not to put anything sickly in my mouth to begin with. Secondly, the country is full of masseuses, prostitutes and HIV carriers; I think it's more menacing for men.

In the case of the Philippines, I think it's threatening for violent crimes; kidnapping and police corruption rates are high. More importantly, the country has 7,600 small islands, so it's easier for criminals to escape and hide. **It's a social**

issue that Korean felons kidnap Korean tourists there. In most cases, the victims end up getting murdered one way or another.

* * *

Personally, I think that Koreans are geniuses for two reasons; they invented Hangul and Bibim Naengmyeon. Hangul is the Korean alphabet currently used in North and South Korea; it's easy to learn, but more accurate to write specific sounds than Roman alphabets or other letters. In a sense, inventing Hangul was a triumph for the entire human race; it has upgraded human legacy and culture overall. Korea will never exchange it with Egyption pyramids or India.

Bibim-Naengmyeon is a spicy cold noodle dish that originated from northern Korea 500 years ago. I always felt high quality at the first bite; I noticed there are cheap and expensive tastes only after I tried diverse foods. It is very unique, so I cannot compare the taste with other foods in America.

Surprisingly, Koreans invented this dish even though there are not many ingredients in the country. The nation has long winters and less futile farm lands without pastures. As a result, being hungry to death had been periodic for thousands of years until the 1960s; I know that it's hard to believe it now. In a sense, having the dish in Korea is like a prison made the best cake in America; prisons do not have better ingredients; this is just an analogy I saw in a movie, but I would say that they invented one fabulous dish despite obstacles.

* * *

While I believe the people may be smart, I believe Korea has more hostile environments to survive; it has only one harvest a year due to winter while Southeast Asian countries have three harvests; Korea has floods and typhoons regularly, which sweep grains away before autumn. Besides, it has so many steep mountains (70% of the country), so there are less pastures to breed farm animals. **It was possible that physical habitats made the people poor.**

As far as crime goes, it definitely is one of the safest countries on Earth. We can check statistics or feel that by instinct if we get there. Still, I do not recommend any foreigner to settle since housing prices are crazily expensive: A small territory with too many people. We cannot see many houses since all the residences are condos or any type of multi-units; these have been the sole choices since it has been outrageously packed.

* * *

I think some jobs are hazardous and can take money away from us. When I worked for the weekend dishwasher at the nursing home, I often took the position called *pot cleaning* in the morning. When they cleaned the large amount of pots, they used very hot water and strong detergents. I honestly feel like all the food contained in those pots are contaminated by strong soaps; literally, guests are eating soaps and bleaches at the restaurant. Those strong detergents used to give me severe *skin lashes* on my arms; both were all red and itchy since I couldn't avoid touching those detergents for almost seven years. **I was worried that I may get skin cancer someday due to toxic chemicals;** I am just glad that I do not work there any more.

This may not be exactly an area with natural disasters as in this chapter topic, but some Koreans didn't recommend moving into Las Vegas, NV; they said everyone eventually gets into gambling and loses all the life savings there. To me, it's just too hot, so heat shock and drought could be the reason to avoid the area to live.

* * *

I notice that there are people living in particularly *disastrous* areas in America: Tornado alleys in Kansas; Hurricane alleys in Florida; frequent wildfires in California; regular floods in Venice, Italy; Volcanic areas in Hawaii, etc. I just do not know why people do not move out of those, completely; in fact, Florida is getting more populated each year. I guess moving into those places ignorantly could be a reason why some are broke despite working.

If some people were born in these areas, that is understandable; maybe it is time for them to get out. Nonetheless, I see a lot of people moving into California in the year of 2022. One of my coworkers named Vincente moved into California with his five kids in 2019; I heard that he is in construction now; maybe he thought there was no hope in Illinois. Yet it was still a mistake in my opinion; at least, IL is a few times cheaper than CA.

Unfortunately, I don't think that disasters just include natural ones. Some areas have higher crime rates (e.g., Compton, NJ); some have severe economic depression (e.g., Rustbelt in PA). Also, some areas like Kensington Avenue in Philadelphia are heavily infested with drugs including *Fentanyl*; needles were everywhere on the ground of some parks as they actually call them *needle parks*. I guess that some people move there without having much sense or knowledge. Regardless, staying there will not help anyone financially.

To me, it does not make sense to immigrate to a poor country from a wealthy one to begin with. I am not saying that we must go crazy about money. But I feel that some seem to forget that wealth is still a great blessing; some may not know this unless they were in desperation. If someone thinks that being poor is funny, interesting or romantic, he or she has never been destitute. **There is only pain in impoverishment:** Nothing more. I assume that we can learn this in an easy or hard way.

* * *

Summary

1. Some people can be poor since they live in disastrous locations.
2. It is nonsense that citizens from wealthy countries immigrate to poor countries.
3. Do not just move into a new area without checking a couple of statistics.

62

Investing Wrong Way

Stock investing is a strange game
where lazy people are the winners.
-Brad Kong

The best investment I made so far was buying my condo with full cash. The money I have saved for not paying a mortgage or rent has been bigger than stock market profit in the last ten years; it has been more than $2,000 saving a month; it will be like this as long as I live in this unit; it can be the next 50 years since I'm not very old. On top of that, this property price has almost tripled since 2013. **The profit from real estate has been solid while that from stocks has fluctuated.**

Some people suggest buying a residence with a mortgage and putting all the money and future income in the stock market, instead: **These people can end up losing both their houses and stocks.** I think that it is better to put more money in safe places and less in risky ones.

* * *

I sold JPM stock at $125 in August, 2022; this Chase bank has been the market leader in bankings, but the stock review has gotten bad lately; I do not believe people get a lot of housing loans due to high interest and recession for a while. I made only +$260 profit out of selling 40 shares of JPM and put all the money in GSK (GlaxoSmithKline), which is a

$90 B Pharmaceutical company; its stock price was strangely low at $35, recently; besides, GSK comes with a 5% annual dividend.

A lot of people fail at investing; some do it, aggressively or unreasonably: **I usually focus on minimizing loss**. I have never really tried to make huge profits; I just do my best to get rid of bad stocks from my portfolio. I used to have up to 230 company stocks in 2019; the prices of all the stocks were cheaper back then (market crashed by Covid). Now I have only 90 company stocks as of April, 2023; I have sold bad stocks little by little and made about +$70,000 profit as capital gains in the last five years. After selling out stocks of less profitable companies, I have moved all the money into the dividend stocks from better companies.

The stock markets have been oddly up in August, 2022. It seems some started believing that the economy will get better from then on. These people are inexperienced in my opinion; most do not have any solid calculation or logic. I don't see that there is a certain reason for the economy to get better soon; impatient investors could be possible candidates for suicider for investment failures.

I can say that Covid has never been under real control and it can spread out again any time; hospitals can be crowded again. Economic collapse may come by December, 2023. That is why I have sold 145 company stocks, all with profits, in the past 5 years; I predict that all stock prices will go down next year, anyway. Conclusively, **I believe that it's the right strategy to focus more on eliminating losses than trying to gain more**; it won't hurt even if the economy gets better.

* * *

One of the best ways to live a peaceful life is to perceive that we own a lot of things and have accomplished many goals so far; I think that it is key to insist on this idea even if it might not be absolutely true. When we have more peace and calmness in our minds, things will get better; we may make more money as well; eventually, we can reach the point to breathe and take a look around slowly. We may notice something we have never; this can be good money making opportunities, too. Close your eyes and think; do meditation. Keeping cool particularly matters when we need to make money.

I have a $650,000 portfolio of stocks, bonds, ETFs and CDs in 2023; it brought me $24,000 dividend and interest income last year. I have a wife, who has a doctorate degree, and daughter; I have a nice condo with a swimming pool right in front of it; the pool always has a lifeguard in a red suit; I feel like I live in a luxury resort every summer. I think being alive by 50 is an achievement; being able to support myself is awesome. **I think it's important to be happy at how many things we have accomplished.** Knowing how to speak a foreign language is incredible. Having your own child is a big triumph. I think we should stop asking for more and more. We do not need more things to live better lives.

* * *

There is an American movie theater company named AMC; their stock ticker is "AMC", which does not have a dividend. In March, 2022, suddenly AMC stock went up to $29 from $14 for about two weeks. Some Koreans explained that short squeeze or gamma squeeze will burst; I honestly do not know what these mean; part of the reason is that I intentionally keep myself away from option, reverse or inverse tradings.

But suddenly a strangely "bright" idea hit me out of the blue. "The $89,000 amount of my bank CDs will mature soon. Can I put all these in AMC stocks? Can that make my money double? They said the trading volume of AMC stock has been 10 times bigger than average these days."

According to my experience, when there is a high volume in trades, usually my chance to make quick cash gets higher; higher volume (for example, 100 million shares a day) means there are a lot of people buying and selling stocks of a specific company; prices go up and down really fast every second; it fluctuates crazily mostly because the stock is extremely popular. If we can buy those shares at a low enough price, it may go up swiftly for no solid reason; this happens all day, sometimes.

When I googled "stocks with the highest volume," Yahoo stock site came out: "The most active stocks today." When I clicked it, the page showed 25 stocks with the highest volume on that day; I remember AMC was one of them in March, 2022. Then, I noticed something was strange.

* * *

There were other stocks listed as well and some of them were dividend stocks: Ford (F), Energy Transfer (ET), At&t (T), Annaly (NLY), etc; some suggested a crazily high dividends though these were high volume stocks; ET had 9% and NLY had 11% of dividends. These were like 5 times bigger than bank interests, then.

This was the conclusion I made on that day: "Why don't I bet on high dividend stocks instead of AMC? **Even if my**

predictions go wrong, I can still get dividends. If I buy those at a low enough price, I will never lose money." You know what? My guess was correct.

First of all, the AMC stock price went back to $14 in May, 2022. When I saw it in March, 2022, it was $29 from $14 and I expected it would go up much higher from $29; that is what those squeeze things are about. But that did not happen. And I told you that AMC stock does not have a dividend, so I could have been in loss for nothing.

Instead, I bought a lot of AT&T (T) and Annaly (NLY) stocks coming with 5% and 11% dividends respectively in April, 2022. So far, these are 20% down each as of May, 2023, but I am getting high dividends at least. Still, these two are stocks with super high volumes, so I believe I can make money someday. Or, at least, I will not lose money. As I explained in Chapter 17, this is how I recovered money from the hopeless PBI investment: **Wait for the right moment while I am getting dividends.** It sounds easy, but some never get it, lose a lot or even commint suicide.

Remember: "**Do crazy investments as long as you get dividends**." After spending 12 years in trading, I learned that no one really can predict stock price. We cannot just bet only on the stock price changes: We need some safety nets.

* * *

My deepest secret to enduring a stock market crash is the dividend. If a market crash happens, we need to get dividends or interests for a while until markets recover. If we do not invest, our money would have been in the bank to get some interest. In general, stock dividends are bigger than bank interest.

So even after market depression happens, we do not lose anything this way. While history shows that stock markets usually recover within three years even after the worst crash, investment is not a patience test: **We need to get some dividends as if we get interest from a bank while waiting.** Not only is it more profitable, it is mentally less stressful. FYI, dividends from stocks or interests from bonds usually come out regardless of market conditions. It is just easier to pass time during recessions this way.

* * *

Summary

1. Buying a condo in full was the best investment of my life.
2. Choose the "dividend" stocks instead of the ones without it.
3. It's easier to pass a recession when we get dividends regularly.

63

Living in an Excessive Comfort Zone

Antoinette was executed one day
after living lavishly for decades.
-Brad Kong

Do you know what the main cause was whenever I got deceived or lost money? Not being suspicious enough and trying to get things done in a rush. I believe that I have lost over $3,000 for nothing in the last 20 years; there could be more, but some had been more likely overcharges; a lot of those deceptions had been related to automobiles, so I am finally living without a car now. **In my opinion, there are three fields giving us the most deceits in America: automobiles (particularly mechanics), dentistries and mortgages.** Luckily, I have never gotten involved with a mortgage as well since I bought my house with cash.

In 2005, I found that a guy named Justin was selling his car for $2,500 in Buffalo. I was too excited and bought it right away without even having a test drive; it looked nice outside, but was junk inside. I ended up donating the car to a kidney foundation after spending an extra $500 on repairs. The seller was trash and made me impatient by intentionally delaying the purchase meeting. I wished that I was calmer, had checked all documents thoroughly and had a test drive, too.

Another major loss happened to me in a dental office in 2019; I had a root canal infection in my left lower molar. I paid over $2,000 for a crown procedure, but the lady dentist placed an inlay crown too high on the molar; it made a crack on the tooth root by biting down. I had mild tooth pain for the last four years. Finally, I extracted that tooth in 2022 as it was cracked big vertically one night. I wish I could double check reviews of the dentistry on Google or have a second opinion on my molar. I trusted those two dental ladies too much; I am glad I did not go back there for more services though they called me several times.

* * *

I realize that money does not always solve every problem. I heard that one Mongolian guy got a tooth extraction, but his dentist broke the tooth root accidently and left it in his jaw; that eventually infected his mandible bone; he got jaw replacement surgery, eventually. In my case, I thought I was investing some money on my dentition, but it only provided a reason to crack my molar due to the height of the inlay crown I got. Spending more does not guarantee anything; it can actually bring a problem.

Now I have a habit of double or triple checking. I can lose chances this way, but I prefer to move slowly as I get old. Frauds can hate us when we are holding up or rethinking. Do not act quickly only because everything looks good, especially when you handle money. Still, the good news can be that having a small fraud once in a decade can make us alert and prevent bigger losses.

I have been living without a car in the last six years; it has prevented further losses like mechanics overcharges or auto thefts. A similar thing has gone for my fangs. It's been hard, but I have eliminated sugars and carbohydrates; I drink only water strictly. And I do brushing, flossing and oil pulling every day, which blocks gum recession. Dentistry is known to overcharge in general although my case was a malpractice. **We are the ones who have made our teeth rot to begin with;** sometimes, we need to change things (i.e. eating habit) completely.

* * *

I propose that people can be poor when they don't live in challenging ways; some enjoy only the present moment, be happy while accepting who they are and indulge into comfort. Some tend to live in their home country for good; some eat only home menus; some men marry wives less educated than them; some people never learn how to speak a foreign language. We see that there are Mexicans eating only Tacos or blacks eating only fried chicken; some never try Thai or Indian foods. It shows that a growing number of old white Americans live in vans, trailers or RVs these days; they are virtually homeless; those who resist changes can move down to the low income class gradually.

What I mean by *challenge* is not an extreme one. For example, I got married to a wife who has a doctorate while I have a bachelor's; a lot of men with my degree choose women who graduated highschools. I am writing a book in English although Korean is much easier for me; the Korean speaking population is 80 times less than all the English speakers in the world (only the American population is 7 times bigger than South Korean one); Korean books can bring me less money from sales; I have learned English for life, anyway.

There are Korean Americans who have only Korean friends; ironically, they tend to be poorer than Koreans having American friends. Also, there are Koreans who never leave Korea; they are poorer, but comfortable with eating traditional meals including *kimchi* and rice. **Worse than that is there are Koreans visiting only poorer South Asian countries**; specifically, they visit Thailand or Philippine mainly for prostitution. It's up to them, but here is one thing for sure: Wealths never grow that way; a lot of them erode their savings by looking down, being wasteful or too comfortable. Committing suicides due to poverty among senior citizens has been bigger in Korea, lately.

* * *

I watched a video about expats' life in Thailand the other day; the guy tried to go to a laundromat located on the backstreet in Bangkok. Suddenly, a tall woman came to him and tried to walk together. I believe she might be actually a transgender and it was a prostitution area. Regardless, I immediately felt sorry for the lady. It must have been hard for her; I observed that she didn't find many customers to begin with; not many men are into that; if even they do, they may not choose her especially during the daytime. There must be some reason why she did that; I cannot help, I felt sorry.

Humans are social animals; even a king is concerned about what others think of him; he wants to know what's going on in the palace. Most people are considerate and thoughtful about others' feelings. **But history shows that some live carelessly, enjoy only their lives to the max and get punished to death one day.** One Korean guy showed off that he bought $1 M houses with a *huge* mortgage in 2022 while it was obvious that the stock market crash was imminent. We need to care for other people, society and environments to be alive; that is how *Homo sapiens* has evolved from *Homo heidelbergensis* in the last six million years. Women usually have the stronger instinct to read emotions; they certainly live longer than men everywhere.

* * *

One of the most dangerous hobbies in the world would be skydiving; a mistake can mean death. When I checked accident news regarding it, I found one strange fact: **Not many people die on the first try;** I learned that most people die after hundreds of jumps if not thousands. The official statistics insist that there is only one death out of 500,000 jumps. Nonetheless, I found out that the skydiving accident news is non-stop in America every week.

There was an impressively pretty girl named Romane Hourcastagnou from Strasbourg, France; she was considered as an experienced diver with over 100 jumps from planes; she died due to a parachute malfunction in May, 2022; she was only 23. One hundred jumps is a lot since people don't do skydiving everyday; she probably thought she had years of experience.

There were also men named Harrington, Sheppard and Loftis who died in skydiving accidents, recently. Common point? It showed that all those three men had more than 3,000 jumping experiences from the sky; one of them was even a pioneer and instructor as well. Even though something is extremely dangerous, if no accident happens for a long time, people tend to think it is secure. And this could be the reason for poverty, too.

I think another well-known example for living a too relaxed life and being extinct is the Dodo bird. The only place they were found was Mauritius Island near Africa in 1598. The small island is 1,200 miles from the African continent; it did not have any enemy for the birds for millions of years. As a result, they lost capability to fly and even approached humans without suspicion voluntarily. The record shows that the meat of dodo was tremendously *untasty*. So scientists believed that people killed the birds for fun and they were completely gone in 1698.

* * *

I read the book titled *Nomadland* and it showed many interviews with "houseless" senior citizens; surprisingly, only less than half of them have been poor for life; the other half had been at least in the middle class or even wealthy. Then, what happened to them to be houseless and work to death after their retirement ages? Basically, I believe that they have dangled housing problems without solving them in a timely manner.

I noticed that all had mortgage or rent problems before being homeless in common. None of them bought a small condo with cash and solved their home issues quickly. Many Americans try to buy pricey houses with 30-year home loans nowadays. But 30-years is a long time and people can lose residences if something happens: economic depression, Covid outbreak, job transitions, natural disasters, wars, etc. Some ended up living in trailers, RVs or vans full-time.

Some interviewers had divorce and their spouses took their house. But when we look carefully, this is the mortgage problem again: They pour all their money in the 30-year mortgages and nothing left after their spouses took the houses; we pay double for the same house when we use the mortgages instead of cash.

Some seniors lost all their savings after the stock market collapsed; this is something I should be aware of, too. Still, paying a large sum of money every month in the next 30 years is dangerous; I don't see there is any real protection; they just have to come up with cash each month somehow. Some do not think this way: **Some automatically assume that**

everyone in America has a mortgage. The fact is that only half of Americans have house loans, statistically.

* * *

When we get familiar, risky things do not look very perilous; let's take driving for an instance. A car accident can cause serious injury, but no one realizes that; it is merely a part of our lives. Having an automobile has become like having a pair of shoes in America; people do not perceive that a car is a traditionally expensive item (cars are more expensive than ever now). And the gas is at least $4 a gallon in May, 2023; spending $5 whenever we move is expensive. Moving around has been perfectly free in the past six million years of human history. I wonder if people will need to pay for breathing someday. I guess that only a few people notice that something is very wrong now.

As a Korean, I had eaten sushi for more than thirty years. But I decided to quit eating it one day in 2019. I saw on the news that one guy got a whale worm from salmon sushi and was hospitalized. When I think about it, eating raw fish is unsanitary or even disgusting; actually, eating any kind of raw meat is dangerous. I just had not realized that until that day.

* * *

Summary

1. Too much comfort can kill us.
2. Do not get familiar with dangerous things; they may look safe, which is not true.
3. Try to solve life problems in timely manners.

64

Being Overly Jealous

Being easily jealous is the biggest curse in everyday life.
-Brad Kong

It shows that Cosimo Medici was an Italian banker who established the Medici family as effective rulers of Florence during the Italian Renaissance in the 15th century. He was the son of the bank founder, but he was the one who promoted the average Medici family to rulers who supported artists, including Da Vinci and Michelangelo, eventually. History says that he dressed modestly, carried only one servant and rode a mule instead of a horse in public. He also intentionally chose a simple and modest design for his palace named "Palazzo Medici Riccardi." He repeatedly said, "**Envy is a weed that should not be watered.**" Apparently, he had been extremely careful not to make others jealous.

There are people who get jealous too easily everywhere; they are cursed and born that way; these often waste a large amount of time on being envious. It's more productive to concern our own profits than the gain or loss of others.

* * *

I did not know the Canadian psychologist, Peterson's daughter had a severe ankle problem for life; he described that his daughter couldn't walk for decades without painkillers in the book *12 Lessons for Life*; I had a similar problem momentarily myself, so I can guess what pain they had been through. Apparently, her photos online look just fine to me, so we cannot guess what misery others actually have in their lives. **In this sense, we absolutely don't not have to be jealous of anyone**. As Plato said, everyone has his or her own struggle; this may be surprisingly equal to all the people on Earth, according to my experiences.

The third daughter of Lee Kun-hee committed suicide in Manhattan, NY in November, 2005; Lee was the richest man in Korea when he was alive and one of the company he owned was *Samsung* Electronics. Samsung used to be a no big deal when his father founded it, originally; Lee was the one who inherited and upgraded it to a super conglomerate; his net worth was up to $26 billions by 2020. His daughter was only 26 years old in 2005; her online photo looked pretty; her net worth was about $190 millions since she received some stocks already from her parents in her 20s. **Theoritically, she was supposed to be the last person who will commit suicide;** I am not sure what happened to her and I do not want to know, either. All I can say is that every family has its own pain and this could be fair and equal to all.

* * *

As one Buddhist monk suggested, those romantic novels and soap operas could be the reason why so many marriages fail these days. Let's assume that we read a lot of novels fantasizing about office jobs; these may describe how working in a company is interesting, funny or fulfilling everyday; guys will have chances to speak with intelligent but beautiful girls working together. Yet we can be disappointed when the bosses assign an incredible amount of work with little wage: **When we expect more, we get disappointed easier.** When people do not expect much, they tend to stay longer in work or marriage.

I assume that the brain difference between men and women can be like *self-help books* vs *novels*. Self-helps are all about how to (e.g., how to make more money); they require more logic and reasons to write about. On the contrary, novels are more likely about emotions. It's no coincidence that I am a male who reads and writes self-helps all the time.

Reading novels for adults is a little useless from a financial point of view. Watching drama is also a waste as many are based on novels. Some said that women wasting time on watching drama are like men wasting time on pornographies; I do not disagree. Personally, I prefer to watch comedies or short funny clips on YouTube. And, in my opinion, jealousy is more likely an emotion that is not beneficial for anyone on many occasions.

Jealousy may help our lives to some extent; it can promote our motivation to grow. But being overly jealous is a total waste; it helps nothing.

* * *

There are people wasting even decades on being jealous. I personally think their lives are doomed: **Being born with too much jealousy is the biggest curse in real life.** I would not be surprised if they wound up being poor since jealousy is a negative mental aggravation, after all.

As I said before, I have written on diverse websites *for free* over the last twenty years. One of the sites was called *"dcinside";* it is something like the reddit in America and tons of people visit there everyday. I had owned the video game store[53] in 2009 and had written plenty of articles in the *small business* sub-group on that site. There was one troll overly

---

[53] Cyb Knight

jealous of my profit from the store and wrote unpleasant comments on my articles; I guess I attacked him back, too. I notice that he has continually followed me everywhere and tried to get revenge on me, which has not been successful.

I do not know how the troll has been able to waste whole day only checking online for decades; I usually go for only one site to write my articles if I was fed up with others; nonetheless, he spotted me a few months after I started writing on any site (I have used the same nickname everywhere: "brad"). One day, he finally burst into anger after he found out that my portfolio was over $500,000. Then, I pointed out that the only thing he did was wasting time being jealous of others' accomplishments; this is why a person like him cannot buy a house. I believe he still pays over $3,000 a month for apartment rent, which is common in CA. I guess I will not write an article for free any more; I will let trolls keep being wasteful.

* * *

There is no cure for jealous people. There was another Korean community site where I used to write regularly: *Workingus.com*. There was another guy wasting on writing nasty replies all the time on that site. He had paid a huge amount of mortgage every month, but his house was not even close to a library; his house was probably in the middle of nowhere. He paid almost double the amount for his house price with a 30-year-mortgage than cash buyers, which is fine. Still, instead of worrying about his own loss, he always wasted time on leaving annoying replies on others' postings. I decided to stop writing on that site in 2022, too.

To be born with intensive jealousy is a huge curse: In the above case, the troll will be a homeowner 39 years slower than me. According to his replies, he just moved into a bigger but pointless house with a bigger *house debt* in 2022; I bought my *big enough* condo 10 years ago in 2013; he may end up paying his debt off in 2052. **This will make him 39 years slower than me to be a homeowner.**

Here is one more bad news for him, though: He told people that he has a $2.5M mortgage left for his new big house starting from 2022; this means he should pay $4 M total to the bank, including the mortgage interest in the next 30 years. In my opinion, he may or may not be able to complete the slavery system of mortgage successfully; simply, 30 years is a damn long time. Most of us don't even know what's going to happen exactly tomorrow. If something goes wrong, he can lose his house and move straight back to a rental apartment. **Some people never be able to own a house for life this way**; they may live there for a while, but never be able to get the deed, which requires the completion of 30 years of payments.

* * *

When I used to work in the video game store, a travel agency was right next door. About five agents worked there and I did not like one particular woman for any reason I didn't understand; I always felt that she was a jealous type.

I used to take their mail from the post office and give it to them as a favor whenever the agency was closed. One day, I found a magazine that was delivered to the address with her name: People magazine. Apparently, I felt from the cover that the magazine was all about gossipping; I learned that the periodical was the home-ground of Paparazzis. That woman looked like a type talking about others all the time. I was disgusted that some people actually pay *money* to read those: **I thought people should tattle for *free*, at least.**

Being born with more jealousy is a malediction. We can still be poor even if we live constructively: **Jealous people tend to get more debt to show off**; the Korean guy I mentioned above had too much debt: a big mortgage, few car loans and some credit card balances, etc. Still, that could have been ok if he just shut up and enjoyed his life without writing negative comments.

* * *

Summary

1. Jealousy is more than an emotion: It is a curse.
2. Some people spend money to gossip more; it is more than disgusting.
3. Everyone has his or her own pain; there is no point in being jealous of others.

65

Not Breaking Prejudices

Anyone can make money;
humble people keep it.

-Brad Kong

There is a German investor named Nicolas Berggruen; he used to be known as a *homeless billionaire*. Wiki shows that his net worth was about $3 billion as of 2022, but he had lived in hotels without a residence for a while. It shows he sold off his house and all the belongings in early 2000; he did not own a home, car or watch at the age of 40; instead, he traveled – staying in different hotels with only a small bag of clothes and a BlackBerry phone, then.

His case is peculiar; I can travel the world for ten years from hotel to hotel if I have $ 10 million, too. Still, I will keep my condo since I may have to come back to set up my next flight schedule, file a VISA application for other foreign countries or take some breaks. I do not want to continue traveling mindlessly from one place to another; I would need some time to pull myself together, occasionally.

A lot of people live opinion-lessly nowadays; many live prescribed lives by society without suspicion. I like to give you some examples of when I get more benefits after breaking some prejudices.

* * *

Do you know what my favorite restaurant is in Chicagoland? Ikea; we all know that this is a furniture store. But it has two restaurants in the building of the Chicagoland location; their salmon sandwich ($4) and veggie balls ($4) are my favorites. I would say that their dishes taste better than average restaurants, sometimes. It also has Greek salad ($5) with a huge portion, Veggie hotdogs ($1) and Pizza ($2); I do not know how they come up with these low prices; maybe they sell food with no margins to furniture customers.

Have you seen the forks used in Ikea restaurants? It is made of very thin wood and their drink section also includes Swedish beverages. I see that they put a lot of effort in the place. Regardless, I always wish that we had one of those in front of my home.

Where do I buy sushi all the time? The Polish market in front of my home; sushi is a traditional Japanese dish; ironically, I found that this place sells the best ones in town. There is a small sushi corner in the market; one Japanese chef owns it. To me, the taste is as good as a top rated restaurant while he uses more ingredients. Luckily, every sushi is 50% off after 7:00 PM there; I feel sorry that he charges less only because it is not in a popular location.

This is the place I usually go whenever I crave salads: Portillo's; this place is known as a hot dog joint, but its garden salad is my favorite; it is not on the salad menu, but on the side menu ($4.50). The size is still a full portion with extra bread and a dressing. Where is the best coffee shop in downtown Chicago? The "Whole Foods" on State street; this location opened recently in 2022; they set up the entire first floor with new chairs and tables for its own coffee shop.

Do you know the fastest way to go to downtown Chicago from my home? Metra trains to Chicago at 7:50 AM. Some people may think of a racing car, but it still needs to make millions of stop signals; besides, highways are typically crowded. The metra train would not make a stop from Roselle to downtown Chicago for $6.75; it may go slow, but never stops. I felt like I was in the presidential parade as I could see through the windows that all the cars were waiting until the train passed.

* * *

I visited the dentist the other day; the Korean lady endodontist suddenly warned me about my fasting plan; she said she had several patients who had lost multiple teeth all at once after fasting. I checked so many articles online, but couldn't find any evidence supporting her claim. We have TV shows like *The Biggest Loser,* but I have never heard of any contestant who lost a tooth after huge weight losses. Instead, I found results showing that fat people can lose teeth due to sugar eating or diabetes.

I thought that her tip was nonsense in the beginning. Some bears hibernate every winter; it's similar to how humans fast for a month. I could not find any article about bears losing a tooth because of that; besides, according to my common sense, I thought that it cannot be possible since bears need teeth to hunt. Mammal bodies are not designed to lose a tooth easily since they need it critically to survive. I thought that her patients possibly lost teeth for other reasons: alcoholism, not drinking enough water during fastings, etc. Eventually, I found out that people can lose teeth due to vitamin deficiency caused by fasting.

* * *

In my opinion, this could be the biggest prejudice in real estate investing: Buying an expensive house will bring more money in the end. ***No, it may not.*** I think that most people do not deduct expenses thoroughly; debtors often get mortgages blindly and double their housing costs because it seems their parents made money out of selling homes after retirement; this is simply an "*illusion.*" People only compare the original home prices, which was 30 years ago, with current ones; they often don't consider inflation, property taxes, mortgage interests, maintenance or repair costs paid during the 30 years of ownership. We can buy a big house; we may live happily, but it will never be profitable.

Another prejudice is this: Buying stocks will make us rich: ***It may or may not.*** I used to own stocks of 230 companies by 2019; I sold 110 of them with over +$72,000 capital gain profit in the last 5 years; now I have 130 companies left as of May, 2023; I am planning to sell 10 more if I can make profits. Now the CD interests are up to 4.2%; I think I may save money in the bank for a while.

* * *

There is one famous English idiom: "Do not judge a book by its cover." I watched a TV program about some weird cultures in Sweden the other day; it showed that Swedishes do not give guests food for free; guests have to bring their own meals since hosts will not give anything. Also, it said that it is common that kids pay money to their friend's parents when they spend some time together with them; it shows that these adults can order pizza comfortably in that case.

This was disgusting in my opinion. At least, it did not look very attractive. Maybe adults can push kids to pay some money somehow: Is it a fair thing to do? Probably not. Does it look good? Never. What is the reason we need to visit a friend's house this way? I wrote in Chapter 20 that I have had a good feeling about Finland since I felt welcomed in 1998. People were very kind, so I even imagined that it would be nice if I kept living there. I thought Sweden is similar since it's the neighbor. We do not know the true face unless you actually live there.

By the way, a Mexican guy on that show said this: "If you bring your own food to my home, my mom will worry if you do not like her food." I think Mexico is a much wealthier country than Sweden in a sense: **A lot of people think that wealth is just the amount of cash stacked or number increased in a bank account;** this is a delusion. This paper money is nothing but a social promise, at best. I strongly believe real wealths is kindness, generosity and sufficiency.

* * *

Prejudices apply to women, too. When I worked in the nursing home, there was a girl from an Italian family who never really spoke; I thought she was a pretty but quiet one. A few months later, I learned that she has a strange habit of screaming for any reason; she freaked me out several times. Suppose that a guy marries her and finds out this later on. It will not be pleasant if a man has to hear an old woman's scream; this can happen until he divorces.

Some lose money since they are obsessed with old ideas; rarely, it is a loss of entire life savings. In the book *Nomadland*, a guy named Bob Wells was interviewed; it shows that he is one of the pioneers of the van life movement and considered as a guru in that community. And I believe he is wealthy since his Youtube channel has a good amount of viewers. This is what he said during the interview: "**When I moved into the Van, I realized that everything that**

society had told me was a lie – that I had to get married and live in a house with a white picket fence and go to work, and then be happy at the very end of my life, but be miserable until then."

FYI, Bob was married and had two sons, but divorced; he said he is living happier in a van now. The point is that a lot of people follow traditions senselessly as if they are fixed destinies without objection. In particular, I notice that some Korean parents push marriage vigorously to their children; I was one of the victims who were pushed to do many things for decades. I just decided to have one child since nothing special happened in my life until I became 37. But I decided not to get pushed any more after another child. It is not like I do not love my daughter; she is great and better than other children, honestly. But I didn't particularly enjoy playing with a baby 24/7 and just do not want to live a life that I did not plan, originally.

* * *

In my opinion, there are a few prejudices we must break to get out of poverty; this might be especially true for Latin Americans in America:

- Having a lot of children is blessing
- We will be rich if we work hard
- You will be very rich if you invest in real estates
- Expensive things are better
- Hiring a tutor solves academic problem of my child
- Going to Ivy League with debt is a good choice
- Never skip meals
- Rice is the healthiest food in the world (Korea)
- Ukrainians are weak people (Russia)

We can save tons of money only by breaking some misconceptions and seeing real things. Whenever I go to libraries, I hardly see Latin Americans studying even though Latin Americans are over 15% of the American population; I honestly do not think their future is glamorously bright; some of them blindly go for more kids no matter what. The Hispanics born in the USA often do not do that, though. Some Mexican coworkers who spoke English fluently were single; I guess they have brains; they did not live mindlessly only by imitating their parents. And I think that was a good sign to be wealthy. Yet, those native Mexicans were crazy; they acted rashly as if producing more children was a religious practice.

* * *

This is the biggest lie in our lifetime: "You will be rich if you work longer." The truth is that many are poor even though they work to death. Also, some are rich though they do not work at all. The secret is how to set up the system; it's called building assets in other words.

Do you know what the best way is to start developing assets? "Thinking" in my opinion. I notice that a lot of blue collar workers blast music by habit and never really have quiet time on their own. Instead of turning on music, I think we should have one hour of quiet time to think alone a day. Sometimes, people call it meditation or praying; this time can rescue us, eventually.

In the real world, we need to find solutions for our specific situations. One hour of thinking can be equivalent to ten hours of laboring in a wage sense. This is why some dishwashers never even own a house after thirty years of service; they pump up music in the kitchens, so never have chances to deliberate as the noise interrupts them. I do not believe anyone can get out of poverty that way.

* * *

Summary

1. Prejudices interrupt us to see truths.
2. Forget everything, sometimes.
3. Never live a life suggested by others.

66

Being Unlucky

Those who are prepared or recognize opportunities make money.
-Brad Kong

Fasting is an abstention from eating for a while; I strongly believe that keeping this habit makes us lucky. We can save some lives by not eating them. Fasting also can bring us health benefits like weight loss; which can even improve mental conditions, including depression or cognitive performance; in other words, we feel better when we lose weight. **I believe people generally get more chances when they look in shape or joyful.** I am only doing 12 hours of fasting everyday overnight (9:00 PM - 9:00 AM) and try to do two days of fasting a week (Monday and Thursday).

Being unlucky can make us financially poor. Probably, most people are unlucky because of themselves. But, sometimes, we keep being poor because we have toxic people nearby; occasionally, these can be our family members. Unfortunately, we have to consider cutting these people off depending on the situation; they can be dead, but we don't have to die together.

There is a Kpop star and model named Tiffany in Korea; she was born in America. Her father had been known for getting debt from everywhere with *her name*; when this rumor was in multiple newspapers, she had interviews and said that this was true and she had to let her father go. This may sound cruel in some cultures, but remember one thing: **We have the right**

to live our lives without worry as long as we don't bother others.

* * *

Still, I believe most of these kinds of issues happen because of people we meet outside our families. It is not rare that a man goes bankrupt since he met the wrong woman or was greedy about women. It is true that women, who make a living by taking advantage of men, exist; they are called flower snakes in Korea or gold diggers in America; the opera *Carmen* is one example. There are women bringing misfortune to men, even regardless of money. There is only one reason why men are attracted to them: They are good looking. Writer Greene took an example of Lola Montez in his book, *The 48 Laws of Power*; let me summarize her story.

A woman named Lola Montez was born in Ireland in 1821. She moved to Paris, France in the 1840s; she wanted to be a dancer, but it didn't work out well. So she addressed a man named Alexandre Dujarier, who owned the newspaper company with the highest circulation in France at that time; her career started taking off thanks to nice reviews from the newspaper. Although she was married to an English man in Ireland already, Montez decided to get married to this journalist again. She had acted arrogantly and had a bad reputation; Dujarier's friends started to avoid him. One day, Dujarier had a fight with a drama critic over Lola's performance; they had a duel and Dujarier was shot to death in March, 1845.

Then, Lola Montez moved to Munich in 1846 and decided to seduce King Ludwig of Bavaria. She seduced Count Rechberg first and he introduced her to the King; it shows that she showed her breasts to the king at the first meeting. He helped her to perform dancing on the Bavarian stage; reviews were terrible, but he supported her career, regardless. On top of it, King Ludwig started spending a lot of money on her while she had acted rudely to the public. People became more than angry and Ludwig eventually stepped down in March, 1848. It shows that he used to be a beloved king, but one woman made him lose his throne, permanently.

After that, she moved back to England. She married a young army cavalry officer named Heald, who was 8 years younger than her in 1849. They were arrested for bigamy since Lola had been married in Ireland already as I mentioned; they managed to escape to Spain together. They had horrible fights during their relationship; Lola attacked the man with a knife one day. Heald returned to England alone and found he lost his position in the Army; he moved to Portugal in depression, lived in poverty for a while and died in a boating accident in 1853; he was only 25 years old.

Regardless of Heald's death, Lola moved to California on her own in 1853. She started a relationship with a married man named Pat Hull, a local newspaperman. After she left him, he got depressed and died of alcoholism; he was only 33 years old. After that, Lola died of Syphilis, which is a sexually transmitted disease, in 1861; she was only 39 years old. It says that one writer published the autobiography of Lola a few years later; he filed a bankruptcy as well. In conclusion, this woman had brought misfortune to a lot of men and died of STD herself. There are these types of people only hurting others; all those stupid men wouldn't have started relationships from the start, unless she was good looking.

* * *

What can we learn from this? Do not go crazy about women: **It is OK if we do not have a relationship or not bring one more child to Earth in the age of overpopulation.**

It actually looks cool when a man rejects a woman; if you have a wife already, have some mindfulness and be happy that you have more than enough; don't go for more women, desperately. Women do not bring men benefits all the time.

I still remember one old stupid dishwasher who had been greedy for women all the time; he had lived in a rental apartment at the age of 60. Do not necessarily think that it is a lucky thing that a pretty girl approaches you; think reasonably if she can be helpful for your life. One obvious sign of a gold digger is that she never spends money on you.

There was a Korean idol band named *High4*; the group had four young boys. I like their music, but I do not know why they were unpopular and finally disappeared. All I can see is that their management, N.A.P Entertainment, was not very powerful; most of the entertainers from the company failed. While I see some disqualified Korean musicians are successful even in America, I think these boys were simply unlucky.

* * *

"7 Luck" Chinese restaurant was the most unlucky business I have seen, personally; unfortunately, it was completely closed out in May, 2022. I liked their food, so I had probably been there thirty times in the last 15 years; I think they made some bad business decisions, but also they got pretty unlucky, too.

Originally, this eatery was a small take out place in a strip mall by 2019; the size was about 1,000 square feet; it did not have any room for tables, yet it had some chairs, so customers could sit and wait to pick up meals. I think the restaurant itself had been there more than 20 years; the owners had been changed at least three times. While food had been fine all along, I guess that keeping a business profitable is a hard thing; especially, restaurants are brutally competitive.

I think the last owners came in 2017; they were a young Chinese couple and had a son (a family of three). I assume that they must have gotten the same problem all the previous owners ran into a year later: The business was not profitable. **They probably had to sell the place to others or make some changes in the place to be successful.** They chose the second option regrettably and it was disastrous.

In 2019, they suddenly rented another 1,000 sf next door and expanded the place. I do not understand where they got the idea: If they did not have enough take out customers, how could they have more only because they created an extra dine-in area? **In my opinion, they only made their rent *double*.**

Besides, the place was closed for several months for renovation; that was a waste of rent for many months. When I used their restroom, I found out that they spent a fortune to renovate it. Result? No one really came to dine in. The most *unlucky* thing above all was this: **The Corona virus came in a few months after they reopened the dining area.** I think they just completed their store lease and closed out in 2022; a new sushi restaurant came in right after that.

* * *

The first mistake I could see was that 7 Luck went in the direction of spending more money for better results: They should have thought about what they can do without spending extra cash. A lot of people just spend money first no matter what: **Some believe that money can solve all problems.** My video game store was 900 sf and I know 1,000 sf is not extremely small. If they felt like they could have more customers by providing a dine-in area, they should have renovated their space without renting more; for most business owners, rent is the top expense. I would have made the kitchen area to 500 sf and provide the rest 500 sf for dine-in if I were them; having bars around the wall instead of tables can help several guests sit and eat. It is crazy if they thought the profit would go up with spending more on rent.

The second reason must have been vanity in my opinion. I think the owner probably had a dream to have a luxury restaurant someday. **After seeing some lavish features, I actually ordered less from the place**; I felt like they may charge me more for those expensive interiors. For this reason, I know that some joint owners keep their eateries looking cheezy intentionally; some hotdog stands look cheap; still, people can enter those without getting intimidated by Chinese emperor paints framed by gold as in 7 Luck.

The third reason was stupidity, immaturity and lack of business intuition in general. If they were mature enough to know that peace of mind is the best (rather than bigger profit), they would have not tried what they did. The original take out place could have made more money since food delivery increased after Covid came: Mental growths are needed to make better decisions.

* * *

Personally, I think I am the luckiest guy in the world. I was born in South Korea, which is one of the wealthiest countries (being born in North Korea could have been a 50% chance for me). Now I live in America, which is the richest country on the globe. Having lived in two richest countries is an extremely lucky case: **Even being born on Earth is lucky in a sense.**

I have not had a hereditary disease; this is an exceedingly lucky thing again; it could have cost more than a fortune if something wrong happened. There was one time I saw one very short guy at the bus terminal. While I am against heightism (I actually respect Peter Dinklage), I felt lucky instantly since it was not his fault. It is like a bad lottery ticket or Russian roulette with lower probability. In fact, even he is lucky as well since there are people who never get out of bed.

I also met a nice woman who won a doctorate degree and we have a daughter (I only have a bachelor). This is impressively lucky again since some guys meet the wrong women and experience hellish divorces; besides, some do not meet a woman at all. There are plenty of people who want a daughter, especially in Korea, but end up having only sons, too.

There are people who do not know how lucky they are, always complain, want more and cause trouble: Being born in America is incredibly lucky by itself; there are myriads of people trying to get U.S. citizenship. Some Americans do not know this, commit crime and spend time in prison though citizenship was automatically given to them without making any effort at all.

* * *

I read about one teenage girl who drove off her father's Porsche after taking drugs, got into an accident and died instantly in CA in 2006. For some reason, her disfigured corpse photos were published online and kept being sent to her parents; as a result, the parents sued the highway accident department for leaking the photos and beated the trial.

This is an extreme case, but I believe she could have lived a heavenly life without getting much interruption: being born in America, having white parents, owning a Porsche in her family, having a chance to get good educations and fat salaries, etc. Apparently, she was a cocaine addict at the age of 18 and it shows that the accident was her revenge on her parents; it says that her parents tried to admit her to a rehab hospital on the night before that accident. She did not have to touch the drug to begin with; some people just want more, more and more. I think she chose her destiny; she chose to blow out everything into an accident.

* * *

History says that Julius Caesar had a habit of saying that he was lucky. I can see that extremely lucky things happened repeatedly throughout the emperor's life: We become lucky when we think that way. Some are broke all the time since they are unlucky; they think that being unlucky is nothing they can do about, but that is not true. **We can try to be lucky**; at least, we can choose not to be unlucky.

Some say that luck happens when preparation meets opportunities. That means no luck will happen if there is no preparation or taking chances. Some people just do not prepare much for the future: no education, license, etc. Or they just pass up good opportunities since they do not recognize them. I would say that being unlucky can be our own faults in a way.

* * *

Summary

1. Many of us are quite lucky already.
2. We can try to be more charmed.
3. We can avoid being hapless.

67

Not Solving Housing Problems Quickly

Owning a home "free and clear" is like getting an extra $50,000 salary a year by itself.
-Brad Kong

Have you heard of "Whitewashing a house?" It is a term to describe "a practice of black homeowners erasing themselves from their home." Nathan and Shani are a black couple, who were both professors at Johns Hopkins University; they owned a 2,600-square-foot home in Baltimore, MD. When they tried to sell it, they had an appraisal of $450,000 in 2022. When they asked their white friends to pretend to be the owners of the house, they got an appraisal of $750,000.

I am not a black, but I suppose that this is absurd. Nonetheless, I think that we can take advantage of it the other way around. When we buy a house, maybe we should avoid the one occupied by white people. Who knows if we can save $300,000? For the same reason, **I think that we should avoid a neighborhood with inflated fame like Beverly Hills**; it does not really have a better library or school. I think it's more wise to choose a less known village as long as it's safe and clean.

* * *

I thought that this black lady named Jessica did a good job of owning her place early. I originally found her videos when I searched for "small space for a family of three" on YouTube; she said she bought her one-bedroom condo only for $44,000 in Detroit, MI. I was impressed since she is almost the only one I met who bought a condo cheaper than me ($60,000 in 2013). There must be people paying less than us, but no one had an interview with CNBC like her.

On YouTube, she said she traveled to 195 countries on Earth; I don't see any hard verification, but she published a book regarding her visitings only to 100 countries. And it seems the book is selling fine on Amazon; it was ranked in the list of 30,000 bestsellers in May, 2023; I hope my books will be like hers. The only difference is that her parents were from Uganda and she seems to be an alcoholic; I see that she has a huge bar in her place, holds wine glasses all the time, and her skin looks damaged; personally, I do not drink alcohol at all, starting with to protect my teeth.

Apparently, she is single and does not seem to plan to have a family although she is close to 40; I am married and have a daughter; my wife has a doctorate from UIUC. It seems her book photos are mainly about luxury life from her Instagram: expensive hotels, extravaganza meals, etc. I prefer to write about frugality. As a life choice, **I would rather choose a family than more indulgence for the same amount of money.**

* * *

Apartment rent had been the biggest waste of my life until I became 40. I am not sure of a big house, but when we buy a small condo, we can save up to

10 times from rents as association fees are smaller. I am paying about $367 a month for HOA fees in the Midwest as of 2023; it includes heating, water, garbage collection, etc. It shows that Californians pay from $3,000 a month for apt now.

I believe true comfort comes from home ownership; when there is a problem with housing, we cannot feel actual peace. One of the mental intruders is a mortgage; we won't feel honest tranquility until we pay it off. Also when the combination of association fees, property taxes, maintenance fee, etc are too large in our budgets, we won't feel relaxed.

* * *

When I used to have my own business, the rent was the biggest problem, too. Paying $1,200 a month for a store doesn't sound like a lot; I ended up paying $120,000 over the course of 8 years. How much can we make out of selling video games? I could have bought two condos with that money in 2013; no wonder I had always been broke.

Maybe I should not have kept the business that long. Initially, I made a lease contract that way, but I did not want to give up so easily, too. Now I can let it go without regret since I believe I had tried everything to save it by 2014. Then, I had intensively researched store rents around the world: **I was deeply suffering, so the only comfort I could get was the fact that there are people paying more than I do;** despite comfort, it did not help me, financially. I had to squeeze everything out only to pay rent every month particularly after the 2009 depression.

During the eight years of business ownership, I mostly paid two rents, by the way: my store rent and apartment rent. **Yet there were times, for about six months, I used to pay three rents**: my store rent, apartment rent and my girlfriend's apt rent; that girl is mother of my daughter now; I used to joke about myself as "three rent man" and made a song about it. While the three rent periods were short, my two rent periods were about 7.5 years; I finally bought out my condo six months before I closed my store. I saw that leakage from savings stopped immediately as soon as I bought the condo; it had been always decreasing for a decade.

Solving the housing issue means getting out of rent or mortgage completely. My recommendation is buying out a small condo with cash at one time; I know it is extremely hard. **But dangling a housing mess unsolved will only bring more losses and stress;** it costs more if we do not solve it asap; the longer we hold a rent or mortgage, the more money we lose on it.

* * *

There is a book titled *Everyday Millionaires* written by Hogan. The author conducted research on about 10,600 millionaires and provided solid data. I actually heard of it when I watched the Ramsey show: **85% of these millionaires bought their houses with full cash, according to this book.**

We know that it is never easy to buy a home with a single payment. **Yet I notice that there are people buying a bigger house with a mortgage even though they can afford a smaller one with cash.** They might have thought they could have better lives in bigger houses. Or they thought these were better investments, at least: Neither is correct. Bigger houses guarantee to bring more repairs and bills; a bigger house can be an investment, but may not be a good one after deducting all the expenses like higher property taxes, maintenance, etc.

After getting a mortgage for a big house, people may pay off the mortgage within 30 years. But in my opinion, **30-years is too long from the start.** We will never know what will occur exactly during the period. Even if things go smoothly, people end up losing way more than cash buyers: it is pointless to work longer while having a rent or mortgage. Let me give you three reasons in detail why solving the house issue ASAP is more vital than we assume.

* * *

First of all, a rent or mortgage costs way more than condo HOA fees a month. Most people in Chicagoland pay $1,200 a month for one-bedroom apartment rent in 2022. I have paid a $350 association fee a month since I bought out a one-bedroom condo in 2013; this monthly HOA fee includes heating, water, garbage, cleaning, landscaping, swimming pool, cooking gas, etc. This is about $800 saving a month after deducting property tax ($1,700) a year; it is $10,000 saving a year while some apartments do not include utilities at all. I would say that I have saved about $100,000 in the last decade.

Comparing a condo owner with a mortgage payer for a big house, the result gets even more ridiculous. There was a Korean community site; most Koreans there were from the east and west regions in America. In general, the house prices there are three times higher than Midwest due to more populations; they talked about "$200,000 salary" or "$1,000,000 houses in SF" all the time; I notice that some went for bigger houses to show off.

I would say that paying off a house and living there without moving out is like getting an extra $50,000 salary by itself: In a money sense, there is no difference between "making $100,000 and spending half on a mortgage" and "owning a house completely and not having a job." I am not saying that we should not have jobs: If we make money while owning houses completely, we have superpowers; we can accumulate savings faster.

Secondly, did you know that we can end up paying double the amount of houses when we pay off 30-years mortgages? **The longer it takes, the more we pay totally;** the total amount would get noticeably cheaper if we choose shorter terms. Shorter than any mortgage is cash upfront; we can actually get a discount on houses since sellers want to get paid quickly; they do not want to wait for a couple of months until buyers get approval from a bank and process everything.

Thirdly, it is a huge mental relief when we do not have a mortgage and never have to worry about it. There is a Buddhist monk named "Venerable Ajahn Siripanyo." He is a Thai monk from Malaysia and known as the son of Malaysia's third richest man, Ananda Krishnan. This is the first thing he said in his lecture: "There is nothing more important than peace of mind." Believe it or not, our brains have limited room to worry about things: **We cannot worry limitlessly.** When we have one less thing to worry about, we can use that portion of brains to focus on something else.

I watched the movie *Ali* starring Will Smith the other day; there was a scene where Ali got a phone call from the Supreme Court amid he had been taking care of kids at home for months. He finally got a court decision as he had waited for it for a long time. I am not sure why he was blocked from boxing, but it is common that we cannot do our day jobs normally when our case is hanging in court. Having a mortgage could be something like that; it can be a minor worry we carry all the time; we cannot concentrate 100% on our jobs. We would not worry much if the mortgage is 10% of our salaries. A lot of people pay 40% of monthly incomes on mortgages and cannot emphasize on work: That is a big drain of mental energy only for shelters.

* * *

Summary

1. Get rid of rent or mortgage ASAP.
2. Do not buy a big house with a mortgage when you can buy out a small condo with full cash.
3. Having the house problem solved completely can be a financial cushion for life.

68

Spending Too Much on Ceremonies and Anniversaries

"Wedding poor" are more stupid than house poor.
-Brad Kong

The most expensive yet tragic wedding ceremony happened in Sao Paulo, Brazil in 2017. A 32-year-old bride named Rosemere rented a helicopter for her wedding day and it crashed before her event due to bad weather. The news shows that four people in the chopper were killed instantly: her brother, a pilot, a photographer, who was unfortunately pregnant, and herself. At least, I think Kim Kadashian made money out of her weddings on TV thanks to paparazzis: I just do not see a point from the Brazilian boisterousness. To me, wasting a fortune on a wedding is already bad enough; dying at the age of thirty-two as a result of overspending is more than being absurd.

Lately, the term "wedding poor" has been trending in Korea; it means that people who become poor after spending a lot on weddings; they are kind of similar to "house poor", but one level down and more degenerated in my opinion. Those *house-poor* people at least have the option to sell their houses in the end; it can bring them profits despite huge mortgages they carry in common, especially in Korea. "Wedding poor" are simply idiotic in a financial sense: No couple makes money out of their own weddings. **In fact, I believe that an expensive wedding can cause a divorce since money problems are the biggest reasons for fights in marriages.**

The top reason why I hate expensive ceremonies in general is not money. Maybe I am superstitious, but I felt whenever I did something unnecessarily loud or boisterous before important events (e.g., exams, marriages), usually things didn't go very well for me. Maybe this is not just true for me; people get injured during crazy spring breaks. My wife and I couldn't have the ceremony at all, but we have lived just fine in the last 24 years.

* * *

In my opinion, there is no practical benefit we can get by showing off in any case. Thoreau once said, "Envy is the tax which all the winners must pay." This means making others envious can actually be a loss. **While smart people try to hide what they have, stupid ones try to show them off even after getting debts to buy those**; some borrow money to brag items; they often buy a luxury car or oversized house with a car loan or mortgage.

To me, having a lavish ceremony can be another creative way to waste money; in fact, I think that it is the climax of pointless spendings; realistically, the only things left after expensive celebrations are some photos, which is ideal for Instagram. Personally, I think men should stay away from those women insisting on huge weddings: **It's pathetic for losers to make themselves stars by spending their own money.** Media would not care for ordinary people, so some decided to spend bucks on their own. I like to be a bestseller author. But I am not going to spend a fortune on advertisements to look like one.

* * *

Blowing a fortune on a big wedding will not make a marriage life better. In fact, it can make marriage worse since it will bring more bills if not debts. Arguing about money has been the number one reason for a divorce worldwide.

Kris was the second husband of celebrity Kim; the news showed that they spent over $10 million on their wedding, but the marriage lasted only for 72 days. Is it too much to think that if they had a quiet wedding, they would have stayed together now? When a man really wants a woman, he does not care for the scale of the wedding; men are not interested in the wedding thing by nature and never dream about tuxedos, rings, etc. I assume that it could be similar to women; if she is really interested in grabbing a man before other ladies do, she may be less interested in a high-cost ceremony which requires millions of plans, schedules or appointments; she may not be able to divert her attention if she is truly interested in the bridegroom himself.

* * *

There are always women spending too much on weddings; occasionally, their men are opinion-less idiots not interrupting their brides; some of these women choose those kinds of men instead of smart guys, so she can control more in the future. These wives can make entire households more advantageous for them or their side of the family; it is possible that they won't benefit their men or men's side of the family much.

There was a TV show titled "Newlyweds: Nick and Jessica" released in 2003. I felt that Nick was the example of one of those powerless men; he was a no-big star while Jessica was famous then; I assume she chose him since she believed in controlling him easily; I notice that no one was really happy except the bride during the entire show. They divorced only after four years.

* * *

I believe spending too much on a wedding is like doing too much on an introduction to a drama. Imagine *the Sopranos* starts with five minutes of song and the production spent half of their budget on it. Marriage can cost a lot later on, especially after a child is born.

I personally do not think there is much point in high wedding costs, especially when divorce rate is quite high these days. It shows that celebrity Kim spent over $20 millions on her three weddings combined; this is high, particularly because all her three weddings ended in divorces. If I put $10 M in a stock giving out 5% annual dividends, I can get $500,000 a year until I die. If my daughter inherits it, she can get the $500,000 until she dies, too. While most men do not care about the wedding ceremonies, a lot of women go crazy about those. Let me tell you one painful truth: Stupid men choose those kinds of women more.

If a bride insists on getting a diamond ring instead of a big ceremony, I guess that makes more sense in finance. Diamond rings hold values; couples can sell them when they need money. The ceremonies leave valuable photos. Still, in case a divorce happens, which is true for half of all marriages in America, no one will even take a look at those.

* * *

The Brazilian world cup soccer team visited South Korea in June, 2022; they came to have a friendly match with the Korean team. The Qatar world cup 2022 game will start in

November, which is not very far and we know that the Brazil team is the number one in the world. So every Koreans' eyes were on the game.

Coincidentally, a huge wild fire broke out in the Southeast region in Korea and it damaged a large amount of forests then. Strangely, the stupid South Korean president Yoon visited the Korean World cup stadium suddenly. People were wondering why he was there instead of taking care of the wild fire. More ridiculous thing was that he started unnecessary ceremonies. There is one famous Korean player named Sohn. The president started a show to give a medal of honor to the player in the middle of the stadium; that is not even his job as usually the Minister of Sports does it. We believe this president did it to make himself popular; it happened right before the game; apparently, that only disturbed the psychology of Korean players. Then, you know what? Korea lost 5-1 to Brazil that night. We believe that if these players could have taken more rest and prepared the game quietly in their ways, the result could have been different.

Personally, I am not going to do any boisterous event or advertisement for the release of my books. Maybe I could sell more copies that way. But I can make more enemies as well since not everyone will be happy with the contents. I will be honest with my opinion, but I do not want to make any hustle and bustle ceremonies: To me, that is bad luck, not to mention it costs more money and energy.

If we want to be successful, I suggest that we should do things less loudly. Do not spend any extra money to call for unnecessary jealousy or bad luck. We can still be poor even without getting ill omens.

* * *

Summary

1. Wasting money to be more loud is pointless.
2. Spending too much on weddings is nonsense when people divorce a lot these days.
3. An expensive ceremony can provide a reason to get divorce.

69

Not Using Infrastructure Already Built

We need to use up what's available first.
-Brad Kong

I think that it is important to take a "train" early; time flies fast after that. For example, I bought my house in full in 2013; tons of money have been saved for not paying rent every month; I cannot believe that 10 years have passed already.

If we are successful in building a good asset system, we should be able to automatically make money afterwards. It shows that the British empire focused on setting, expanding and securing trading routes in the Ocean while the Spanish focused on getting gold from the Aztec in the 16th century. History proved that the desire for gold from "El Dorado" ruined the Spanish armadas eventually: The English believed that there was something great beyond the seas; English is spoken in 59 countries now thanks to their heavy concentration on keeping routes rather than gold.

Similarly, I read that Genghis Khan had emphasized on keeping the Silk Roads in the 13th century. He knew wealth would come as long as Mongols were able to keep the routes.

* * *

It is possible that other people may envy us for things we own while we do not notice; strangely, these could be our arms and legs. When I used to work as the healthcare wait staff, there was a waitress who was physically challenging; she had some underdevelopment issues with one arm and hand. I am pretty sure that she wished she would have the same arm like others; most of us may have $1-million arms in her point of view. **Still, we keep complaining, being frustrated or even committing suicides despite having miraculous advantages.**

Another example could be my condo purchased 10 years ago. I used to live in a one-bedroom rental apartment on the second floor (it was a three-story building). I had always envied people living on the third floor; which was more quiet and clean; I thought that I could live there forever if I could get a unit on the top third floor, then.

Now I live on the third floor of a condo building with a pond view. My unit is surrounded by big trees, and definitely better than lower units: **Still, I realize that I do not appreciate it as much as before.** I got a roof leak when there was a hail storm in 2017; it was a hassle to stay in hotels for a couple of weeks twice for huge roof repairs in our unit. I learned that not everything is as it looks outside.

* * *

This is the definition of infrastructure: The set of facilities or systems that serve a country, city, or other area. People often do not recognize that a language is also an infrastructure; it serves as a communication tool in a society; I think that the most obvious example for this is English.

I am not saying that all English-speaking countries are great. Nevertheless, England certainly has made a huge effort to build this structure; it's important to be aware that we can take advantage of this. As I noted before, some Korean authors write books only in Korean only because they are poor in English; some never learn it even after living in America for a decade.

Learning English does not cost us money, but people can lose some when they do not learn; Korean writers can lose a huge amount of readers since less than 1% of people in the world speak Korean. I assume writing in English is the only way to approach 100% of readers on Earth, including Korea.

If we are not good at English ourselves, we have to pay a translator to write an English book; this is an extra expense. **Some people are broke since they fail to use infrastructure already built.**

* * *

It shows that there is a famous road called "Santiago Pilgrimage" in Northern Spain; it is a 500-miles-long religious pathway; it's also known as "Routes of Santiago de Compostela" in Spanish and "Way of St. James" in English. It says that this road has millions of yellow signs from France to the west coast in Spain. No one loses direction there as long as he or she just follows the signs.

For some reasons, visiting the Santiago road and finishing the trekking within two months has become largely popular in Korea since 2017. A lot of Korean celebrities did it and made documentaries along the way, too. In general, I believe Koreans like to walk as the country has similar tourism routes in the country; the most famous one is Olle Trail in Jeju Island. And the trend seems to be that more Koreans choose the pilgrimage route from France rather than visiting the Eiffel Tower or other museums in Paris these days. I think another good reason is that Koreans believe walking is extremely good for health, which is true.

As I wrote before, I am a walking maniac myself as I do not even own a car any more. And I thought I will go to Santiago Pilgrimage myself someday. But, soon, I realized that this plan was kind of pointless.

* * *

Although they are not famous, Chicagoland has plenty of pleasant trails already: Salt Creek Trail, Lakefront Trail, Great Western Trail, Illinois prairie paths, Valley Line Trail, Sauganash Trail, Bloomingdale Trail, etc; these are only a few examples near my home; most of them are surprisingly well built and long; most are about 20 feet wide paved endless roads (with asphalt or cement).

I do not know how they did it, but these trails pass in the middle of woods, parks or some villages without stop signs or signals. The governments even built quality bridges over major highways only to connect those trails. When I used to drive on highways, I always wondered what these bridges were for; I thought that I had never been on those, but they looked cool.

Certainly, I can spend airfare and hotel fees to walk on the Santiago road since they said it's famous. Or I can imagine that I am on it and walking on one of these nature trails, which are not far from my home: What are exact differences, really?

Apparently, Santiago trail does not have many trees or shades due to the desert nature of Northern Spain. As far as I have checked blogs, it seems people just needed some time to walk alone and think for a month. Of course, we can have some unique experiences with Spanish food or bed bugs in hostels. But I do not think it is worth all those labors and costs. I know this since I have traveled a lot myself for decades: In the end, I concluded that all the places are the same after all. At the same time, I suggest that we can save a lot of money if we enjoy the infrastructure already built nearby.

* * *

I notice that I have less fantasy about tourist attractions as I get older. We would not have much fantasy about shopping malls if we had worked in several malls for a decade; all the malls could look the same after all.

In a sense, I think that getting mature is getting rid of unnecessary fantasies. Men who have never dated a woman before tend to have more fantasies about women. After they meet a lot of women, they may realize that women poop and fart all the time just like men. Then, finally, they start to tell which type of woman is good or bad. Having unnecessary fantasies can cost us fortune if not life.

* * *

Summary

1. Keeping fantasies often does not help our wallets.
2. Getting mature means having less vain fantasies.
3. Nothing is better than what we have already.

70

Not Working While Being Wealthy

Try not to stop working completely.
-Brad Kong

The biggest advantage we can get from working while being wealthy is not wages: We can have chances to see the true faces of people. Let's suppose that you are rich, but got a server job in a restaurant to get out of boredom. Your horrible boss could be a kind manager only to customers in the cafe. When we see the harsh realities, we learn that it's not easy to make money: **Our wealth may last longer as a result.**

Whenever I see some Mexican cooks in a restaurant, they remind me of the horrible sous chef in the nursing home kitchen where I used to work; he treated dishwashers rudely. While I don't want to get back to that horrid job, I am glad I had that experience of 7 years. I believe that I have more understanding of human nature; probably my wealth will last longer as a consequence.

* * *

I believe modern *drudgery* might have been created with the Industrial Revolution in the 1760s. Have you ever worked in a commercial kitchen before? It is not natural to do brutally repetitive jobs for over 8 hours a day: **Humans have never lived like this in the first 6 million years of our**

history. Life has always been slow until recently, if we compare it with that of modern industry.

There was a Chinese nobleman named Jiang Ziya 3,000 years ago; he was a well-known duke and strategist at that time. It shows that he got forced to get divorced by his wife when he was a student; his wife asked him to watch beans getting dried under sunlight one day; rain came and swept away all the crops while he was focusing on his reading; his wife finally bursted into a massive anger and left him; unfortunately, he could not brought any salary to home for a long time. It shows that she regretted it after he became an official years later. Nonetheless, I realized this is how people used to live: drying beans slowly and eating them. Simple lives. "Being ten minutes late or not" is pretty much a modern thing and I do not like it.

* * *

While I disfavor too hard work, there are people who never work forever, too; some are dependent on their parents even at their late ages; it's their parents' fault as well in a sense. I heard that these types of young people are increasing in Korea; this "Kangaroo tribe" actually has become a social issue, lately; those youngsters are like baby kangaroos living in their parents' pouches. I perceived the real problem is that these dependent people keep bothering others until they die. As I wrote before, being poor is not just about money; poor people tend to bother others more while they don't notice. Sometimes, they make others miserable, too: Especially their own families.

After seeing tons of internet trolls, I decided not to be sympathetic for old poor people all the time; they can be the future of those wasteful trolls. I understand that there are exceptions; some people are broke after pure struggling. But, in common sense, it is not normal for people born in America or Korea without a disability to despair after working honestly for life. There could be reasons to be in impoverishment; one reason may be that some bother others in unproductive ways for long; once in a while, a few just deserve to be poor.

* * *

There is a series of videos tagged “the gold digger pranks” on YouTube. The first of this series was originally published by Zdorovetskiy, who owns a channel VitalyzdTv, but millions of others have copied him and revived the series. All the plots are similar in videos: Usually, a guy approaches a girl to ask for a dinner or date on the street; the girl usually declines his offer; then, the guy gets into a luxury car parked nearby; then, usually the girl stops the guy and says, “Is this your car? I can have dinner with you.” Then, the guy announces, “You're a gold digger” and drives away.

Maybe every woman in the world is a gold digger as these *social experiments* suggest. But do you really believe it? After I thought about it, I figured that there are other reasons than money why those women prefer rich men. Conclusively, I think that a girl may prefer an affluent guy even when she is wealthy herself; in fact, many professional women still like the rich. Here are the reasons I figured.

Being wealthy can be a barometer of a healthy human condition; it may not be absolute, but reasonably true; being well-off is the result of a diverse combination of lifestyle, personality and qualities. And I believe these qualities are what women look for and chase at. Rich guy may be a hard worker; he may be trustworthy or responsible. **More importantly, he may not be an internet troll who wastes time online leaving pointless comments for hours.** He may be more constructive; he is less likely to harass a girl for no apparent benefit; he may not catcall women on the street since no one can make more money that way.

The only problem in those videos is that some ignorant women think a guy with a luxury car is rich: A smart woman knows that this is not always the case. If a woman goes purely for money, Bill Gates must have been the most popular guy in America; we all know that this is not true. **I think women go for good qualities of a man and wealth could be a *quick* indicator for those**; not many people get rich by accident.

* * *

Prosperity may not last forever; when things are going well, people tend to assume that the success will last for good; we can only try, but there is no guarantee.

I was in Northbrook shopping center the other day. It was a luxury mall with a Louis Vuitton shop inside. The last time I visited was around 2018, and I remember the mall was full with stores. This time I was surprised that the mall was half empty after three years of Covid pandemic. Even the food court was all empty except one place named Bruno's pizza. I am shocked that this happened even in a wealthy Jewish town; FYI, there were still a few luxury brand stores left in the plaza.

* * *

Working despite being wealthy may not be necessary for everyone. **But it will be helpful for people who are about to blow money after getting a fortune.** Some may think getting a fortune or a good amount of money will never happen to them. But it does happen to anyone, though it's not common: inheriting money from parents or relatives;

increased value of stocks, bonds, coins or other assets; real estate boom; sudden business success; marrying or divorcing a wealthy spouse; getting a good job or promotion; winning a gamble or lottery; winning an award or prize; finding some money by accident; etc.

Most people waste all the money quickly when one of those happens. **But it's crucial to know that the consumption desire is particularly strong only in the beginning when we get some money.** According to my experience, this desire to spend diminishes exponentially as time goes on. A year later, we may be angry if we do not have the original amount of money in the bank account any more; our brains change that having the money feels very natural, eventually; we feel that it's a loss if we do not have the original fortune any more. I can say that it takes about a year to feel that way and make the money to be truly ours.

How can you spend a year without touching a large portion of the money? **In my opinion, the best way is not quitting our current jobs immediately or even getting one if we are not employed.** We have less chances to touch the money if we have a steady income from a job. More importantly, we will see how hard it is to make money in the workplaces everyday: That will prevent us from spending a large portion of our fortunes. We can quit our jobs after a year. The fortune will be finally ours by then. We may not feel like blowing it quickly. Alternatively, you can put the money in some places no one can touch.

I have inherited a good amount of money from my parents in my 40s. Having the weekend dishwasher job for seven years helped me not to touch the money. I couldn't spend that half a million dollars at all since I knew how hard it was to make $16 an hour in the kitchen by 2022.

* * *

Summary

1. Anyone can get a fortune unexpectedly.
2. Spending desire is super strong only in the beginning.
3. Do not touch a large amount of money at least for one year; it will be truly yours after that.

71

Going Too Big

The simpler, the happier.
-Brad Kong

I think that it was the start of unfortunate events that Germans supported Bismarck to unite their states in the 19th century. The chancellor initiated wars against Denmark, Austria and France to unite 39 small German states under *Prussian* leadership; as a result, the unified German Reich was born in 1871. Subsequently, the united Germany triggered World War I and II in the 20th century. Consequently, millions of Germans died themselves; totally, more than 70 million people died worldwide during these two wars. Sometimes, I guess that it's better to stay small. **Things going well, bigger or better is not always good**; it can provide reasons for misery or even extinction.

Lately, I regretted ordering too many xylitol gums from Amazon. I thought that they are good for my teeth; these are supposed to prevent decaying. Strangely, I started feeling weird pain after chewing them for 10 minutes. I should have chosen the package of 500 gums, even though my daughter ended up finishing the package of 1,000, lately.

What I mean by "going too big" means bigger spendings here; there is nothing wrong with having bigger incomes. Regardless, there are flops spending money first, no matter what. Do you know how to know if you are one of those? See how much debt you have now. This may shock some: **Not having a debt is perfectly normal.** Humans have lived without it in the first six million years throughout our evolution.

* * *

Did you know that there are a lot of natural disasters in Japan? I heard that earthquakes are part of daily life in Tokyo; it also has frequent tsunamis, typhoons and floods as it is an island facing the violent Pacific ocean. As a result, **I believe these natural disasters have made Japanese people nervous**; *they have seeked for peace of mind more eagerly than others and preferred something stable.* I figure this is why the Japanese do not invest in stocks much; it's a cash oriented country with less credit card usage. Stock markets are small since they cannot afford anything more dangerous; their lives are already in threat due to disasters. It is a fact that the Japanese save more cash in the bank than others; which is a more conservative way of building wealth.

Japan has a tradition to inherit parent's professions, even for generations. **I believe the reason is that they feel more stable that way.** Consequently, it has more old businesses with longer histories than others. What I mean by "old" is like 500 years old in Japan. I deduce that they feel more comfortable when there are things never changing but benefiting, while their environments are dynamic.

Do you know what is the most common point of those old Japanese restaurants? Above all, their sizes are small in general. I have seen photos of a 500 year old Owariya udon place; their space is pretty small, too; guests have to wait in line basically forever; no seat is available until someone finishes his or her meal. Google shows that 80% of over 100 years old restaurants in the world are in Japan, statistically. And their spaces are all small compared with those in Korea or America: **Why?**

In my opinion, being small is the reason why they have survived for so long. Naturally, a small place pays small rent, which is good for the business. They can manage to keep their doors open during hard times since small overheads help. Probably, old restaurants already bought their buildings hundreds of years ago. Still, being small helps since they pay cheaper mortgage, property tax, etc for their buildings.

* * *

In a sense, I believe that managing personal finance is similar to running a business. I notice that some people, particularly Mexicans, try to have large families, no matter what. It is obvious that large families require bigger houses to live in; we need more money to buy them, but many go for bigger houses, cars, TVs, etc, regardless; many do not seem to have a plan; as a result, some stay broke for life.

Science shows that 75% of all the animals on Earth are insects. Humans have been on Earth, for about six million years, from the common ancestors with chimpanzees. But many insects have been on Earth for over 300 million years: What is the common point of insects? I think that their sizes are small in general. They require less food and resources to survive. There are particularly dominating insects than others: ants, beetles, flies, bees, wasps, moths and butterflies; these are all small.

On the contrary, we all know that dinosaurs went extinct. One shared character was that they were generally large creatures. When I was in the Field Museum in Chicago, I found out that some of their body sizes were like houses. **I believe being too big was the reason for extinction**. Some dinosaurs are still alive after evolving into birds, I read that all the birds are from dinosaurs. We know the sizes of birds. Most are much smaller than humans.

I believe that we will see a lot of economic turbulence from now on. I know that some bought bigger stuff with debts (mortgages, car loans, credit card debt, etc). I remember that there is one Korean troll having all three of these loans (maybe more). It is up to us how we will live our lives. Personally, I am more than happy to have only one child and a small condo purchased in full.

* * *

There is a franchise mogul named Baek in Korea; he owns more than 20 franchise restaurants and hotels as of 2018; it was reported that his net worth is $830 M. He is also a media personality like Gordon Ramsey. There was a TV program called *Solutions by Baek;* struggling small restaurant owners visit him on the show and he suggests things to improve their businesses.

I remember one food truck guy visited Baek in 2017; his main menus were green pepper corn dogs and curry corn dogs. Certainly, the problem was that he couldn't sell many of these. Baek suggested mixing the sliced peppers in the dough before frying; also, he suggested using cumin powder instead of curry powder to give a stronger curry taste. Luckily, his suggestion was successful and the food truck owner Park worked even harder to make more money.

But here is one sad news, unfortunately. Park was actually 64 years old in 2017 and died from cancer in 2022. I remember that he was smiling and even crying after seeing a long line of customers waiting in front of his truck. *Still, if he knew he could be dead soon, he would not have tried so hard to make more dogs, even skipping his own meals*; he worked

9 hours straight a day. It shows that he worked until May, 2022 although he passed away in July, 2022. We have to see what we are doing since this kind of thing can happen to anyone. I am glad that I do not work for the nursing home anymore in a sense, especially when I have enough money; one sous chef made everyone miserable there. I am glad I gave up before things went too far; I am glad I walked away in 2022.

There was another guy named Lee in Korea; his nickname was "the King of part timers." He was a businessman originally, but wounded up getting a $350,000 debt from management failure in early 2000. **He was known to work *seven part time* jobs a day to pay off his debt for eight years**; he said that he *often slept only two hours* a day due to multiple jobs. TV showed his unbelievable daily routines in detail; it also showed the last moment when he paid off the final portion of debt in tears and became debt free at last in 2008; he became a national star in Korea, after all.

Again, here is the sorrowful news. **He suffered from colon cancer since 2012 and finally passed away in 2014**; he was only 54 years old; this was only six years after he paid off his big debt. *Doctors said colon cancer has a strong relationship with lack of sleep in general.* This story gave me a lot of things to think about then. I guess that he could have filed bankruptcy; I know there must be some disadvantages for that, but he wouldn't have to work that much cruelly if he knew that he would die too early. I feel that these two just worked to the extreme until the last and expired.

* * *

I think that the most dangerous moment in our lives is when we accomplish a small success; it is possible that it can bring us a failure. Oddly, I don't think small failures bring us bigger defeats; often we stop and don't do anything after that. Arrogance caused by little successes can bring us serious collapses.

I already told you that I made +$20,000 profit after selling all my PBI stock shares in 2021. Originally, I had 6,500 shares of PBI stock at the average purchase of $10.40; these were all sold out at $13.45. Price had spiked up only for a couple of days in January, 2021.

Now PBI stock is back to $3.50 in June, 2023. I had the urge to break my $60,000 CD from the bank and put the money in PBI stock again, but decided not to. First, I can lose $900 for the early withdrawal fee for the CD. Second, I think it's risky to put any money in there again. I can lose a new $60,000 only because I made +$20,000 profit from it before. Thirdly, the CD itself gives me 3.1% interest, which I do not want to lose. Still, I believe PBI does essential things for shipping industries; I decided to buy 5% bonds from the company.

* * *

I did not intend to make *UnBrokable** a long series in the beginning. But I noticed that a lot of top sellers on Amazon are over 500 pages. My draft has gotten over 400 pages already after writing only for four months in 2022. Suddenly, I decided to make the final book close to 700 pages.

To sell a book, I believe that it should be a little different from other books. There are 4 millions of new books published every year, but I found out that 90% of them are under 400 pages. I learned that there is a big population preferring thick books; many individual books from the Harry Potter, Outlander or Game of Thrones series are over 700 pages. Since I have written a good amount already and still have many things to point out, I thought that I might just go for a super thick one. Anyone can write a thin book; **I have to do something most others cannot**.

On top of it, this is what most do not know: the cost to publish a thick book is not that much higher than that of a thin one. I would say that I pay about $1 more for an additional 100 pages, but we can charge more for that, too. And this is the same, regardless of the page sizes; some books are *small, but thick* and some books are *large, but thick*; these cost exactly the same in Amazon KDP printing. I decided to choose a font size 12pt for now, which is the largest for a regular print; some people cannot read small fonts well. And I decided to go for a *large, but thick* book since it does not cost me more. In this case, I guess going bigger works out fine.

* * *

Some people end up failing after they go too far or big; this is happening in businesses, too. The price of Amazon stock dropped significantly a few times last year; they splitted the share 20 : 1 in June, 2022, but it did not help. Did the company work hard? Yes. Has it been helpful to customers? Of course; this online retailer has been supportive, especially for people not owning a car.

I strongly believe the loss is from overextending their businesses to supermarkets: Whole Foods and Amazon Fresh; I read on the news that they actually shut down several Whole Foods locations last year. They should have focused on book sales, publishings or other IT related fields. They did not have to get into all the traditional businesses, which has been mundane and competitive. Supermarkets seem to have too much real work with low profit to me. Besides, anyone can do it, so Amazon should have focused more on some cloud or other ITs no one can imitate quickly.

* * *

Summary

1. Being small increases the chance of survival.
2. Good things now may not be good later.
3. It is important not to increase size or spending only after tiny successes.

72

Not Being Awake

Sometimes, we are the biggest enemies to ourselves.
-Brad Kong

I decided *not* to interrupt my daughter's life forever; she is 13 years old now in 2023. Originally, I hoped that she would live peacefully without getting married. Personally, my parents had not been in harmony and ended up in divorce. I met my wife 24 years ago when I was 26 in 1999; occasionally, I wish I would have had more freedom; not everything has been great. Population is growing super fast now, so I thought that my daughter has more reasons not to get married.

During the time I worked at the nursing home for 7 years, I had a hard time every now and then since many women addressed me while I was focusing on my jobs (the facility had over 1,000 employees). Most of these were coworkers, but some of them were patients or residents, too. I noticed that the biggest pains came from old but unmarried ladies; I realized that they approached me the most aggressively. I still remember one fat Filipina in her 40s, who was a dietary care worker. I had been annoyed repeatedly since she always came onto me while I worked, but eventually she ended up quitting her job. I noticed that most of those approachers knew how to stop on their own at some point if they are married or have a child. It seems they acted a little easier since they got what they wanted (child) already in a biological sense; there is less need to bother another man to get more children. But those old unmarried women seemed to act more desperate; often it is the last chance for them to meet a man and get pregnant; they are less likely to stop annoying other men.

The only problem is that my daughter can be in that situation, too. I honestly hope that she can live relaxed for good. Technically, I believe that there is no reason for anyone to date anyone any more; the population is bursting. **But human instincts won't fade away, all at once.** I just do not want her to be in the Filipina's situation because of my encouragement. If she wounds up being like that, that's perfectly fine with me. I just do not want to provide her direct reasons.

* * *

Once in a while, I see exceptionally attractive women, too. But the feeling of being attached to her goes away relatively easily. It's not because I am a morally right or self controlling person; it's because I have a wife and daughter already. **While I am not 100% happy with them, I fulfilled my obligation in the DNA survival sense**; I finished my homework from nature to send my DNA to the next generation; psychologically, it gives animals more comfort.

I believe that this could be a mind boggling problem, especially for women than men; they have a shorter time left to get pregnant during their lives. I do not want my daughter to suffer because of inspiration from me, though: *It's perfectly fine if she lives as a single for life and enjoys my inheritance.* From a perspective, it can benefit everyone the most, including herself, on Earth. Regardless, I made up my mind to leave her alone for whatever she does.

Initially, I got an inspiration for this decision from a posting on a Korean woman's site. One single lady in her 40s wrote that she ended up being in love with an auto salesman in his 20s after she bought a luxury car from him. She asked how she can form a closer relationship with him: "Can I ask him for driving lessons and pay extra money?" Hundreds of other ladies replied to her, "Are you crazy?" or "Don't be an ugly customer," etc. Personally, I felt sorry for her since I have been in similar situations before; in fact, we all have been in those moments. **Only difference is that she was single, so I guess that it must have been harder for her.** In those cases, I assume that people having their own families suffer less; they *instinctively* know that they are done with the biological obligation. I thought about my daughter and decided not to affect her; she is more than welcome to live as a single for life, though.

* * *

What type of people would get deceived by frauds the most? Stupid or greedy people in my opinion. **I think that con artists use gluttony in people to defraud them**; people do not even see easy deception once they get blinded by their own desires. For example, even a child can know that paying a house double the amount is a loss; often people accept mortgages once they get obsessed with some houses; people buy pointless stocks when they believe it's a chance to make easy money. Not being avaricious is one way to protect ourselves; not being gluttony will make us safer.

Also, I think that not being acquisitive can make us stronger. People usually value something not easily acquirable; when we do not move easily by money, others will respect us; we can actually gain more power that way. People who can control their rapacity can handle everything; they will be the ultimate winners. It is a key to know that there is a limited amount of money we can spend during our lifetimes;

there is no point to working longer for more money endlessly: **"A little more" can eventually kill us.**

Personally, I had not recognized that I have so much *desire* to write. It has been with me all along; it was why I had problems with so many internet trolls; I had written too many articles for free. **I had not been awake to realize that I could use my gift in a better way**; finally, I decided to write a book.

* * *

We do not usually meet criminals all the time unless we live in a slum or prison. If we get paid $60,000 a year and live in an apartment in the Midwest suburbs, probably we will live peacefully until we die. *Yet here is one way we can run into criminals frequently:* Buying a Ferrari with savings. We may have to meet all sorts of low lives: car thieves, gold diggers, beggars, door-to-door salesmen, etc. It would be even more ridiculous if we buy that car with a loan; people actually do that along with living in upscale houses with mortgages: I am sure that they will meet more offenders than me; delinquents will never leave rich people alone (fake riches in this case).

There is a legend called *Pied Piper of Hamelin* in Germany; a lot of mice were hallucinated by his music, and fell into a river and died; a lot of children followed him while he was playing flute and disappeared for good, too. **Some people just follow the music of trends and crash their lives that way.** They may live harmoniously without making many conflicts; they may agree with everyone and follow the most dominant opinions. But this can lead to poverty. Not being awake or having our own opinions is extremely bad particularly in investment. Let me give you an actual example.

* * *

There is a Korean community website called "Missy USA." It is big, but, strangely, only women can write on this site; it is notorious for being occlusive. I have no idea how they have wound up having so many members, but no one can join it any more. And it has a stock subsection; whenever I see it, **I can see how keeping opinions in a confined place is dangerous**; many women follow the major trend there blindly.

In 2020, out of the blue, Inovio Pharmaceuticals stock got popular there (ticker: INO). Have you heard of that company? Probably not; I have not, either. I do have stocks and bonds of 120 companies as of 2023, and have bought and sold 450 companies so far. Still, I would have not known there was such a stock unless they mentioned it crazily. Apparently, there are two reasons why it got extreme popularity there:

1. The CEO of the company is Korean.
2. This company may be able to make COVID vaccine successfully (which they didn't).

Then, I sold out PBI stocks with +$20,000 profit and got $90,000 cash totally in hand by January, 2021; I put a large chunk of it in Pfizer stocks. By 2021, Pfizer already launched COVID vaccine; I was impressed by the shot I got; I had pain for a couple of days and it was gone perfectly. Since Pfizer stock gives out good dividends and the company makes plenty of other drugs as well, I thought it was a safe investment. I would say it has been fine so far with quarterly dividends.

When I saw INO was extremely popular on that site, I wanted to write that it is too risky: **Having a Korean CEO is not a reason for investing.** The company is small, and the stock has no dividend; the possibility they can successfully release a vaccine was slim. Even if they do, there were vaccines from Pfizer, Moderna and J&J already in 2021. Besides, the company does not make any other drug and, in fact, never has even attempted doing so. The stock was over $20 in January, 2021; I read that some women invested $50,000; it is only $0.58 a share in June, 2023.

No one talks about INO any more there. But if I dig, I am sure I can find plenty of bankruptcy stories there. *I notice that women go for the general trends, dominant opinions or popularity blindly more.* This happens everywhere and I believe that it is particularly bad in investment. Now they talk about Coins there, which is another bubble from my point. In general, I know that women do not like anything risky and Korean women are more conservative about it. I have no idea where these female gamblers come from.

Some automatically assume that opinions from the majority of people are right. In my opinion, this can be true probably only in half of all cases. Trump was elected with the majority of votes: Was he the right choice for America? Or are you happy with all the presidents elected? I do not drink or own a car; most people drink beers or own cars. Are they right and am I wrong? I think I am right to drink no alcohol and walk more without driving. Now the gas is close to $5 a gallon everywhere in 2022. I cannot spend $5 only to move around all the time. Who knows how much oil is left on Earth, anyway?

* * *

Summary

1. Never do what others do blindly.
2. It's especially bad in investment.
3. "A little more" can kill us.

73

Too Fantasizing Wealth

If we are not excellent,
we need to be patient, at least.
-Brad Kong

Portillo's Hot Dog is an American fast food chain founded by Dick Portillo in Villa Park, IL in 1963; it had 67 locations by 2022. I would say that this place virtually invented the Chicago-style hot dog, which comes with diverse vegetables. And I believe the net worth of Mr. Portillo is over $ 1 billion since it was the amount of cash he received after selling 50 locations to Berkshire Partners in 2014. I still remember his interview with PBS a couple of decades ago: "A lot of people ask me about our secret to success. **There is no secret.** It just tastes good."

I believe that the same thing goes for our wealths. There is no secret to getting rich quickly: **The only way is to make more money and spend less;** this may sound simple, but it is the only way. A lot of people lease a luxury car as soon as they start getting paid from salaries; they believe that steady incomes will come forever. Being in a fantasy which is not based on ground is one way to get broke.

* * *

In my opinion, there are two types of rich people in the world: **Bill Gates type** and **Warren Buffett type.** The Forbes magazine shows that the net worth of Gates is $122 Billions and that of Buffet is $100 Billions in 2022. These meet regularly and have a close relationship in donation as well, so people may mistakenly think they are similar: Wrong! The ways to build their wealths have been completely different.

And here is my shocking conclusion and possibly good news for you: **No one can be like the Gates, but everyone can be a Buffett.** Realistically, I think only 0.1% of Americans can be another Gates, but 70% of people can be like Buffett: Why? If we cannot be excellent, I think we need to be persistent, at least. If we are neither, we will never be rich.

Bill Gates marketed the operating system of all the personal computers in the world when he was young: Very revolutionary back then. He founded Microsoft and has been CEO all along. What is the possibility we can do the same thing now? 0%. Or maybe 0.1%? Let's be honest. Not many people will do this kind of thing during our lifetimes.

On the contrary, I believe that almost everyone or about 70% of the population can be like Buffett if he or she tries. I am not saying that we will be a billionaire. But I think we can be a millionaire at least and live far above the poverty line only to benchmark him. Here are three things we can learn from this billionaire.

First of all, Buffett bought his house with “full cash” in 1958. Wiki shows that he purchased the five-bedroom house in Omaha, Nebraska for $31,500. In my opinion, this could be the key foundation of his wealth; he still lives in the same house as of 2023, and the house is worth $900,000 now after living over sixty years. I can see similar examples and some people get richer only because they bought houses in full a long time ago and lived there without moving out.

There is one English maxim: “A rolling stone never gathers moss.” Google translates it as “A person who does not settle in one place never accumulates wealth.” I think this applies exactly to housing issues. Since mortgage interests are high over the course of thirty years, it is important to buy a small, but decent house in full. People buy luxury or big houses with mortgages these days and I believe that it is the starting point of doomsday. Policyadvice.net shows that “**Nearly 40% of American homes are completely mortgage-free.**” I think it is possible for many people to buy a small condo with full cash. If you are serious about becoming a millionaire, I think this is a seriously important first step.

Secondly, Buffett has been a long term investor for life. Probably, he is one of the *longest* since he is 92 years old now in 2023. We cannot build a company like Microsoft, suddenly. **But we can buy stocks and hold them for forty years as Buffett has, can't we?** This is why I am saying that 70% of folks can be rich in Buffett’s way. If you are not sure which stock you choose, just choose a high dividend ETF including S&P 500 companies. Dividend compounding will seriously help us in the long run. Or we can choose the biggest company in a specific field; we can choose Chase in banking or Exxon in oil, both of which give us dividends. A lot of people just buy and sell stocks immediately these days. *If we are not excellent, we need to be patient, at least.* Thirdly, we have to notice that Buffett has been extremely frugal for life.

If we can make these three characters our own, I am pretty sure we will wound up being millionaires one way or another. No need to live in a van in cold temperature as in the book “Nomadland” and argue about “we are not homeless, but only houseless” crap; unfortunately, these are virtually all homeless to me in a sense. I am sure at least 70% of Americans will be moneyed only to follow Buffett’s lifestyle.

* * *

A girl some men are interested in now may not be a fantastic woman as they presume. With 99% chance, she is probably a farting normal girl anyone can find anywhere anytime: Then, what's happening in men's brains? I think human brains just evolved that way, so we can keep producing offspring; **it is merely an extinction prevention mechanism.** There are only two problems with it, though: One is that there are too many humans on Earth already and the population is still growing super fast. The other is that this unnecessary fantasy can make us go broke.

Do you know why *remarried* couples divorce more? Statistics show that 50% percent of first-time marriages and 67% of second marriages end in divorce in America; the divorce rate of third marriages is 74%, which is even higher. This is my theory for this.

When a second marriage is about to happen, men tend to think that everything about his current wife is bad and everything about his new wife will be good; men are stupid. There is no woman who is much better than another; **every girl has ups and downs on her own.** The main difference is that his previous wife showed him everything, but he does not know anything about new wife yet. Surely, there could be some character discrepancies between you and your partner; for example, I like to be in a quiet environment, but some women blast music all the time. It is imprudent if someone does not even check these kinds of things before marriage. Except for personal preferences, all the women are similar in terms of advantages and flaws to some extent.

Still, getting married the second time means a man has to spend extra money and go through tons of hassles again: new wedding ceremony, new honeymoon, new relationships with in-laws, possibly more babies, etc; a mountainous amount of new bills and debt may come. **Subconsciously, he *expects* more from his second wife**: Why? Otherwise, he did not have to go through all those hassles again, including divorcing his first wife. Chances are the second wife will not be way better than the first; sometimes, she could be actually worse. In the case of his first wife, he did not have anyone to compare precisely. For his second wife, he will always compare her with the first one: If she is better than the first, it is barely even to a man; he spent all that money for this; if she is the same as or worse, it will be a loss to him. The unrealistic *fantasy* of "a much better woman for a better life" can damage him financially.

I took marriages as instances, but the same goes for jobs, too. **There could be a better *paying* job, but there is not really a better job**. Chances are we won't have enjoyable work anywhere; if there is one, it will not be available to the public; the owner families of corporations already took it. Besides, higher paying jobs are often available in expensive areas, so people end up not saving much. In the case of travels, there is no really more fantastic destination than where we are now (unless you live in a prison or refugee camp). In a sense, even Mars is not very different from Earth.

* * *

It is important not to fantasize about wealth. Buying a house with cash means having no debt. Consequently, I strongly suggest that there are only three rudimentary stepping stones to becoming rich: **No debt, long term investment and frugality**. If you can become like Bill Gates, I won't stop you, so please go ahead. Chances will be slim though in my opinion. People who fantasize too much tend to gamble or fall into quick rich schemes.

Again, this type of fantasy applies to relationships, too. Some men, usually the stupids, daydream about women too much. They usually get deceived, dumped or divorced, or lose money somehow. The more we hallucinate, the poorer we become: This will be true in everything.

* * *

Summary

1. If we cannot be a Gates, we can try to be a Buffett, at least; these two have similar net worths, anyway.
2. If we are not excellent, we need to be patient.
3. No debt, long term investment and frugality.

74

No Long Term Vision

YOLO can be *a short term vision;*
some people die because of it.
-Brad Kong

Isabella I was the Queen of Spain in the 15th century. History tells that she had to sell a lot of her jewelry and even her crown to finance Christopher Columbus's voyage in 1492. **The voyage was not profitable in the beginning**; the Bahama Islands in the Caribbean, where Columbus arrived at, did not really have gold. It shows that the selfish bastard pushed and killed many natives to squeeze some profits out of the expedition, but it never worked out until he died.

But, eventually, Spain had made huge fortunes out of sugar and silver imports from the new continent; it ultimately had made the country powerful and wealthy; they were able to build the famous Spanish Armadas[54] later on. Subsequently, Spain dominated the oceans during the Age of Discovery. The queen's investment must have been a loss in the beginning, but the mission has ended up benefiting the country all the way up until even now.

James Clear suggested that **if we can improve 0.1% a day, we can be 37% better every year** in his book *Atomic Habits*. He took air travel as an example: Let's

---

[54] Navy

imagine there is an airplane traveling from NYC to LA; if the plane changes its angle only 3 degrees down to south, it will arrive in Tijuana, Mexico, which is 140 miles south from L.A. Little things are not little; it accumulates 140 mile difference out of only a five-hour flight. We have to see what changes our actions can make in the future; poor people often fail to recognize this.

* * *

Have you ever felt insecurity or nervousness before? Bottomless restlessness is getting common nowadays. One Korean Buddhist monk[55] suggested that keeping a hard physical job for at least three years (without quitting) would help cure this symptom: **Continuing something despite difficulties helps mental stability.** I agree with him and it seems we can make money as well instead of wasting money on psychiatric therapies this way.

I believe keeping long relationships with people helps in the same sense. For example, I met my wife in 1999 and it's 2023 now; having old friends should give us similar comfort; probably, living in the same house for long would do the same. **When we have a long term relationship with anything (e.g., a pet, career or hobby), we generally feel more relieved.** People tend to feel comfortable when they visit their hometowns. Having a long term relationship or vision should bring us more profits. But, at the same time, I believe that it bring more mental stability along the way.

* * *

---

[55] Pomnyun

Most authors cannot write their books in a series; one reason is that they do not see things in the *long* term. If they plan to publish their books in a series from the start and write books that way, most can make way more money; readers can buy more in a franchise if they like one of them. I think that one example would be the *Fifty Shades of Grey* series; this lady has written seven books by 2022, but never written a book other than in this series. Imagine all these books have independent titles like this: *Fifty Shades of Grey, Mister, A Rich Woman's Life*, etc. **I am sure these books could have sold 10 times less in total.** Instead, she made all the titles somewhat similar to each other to make them all in a series: *Fifty Shades of Grey, Fifty Shades Darker, Fifty Shades Freed,* etc. I saw that all the books were exactly the same size, similar thickness and colors, so I believe she must have planned it long ago.

Alternatively, I think it's important to find what we like (or are obsessed with), and stick to it. There is a book series *The Hotel Nantucket* written by Hilderbrand; those books were relatively thin, but ranked high in Amazon sales in 2022. I thought it's unusual, but what I found was that this lady has focused on romances in the Nantucket beach area for the last 23 years (32 books). I do not know what's so great about the beach hotel in the tourism area, but it doesn't matter. It seems she found what she truly loves and made $ millions out of it.

* * *

Did you know that Nikola Tesla died penniless in a small hotel room in NYC in 1943? Many admit that this Serbian guy was the greatest inventor in human history. But it shows that he had been robbed of virtually all his credits and patents from research by other scientists like

Edison or Marconi. He had never even got married: no scientific credit, award, wife, child, money or even a house; he only worked, worked and worked up to 18 hours a day like a slave.

I think that it is our minimum obligation to protect ourselves first; that's the only way, so we can help others, furthermore. It says that Tesla had been alone in America for life as an immigrant. Regardless, if we never protect ourselves properly, no one will do that for us. Little things are not little; little incomes are not little. **When people let others keep taking their profits, even the world's greatest genius can pass away as a homeless person.**

* * *

Bhumibol Adulyadej was the *longest* reigned emperor in Thailand history; he was the father of the current king in 2023 and had governed the country for 70 years (1946 - 2016); this term is longer than Queen Elizabeth II of the UK. Nonetheless, I found one unique thing about this Thai King: This Siam emperor had only one wife even though the country allows multiple; his son has had four wives, for example. Most people do not realize how unusual this is, so let me explain.

I consider myself a person not very interested in women; still I see an extraordinarily pretty woman once in a while; I think this is similar for other guys, including the emperor. Nothing really happens to me since I am not a very handsome or rich guy; most importantly, Korean or American culture does not recommend that I see other women; people will blame me if I do; actually, it had been against law in Korea even until the 1990s. But the emperor has everything including the legal system supporting him to do so without any objection. Yet he did not have more than one wife and I analyzed a couple of reasons why.

First of all, it is possible that he is actually an hardcore Buddhist monk beyond all human desires; 98% of Thais believe in Buddhism and they expect their king would be a sort of Buddha. Secondly, it is probable that he decided to sacrifice himself for his country. He knew that having more women causes unnecessary jealousy and chaos. To keep the country united and organized, he knew that he should not make any enemies. I think I can sacrifice if I am an emperor, too. Still, this is unusual if you know old Asian histories; there had been so many kings murdered or executed and there were always women behind those messes. I have never been to Thailand, but I would say that the king is very wise; this could be the reason why the country is more developed than other southeast Asian neighbors.

There are people spending money as soon as they get some; unfortunately, this includes a huge amount of Thai people; they live notoriously more lavishly than Japanese or Koreans. And I believe the reason is that Thailand does not have any cold winters.

* * *

To me, the best way to get rid of cash is putting it in savings: preferably, in my stock and bond portfolio rather than the actual savings account. Maybe it is *not really removing*; getting dividends from stocks, and interests from bonds and CDs are the best for me now. I assume that there will still be plenty of chances to spend money for the rest of my life. I got close to $24,000 dividends and interests a year, as of 2022; I don't see that there is a need to rush spending money. I will spend little by little whenever it's necessary.

Poor people tend not to have long term vision; some go for instant satisfactions; this causes chronic brokenness. For example, my wife just came back from the mall and brought those caramel popcorn and Stan's doughnuts again. She couldn't control herself despite losing two teeth. Honestly, she is not really close to being financially wealthy. Do you know who else goes for instant satisfaction? **Drug addicts.**

Some people invest money for quick results. Poor people buy and sell stocks usually for quick capital gains. Ironically, their predictions in stock markets are mostly wrong. Some people buy a house with a mortgage only because they can afford monthly payments. They do not see the total amount of money they spent for 30 years can be twice more than that of cash buyers.

* * *

Summary

1. Long term plans do not always bring instant profits.
2. Poor people tend to focus on short-term gains.
3. Drug addicts look for quick satisfactions.

75

Being Deceptive

Some choose to be poor.
-Brad Kong

Kimbap (gimbop) is a Korean dish made of steamed rice and vegetable ingredients rolled in *gim* which is dried sheets of seaweed; the similar food is Japanese *maki rolls.* South Korea has millions of *gimbap* houses as it is a popular lunch menu; most of these restaurants are struggling to make ends meet, especially after COVID came in 2020.

I saw on the news that a Korean man in his 50s was arrested since he ordered 40 rolls of *gimbap* to take out in many places and disappeared without payment. This dismal loser wickedly planned this; he ate in a restaurant first, praised that it's so tasty and ordered 40 rolls to pick up on the next day; surely, he didn't come back. **No one gets benefit out of this type of prank**. I understand that it's the owners' fault not to ask for any deposit or full payment in advance; some Koreans think it's rude to ask for money too early; probably, some were afraid that he would be offended and cancel the order. *No one takes advantage of anyone here*; he only damaged 20 restaurant owners financially.

This is what I wrote upfront in the prologue: *Dying poor is not all about money; it shows how we have lived.* Would that prankster be poor or rich? According to my experience, rich people don't really waste time on something unbeneficial; they focus on profits more. They tend not to commit petty crimes since, if they get caught, riches get more damages than the poor for higher lawyer fees, bail money, etc. I observed that the poor waste more on pranks. At the same time, people not focusing on profits tend to be broke, too. Regardless, I don't think that the poor benefit society, financially; being wasteful can be a solid reason some get poor in wealthy countries.

On the contrary, I can say that riches benefit societies more, while they do not even intend to. I do not like Trump well, but see how many people he hires or how much property taxes he pays for all the houses, condos or hotels every year? It is possible that broke people bother others more.

* * *

What goes around comes around: Did you know that Caesar was the person who promoted chariot race, wild beast hunt and gladiator fights staged in the Colosseum in Rome in 70 B.C.? He eventually got stabbed to death at 55. This could be fair after being cruel on others for decades.

People know that being duped can make us poor. But did you know that being fraudulent makes us poor, too? Other people are not fools; they can notice bad intentions from someone else. **There are people losing credentials or**

known for taking advantages; they never really make any money, according to my experience.

The point often missed is that we can be deceived because of ourselves: Our greed can be the one putting us in jeopardy. Cleopatra VII used two Roman generals to take over the political power of Egypt solely for herself instead of sharing it with siblings; she used Caesar and Antonius. Her plan did not worked out smoothly; she wounded up committing suicide at the age of 39 in Egypt in 30 B.C.

* * *

In my opinion, there are advantages for wives to have a stingy husband; he will be less likely to meet another woman; women never like a stingy guy in general. Also, he will save money continuously since men tend to be obsessed with it; some do not think cash is a tool to buy things; they think it is a barometer showing their power or amount of achievement they have accomplished for life. When men meet another woman, they spend more in general; some men even upgrade their automobiles to show off. While they do those, they generally give more money to wives as well. There are always ups and downs for everything; women like a rich, handsome and generous guy; wise girls know it and some avoid a perfect man intentionally.

"The opposite of truth is oblivion in Greek," one Korean professor said; oblivion means being forgotten forever; this means people only remember the truth. If we start lying, we won't remember what we said. **I think that a couple of common deceptions these days are social media and plastic surgeries.** I was passing by a small village in Chicagoland the other day and checked out its downtown. I found a $9.95 lunch special at a Thai restaurant, so I decided to try. But I was shocked that the waitress was impressively pretty; in general, I have a high *standard* for women (*out of nowhere*). The restaurant was humble; we don't get shocked by a diamond in a jewelry store; we may do, if we find it on a table at McDonalds. She looked like she had cosmetic surgeries. But I thought that was not possible; she could be a daughter of her parents' tacky restaurant. I thought that people working there would not get plastic surgeries.

After coming home, out of curiosity, I checked the restaurant on Facebook and all the family accounts came out as well. **I would say that these people seemed to live in lies**: Vegas trip, Disney world 50th anniversary, Ice Castle hotel, Mt. Rushmore and other upscale places I could not recognize; I didn't understand where all the money came from. And it was a mistake for the waitress to post all her photos since young. She looked like a typical mundane Asian originally, but has changed to look European, lately; I know this does not happen naturally.

None of the family accounts were directly connected to the restaurant business: What a waste of postings. I thought I would help the place after eating since I had a hard time myself when I owned Cyb Knight; they kept posting unnecessarily lavish lifestyle photos; all the FB friends seemed to live in Thailand, so I guess that these are the ones who they want to show off to. This is the second time I felt Thai people frequently do this; I suddenly didn't feel like helping the business; the food was barely average, anyway. I realized that social media can remove good images about people and plant bad emotions against them; boys can walk away after seeing girls' old ugly pictures or luxurious spendings, which will cost future husbands a ton of money.

* * *

There used to be a Chinese restaurant near the library in our town; it used to have special lunch menus for $8.25 in 2018. I had been there probably over 150 times while I had studied for the Medical Coder exam. I ordered all sorts of menus, but my favorite menu was Mongolian shrimps: steamed rice, one egg roll, Mongolian shrimp and one bottle of water for $7; I thought that that is too little, so I always ordered one extra bottle of water to make the total $8.25.

Sometimes, I ordered Mango smoothies as well when I had enough money; in that case, the total was about $11. I learned that the lady owner did not bring me the water included in the menu whenever I ordered the smoothies. Stupidly, I did not catch it at that time. The place closed out in 2020; I found out that she was not completely honest with me years later. Maybe she forgot, but I experienced that there are a lot of Chinese places that intentionally do not include egg rolls from lunch specials; I guess that many of these do not stay in business for long. *People might get deceived temporarily, but realize the truth eventually.* I believe being deceptive is one way to make ourselves poor.

* * *

I found a book titled *Cheatinglands* by "Anonymous" at the library the other day. It has some statistics about cheaters in married life in America. Obviously, divorces cost a lot; it is a major reason for bankruptcy these days. It is true that humans have been on Earth over 6 million years; they started from the common ancestors with apes. But agriculture started only 10,000 years ago; it has developed gatherings, communities and societies ever since. Marriage does not exist in wild animals and they include humans as well until recently. *I believe that the concept of marriage might have developed along with agriculture.* Probably, humans have lived freely for most of six million years like other animals:

none has the concept of restricted relationship. As we have lived in groups, people found some efficient ways to produce and grow new members without conflicts in society.

Maybe we can blame cheaters in a marriage sense. But we have to admit that it is not natural if we expect that a man or woman cannot meet others for life mandatorily in a free world; at least, it has never happened for the last 6 million years. I am not defending cheaters, but it is a key to understanding human instincts to solve dilemmas. Imagine a person who cannot move out of a room for life; it is not natural for an animal with legs. Marriage can be a social prison in modern society; it is the ideal way to assign one partner to one person to avoid fights in a crammed society (it has been crowded only after agriculture); I agree that it is fair. Still, it has nothing to do with or even goes against animal instincts.

I read that particularly women get upset after realizing they were cheated on. These are my recommendations for ladies on how to find honest husbands if that is the top priority. First of all, see if the man you are interested in has less stamina physically; there are men not interested in meeting new women by nature. Some girls choose inferior men with the hope that they can focus only on their wives: *Wrong!* Stupid, ugly men cheat on their wives, too. But there are men less interested in being social, genuinely; just like some eat less foods for life, they were born with less sexual desire; they tend not to have a huge amount of steroid hormones as well. We cannot expect a guy with a lot of muscles and stamina to see only his wife by marriage vows; these guys are athletes, sometimes; they tend to go to the gym everyday or ride muscle cars. There are noticeable signs that some men have more testosterone. Just avoid them to begin with.

Secondly, choose a guy who does not drink or smoke. This helps financially; at the same time, he won't go to bars where men can meet new women, occasionally. Thirdly, choose a guy who doesn't like to be gregarious; he will have less chances to meet women in reality, too. Fourthly, try to meet an early riser; they do not hang out much with others at night. Fifthly, try to meet a little stingy guy. Meeting a woman always costs money. There are people who prefer keeping money to meeting others; they do not like to spend money. These may not be ideal husbands for housewives not making any money, but less likely they will cheat on their partners as well.

Sixthly, try to choose a guy not extremely popular among women. If many women keep approaching him, the chance of cheating will go up exponentially. Honestly, most men do not cheat on their wives not because they are honest, but because they do not get chances to do so. Seventhly, see if your future husband is old enough. According to my experience, sexual desire drops dramatically after 45. If your partner is young, there are more chances that he will meet other women simply because he has more hormones to release. Eightly, see if you can find a guy who is into religion. They tend not to go into any type of trouble. It is possible that they already know that there is no point to desires.

Ninthly, I think it is important to change your view as well if you are a wife. Most men are not necessarily in love with the women they have sex; some do not even meet the same women twice. Remember one thing: While your man is attractive and has high sexual desire, if you want to keep him only to yourself, I think you are on an impossible mission; you go strongly against animal instincts; you are challenging the nature.

On the men's side, this is my suggestion. Think about this: What is really a sexual desire? It is merely a sort of emotion needed to produce a baby; it was created only for that reason. Having too much of it without making an offspring is just a waste. Some think there is something great or mysterious about sex: There is not. When we think logically or get rid of useless fantasies, we can see the truth and avoid troubles. We won't be broke, at least, as a result; flirting continuously is a waste, after all. It shows that cheaters tend to be obsessed with their mobile phones. See if your partner sticks to his or her smart phone all the time. Regardless, that is not a good sign in any sense.

* * *

Summary

1. Poor people waste more on pranks.
2. Being deceptive can make us broke.
3. Disputing being chaste in marriage may not have a huge point as much as we think.

76

Being On the Wrong Side

Some people make money automatically
only because they are on the right side.
-Brad Kong

In the financial world, I think people are divided into two groups: those who get interest or pay interest. If we are on the side paying interests, we are on the wrong side; more likely we will be poor in the future. **Regardless of how much we have now, we can get wealthy if we choose the right side**: The side where people get interest.

Money is not a fixed thing; it has been always moving around. *So which direction we are going is more important than how much we have now.* We have to make sure that the train we are on is to the right destination. It is pointless working hard while being on the wrong train to poverty; millions of people literally work to death and die poor. **In my opinion, many of those stood in the wrong line to buy doomed tickets from the start.**

* * *

Let's suppose that there are two people possessing $200,000 each: A and B; they have the same incomes, too. Person A bought a $100,000 condo and saved the other $100,000 in a CD in the bank. Now the bank will give him monthly interest, so **A is on the side *getting interest.***

Meanwhile, let's say that B decided to buy a $300,000 house. Now all of his $200,000 is gone for the home. On top of that, B has to borrow $100,000 from a bank in the name of a mortgage (it is not his residence until he pays it off to the bank). As a result, he has $0 in his bank account as of now. Besides, he has to *pay monthly interest* to the bank where he owes his mortgage to. **B is on the side *paying interest.*** Bank interest is 5% and mortgage interest is 7% in 2023, so here is their finances.

A: getting +$6,000 a year as the CD interest
B: losing -$7,000 a year as the mortgage interest

We can see that A is gaining +$13,000 more profit than B every year; it means that **A will keep +$390,000 more than B over the course of 30 years of the mortgage.** But this is not all.

Since B bought a three times more expensive house, he will spend more money on property tax, maintenance, insurance, utility, etc. Let's say that B loses $10,000 more than A for those every year; it means A will keep +$300,000 more than B during the 30 years. **Totally, A can have +$690,000 more profit than B**, but these are still not all.

* * *

Let's say that A starts investing those bank interests in the stock market for the next 30 years. His interests (+$6,000 a year) for 30 years would be $180,000 by itself. Depending on where he put this, it can be easily $1,000,000 after 30 years. **Now A will have totally $1,690,000 more profit than B.** It is possible that B is a hard worker; he just waited in the wrong line to take a train. He made a lifetime mistake, and it will cause chain reactions to financial disaster.

I just used the term "interest" to simplify things. But there are people always getting something (out of assets) while others are paying. This "interest" could be stock dividend, bond interest, rental income, royalty, etc. If we do not pay anything at least, that is better. Nowadays, people get debt too easily; some mistakenly think that getting it is a sort of qualification by a bank: No, it is not. **While most qualifications come with any type of benefit, the only thing we get by bank qualification is paying more money.** People often pay their houses double the price with 30-year mortgages than cash buyers.

* * *

I was stupid when I was in the Korean Army; I started my mandatory service of 26 months in November, 1994. At that time, Korean soldiers were getting paid about $10 a month; it shows that they get paid over $1,000 a month now in 2023. South Korea was not extremely wealthy back then. While the Army provided everything we needed (i.e., housing, clothes, rifles, other equipment, etc), they didn't give us much wages. Basically, it was free services from young boys for the country.

My particular position was ammunition counting in the military. Magazines are storage building units for explosives and I believe we had about 150 of those in our battalion. My job was to count the exact number of ammunition. It was a relatively easy job since the inventories had hardly changed. They had never used the majority of bombs since there has been no war between Koreas since the 1950s. We only had to make sure the numbers were the same, though.

Before I took the job, two people, who were a public official and a soldier, did the counting job together. I remember they said it had been like that for decades before I came. But I was reliable and did the job well, so they decided to give the entire job only to me. I believe the military official was laid off for budget reasons in the middle. When I did the job on my own, I was very proud in the beginning; I did two people's jobs even though I was merely a low ranked soldier. I showed that off to fellow soldiers and they envied me, too. But when I think about it now, I was plainly idiotic: **I was getting paid the same, but I was working more for two people.**

* * *

John D. Rockefeller Sr. (1839 – 1937) was an American business magnate, who has been the richest human ever to exist on Earth, according to *Outliers* by Gladwell. It shows that he tried to dominate the oil industry in the 1860s. Strangely, what he did first was buying up railroad companies; all the oils were distributed on the railways, then. Whenever a small oil company refused to be sold to Rockefeller's Standard Oil, he didn't let it use railroads or raise the transportation fees. I think it was a mean, but clever way to control everything without having direct conflicts.

I believe lots of people spend money the wrong way these days. I think the first thing we need to do is stop working or work less if we get enough money in our hands: Buying freedom to work less, choice to reject a bad job or courage to say no is priceless. A majority of people just buy new cars or upgrade their houses, instead: **Some actually become poorer by getting new debts only because they made some money.**

* * *

In my opinion, one of the common mistakes people make when buying houses is choosing ones in upscale neighborhoods with poor libraries; they will pay a lot of property taxes, but won't get much benefit from the village. I know how important having libraries nearby is; **I passed two certificate exams after moving into my home, which is near a big library**; it was pure luck since I had no idea when I bought my condo in 2013. Our library helps me to be a writer, too. Most wealthy areas come with reasonably good libraries in Chicagoland, but there are a few exceptions.

Glencoe is one of the richest neighborhoods in Northern Chicago; the houses are at least $ a few million dollar$ there; the Coldwell shows that the most expensive one is $10 M there in 2022. I have been to the area a few times since it is located on top of a cliff in front of Michigan lake; it is scenic to see the lake from a mountain top view. The downtown has upscale restaurants, which I do not care much about. But the library in the town is really small; it was not even a commercial building; it was merely a family house donated by a rich man a long time ago. It must have been a big residence. But, it is 10 times smaller than that of Highland park, which is located right above the town. I would not pay high property tax every year only for meaningless views. Besides, I did not like the tiny supermarket there; all it sold was pricey drinks instead of water.

Another example is Glen Ellyn. It has a lot of houses ranging from $1 to $2 M worth, but the library in town was crammed and inconvenient. Since the space was small, the building has three stories, but only staff can go to the top floor. Apparently, it is a compact, crowded library with a huge staff area. Bathrooms were limited as well, so I did not feel comfortable staying there for the whole day. I will definitely not choose the village for that amount of money.

Another example is Roselle library. It is not a wealthy area to begin with, but I know that people pay a lot of property tax there; the library was simply old and outdated. I saw only three computers running slow in the entire place. The building, walls and doors were aged; desks and chairs needed repair and water leaked. I wondered if I was even in America. I know a lot of houses pay over $10,000 property tax a year in the town; I am not even sure where they spend all that money.

* * *

Summary

1. It doesn't matter if we work hard or not. Standing in the right lane matters.
2. Getting interests or debts early makes a huge lifetime difference.
3. Check if the village has a decent library nearby before buying a house.

77

Not Going Straight to "Profitable or Not"

Being extremely practical is the only way to survive.
-Brad Kong

I read the novel, *Empire of the Ants* written by French writer Bernard Werber when I was in high school. That was over thirty years ago, but I still remember one insight: "When a problem happens, humans discuss whose fault it is, first: **Ants go straight to solve the problem;** they never waste time to see who caused this; that is why ants are the most successful insects on Earth." I agree since the population of ants is the biggest among all the bugs while insects already account for 75% of animals on Earth. This lesson has impacted on my life all along for decades since high school.

Did you know that new palaces are often built before dynasties fall in China? Forbidden City is a gigantic palace complex in Beijing, built by the Ming dynasty before it collapsed; it was used as the Imperial palace for the next Qing dynasty. The Qing was super strong in the beginning since I believe they didn't spend any money on new constructions. Later on, it was defeated by the English navy after Empress Dowager Cixi built a new huge summer palace to show off: **Being lavish means death, sometimes.**

I assume Werber pointed out that the practicality of ants increases their survivability. In life, I observe that some people never get into points straightly; they don't think whether their actions are profitable or not upfront. Extinction of an animal can happen as a result when it is not practical: **Vanity can make us vanish, which has been proven throughout history.** When a problem happens, less people go directly to "how can I solve this?" instead of "whose fault is this?" Occasionally, impracticality happens on a national scale; that is why some countries like the Philippines or Mexico are in a mess despite diligent people.

Similarly, some women check other people's loss first before their own gain: **Celebrity divorce or break up news won't bring us any profit.** Nonetheless, some even spend money on gossip magazines. If a man sees these types of papers at a girl's place, I think he should start a process of cutting her off, eventually (do it, slowly). Those types of ladies will never ever bring men a benefit, advantage or happiness.

* * *

One of the reasons why I decided not to have any more children after my daughter was my younger brother in Korea. I am not saying that he is a bad person; he is probably a good, generous guy. But he has been an assiduous spender and brought all sorts of problems to my parents. I guess it's our parents' faults as well to have raised him that way, which made my childhood miserable. I do not understand why, but they had cared so much about him for over four decades. It seems my parents considered him as a loser who needs intensive care, constantly; their assumption was simply wrong.

Now my own daughter is 13 years old and I try to leave her alone as much as I can: If something wrong happens to her, I guess that it's her fault. My brother and I are both in our 40s now. Sooner or later, hopefully, both of us will be free from our competently caring mom and pop: I suggest it is impractical for them to worry about their adult children; getting to real issues quickly is the key since time is limited.

* * *

Do you know how to get out of an attachment to a girl? Realize that she won't be pretty forever; she will be old and ugly someday; every woman will be one way or another. The easiest way to visualize this is seeing her mother; the girl will be like her mother with 90% of chance later. If you cannot meet her old lady in person, check the girl's social media.

Even if her mother is gorgeous, here is another problem: Men eventually may not feel anything if they spend years *even* with beauty queens. Most people perceive that water does not have any taste; about 70% of the human body is water. **We drink water all the time, so we don't feel anything any more.**

Before getting married, I think it's important for men to check if they get attracted to women for something other than appearance; for example, my wife has a doctorate while I have never been to a graduate school. Is your girl funny while you are gloomy? Is she wealthy? Does she have a good career? We will most likely feel miserable after the wedding only because marriage custom goes against human nature itself: We all need a solid reason to stay in marriage.

I think a man should check if his fiance makes enough money to support herself, at least; actually, it doesn't matter which job she has as long as she is independent. Do you pay for everything when you go out with her, which is common in Korea? If not, how much do you share? What's happening during dates probably will happen after the wedding, too. Most people divorce since there is no reason to save their marriage; no one keeps it since it is easy; it is hard for everyone. **Woman's beauty is like a car; the value *only* goes down.**

* * *

I notice that there are people who don't even care if things are profitable or not: trolls, pranksters and flops. These people do not even commit crime to gain benefits; some do it for fun or entertainment; their lifestyles are prodigal; as a result, many of these have no money left in their late years. This is why I don't feel sorry for poor *old* people any more. There must be some exceptions; still, I mostly believe that those have bothered others for long to be in that position.

I saw on the news that one middle-aged man had kept ordering a large amount of food in restaurants and disappeared in Korea; he kept ordering 40 rolls of kimbaps (maki) and never came back. Those struggling small restaurant owners usually never be suspicious when an order is placed by a middle aged man face to face; an oldman has a stereotype of not making a joke in Korea, so they did not ask for any deposit or payment in advance. The man eventually got arrested, but this is a type of crime not to bring anyone any benefit; at least, an offender tries to get a sort of benefit in most crimes. **I think this is the most stupid type of crime since no one gets anything, but only offenders get punishments.**

* * *

I think one way to get revenge on internet trolls[56] is to stop writing; it was stupid for me to keep writing and suffer from

[56] A person who posts inflammatory, insincere, digressive, extraneous or off-topic messages in an online community.

negative conflict with no gain. Nasty trolls are serious problems nowadays; they write anything only to hurt others' feelings. They believe they can be completely hidden, hit and run safely: Wrong! If we keep writing on a specific website on a regular basis, that means we are kind of addicted to doing it; that is the same for trolls, too. If we have written on a site for a while, the chances are they are also addicted to reading our articles and putting comments on them.

I assume that it is the endurance game from that point; writing something they can be offended by and run away; there is no real way they can know what we are doing now or when we will be back; make them wonder and go crazy; do not write anything, so there is no clue or trace. **Just stop writing and do our job for the rest of our lives is the biggest revenge after all**; let them waste time and stay poor. People who think about profit must have not wasted time on trolling to begin with.

* * *

Summary

1. When you see a problem, try to solve it first, instead of asking, "who is responsible for this?"
2. Being practical is key to survivorship.
3. Living our lives well is the best revenge.

78

Having Low Self Esteem

Lowering ourselves costs money.
-Brad Kong

History shows that the explorer Christopher Columbus was a bold, arrogant man. He was not a good cartographer, in fact; he believed that the Bahama Island in the Caribbean he reached in 1492 was India until he died. His father was a wine and cheese seller, but he made up a fake noble background to sell himself; he showed off that he was a descendant of Roman general Colonius, who is grandson of the emperor of Constantinople. He asked for too much money for his voyage, so couldn't find a patron for a long time. When Queen Isabella I in Spain decided to support him, she had to sell a lot of her jewelry, including her crown. *Still, he didn't negotiate for any discount on his expedition*; it's explained in *The 48 Laws of Power* by Greene.

I think that people buy expensive things to cover up their inferiority complex or low self-esteem; those won't make them better or rich; they will end up only draining more money. I believe that the best way to increase our self esteem is to accomplish little goals and accumulate successes; the tasks do not have to be super hard. How about reading 50 books this year? It won't cost much money. I bought the book *Nomadland* for $2 at Half price books store the other day. It was in the bargain shelves; I picked that up only because I heard about the movie based on it. I was able to read it completely and it should be remembered as the first English book I have completely finished though it took almost a month; the book was boring and the lady author didn't seem to be a good talker on YouTube; nonetheless, it helped me achieve a small mission of reading.

After that, I finished reading *The Alchemist* by Coelho and *Let's go to a better place* by Jung; I am reading *12 Rules for Life* by Peterson now. Reading some books you have always wondered about could be a great mission to give us a feeling of victory; it requires patience and time. What if we make more money after reading all those? In *12 rules for life*, Peterson summarized some self-matters: "We do not own our bodies; we do not have the right to torture ourselves. When all of us respect ourselves, the world would be a better place as a whole." **Some people keep disrespecting themselves beyond modesty and damage their wealth.**

* * *

Many people automatically think that the bigger or more expensive things are the better; they subconsciously assume that there could be a reason for high prices of anything; this is the default setting in our minds. As a result, people try to make more money for bigger houses, cars or even bigger families, including more children; many are not afraid to get into debt since they firmly believe that more expensive stuff will bring them more joy.

I don't think that this belief is true, though: There is always the right size, price or quality for everything. If a bigger car is better, why didn't *Porsche* file a bankruptcy yet? It is smaller than a Corvette, but twice more expensive. If a bigger car is always better, why doesn't Trump drive a trailer to work? He ain't in the delivery service. There is always an appropriate size and price for everything; this is especially true for the house as well.

Before moving into my condo in 2013, this is what I thought: "Do I really have to buy the smallest home in town? Maybe I will buy this one for now only to avoid apartment rent for good. I have paid the rent in the last thirteen years and I cannot do it forever. Let me move into a bigger place later on." That was 10 years ago as it's 2023 now; I have more than enough money to buy virtually any house with cash in this town. Yet, frankly, this is what I am thinking now: "Do I really have to move into a bigger house? I feel comfortable since it turned out to be more quiet and decent than I expected before moving in; 850 sf is enough for a family of three. My wife and daughter have many local friends in this complex. I will only pay more property tax and have more work to maintain it if I move to a bigger house."

* * *

Psychologically, the reason why I feel comfortable with a small condo is that I do not have any mental shame against poverty. Since I was young in Korea, everyone knew that I was from a wealthy family. This is not particularly true in America because not many people know where I am exactly from. Since I had been a video game shop owner and nursing home worker before, some might even think I am from a poor family. This is not true, but it does not bother me, either. I am accustomed to being considered a rich boy for a long time, so I guess that I do not have this type of complex.

There was a Korean community site that I do not visit any more; one nasty troll always insisted that he was proud of living in a $1 M house with a huge mortgage debt. My point was that there should not be anything to be proud of being in loan, at least: **A lot of debts in his case.** I had arguments with that trash repeatedly since he commented on everyone's article unpleasantly. And this was my firm opinion: Maybe nothing wrong with being in debt, but do not show it off or insist that getting a massive mortgage is the right thing to do.

But when I think about it, I think he might have had a poverty complex or scar; maybe people have disrespected him for his poor parents when he was young. I would say that low self esteem can cost money unnecessarily this way: a lot of money, sometimes.

* * *

I have seen people not meeting others richer than them; that includes my father. *Some avoid meeting successful people, even unconsciously, and lose chances to get better*; some do not read books by inspiring writers; it won't help for us, financially. Nonetheless, I notice that these self esteem and complex matters happen more, particularly to women.

When I was in a college in Korea, there was a girl only dating failed older students. The college entrance exam had been competitive in that country; it was common that a student studies one more year, takes the exam again and gets accepted the next year if he or she fails to get admitted by the first try; some fail twice or more. As a result, some colleagues were two years older than most of the students and subtly considered as losers in the class. It was similar to the fact that some students cannot graduate from colleges within four years in America; it takes six years for some. And there was a Korean girl who dated only those two time losers.

"Failing the exam" didn't mean that these older students did not study hard in Korea; it was that the exams were merciless about thirty years ago. There were 60 students in our genetic engineering department in the class of 1992. I remember 31 students passed the entrance exam without a failure; 15 students failed once, so they were a year older than me. The rest failed twice or more. I believe that girl entered the school without failing. She dated a few times only with those older failures (a two years difference is nothing in my age though it felt like ten years that time).

Why do you think she did that? Basically, she did not have much self confidence. Only thing she was confident about herself was that she passed the college exam at the first try; I remember that most girls preferred someone her age; most preferred a guy without failing. *Why would anyone prefer a partner with a failed record?* Nonetheless, is it helpful for our lives?

I studied fine enough to pass the college exam without failing; it was like finishing a college within four years in America. But I have preferred a girl studying better than me. In fact, I have been married to a girl who got a doctorate by scholarship in America; we have a daughter. Isn't it natural for an animal to choose a mate better than others in a species? If I chose a girl who did poorly in academics, would it be more profitable? Or would I be happier now?

I think some people are poor since they avoid better people intentionally. Some girls are broke since they avoid talented men to marry: Why is this happening? I believe that some have low self-esteem to cover; some may feel inferior that they do not even deserve ordinary guys, not to mention excellent ones. Personally, I assume that I have had high self esteem all along. I have only a bachelor's degree, but I have always thought that I could not marry a normal girl; my partner needed to be attractive or excellent somehow; she could be from a rich family; she might be a supermodel; she finished famous school with a full grant, etc. I knew that I would not marry an average one, not to mention less than ordinary.

Now I see things differently and strongly believe an average girl, who is really owned by me, is good enough. Some girls are not into their partners; I don't prefer that. I just feel comfortable not being with an outstanding woman asking and costing too much. For sure, I will never be a sugar daddy for a young girl who is not into me; I will never worry if she will leave me or not after spending my own money. It was just different back then when I met my wife twenty four years ago. Regardless, choosing her has been financially helpful for me; I am just mentioning this because some, particularly girls, intentionally avoid better choices. Some choose stupid guys with hope that they will never meet other women: Wrong! Meeting other women has nothing to do with men's capability to work or make money. Actually, as far as I have observed, broke men flirt with other women more.

* * *

I learned that fasting has health benefits; it helps injuries heal faster, too. After having my rotten molar removed a week ago, I still felt my jaw have *Streptococcus* infection left, so I decided to fast and lose more weight: **Losing weight means my body eats the infected tissue in my jaw, priorly.** I am already 125 LB, but my new target is 120 LB for now.

I found out that I have to wait until my hunger goes away to lose weight. After we skip a couple of meals, the moment we cannot resist food comes; after hearing some stomach growling sounds and passing those moments, we can see that suddenly abdomens feel comfortable; we won't feel our teeth sensitive any more in case of having decay. We can literally feel having more white blood cells to kill tooth bacteria. After a couple days, I noticed that I didn't even feel hunger itself any more.

I think that this is the characteristic of all desires. After passing some insisting moments, we may see that a desire itself is gone. And just like fasting is good for our body, not having a strong desire can be good for our soul as well. Nevertheless, I can say that the fastest way to get rid of low self-esteem could be losing weight. Just pass some hungry moments a few times. I strongly believe that anyone can do a week of fasting while we can save more money.

* * *

Summary

1. Having low self-esteem can bring us less profits.
2. Achieving small goals can promote confidence.
3. Losing weight is one costless way to feel good about ourselves.

79

Not Being Constructive

No reason to get busy; no reason to be wasteful, either.
-Brad Kong

Why had Germany lost WWII? I think that Germans focused on something not bringing them direct profits; they didn't fight in constructive ways. Killing Jewish people did not bring them any gain; it only created miseries on others; it was merely a waste of time, energy and resources from the German side. Deutschs could have used those to fight against enemies or defend their country. **Unless we strictly pursue our profits, we will lose one way or another.**

I think that people get poor when they waste their talents. My daughter just finished her elementary school this June, 2023. She reads multiple swimsuit catalogs delivered from “Lands' End” repeatedly these days; she asks a lot of questions about modeling. I told her that most of these models are part timers; often, their real jobs are actresses, singers or entertainers, especially in Korea. I told her that she can do it as well, at least for side jobs. When I walked on the River Walks Chicago the other day, I saw some professional models having their photos taken; they were incredibly bony. My daughter is skinny, too; I told her that keeping her in shape will matter if she is serious about that job.

* * *

Do you know what is the most common trait among all the losers? **They waste time**; probably, they waste energy and money, too. It doesn't mean that winners should work to exhaustion. Yet I notice that winners do not waste time much, at least not at the level losers do. In fact, most successful people hate to misspend. Degenerates waste time even in critical moments; some go extinct as a result; this happened many times throughout history.

I used to go to a Korean discussion website; I must say that trolls there were geniuses of wasting. In fact, it is a social problem that a good portion of young people don't do anything in Korea; they get little allowances from parents and live on them, but that is all. Obviously, those trolls never wrote anything meaningful on the site for years; they never graduated from a college having reasonable reputations; no assets, marriages or children, etc. I agree that it is a good idea not to live too diligently. But I notice that those trolls have squandered for decades; astonishingly, they find me as soon as I start writing somewhere else online; my writing ID has been always "brad" for decades, though; still I do not understand how they can visit millions of sites. I decided to stay away from them only to be sane.

What I usually feel after coming back from a leisure trip is regret: The feeling that I wasted my time and money. I get a similar feeling after checking social media or watching movies for long; strangely, I never get that feeling after reading books. We cannot change everything all at once. But I think it is important to increase the time giving us fulfillment and decrease the time giving us futility, gradually.

* * *

There was one idiot I particularly did not like on the Korean site; he envied people who bought a house in full; I was one of them. He had wasted time being jealous for several years; he never wrote a single constructive article expressing his own idea. Nonetheless, he was there all the time; he wrote nasty comments as soon as anyone wrote an article.

Despite being jealous, he never made an extra effort to pay his mortgage early. He had a 30-year loan on a mundane house. Then, he said he moved to a bigger house and started another new 30-year debt from 2022. I bought out my condo in full 10 years ago in 2013. This means he will pay off his house "39 years" later than me: I mean, how long can a human live? **How come one person is "39 years" slower than another to buy a house?** I am not a super efficient genius; I am actually stupid since the only thing I did was get money from my parents and buy a home.

At the same time, I have never been wasteful enough to write only comments without writing my own articles. I have always written unique ideas and opinions; I did not rush to do it; I do not write eight hours a day diligently like the writer Armentrout. I just have never wasted time, particularly; I can waste time, but it is not going to be for years like the loser.

Whenever I see my daughter, she is always doing something. She is not an excellent student and I don't expect her to be. But I can see that she is the type of person minding her own business; she will never waste time concerning others' lives. As a middle aged man, I know that this attitude can make a huge difference in the end; **I know why some wound up buying houses 39 years slower than others.** Some people are poor for no outstanding reason; they just have wasted time all along.

* * *

I went to Heritage Farm in our village with my daughter the other day. I have passed the place by millions of times alone. It was on my way to the bus terminal from my home, so I always rushed to glide by it on my kick-scooter. Finally, I had a chance to stop there thanks to her and spent three hours checking everything out.

The Heritage Farm is an old settlement place, including a tiny museum, 200 years old houses, animal farms and forests. It was crowded since little students were on summer vacation. The old houses include several buildings: the main two story house, a wine cellar, a barbecue house, a hay barn, a seed basement, blacksmith forge, etc. Everything in the main house was set up in the traditional style with three stoves; there were a couple of ladies wearing old clothes in the 19 century-style, so I could see how people used to live 200 years ago.

My impression was that it must have been a lot of work only to maintain a daily life, back then. There was no supermarket since people just settled in empty spaces. So, basically, all they ate was what they grew; people wore the clothes they made. Besides, there was no home depot at that time: **Can you imagine how hard it would be to get a piece of wood from a real tree?** It shows that four generations had lived in those houses. I think one of the major reasons is that it must have been incredibly hard to get building materials to begin with.

After a few hours of browsing, I have come to a solid conclusion: **Everyone has too much free time nowadays.** Even if I have ten children to take care of, I would say that I still have too much free time compared with people born then. I can say that success nowadays virtually depends on how to handle this huge amount of free time.

* * *

When I watched the movie "Undisputed," staring Wesley Snipes, there was a scene where he was building miniature bridges by matches and glues; the movie was about a boxing match in a huge prison. The match was legal, but the boxer was a powerful but dangerous guy, so he was in solitary confinement. He spent all his free time building all sorts of miniature buildings there. I thought it was a constructive way of doing time. Even in the worst case, I guess he can still sell those for money, at least.

Recently, I have thought about what could be the best way to spend free time: Thinking. Some people call it meditation, and I believe this will bring me solutions, profits or better articles from now on. **It won't cost to think.** But I believe that this is what we are lacking the most in modern society.

Poverty is not all bad since people tend to start thinking only when their lives are free from consumption; they start to imagine or study only when they do not have money to spend; most will read books when they cannot afford TV subscription. **It is important to put all our money in the bank and act as if we do not have any;** we will start to think and our life will go in a more positive direction from that point. How was I able to write 24 books? *I imagined I do not have any money left*; that made it possible for me to stay at home with a chunk of free time: All the time in the world. I have had no choice but to write something somehow.

* * *

Summary

1. Unless we become practical, we die.
2. Not wasting time is more important than working hard.

3. Imagine you do not own any money. Life can be more constructive from that point.

80

Not Having Enough Room To Breathe

Being too sensitive is
a guaranteed way to live miserably.
-Brad Kong

Speedometers of most cars show 140 miles though most people don't drive more than 80 miles an hour: Why is that? There is a Korean word called "여유[57] [Yeo-yu]"; it can be translated into "enough space." If we have enough money or extra time, that is 여유 (*Yeo-yu)*, too. Did you know that "not having enough" can cause poverty as well? If we are always short of things, that can cause a chain of unfortunate events, which can be led into brokeness. On the contrary, when we have enough of anything, it can bring us more profit as well.

I read a Korean book titled "Let's go to a better place" by Jung. The author wrote that she got hit by a car in a big accident years ago. She said she could not move for five months; an insurance agent of the offender side came and suggested $20,000 initially for settlement right after the accident; she declined since she was not in condition to talk about money at that time; she was deeply concerned about her physical condition. **The agent came a few times more after that and she learned that he suggested more and**

[57] Unfortunately, this Korean word is not visible on Kindle due to tech error.

more money for settlement as time passed. She said she had no idea how the settlement works. When she finally was able to walk a little bit five months later, she talked with the agent and accepted $50,000 for the final settlement; she got the money in her bank account a day after she agreed to the amount.

This was her conclusion: If she did not have enough money saved at that time of the accident, she would have accepted $20,000 quickly in the beginning. FYI, medical expenses are not extremely high in Korea and probably $20,000 could have been still enough for her treatments. **But she realized that she was able to get $30,000 more only because she had enough in savings and could have delayed the settlement talk.**

I think this is happening all the time in our lives, too. Some people lose more money since they do not have much; **some make more money since they have some.** For example, some who cannot afford apartments, also called *Hidden Americans,* rent motel rooms by the week; they end up paying way more than apts rent. Once we fall into a poverty swamp, it is hard to get out. I think it is important not to get into it by disconnecting all the poverty habits to begin with.

* * *

Recently, I found a new French word: *Flâneur*; it means an idler or stroller, who does not work a lot. Ironically, I believe this is the reason why Frenchs have been creative and accumulated wealths throughout centuries: **The more we get desperate about money, the farther fortunes go away.** The funny thing is that only rich people can afford to be lazy and walk instead of driving; still, this could be the reason why they stay wealthy.

The French conqueror, Napoleon once said, “The greatest danger occurs at the moment of victory.” **I think it’s important to take some time off from being successful and have some moments to restore calmness**; we need some time to think quietly before moving forward. Our success can be a trap set by others; it is possible that some make us feel successful to utilize us. If that is the case, those enemies will be nervous when we stand still and do not move; we won’t get deeper into traps by moving slowly or not at all.

* * *

When we look desperate, we must lose; in my opinion, the best way not to look distressed is not to be in despair, actually. I think we shouldn’t put ourselves in that bad financial situation by removing bad habits, to begin with. On top of that, I assume that it’s important to realize that we have more than enough. **The feeling of having enough is not dependent on the amount of things we have**; it’s simply the state of mind; religions may help us get into that, sometimes.

There was a squirrel trapped in my condo once; I found it when I came home from work one night. This happened when my cat was still alive in October, 2019; it seems they had fought for hours already; I found blood stains everywhere on the walls. At that time, I used to leave my living room window open just a little bit (4 inches) from spring to late fall, so my cat could go out to the balcony freely. When it didn’t rain, I used to leave his litter box on the balcony as well, so he could take care of his business outside; I thought it’s cleaner that way.

The only problem was that once an animal (i.e., sparrows) comes from the opening, it never finds the way out while no one closes the window. It was not a big opening, but big enough that a cat could pass in and out without a problem. But those animals, like a squirrel or mouse, just lost direction once they came into the house and ran into my cat; they just got shocked by the predator and puzzled.

As soon as I saw the squirrel on that night, I made all the windows in the house completely wide open; the opening size was more than 2 feet each window; still the squirrel couldn't find his way out. It took over 20 minutes for me to let the squirrel out by pushing him with a long stick gently; he finally jumped out to the pine tree right in front of my house through the bedroom window; I could not believe it since he was moving around the window, which was totally widely open, for over 10 minutes. Then, it took a few hours for me to clean up all the blood stains that night.

* * *

We cannot be desperate to be successful: **Destitution disrupts time to think quietly.** *When we are perplexed by a problem right in front of us, we often do not see other chances, exits or solutions.* This is why I used to blame mortgage paying Korean trolls all the time. Maybe I am blaming them once again now since those offensive trolls were all mortgage payers, coincidently. Having a mortgage debt itself is a way to double the house costs, mathematically. But, more importantly, they lose chances to get involved in other investment opportunities continually during the 30-year term.

For example, PBI stock price has dropped to $3.50 back this morning, so I bought 100 shares again in 2022. Most people paying rents or mortgages don't do this; they are mostly worrying about their payment deadlines as it is at the end of the month; these obligations can take away moments to think alone, peacefully. As a result, people can miss the kind of opportunity I got this morning for as long as 30 years.

I understand if someone is paying rent or mortgage because he or she does not have enough money. **The real problem happens to those who go for a bigger house in vanity even though they can afford a smaller house with cash.** Some Koreans have a blind theory they insist: A bigger house will bring me more money no matter what; this has been true only in Korea, especially in the 1980s. These people simply failed to adapt in America; the property tax in America is 11 times bigger than that in Korea on average; it is nonsense to invest in bigger houses or rental businesses here; some are poor since they failed to be Americanized.

* * *

Being desperate always makes ourselves less profitable; it makes us narrow sighted; people choose any option even though it is not the best one in this case. We have to avoid that situation as much as we can; that is why it is important to have enough money or some savings just in case. Also, it is important not to waste energy; for example, I planned to take some time off after working at the nursing home for seven years, but still write a book, instead. **When we work when we don't have to, we tend to make wiser decisions since they have some room to think.**

Some people are desperate after having too many failures. **Having more failures is actually a good thing**; it means we have tried more things and harder than others; getting frustrated means we tried something, at least. *I don't think we should be desperate only because we failed some times.* I saw the SpaceX launch failure the other day in 2020; the spacecraft exploded in a second. The record showed that the company had five complete failures, four partial failures, and one partial success, for a total of ten trials since 2006. Musk is still the richest man on Earth with $225 billion net worth; this is almost $100 billion more than the second richest man, Bezos as of 2022.

I passed through the big Indian street on Devon in Chicago the other day. I tried to stop by my favorite Indian restaurant, Ghareeb for veggie thali for $7. But the ca$hier said they accept ca$h only in this location. I thought about going to the bank and coming back, but decided to try a different one; there are about 30 restaurants, anyway. On the way home, I found a place called Sukhadia and ordered veggie thali for $10. It was $3 more expensive, but the quality was far better; it included Indian sweets, too; it was the first time I tried an Indian dessert and it was unique; now I see where I can go if I crave for Indian food. **By trying a new place, we have more risk of failure**; the one I choose can be worse. But, without trying other options, there is no better deal or improvement, either.

* * *

Summary

1. Not having enough can cause more shortages.
2. Having sufficient time or money can bring more profit.
3. Don't put yourself in a barely making situation (i.e., have one child though you can afford two).

About Brad

Making a little effort everyday makes a huge difference.
-Brad K.

- Philosopher, writer, book cover designer and investor
- Certified Pharmacy Technician at PTCB (2022)
- Certified Professional Medical Coder at AAPC (2018)
- Nursing Home (2015-2022)
- Father of one child (2010)
- Founder of Cyb Knight Games and Top Rated seller at eBay (2006-2014)
- Bachelor of Science degree at State University of New York at Buffalo: Major in Biology (2001-2005)
- Bachelor of Science degree at Hallym University in Korea: Major in Genetic Engineering and Minor in Computer Engineering (1992-1999)
- Army Ammunition and Magazine Management Soldier (1994-1997)
- I used to have a cat. I like to read, think and write. The "*Unbrokable**" series is my first book.
- https://amazon.com/author/bradkong

Author's Note

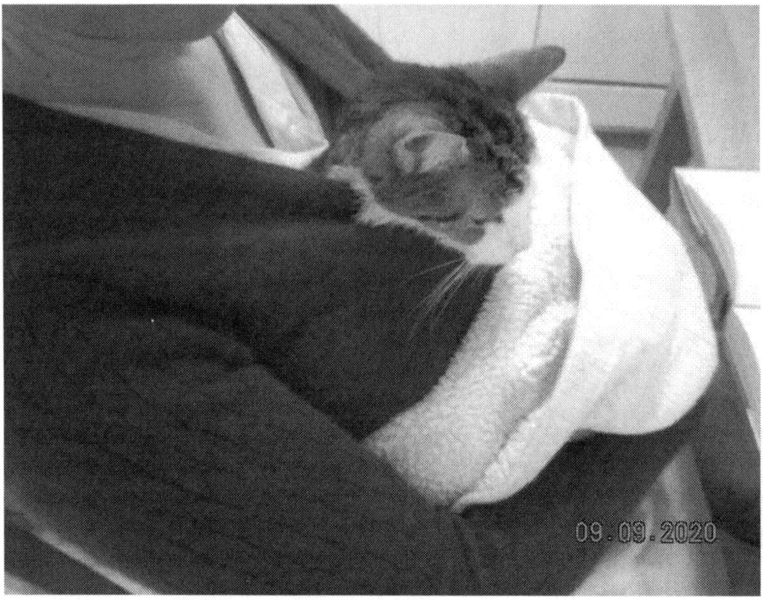

Congratulations: I truly appreciate you finishing my book until the end. The cat in the photo is Yang (Oscar) who I mentioned many times in Chapter 21 of *UnBrokable* III*; it was taken only a few days before he passed away. We had so many memories, but he couldn't get over the blood cancer in the end.

I was born and raised in Korea and immigrated to America in my 20s; that was 24 years ago since it's 2023 now. In the beginning, I failed getting accepted to prestigious Ivy league schools although SUNYat Buffalo is a great school. Then I graduated from college with a 2.5 GPA by 2005, so I couldn't get into any graduate school as well. Then I started my own business, but it wasn't very successful for 8 years. Subsequently, my career at the nursing home also didn't work out as I planned even though I won two certificates during the 7 years; now I try to be a writer at the age of 49.

If you believe this book can be helpful to others and have a minute to spare, ***I would truly appreciate a rating.*** Your help in spreading the word is greatly appreciated. Believe it or not, *I do read all the reviews and use them to improve my writings.* Reviews from readers like you make a huge difference; please let me know what you think. I sincerely wish my best luck to you.

Made in the USA
Coppell, TX
05 November 2026

11289016R10414